Jack Lawrence Luzkow

Monopoly Restored

How the Super-Rich Robbed Main Street

palgrave
macmillan

Jack Lawrence Luzkow
Fontbonne University
St. Louis, MO, USA

ISBN 978-3-030-06767-0 ISBN 978-3-319-93994-0 (eBook)
https://doi.org/10.1007/978-3-319-93994-0

Cover image: © onfilm, istock/Getty Images Plus
Cover design by Akihiro Nakayama

Printed on acid-free paper

This Palgrave Macmillan imprint is published by the registered company Springer International Publishing AG part of Springer Nature
The registered company address is: Gewerbestrasse 11, 6330 Cham, Switzerland

Monopoly Restored

For Roberto Giammanco, who taught me to see

Contents

CHAPTER 1

Introduction

Like the majority of Americans, I did not expect Donald J. Trump to be elected president of the USA. No more than many in Britain expected Brexit to win the approval of British voters. Yet, like many others, I could also see the possibility that both Brexit and Trump would be triumphant. It did not take great insight or foresight to see that the press, the media generally, many politicians, and virtually all major political parties on both sides of the Atlantic were missing massive populist revolts that seemed all but invisible to the parade of public commentators.

Even while there was much talk of economic recovery, the rate of poverty in the USA reached 17% in 2016. A percentage roughly double that had been in poverty at some point between 2010 and 2013: the same was true for the UK. The official rate of unemployment may have been reduced to below 5% in the US and almost as low in the UK by 2017, but these calculations were badly flawed. If part-time employment was not counted as being in-work, if people were not counted as working when they were nominally "self-employed," then the rate of "official" unemployment doubled or worse, in the USA and the UK.

In both countries, wages have remained stagnant for the middle classes and have been so for decades. The working classes practically have become invisible in both countries—at least prior to Brexit and the election of Donald Trump—as both nations have abandoned manufacturing, arguing that blue-collar industrial jobs were best done in low-wage countries. The irony is that for many, the UK and the USA have become low-wage countries themselves. But it is worse than that. The

J. L. Luzkow, *Monopoly Restored*,
https://doi.org/10.1007/978-3-319-93994-0_1

middle classes on both sides of the Atlantic have been struggling for decades, facing stagnating incomes at best, or long-term unemployment as many so-called middle-class jobs have either evaporated or been exported abroad.

Conservatives on both sides of the Atlantic point out that this was the inevitable result of globalization and automation. Some say it is because of poor decisions made by the less successful, the impoverished and the uneducated: they failed to get the right skills, or education, their productivity was low, and American and British workers were not competitive. Moreover, Republicans and Tories have argued for decades that labor unions are greedy, practice class conflict, and advocate unreasonable wage hikes that raise prices, lead to inflation, and make products more and more unaffordable. Inevitably, as jobs have disappeared, as wages have stagnated, as millions have failed to participate in so-called recovery, as unions have been eviscerated, and as political parties have failed to respond to the suffering that they have not acknowledged, or simply could not see, the mass parties of the past began to fragment, unsure of who or where their constituencies were.

Constituencies themselves have become more complex, divided by identity politics, regional attachments, social and class divisions, and polarized further by immigration and population movements as both the USA and the UK became less Western, less Christian, and less white. Identity politics have proved especially nettlesome, as gender identity has become more amorphous and ill-defined, and as marriage has become something other than between a man and a woman, challenging traditional white populations already threatened as their neighbors and countries became less Christian and less white. And as whites, particularly the traditional bread-winning male populations, have become more threatened, as their jobs have been eviscerated or exported, as more and more have been displaced, and as they have had to compete with low-wage workers in far-flung countries, Conservatives everywhere have successfully argued that their problems were the result of Big Government: too many taxes, too much support of illegal immigrants, too much protection of trees and certain animal species, too little concern for workers who had nothing to look forward too.

In the midst of these problems, liberals seemed unable to articulate a vision for the future. They became too cozy with Wall Street in the USA and the City in Britain. They became part of the establishment, more and more distant and increasingly unaware of or insensitive toward the suffering of their traditional constituents. On both sides of the Atlantic, the major parties moved to the right, Democrats embracing compromise with Republicans as a way to acquire power, and Tony Blair and Labor doing the same in Britain to accommodate the Tories. For decades, in both the USA and the UK, major political parties accepted the viewpoints of Big Business: keep taxes low, government regulation at a minimum, low or no tariffs at the border, minimal if any carbon tax, weak unions, and strong currencies.

What progressive parties on both sides of the Atlantic failed to do was to adequately acknowledge or grasp the multiple crises at hand. We have been floundering in the USA and the UK now for several decades, following the "end of history," or at the least the End of Communism as a serious historical force, as to what exactly our alternatives should be in the non-Communist West. It is time now to admit and to fully acknowledge that Europe and the USA have been facing dual crises of capitalism and liberal democracy, and for Europe a continuing crisis of unity.[1] More than crises, the West now faces a historical caesura marking the end of liberalism as we have known it, and the beginning of a new era of authoritarianism that is a reminder of things past, if not a return of history. German historian Philipp Ther, though addressing the failures of the Western model of liberal democracy and economic liberalism in Central and Eastern Europe, has inadvertently put the current crisis in the West in historical perspective. Ther has argued that a "neoliberal train" set in motion by Margaret Thatcher in Britain and Ronald Reagan in the USA began to cross into Europe in 1989. He states the problem with clarity:

> Blind belief in the market as an adjudicator in almost all human affairs, irrational reliance on the rationality of market participants, disdain for the state as expressed in the myth of "big government," and the uniform application of the economic recipes of the Washington Consensus.[2]

Ther's thesis was intended to apply to the bungled attempt to transform the former Communist countries of Europe into Western-style capitalist liberal democracies. Yet his thesis uncannily intones some of the notes of the UK and the USA. Both countries are after all the progenitors of neoliberalism and its liberalizing, deregulating, and privatizing progeny, and it is these tenets that have created the mischief that now threatens the very fabric of the social contract in both the UK and the USA, moving both nations toward unintended and unanticipated historical reversions.

The social problem, once thought resolved, has returned with a vengeance, revealing that history may be reversible and that some of the worst riddles of the past have remained—just below the surface.

Which is precisely the argument of *Monopoly Restored: How the Super-Rich Robbed Main Street*. The super-rich—the 1 (or 0.1)% in current lingo—have gotten immensely rich not through sheer ingenuity, or inordinate intellectual ability, but by extracting wealth from the real economy where most of us live and work. Historically, much of the wealth of the ultra-wealthy has been based on inheritance, tax evasion, political influence, or just plain theft. In the last four decades, the menu has expanded. The owners of wealth, whether financial, intellectual, or physical, have largely succeeded in destroying competitive markets and deregulating large parts of the economy, creating large "rents" for themselves. They have forged virtual monopolies in telecommunications and energy, producing outsized profits or "rents" for them. They have insisted that banks retain the right to speculate on derivatives, ensured that credit card companies not be bothered by pesky usury laws, expanded the shadow banking system so that hedge funds and private equity firms remain unregulated and virtually invisible. Their credit card companies have suppressed usury laws limiting interest rates. They have successfully resisted more efficient, less expensive, and fairer single-payer healthcare systems (in the USA), while defending for-profit health insurance that is unaffordable and inequitable for many millions, producing vast rents for their health insurance companies. The super-rich have been granted patents on drugs, even when their drugs are no better than those already on the market. They have won undeserved subsidies for themselves in agribusiness. Their seed companies have established near monopolies over the genetically modified seed market, using political leverage to limit or to eliminate competition. The super-rich who control corporations have practiced wage theft, fought minimum wage laws, weakened unions, outsourced jobs, resorted to temps and contract labor, and preached free trade so the commodities they produce in China and elsewhere can be brought to the USA with minimal duties. The super-rich have lowered (or escaped) inheritance taxes, shifting much of their income to lower-taxed capital gains. They have created tax havens where trillions of dollars remain untaxed and invisible. And multinational corporations have transferred profits of their intellectual and financial property to subsidiaries in low-tax regimes, where they often remain permanently untaxed.

As Chapter 2, "Democracy Corrupted," explains, the super-rich have accumulated great wealth for themselves by corrupting democracy. They have done this by establishing think tanks that masquerade as neutral and scientific. They have poured large and virtually unlimited funds into political campaigns, promoting and helping to elect candidates who support a neoliberal paradigm that has shredded the social contract. In the USA, in 2010, this has been enabled by a majority decision of the Supreme Court in *Citizens United v. Federal Election Commission*, granting deep-pocketed corporations the right to spend whatever they wanted on political election campaigns.[3] The UK has much more restrictive campaign finance laws, but that has hardly prevented the City of London from having lopsided influence over number 10 Downing Street.

By influencing and even controlling political parties through campaign contributions, by ownership of large segments of the print and electronic media, where they run disinformation campaigns that confuse truth and propaganda, by the establishment of so-called disinterested think tanks, by employing armies of lobbyists, the super-rich have established a rentier economy that rewards capital while regulating and diminishing labor.

Corrupting democracy has allowed the corporate super-rich to privatize public assets, to limit government oversight on the financial and banking industry and to build new monopolies in everything from telecommunications to (patented) drugs. The super-rich have used political leverage to create "rents" by obtaining undeserved "subsidies" in everything from healthcare to agribusiness, and then used government to reduce taxes on those rents.

Less than a decade after *Citizens United*, plutocracies in the USA and UK have produced a kind of "extreme" capitalism that has helped transfer considerable financial and political power to Wall Street and the City of London. As is detailed in Chapter 3, "The Rise and Rise of Wall Street and the City of London," the gravitational pull of Wall Street and the City has given the banking and financial sectors continued leverage to make predatory sub-prime loans, to prevent the restoration of usury laws limiting interest rate charges, and to increase debt to capital ratios once thought dangerous and even lethal. Even post-Dodd–Frank, there is no firewall between investment and commercial banks, hedge funds and private equity firms remain unregulated and can legally access pension funds, and derivatives are again widely traded despite the meltdown they caused during the crash of 2007–2008. Meanwhile, banks have gotten even bigger than they were when they were too big to fail, avoiding antitrust laws that might have prevented the crises of 2007–2008 had they only been invoked.

For every additional dollar generated by the economy, some economists, such as Thomas Piketty and Anthony Atkinson, argue that more than 90% goes to the 1%. Chapter 4, "The Ascendancy of the Corporate Elite," explains how this happens. During the "golden age," for several decades following WW II, American and British executives were paid modestly, with rare (and sometimes deserved) exceptions. Beginning with the Reagan and Thatcher eras, executive pay mushroomed while the income of corporate employees stagnated at best. Rising executive compensation was taken as an entitlement: greed was good for the overall health of a firm and the American economy. Corporate executives grew profits—and their personal income—by shifting to short-termism: encouraging employee layoffs, moving companies to low-wage states or countries, evading corporate taxes in the name of greater profitability, acquiring other companies to raise market share and corporate revenues, and using share buybacks to (artificially) raise share value, which was then linked to executive compensation. By packing corporate boards with cronies who were well paid for their services—subsequently raising their own wages completely out of synch with executive performance—and by moving employees into short-term or part-time work, or simply calling them self-employed, the wealth of the corporate 1% was vastly enhanced, much of it at the direct expense of their employees. Corporations also repressed the wages of workers by shifting production—in the USA—to right-to-work states, which are difficult to organize, or by shifting production abroad, made easier by trade agreements mostly favorable to corporations, which in fact help to write those agreements.

The more that the corporate rich take for themselves, the less there is for everybody else: that is what extracting wealth from the real economy means. Chapter 5, "The Decline of Main Street and the Middle Class," examines how corporations have replaced defined-benefit with defined-contribution pensions, shifting much more of the burden of retirement onto employees and away from employers. The super-rich at the helm of the corporate world have resisted pay increases, dropped health insurance—or modified it so it is "cost-effective." They have downsized, outsourced, sub-contracted, moved production abroad, and utilized endless schemes to employ temporary workers who can be hired seasonally, or simply part-time, or as independent contractors who are not called employees—the better to evade employee benefits, anything to avoid fixed employee costs and payment of decent wages with comparable benefits. Companies have used their economic and political leverage to restrict unionization or to bypass unions altogether by shifting operations to right-to-work-states or abroad. They have opposed raising the minimum wage, which remains much lower in the USA than in the UK: in 2017, the minimum wage in the USA has not advanced in real terms for four decades. The result is that workers have less economic security than they had in the 1970s: even middle-class employees have seen their standards of living stagnate at best. And for the most vulnerable workers, corporations have widely practiced wage theft, or deliberately misclassified workers as independents not entitled to healthcare and other benefits.

Not all countries employ the kind of class struggle race-to-the-bottom so characteristic of the USA and the UK. German workers are paid decent wages, enjoy good working conditions, universal healthcare, pensions (that provide as much as 67% of an employee's income when in employment), extensive maternity leave, and more or less permanent employment or training provided by employers or the state. To get these benefits, Germany protects its unions and supports works councils—shop floor groups including workers—that negotiate work conditions and even job classification, and democratic boards of directors on which half the sitting members are workers. Unlike the USA and the UK, in Germany industrial unions are regarded as partners, not adversaries. The result is that German auto—and all industrial—workers rarely use the right to strike for the simple reason that they do not need to. The German model contradicts the wisdom of neoliberals who argue that the labor force has to be flexible, accept low wages to remain competitive, and that government must keep unions weak or else they will distort the market and irrationally drive wages above their "natural" limit.

The tax system in the USA and the UK levies the poor, the middle class and the upper middle class to subsidize the ultra rich. The tax system in both countries, contrary to what the super-rich themselves say, redistributes income toward the top. How the 1% accomplishes this is the topic of Chapter 6, "The Politics of Taxes." The super-rich, over decades, have lowered their income taxes, increasingly shifting the tax burden to regressive sales and value-added taxes. They have successfully reduced inheritance taxes and prevented serious consideration of wealth taxes. Corporate executives have aggressively moved more of their income into stock options, which means lower-taxed capital gains taxes for the super-rich and growing tax burdens for everybody else. And the super-rich, in their capacity as corporate managers, have established subsidiaries globally, many of them in tax havens, avoiding corporate taxes altogether or delaying their payment until they can obtain a tax holiday from a friendly government administration. Corporations have routinely used transfer pricing to shift profits to low-tax regimes, and losses to high tax regimes, allowing them to reduce or eliminate domestic taxes altogether. And some companies have even declared that they have no tax home, and therefore minimal if any tax liabilities because their profits are held somewhere in virtual space.

Tax dodging may help the balance sheet for corporations and improve the value of company shares, but it is costly to the average taxpayer who is subsidizing the tax breaks of multinationals. Every year up to $111 billion in corporate tax revenues in the USA are lost because of tax evasion, meaning less money available for investment in education, infrastructure, research and development (R&D), less revenue to create jobs or to put into poverty reduction programs. It also means regressive taxes to replace revenues lost to corporate tax dodging, and this in turn means higher taxes on the dwindling means of middle-class families, and especially on the poor, who also have to pay escalating sales taxes—caught in the vice of company tax evasion.

Chapter 7, "The Business of Healthcare," shows what happens when healthcare becomes a casino game. According to all legitimate studies, a business model of healthcare such as in the USA is ineffective, unfair, costly, and punitive for those who can least afford healthcare. In a word, a private (competitive) healthcare system is unhealthy. The USA spends at least twice what the UK and France pay for healthcare per capita, yet the USA has the highest morbidity rates among developed nations. In terms of longevity, access, affordability, and geographic uniformity of medical services, the USA ranks last, leading only in cost. Every year about 100,000 people die prematurely in the USA because they lack basic medical care: not because they did not seek care, but because they were denied the care they needed or were afraid to seek because of the expense. Medical bankruptcy still accounts for a majority of individual bankruptcies in the USA a half-decade after adoption of the Affordable Care Act. A Commonwealth study in 2014 ranked the UK healthcare system the best among the twelve nations it studied: but it also found that as the coalition government has privatized some of the corners of the National Health Service (NHS), it has diminished its effectiveness.

Chapter 7 explains that American healthcare is lagging because it has become a massive subsidy of Big Business. Supporting the 1% controlling the healthcare industry has become unsustainable and unhealthy for many if not most of us. Using for-profit health insurers instead of relying on nonprofits, such as France and Germany, and refusing single-payer systems in which the state insures the entire population, such as in Denmark, Norway, Sweden, and the UK is costing America about a half trillion dollars or more annually. Medicare, which is a government program, provides universal coverage for people aged 65 and over, is cost-effective, and is the most efficient and fairest healthcare program in the USA. That is because it has taken profit out of medicine.

Nobody doubts that patenting drugs based on genuine innovation deserves legal protection, otherwise the incentive to innovate might be minimal, especially when large investments are needed to develop new products. But it is not a given that patenting drugs—patents are essentially monopolies—will produce new drugs that are affordable and better than those coming off patent. Drug companies have routinely used the patent system to limit competition, not to innovate. And most innovative drugs by far have been based on government or government-funded research, begging the question of whether government research funded by the taxpayer should be patented by so-called free enterprise.

Chapter 8, "Big and Bigger Agribusiness: Farm to Table," focuses on the super-rich in agribusiness, who benefit from subsidies to corporate farms to protection for the sugar industry to subsidies for the giant seed company, Monsanto, allowing it, for example, to dump cheap corn on foreign markets like Mexico, undercutting and displacing Mexican farmers. Monsanto has used its considerable market power for decades to carve out a near monopoly in certain seed sectors, most notably genetically modified corn. It has been able to do this because of the revolving door syndrome between government and industry. The net effect has been a gigantic welfare scheme favoring Monsanto. It has bought rival seed companies, won the right to patent "life" by convincing lawmakers that anything concocted in a laboratory should be patentable, and has even won legal battles over the labeling of food products containing genetically modified ingredients: in the USA, labels do not have to identify foods containing genetically modified organisms (GMOs). Even though Monsanto controls up to 90% of the USA (genetically modified) corn market, dramatically reducing corn diversity, there has been little or no antitrust actions taken by the USA government.

The Farm Agricultural Act of 2014 was the reform act that was not. Taxpayers were still liable for a significant share of payments that went to producers if they should suffer a "loss" of either revenue or yield. Moreover, under the new law, farmers could actually do better if widespread crop failure occurs, or there is a loss of revenue from price decline (or collapse), since they are fully insured by government subsidy programs. The more that farmers "lose" from drops in yield or price, the greater the cost to the taxpayer. But the taxpayer also is liable when crop prices rose. That is because land values rise with the price of farm commodities, and that means that insurance premiums, largely paid by the federal government, go up.

The British landed elite are also fully subsidized. All they have to do to get their subsidy checks is to own land. They don't have to farm one whit, or at least they didn't. Now they do have to produce at least 5% of their income by farming, but that is a low hurdle, not a real obstacle. Meanwhile, the British landed class does not have to worry about inheritance taxes, they can continue to hold their land as a kind of sinecure, and the checks from Brussels will be in the mail, at least up until Brexit actually occurs. Until it does, the citizens of England will continue to subsidize the super-rich landed quasi-nobility: that is because the average English household annually sends £250 to Brussels in taxes, some of which then gets rerouted to the genteel estates back in England.

In both the USA and the UK, whether considering the financial and banking sector, the tax structure, compensation of "work," healthcare, or agribusiness and the food market, the 1%, the super-rich, have become too expensive to maintain. The so-called free market is a myth, covering the larger truth that much of the wealth of the super-rich is really just an unearned and undeserved subsidy unwittingly supported by taxpayers who are ill-served by their governments.

Chapter 9 "What Can Be Done?" argues that much can be done to restore fairness and social equality. What is lacking is the political will, or a political party that has the will to represent the vast majority of people and not just the privileged few.

Not lacking are precarious populations. They suffer from precarious jobs, precarious education, precarious healthcare, precarious housing, precarious income, and precarious futures. They are the alienated ones. The voiceless. They have no political party. They are on the outside looking in. They believe they have no control over their own lives.

But the precarious populations are not content to fade away. They are defiant. They are the primitive rebels. They are the refuseniks. The occupiers of Wall Street. The angry ones, the *indignados* in Spain, the rebels in Greece.

These primitive rebels share similar narratives of hardship and deprivation, similar voices and grievances, similar rejection of institutions that preach austerity and that preserve inequality. They insist that there are alternatives to radical inequality, to unequal healthcare, and to unequal education. They instinctively assert that rentier capitalism, that perpetual privilege, that eternal subsidies for the very rich, and that untaxed inheritances are unfair and undeserved. They intuitively know that deindustrialization and globalization do not explain the kinds of inequalities that are unprecedented.

That is why they look for (and form) new political parties to represent them, to fight for the economic and social rights they deserve. They are Syriza in Greece, Podemos in Spain, the Scottish National Party, progressive Labor led by Jeremy Corbyn in the UK, progressive Democrats led by Bernie Sanders in the USA.

Chapter 9 demonstrates what "primitive rebels," organized as a political party, can accomplish. Start by insisting on higher inheritance taxes: much higher. Prevent or abolish inheritance tax loopholes. Make earned income taxes much more progressive. Add a wealth tax. This would sop up a lot of unproductive capital, and it would make us much more equal. Count capital gains as earned income: why should the 1% pay less than others? Don't lower corporate taxes, raise them. Don't defer corporate taxes on earnings kept abroad. Better yet, tax corporations where their profits are made, in domestic markets. Finally, impose heavier taxes on energy production: subsidize renewable energy with taxes on dirty energy.

Regulate the banks. Break them up if necessary. Let them fail. If they do, nationalize them and make them whole again, as Sweden once did. Regulate derivatives. Severely regulate or ban sub-prime loans. Don't give banks access to pension funds. Don't give investment banks access to the Treasury window. Prevent this by rebuilding the firewall between investment and commercial banks. Finally, bring back usury laws.

Democratize corporations. Do this by putting workers on the boards of directors. Democratic boards make corporations more responsible to workers and the communities where companies are located. Establish works councils as they do in Europe: this establishes solidarity and equalizes stakeholders.

Privatized healthcare does not work. It is expensive, inefficient, and unfair. Embrace single payer as they do in Scandinavia and the UK. In single payer, virtually all outcomes are better and all people are insured throughout their lives.

Regulate drugs. Single payer makes this feasible and realistic. Force drug companies to share profits if their products are based on government or government-supported research. Don't allow drug companies to patent life. Don't grant patents for "me-too" (copycat) drugs: they are not innovations.

Based on higher tax revenues, establish sovereign wealth funds that can be used for the benefit of entire nations, such as is done in Norway. Establish a Basic Income for all citizens, a minimum that would be paid from birth and that would help people escape the poverty trap. It would also enable workers to reject unsuitable employment. They would, however, have an income floor that might make it possible to accept some jobs as supplemental income. Leave it up to them.

Combining universal healthcare, Basic Income, a more equitable tax system, a more democratic work environment, would raise human dignity and the quality of life for virtually everybody.

Notes

1. Timothy Garton Ash, "Is Europe Disintegrating?" *The New York Review of Books* 64, no. 1 (January 19, 2017): 24.
2. Philipp Ther, *Europe Since 1989: A History*, trans. Charlotte Hughes-Kreutzmüller (Princeton, NJ: Princeton University Press, 2016), x.
3. Robert B. Reich, *Saving Capitalism: For the Many, Not the Few* (New York: Alfred A. Knopf, 2015), 11.

Bibliography

Ash, Timothy Garton. "Is Europe Disintegrating?" *The New York Review of Books*. 64, no. 1. January 19, 2017.

Reich, Robert B. *Saving Capitalism: For the Many, Not the Few*. New York: Alfred A. Knopf, 2015.

Ther, Philipp. *Europe Since 1989: A History*. Translated from the German by Charlotte Hughes-Kreutzmüller. Princeton, NJ: Princeton University Press, 2016.

CHAPTER 2

Democracy Corrupted

Introduction

On January 20, 2009, as Barack Obama prepared to be inaugurated and to begin pursuit of a progressive agenda that he hoped would transform America into a more just society, a group of billionaires was meeting across the continent in California, to develop a strategy to neutralize the results of the recent election and to stop the agenda of the newly elected president.

The billionaires in attendance had been summoned by Charles and David Koch, longtime supporters of libertarianism and minimal government. Guests included like-minded billionaires: Charles Mellon Scaife, heir to Mellon banking and Gulf oil fortunes; Harry and Lynde Bradley, recipients of defense contracts; John M. Olin, a chemical and munitions producer, the Coors brewing family of Colorado; and the Devos family of Michigan and the Amway company.

For this group of billionaires, the election of Barack Obama was catastrophic. Everything he stood for was a threat. He believed in relative equality, and that meant the reform of taxation. Obama wanted universal healthcare, and that not only sounded like socialism, but also seemed a denial of the free market. And among other things Obama advocated for alternative (and clean) energy, and that sounded like government regulation. The Kochs, who had extensive energy interests of their own, and who owned miles of oil pipelines and were early advocates of fracking

J. L. Luzkow, *Monopoly Restored*,
https://doi.org/10.1007/978-3-319-93994-0_2

and traditional energy, were determined to stop Obama. The government, they complained, was intrusive and getting in the way of American freedom. Their billionaire friends agreed.

Super-Rich Rentiers and Inequality

It has become an obvious truth of our times that the super-concentration of wealth has become one of the greatest social threats of the modern era. It is abundantly clear that 2008 was far more than a warranted and necessary correction of the market for most of us. The super-rich, far from learning the necessary lesson that sharing is a good thing, instead have attempted to shift blame onto the classes below them. They have castigated the poor because they bought homes they could not afford, criticized the middle classes because they failed to get properly educated, and almost everybody else because they were not among the truly creative and intelligent. The super-rich do not recognize their contribution to the rise in inequality. They argue on the contrary that their greed—they don't call it that—has contributed to a modern financial and economic revolution. Greed, they argue, is justifiable; they spend much of their wealth arguing the point. After all, the super-wealthy believe they are needed to generate the wealth that the rest of us share, even if we get less and less of it. They do not echo the belief held by the majority of us: the more that the rich take, the less there is for the rest of us. Some among the super-rich even argue that there will always be the 1%, and technically that is true: but there has never been a time in the USA—not in the modern era—when the 1% has controlled upward of 45% of US financial wealth and roughly half of that in income. The figures for the UK are about half that of the USA: the upper 1% in the UK owns almost 23% of the national wealth and about 15% of the national income.[1]

Much of the wealth concentrated at the top is undeserved. It is not the result of competition and a hypothetical free market. On the contrary, what we have seen for some four decades is quite the opposite: a rentier economy in which huge profits are made because of the absence of competition and the suppression of a free market. A considerable portion of this wealth is the result of patents, monopolies, and subsidies of all sorts in everything ranging from energy and telecommunications to banking and finance. But it is in the financial sector especially that the greatest profits have been taken, based on income or rents derived from interest, dividends, and capital gains. In a word, the true winners in the modern era are the rentier class, those who derive income from ownership or control of scarce assets, or assets artificially made scarce, especially rents derived from the ownership of financial assets and intellectual property, including patents.[2]

Even the narrowest definition of financial income shows that across the developed world, for twenty-nine countries studied between the 1960s and 1990s, rentier income accounted for most—in a few cases all—the growth in profits.[3] If only interest and dividends are counted as rent on financial assets, the countries in which the rentier share increased most, from top to bottom were: France, the UK, South Korea, the USA, Germany, Australia, and Belgium. In each of these countries, by 2000, rental income from financial assets accounted for over 20% of total income: the UK and Italy were not far behind.[4]

The USA has become the leading rentier economy by far since 1980, which explains the extreme concentrations of income and wealth in the USA. Between 1980 and 2000, the rentier share rose more than sevenfold, accounting for a third of national income.[5] Almost two decades later, in 2017, financial services, including banking, insurance, and marketing, accounted for more than 40% of all domestic profits. In the USA, if only financial income and dividends are counted as rent, then rents account for 40% of national income. By consensus, this means the USA has become a rentier economy, dominated by a financial sector. If capital gains on financial assets are included as rent—as they should be since nothing of value has been created, then up to half of US national income may be derived from rents, a tidy sum extracted by the financial elite from everybody else.[6]

From the Great Transformation to Neoliberalism and the Rentier Economy

It seems obvious that when there is an obscene concentration of income and wealth at the top, that markets have not been working as advertised by neoliberal economists and Wall Street financiers. It seems equally obvious that when wealthy elites manage to monopolize financial, intellectual, and physical property, as they have in the USA and UK especially, and increasingly elsewhere, that none of this has come about democratically. People do not vote themselves into oblivion. They do not consent to the loss of their jobs, they do not support the evisceration of their health, or applaud the loss of their homes. In a real democracy, there would not be a small elite controlling almost half the financial wealth of a nation, as in the USA, while most others have stagnant incomes, diminishing job security, and bleak futures.

Yet we have rentier capitalism, which defends the institutions that have created and maintained inequality and growing risk for the majority, in everything from healthcare to mortgages to food security.

So how do the financial elites, those who run the large banks, those who own intellectual property, those who own tangible property, often by transferring publicly owned assets to themselves through privatization—do it?

The only way to establish a rentier economy is to capture political power and to commodify politics by creating a rentier state. Politicians rely on rental income to win and remain in office; those who have rental income enter into client relationships with politicians who enable the continuing pursuit of rents. Staying in office means pandering to owners of rents; pursuing rents means supporting pliable politicians. As a result, citizens have become disengaged, political parties have become flattened and abandoned, and those voting have been willing to listen to demagogues who make promises they do not intend to keep. Rarely if ever do politicians mention rentier capitalism: they are too busy defending it. And some rentiers are in the highest office, such as Donald Trump.

Rentier capitalism is fraudulent. Those who practice it, using the rhetoric of neoliberalism, praise free markets. The implication is that their treasure is based on competition in a free market. But this is just rhetoric, there are no free markets: rentier capitalism means unfree markets. That is what rents are all about, avoiding competition. That is also why rentiers require control of media and political parties. It is important to convince the public that wealth has been earned in competitive markets. It is important, also, for political parties to embrace the rhetoric of "free markets." Republicans and Democrats in the USA, and Conservatives and even Labor in the UK have done just that, embracing Wall Street and the City, respectively. We know the result: populist revolts against traditional parties. The Third Way offered by Tony Blair in the UK and by Bill Clinton and then Barack Obama in the USA has been abandoned by voters.

So how did the rentier class, especially the banking and finance sector, but also other rent seekers in real estate, telecommunications, healthcare, energy, and high-tech, get away with it? How did they capture the state and weld it to their neoliberal rhetoric and to policies of deregulation, privatization, financial manipulation, and low taxes? How did they create a system that bestows outlandish rents on the owners of financial, intellectual, and physical property?

The narrative begins with the Mount Pèlerin Society (MPS), a small group of mostly economists that first met in 1947 in Mont Pèlerin, Switzerland. From the beginning, the group pledged itself to an ideological core: free markets and a non-interventionist state. With added refinements such as low tax regimes, privatization of state assets, and deregulation, this has evolved into what is called neoliberalism.

The MPS has had an outsized influence on politics and the economy since at least 1972, when it first began to get traction. Many of its earliest members occupied high positions in politics and finance. Among them were Ludwig Erhard, who became the Chancellor of West Germany; Luigi Einaudi, who became president of Italy; Václav Krause, who became prime minister and then president of the Czech Republic; Arthur Burns, who became chairman of the US Federal Reserve Bank; and Roger Auboin, who became general manager of the Bank for International Settlements (BIS).[7] And as many might know, Charles Koch, the billionaire supporter of libertarian and conservative causes and often the Republican Party, has been a member since 1970.

From the beginning, MPS had an incestuous relationship with financial capital. Its first conference was funded by Crédit Suisse. It is also a club of ideologues: candidates must be nominated by two sitting members, and they must demonstrate fealty to the stated aims of MPS.[8]

MPS economists have been among the leaders promoting neoliberalism. Founding member, Austrian economist Friedrich Hayek, was invited to the London School of Economics in 1931, by Lionel Robbins, another founding member of MPS. Subsequently, Hayek became a professor at the University of Chicago. In 1974, his neoliberal views won a global audience when he was awarded the Nobel Prize for economics. He later defended the Pinochet regime in Chile, though he was aware of the oppressive and murderous nature of that regime. And while Hayek was honorary president of the MPS, he organized the meeting in a Chilean resort that planned the coup bringing Pinochet to power.

Ronald Reagan was a great admirer of Hayek. He claimed that Hayek was one of three people who most influenced him and subsequently invited him to the White House. And then there was George H. W. Bush, who in 1991 awarded Hayek the US Presidential Medal of Freedom. Margaret Thatcher was also a great admirer of Hayek and had been since her student days. She referred to his *The Constitution of Liberty* as a manifesto she could embrace. And what were the principles advanced by Hayek? Hostility to the public sector, objection to any kind of protection provided by the state, and opposition to progressive taxation, which Hayek thought oppressive and unjust.[9]

But it was Milton Friedman who inherited the mantle of the MPS and made neoliberalism into an orthodox faith. He was the youngest inaugural member of the MPS in 1947. Associated with monetarism, Friedman was a supporter of Pinochet, Thatcher, and Reagan. In 1974, he was a recipient of the Nobel Prize for Economics, providing him with a platform to spread the new orthodoxy. Friedman was also professor of economics at the University of Chicago between 1946 and 1977, where he helped train generations of economists in his view of a hands-off state.

Arnold Harberger was far less famous, but his influence at the University of Chicago, where he initiated generations into the new economics, was almost as important as Friedman's. Harberger once boasted that he had helped train more than twenty-five ministers of finance and more than a dozen central bank presidents.[10]

Between 1980 and 2008, there were seventeen winners of the Nobel Prize for Economics who were from the University of Chicago or who were educated there. What had once been a pluralistic academic discipline now became hostage to an ideological paradigm. Critics of neoliberalism were disenfranchised and found themselves estranged from their profession as economists. In the name of market freedom, the market for economics professors suddenly became one-dimensional and anything but a free market. Leading academic journals also became captives of the ascendant free market view: those who did not pass the litmus test could expect not to get published in these prestigious journals, making advancement and tenure ever more tenuous.

Encouraged by MPS, and by the ubiquitous Milton Friedman, some of the most powerful financiers in the world began putting money into alleged think tanks: these included the Heritage Foundation, the Hoover Foundation, the American Enterprise Institute, the CATO Institute in the USA, and the Center for Policy Studies. In Sydney, Australia, the Australian Center for Independent Studies was established by Maurice Newman, a denier of climate-change.

The names of these institutes and centers suggest they are neutral and engaged in scientific research. In fact, what they have in common is that they all advocate the MPS agenda, especially as promoted by Milton Friedman. And what did Friedman promote? Abolishing Social Security, reducing or eliminating corporate taxes, getting rid of progressive taxation, abolishing unions, privatizing everything, including the post office, healthcare, retirement pensions, education, even national parks. Whatever belonged to the public had no value anyway, said Friedman, not until it acquired an exchange value. And, of course, Friedman advocated shrinking government. Inequality? It would not exist, he said, if free market rules were followed.[11] Inequality occurred because of government intervention. It could be solved by withdrawing government and relying on the free market.

The ideas of Friedman and like-minded economists had been around for a while, but had never gained traction. That was because they went against the Great Transformation following the two plus decades after WWII. That period, which we can date between 1945 and 1973, was based on social solidarity, or the notion that labor deserved labor-based (jobs and income) security. During this era, the share of income going to capital as profit and the share going to labor as wages and benefits were stable, and far more equal than it would become later. Government played a large role in maintaining this stability by limiting the income that could be taken by rents, outsized return on assets, whether financial, intellectual, or physical property. This was done in numerous ways: regulating railways and utilities because these could readily become monopolies; and regulating financial markets to deter speculation while encouraging lending for productive purposes.[12] The key to this period was labor peace, for example, the Treaty of Detroit of 1950, a five-year agreement that was negotiated between General Motors and the UAW. This pact was adopted nationally, and it became the model for many industrialized countries. In return for no strikes, labor was given a share of gains in labor productivity, mostly in non-wage benefits, including pensions and health insurance.

This was the height of social democracy. Those in full-time employment could depend on rising real wages, the growth of non-wage benefits—based partially on worker contributions—and entitlements to Social Security. For those not in employment, as long as they stayed a relative minority, they could be supported by a universally available social safety net. It was when this latter group grew, threatening to destabilize the agreements between capital and labor by enlarging the costs of the welfare state, that social democracy began to break down.

The system was hierarchical from the beginning. Those unable to find regular paid employment had to depend on the welfare state, supported by left and right governments, as a way to maintain social stability. Simultaneously, those in full-time employment had to pay more income taxes to maintain that state, and welfare for others, while rising contributions to Social Security also eroded real wages. And as the number of unemployed, or irregularly employed, grew, and as governments, including social democratic governments, applied means testing, the old model in which the fortunate helped support the less fortunate was dead. Means testing meant that what had been an entitlement for all was now a stopgap for the poor. It was the definitive end of the Great Transformation that had countered the previous era of free trade, blamed by many for the Depression. It also meant the end of social democracy as it had been. As Guy Standing put it, "previous generations of social democrats had understood [that] benefits designed only for the poor are invariably poor benefits and stand to lose support among the rest of society."[13]

Labor and social democratic parties everywhere shifted from solidarity, based on a model of mutual support, to the eradication of poverty. In some cases, Left parties even helped foster poverty, mainly by weakening the social safety net, adopting workfare policies that forced workers to apply for jobs that didn't exist or that were demeaning and unsuitable, and diminishing social benefits to encourage taking temporary, low-paying, and poor-benefit jobs: in other words punishing and stigmatizing the unemployed for their unemployment. With worker solidarity increasingly a thing of the past, and as Left parties abandoned a splintering and "disappearing" working class, labor and social democratic parties veered to the right to attract the growing middle class. As for the working class, they were increasingly on their own.

There were other factors that contributed to the end of the Great Transformation. The emergence of Japan and South Korea as industrializing countries produced low-cost competition with the West for manufactured goods, beginning a crisis in balance of payments and manufacturing jobs. The tripling of the price of oil in 1973 following the emergence of the Organization of the Petroleum Exporting Countries (OPEC) only added to the inflationary pressures inherited from Keynesianism, which had relied on stimulating demand to produce full employment. Now too much stimulation, together with rising oil prices and wage gains, would only lead to runaway inflation. Moreover, profit margins were squeezed by energy costs, wage gains, generous benefit packages, and maintaining the welfare state, energizing the corporate world to deploy its ideological paradigm of neoliberalism.

And this was precisely where MPS and Milton Friedman and his acolytes came in. The emergence of a global market, the splintering of labor into organized labor and the "others," difficulties with balance of payments because of emergent developing countries, and the inability of Keynesian policy makers to tame inflation, opened a new era. The closed national economy now had to compete with the open global economy. That provided an opportunity for the neoliberals. But that opportunity depended on gaining power, and that would mean getting the government out of the way of Big Business or simply capturing the government. As the corporate world and their neoliberal economists put it, the time was right for "free-trade," which in corporate lingo meant deregulation and privatization.

Oligarchy and the Commodification of Everything

Milton Friedman's ideas could now be pressed forward globally. There was only one way to grow prosperity in the future: liberalize markets, privatize and commodify everything, and dismantle all institutions that protected people from market forces. Regulations could not be justified if they hindered growth; for Friedman, they hindered growth by definition. Friedman pressed forward. Left alone, he argued, markets rewarded efficient and punished inefficient firms. Friedman did not bemoan all that "creative destruction" brought about by "competition": financiers, he argued, would help transfer assets to efficient companies. The same reasoning advocated for denationalization. After all, transferring assets from public ownership to the more "rational" and "competitive" free market meant more growth. And more jobs. This sounded right, and even New Labor and Tony Blair bought into this.

But financial deregulation didn't quite behave as neoliberals predicted. Once financiers were set free, they had little interest in routing capital into productive activity. Not when it could be much more lucratively employed even if that meant accepting more risk and especially when that risk could be transferred to the taxpayer (pension funds for one). So financiers indulged themselves in frenzies of speculation. They made tons of money from interest, commissions, insider trading, and capital gains. The results as we all know, and as we detail in Chapter 3, were endless rounds of bubble economies. Hot money, foot-fancy capital chasing global opportunities, traveled at high velocity in and out of countries, wherever interest and profits were highest. Inevitably, the bubbles burst: the Latin American financial crisis of the 1980s, the Asian financial crisis of the late 1990s, the financial and banking crisis of 2007, and the real estate bubble of 2008 followed. Yet even after all these crises, even after the collapse of the US hedge fund, Long-Term Capital Management, which had two Nobel Prize-winning board members, neoliberal ideology remained ascendant. And even after daily events and common sense suggested that neoliberal-supported free markets and deregulation were a catastrophe for most of us, the political will to challenge Wall Street and the City never materialized.

The reason was politics. Armed with its free trade slogan, the MPS, associated think tanks, and the upper echelons of the 1% pursued their real agenda: growing rents in finance and banking, growing rents from intellectual property in telecommunications, hi-tech and Big Pharma, and growing rents from physical assets like energy. It turned out that about 80% of books that denied climate change was caused by the activities of mankind were connected to free market think tanks through their authors or publishers.[14] Many of these same think tanks were funded by fossil fuel interests. CATO Institute admitted to funding from Big Oil. In fact, its ties to Big Oil were extensive. The CATO Institute was founded with the oil fortune of Charles Koch, the conservative right-wing billionaire. The 200 top individual contributors included Charles and his brother David Koch, who also contributed through their Charles Lambe Foundation. CATO has received contributions from oil magnate Phillip Anschutz's foundation.[15]

The Heritage Foundation has also consistently denied climate change. Like CATO, it has received extensive support from the Charles Lambe Foundation, $4.8 million between 1998 and 2012. Among its contributors are ExxonMobil and Peabody Coal, fossil fuel companies that have both denied mankind's contribution to climate change. Other major funders have included Amoco, Amway, Chase Manhattan Bank, Chevron, Exxon, Mobil Oil, and SmithKline Beckman, all of whom have had a so-called free trade, deregulation, low-corporate tax agenda: the presence of big oil can again hardly be missed. Not coincidentally, the Heritage Foundation has a long-term relationship with the MPS.

The American Enterprise Institute (AEI) has also clocked in on the free trade agenda. The same Charles Koch, of Big Oil interests, donated at least $8 million to AEI in 2005. ExxonMobil has also been a contributor to AEI: not a surprise that the AEI has consistently denied climate change. In early 2007, the *Guardian* reported that AEI was offering scientists and economists $10,000 each "to undermine a major climate change report" published by the United Nations Intergovernmental Panel on Climate Change.[16] The AEI has also described minimum wage hikes as reckless and Dodd–Frank's attempt to regulate Wall Street as a disaster.[17]

The links between the MPS and the Institute for Economic Affairs are even more direct. The Institute was founded by Antony Fisher on the advice of (no less than) Friedrich Hayek: the explicit idea was to promote free market ideas and deregulation. Although it had a clearly libertarian basis, it presented itself as a neutral think tank whose views were disguised as science. This was hardly the case. It was funded by the Sarah Scaife Foundation and the Mellon family—Richard Mellon Scaife—who inherited his fortune from Big Oil (Gulf). The Institute, unsurprisingly, was opposed to corporate taxes, repeating a pattern we have already seen: inherited fortunes based on concessions of public commons for private profit—oil in this case—being used to dismantle protection of public goods, shift tax burdens to the public, and promote deregulation by calling it free trade.[18]

At the heart of neoliberalism, and of the outlook of MPS, are two incompatible arguments: a belief in so-called unregulated free markets and a belief that trade unions and collective bargaining, any collective body asserting the rights of labor, must be regulated. Whether dismantling regulation, privatizing the public sector, liberalizing capital markets, and deregulating Wall Street, while regulating labor, there is one objective: dismantle democracy, and capture the state, not necessarily in that order. On the one side, there is the religion of free trade, and on the other, the defense of property rights, regardless of how property was acquired, including concessions such as oil being granted by the state.

Plutocrats: Unleashing Capital, Regulating Labor, Capturing the State

What CATO, the Heritage Foundation, and other neoliberal institutions wanted was the free market, deregulation, withdrawal of the state, and the privatization of public goods: in a word, the free rein of capital.

Their attitude toward Labor was the reverse; it had to be regulated or reregulated. It had also to be flexible, that is, shorn of protection, which meant weak unions and which also meant no borders for workers and the free movement of labor. This too was part of the neoliberal argument. Organized labor propped up wages and benefits, and that was a "distortion" of the natural laws of economics: it meant higher prices, lower profits, and the inability to compete in the global market. And what was the best way to tame labor? Capture the state for one. Control the media for another. Use political leverage to dismantle the institutions of liberal democracy. Control the science of energy, the science of dietetics. Use financial leverage to control the state. Operate through powerful financial circuits, largely invisible to the general public, to secure political power. The endgame had one objective: secure rents, extract wealth. Once again, the free market was but a smokescreen.

So how have the super-rich gained access and translated the ownership of assets into political power? Again, we see the MPS front and center. In 1954, it established a long-term relationship with the Bilderberg Group. The avowed aim? Promote "free market" capitalism. Annual Bilderberg meetings at global luxury resorts brought together prime ministers, directors of central banks, CEOs of multinationals and banks, and principals from think tanks and the media. Henry Kissinger has been a member, so has Mario Monti, former Prime Minister of Italy and former European Commissioner.[19] Bilderberg Group is linked to the US Council on Foreign Relations and the Trilateral Commission through its members. Many members or former members of the commission have taken leadership positions in government, industry, and finance, at national and international levels. Several have headed the World Bank.

There are other informal networks of the super-rich: the World Economic Forum that meets in Davos and a number of multinational corporations linking the global (especially financial) elite. Most prominent is Black Rock, the world's largest asset manager. It controls $4.5 trillion in assets, including corporate bonds, sovereign debt, and commodities and shares. With the leverage that comes from holding such assets, Black Rock gets a seat at many tables. It is a major lobbying force in North America and Europe, lobbying for the financial interests of its investors.[20] With global reach, and with its unrivaled assets, it operates almost as an unofficial broker and parallel but unelected government for the interests of the global super-rich.

Another conduit of the global super-rich that includes links to the Saudi royal family is the Carlyle Group, with linkages to military contracts. Carlyle Group qualifies as the world's largest private equity company. Carlyle runs a portfolio of more than 200 companies, with a payroll of more than 675,000 employees. Prominent politicians appointed to its board reveal the links between the world of the global financial super-rich and the global political elite. President George H. W. Bush has been a member: so has former Secretary of State, James A. Baker; and so has former British Prime Minister John Major.[21] What these political figures share is a conservative outlook on how world financial and political interests should be shaped. All are the official representatives of the global financial elite, the owners of assets, be they financial, intellectual, or physical property.

What do Black Rock and Carlyle have in common with each other and with the global super-rich? Their common aim is to minimize tax obligations, build a global rentier economy that rewards capital above all else, and promote "free trade" by allowing private equity to expand assets with minimal government interference. A favorite technique? Establish pass-through entities that move corporate earnings directly to their owners, avoiding corporate taxation. This has been so effective that pass-through corporations now account for more than 25% of US companies. Despite the magnitude of Black Rock and Carlyle, and the assets they control, they remain largely invisible to the larger American public: exactly as they want to be. Such global companies can make effective use of tax havens, hiding both the income of corporations and the individuals who own and run them. That is what a rentier economy means. That is how assets managers can expand the return on capital, while minimizing returns to labor. The fact that the global super-rich have a common agenda, and common objectives, does not mean they are engaged in a clever global conspiracy. But they don't have to be. Everything they do is legal. They are simply leveraging financial clout into political power. But there is something missing in all this. It is called democracy, and nobody gets to vote on all these dealings. And the ideological paradigm that the elitist think tanks are constantly promoting—as we have seen—is that there are no alternatives. This is globalization, a natural outcome of modern technological transformation. Just to be certain there are no reversals or surprises, the super-rich have moved to take over political parties.

Oligarchs: The Party Is Over

By 2016, it had become clear that political parties had reoriented themselves to serve the interests of the super-rich, including financial interests (banking, finance, and real estate) but also owners of intellectual property, especially in healthcare, pharmaceuticals, and telecommunication, and owners of physical property, as in energy producers.

Political parties, beginning in the late nineteenth century, were clearly aligned with their class foundations. The Conservatives in the UK represented the landed class and the new industrial leadership. Labor, from its inception, represented the industrial proletariat. Allegiances were clear and uniform. And both parties had a well-defined platform, more or less ideologically consistent with the classes they represented.

In the USA, Democrats were on the Left and represented the interests of the industrial working class. Republicans represented the landed and industrial classes. In Europe, the social democrats represented the Left, and Christian democrats the Right. When the latter were in power, they generally embraced the policies of the social democrats. Social solidarity was maintained.

Until well into the 1970s, the political balance remained relatively secure. But this changed quickly when national economic borders were challenged, working classes were threatened by automation and cheap labor in emerging economies, and capital could be employed abroad more profitably without any "border" restrictions. Overnight, the class basis of Left parties collapsed. The working classes began to shrink, while those who had benefited from social democratic policies and risen into the middle class reoriented their thinking toward conservative parties.[22]

Social democrats, including Tony Blair in the UK, Bill Clinton in the USA, Gerhard Schröder in Germany, and Göran Persson in Sweden, with a collapsing class basis, realigned themselves in what they called the Third Way. They embraced neoliberal economics and the free market. The class struggle was over, and they seemed to be saying. Wall Street and the City were no longer enemies. The more wealth accumulated by the filthy rich, the better for everybody else. Just redistribute, give the losers enough to keep them off the streets, and don't worry about the loss of manufacturing jobs. As Clinton, Blair, and Gordon Brown put it, those weren't coming back anyway.[23] Not only did the Third Way leaders fail to oppose rentier capitalism, and the moguls of finance especially, they quite literally handed over the reins of power to them. Tony Blair made the Bank of England independent, putting financiers at the helm of economic policy. Bill Clinton abandoned much of the base of the Democrats. He scuttled welfare as it had been known in 1996 with the Personal Responsibility and Work Opportunity Reconciliation Act. This so-called welfare reform was highly punitive toward poor families. It introduced restrictive time limits for entitlement to benefits and extended workfare, forcing people into poverty-wage jobs. For the working class, or what would be left of it, Clinton urged greater flexibility. He cautioned the young to get the education and skills they needed so they could enter the modern workforce.

How Wall Street Crushed Main Street and Corrupted Democracy

But, simultaneously, Clinton advocated the North American Free Trade Agreement (NAFTA), costing hundreds of thousands of American jobs, and later he supported China's entry into the World Trade Organization (WTO), forcing millions of American workers to face-off against cheap Chinese labor. And he was not done. He cravenly put Wall Street at the helm of Treasury, moving Robert Rubin directly from the investment bank Goldman Sachs to Secretary of Treasury. Later, Clinton helped remove the firewall between investment banks and commercial banks, by advocating the end of Glass–Steagall, which had acted to prevent those kinds of mergers since the 1930s. When the separation ended, speculative investment banks had direct access to the Treasury window; they had the same government guarantees as commercial banks once they merged.

Many economists credited the end of Glass–Steagall with the financial and mortgage meltdowns of 2007–2008. At the least, the merger allowed excessive leveraging and fueled speculation in unregulated derivatives. Why they were deregulated had nothing to do with the "free market." While Rubin was unleashing the bankers to make sub-prime loans that produced the inevitable crash, and arguing against regulating derivatives—a major source of profit for Goldman Sachs, his former company—the Deputy Treasury Secretary, Larry Summers, was working hard to maintain unregulated derivative trading, despite their high volatility. In 1998, Summers famously called Brooksley Born, then the head of the Commodity Futures Trading Commission. His message was clear:

thirteen bankers were in his office and they were insisting that if she proposed regulating derivatives she would cause the worst financial crisis since WW II.[24]

The invasion of Washington by Wall Street, led by Goldman Sachs and its neoliberal, so-called free trade philosophy, continued unabated. Derivatives remained unregulated. Hank Paulson, Goldman Sachs' CEO, became the Secretary Treasury in 2006. In 2007, he described the banking system of the USA as "healthy." It was still "safe" as late as July 2008, according to Paulson. Several months later, he noticed that the economy had signs of sudden mortality. The reason was not so much Wall Street and the banking industry, but government inaction and mistakes. Wall Street was fingered for excessive risk-taking. He did not say that excessive risk-taking was the result of government inaction resulting from the pressure of Wall Street, led by Goldman Sachs.

Meanwhile, Goldman Sachs attained a global presence at the highest levels of government. The Governor of the Bank of England, Mark Carney, had been a Goldman Sachs employee. So had William Dudley, chair of the Federal Reserve Bank of New York. So was Jim O'Neill, over in the UK: he was a former chief economist for Goldman Sachs, before being ennobled and becoming a Treasury minister in 2015. O'Neill, with as much clairvoyance as Hank Paulson, predicted—not long before the financial crash of 2008—that many millions more were about to enter the ranks of the globally affluent. Instead, millions lost their jobs and homes and joined the ranks of the unemployed, victims of policies advocated by Goldman Sachs and Wall Street and the City.[25]

Goldman Sachs was a major beneficiary, along with other financial houses, when Lloyd's Bank was re-privatized following the British government's rescue of the bank. Goldman was a major player in the lucrative area of bank bailouts. It and other financial firms profited from quantitative easing, a government policy that was highly beneficial to banks by giving them limitless liquidity. Unsurprisingly, these policies were largely written by the financial industry, further testimony that government at the highest levels bowed to the needs and whims of Wall Street.

During the 2008 crisis, both Goldman Sachs and Morgan Stanley were granted the right by the government to become bank holding companies, giving them access to government liquidity. Translated, this meant direct access to the Treasury window at banker rates—close to zero interest. It seemed there was no limit to Goldman influence at the highest levels of government and no limits to its corruption. In 2014, Goldman Sachs was involved in a deal that merged two oil companies. Normally, this was not a problem. But in this case Goldman had a financial stake in one of the companies, and a Goldman banker had a personal stake. Despite this obvious conflict of interest, the New York Fed hardly raised an eyebrow, an indication that Goldman had ascended to the top of the power ladder.

What was happening in finance was not the so-called free market. It was rentier capitalism, or getting government out of the way so financiers could make even more money, knowing their bets would be covered by the state.[26] The Third Way was the ultimate capitulation to bankers and financiers. It meant the end of liberal values. It meant also that the Left was competing with the Right by copying its values: free market capitalism, telling workers they were on their own, dismantling the protective state, and the lingering shreds of the social contract.

And just as the Left was moving toward the center, the Right was moving further to the right, the hard right. It was also losing its class basis. Formerly, it could appeal to the successful middle class, enlarged by industrialization. But by the 1970s this class also was shrinking, especially in the US and the UK, to a large extent because of deindustrialization. Not able to look at the diminishing middle to win elections, the Right needed to appeal elsewhere. It looked to the world of finance, the world that possessed the wealth to fund elections—and think tanks. And it looked to the growing minions disaffected by the Left, workers left behind by deindustrialization who saw the export of their jobs, or were replaced by machines, or saw Left parties abandon their unions.

As the Left and its base fragmented, the Right moved quickly to seize the advantage caused by financial crises. In the USA and UK, this could be easily followed. The line was always the same: too much government regulation and not enough free market and/or free trade.[27] The Left and the Right seemed to converge on this point. Unleash the bankers, unleash free traders. The market is rational: government is not. Don't trust government planners or regulators. Ironically, 2008 was only a slight burp. Neoliberals continued to dominate government. They were still not held accountable. In fact, they largely invaded government. Even President Obama brought Wall Street into his administration: Timothy Geithner at Treasury, Larry Summers at the National Economic Council.

The New Oligarchs and the Dismantling of Democracy

Just to make certain, Conservatives everywhere began to reorganize the electorate and electoral strategies. Majorities would no longer be needed to win elections, not if enough voters lost the right to vote, not if electoral boundaries were redrawn. Once in power after 2010, British Conservatives moved to strengthen their position by redrawing constituency boundaries. They also extended the franchise to expatriates living abroad for fifteen years, an elderly group previously disenfranchised, but sure to be part of the Conservative electoral base once enfranchised. Another measure changed the voter registration system in place since 1918, which had allowed an individual in each household to register all eligible voters in the same household. This change, made just ahead of the 2016 elections, was projected to lead to a drop of almost two million voters, consisting mostly of the young, students, ethnic minorities, and residents of inner cities, all of whom were most likely to vote for left-wing parties. This new calculus became the basis for redistributing seats away from traditionally Labor urban areas with multiple-occupancy and private rental housing toward suburban and rural areas favoring Conservatives.[28]

The funding of political parties has also been changed to help Conservatives. The ceiling for donations to political parties has been raised, but Labor's funding base has been limited. This has been done by giving union members an opt-in choice for political funding that previously was automatic. This is despite the fact that there is no comparable rule for corporate political donations: shareholders do not have to give consent to opt-in. As a result, Labor loses some £1 million annually.[29]

But when it comes to raising the ceiling on what can be donated to political parties, the USA has again led the way. *Citizens United vs Federal Election Commission* famously led to the verdict that corporations are people and are therefore entitled to First Amendment rights, notably the freedom of speech. This decision by the Supreme Court in 2010, effectively eliminated any ceiling on what a corporation could commit to a political campaign, and ushered in the era of unlimited corporate influence, or the New Oligarchy in the USA. Rentier capitalists, worried about the financial meltdown of 2008, and the possibility this would become global and effect their assets, and also beset by the election of Barack Obama, decided they needed to do more than engage in a war of ideas through their think tank mouthpieces.

In January 2009, a group of eighteen billionaires met, led by Charles and David Koch. Many of these rich elite had long promoted an ultra-conservative, free market, deregulation, privatization agenda, through the think tanks they funded. The election of Barack Obama, however, was a dire warning: the new president did not share the ideological paradigm of the billionaires. Not on taxes. Not on free trade. Certainly not on deregulation, or getting the government out of their way and letting the market make so-called corrections. The market was rational, but an Obama-led government was not.

Altogether the eighteen billionaires in attendance, as of 2015, were worth more than $214 billion. In one room only there were more billionaires than there had been altogether in 1982.[30] The Koch brothers alone had an estimated worth of $14 billion each in 2009. Between them, they owned the second largest private company in the USA. Their assets included four-thousand miles of pipelines, oil refineries in Alaska, Texas, and Minnesota, and coal and chemical companies among other businesses.[31] The Kochs had successfully grown their business, but they had also inherited considerable wealth from their father, Fred, as had a number of the billionaires at their clandestine meeting. In fact, Fred Koch's wealth was not just considerable, much of it was made through deals with Stalin's Russia, and later, he helped Hitler and Nazi Germany build oil refineries that would be useful for Hitler's military machine.[32]

The men in the "conference" with the Kochs were not just rich, they were super-rich, and they were not just the top 1%, they were the top 0.01%. A number were in oil, and some were in finance, especially private equity, the buying and selling of companies. Others were in hedge funds. What they all shared in common was the fear of government intrusion into their business affairs. Virtually, all were climate change deniers. The Kochs led the way, opposing government environmental regulations that would hurt their fossil fuel interests. This elite group was also held together by opposition to government regulation and taxation—hedge funds and private equity firms were virtually unregulated, and they wanted to keep them that way.[33]

Among the better-known financiers attending the meeting were Steven A. Cohen, Paul Singer, and Stephen Schwarzman. Cohen was under criminal investigation for insider trading, and in other words he had done everything to avoid market rules and competition. Singer was an ideological free market conservative who made his fortune by buying distressed debt in economically failing countries and then taking aggressive action to collect that debt. Despite his free market ideology, he pressed government to squeeze impoverished countries to help him collect the debts he had bought. Schwarzman also stood out for excess. He came under government scrutiny after taking advantage of the carried-interest tax loophole, which allowed him to pay lower capital gains taxes on profits.[34] These men were all stunning examples of rentier capitalism, using the free market as a smoke screen to render their financial affairs invisible, evading taxes by avoiding government scrutiny, screaming free market when they wanted the government to remain out of their way, and seeking to influence government when it came to getting energy and other concessions such as military contracts.

Another billionaire attendee at the Koch seminar was Richard Strong, founder of the mutual fund Strong Capital Management. He was banned from the financial industry for life after an investigation by New York attorney general Eliot Spitzer revealed that he had illegally timed trades to benefit his friends and family. He subsequently paid a fine of $60 million and issued a public apology.[35] Philip Anschutz, founder of Qwest Communications, whose net worth in 2015 was estimated by Forbes to be $11.8 billion, was also at the Koch conference. A Christian who funded movies with biblical themes, he once tried to avoid paying any capital gains taxes by using a transaction known as prepaid variable forward contracts: he promised to give shares to investment firms at a later date in return for cash up front—that would be untaxed since no shares actually were transferred. The transaction didn't stand up in court (though on a technicality). But the verdict meant that Anschutz was officially a tax cheat.[36]

It was this group of elite ultra-rich, led by the Kochs, that was instrumental in dismantling democracy as it had been known and practiced in the USA. The most dramatic victory came with the controversial case known as Citizens United. This was a political action committee, founded in 1988, funded largely by the Kochs. Citizens United was from the first a propaganda machine, arguing that it supported "traditional American values of limited government, freedom of enterprise, strong families, and national sovereignty and security."[37] But the objective of Citizens United was anything but traditional. For one, Koch funding was largely concealed. For another, "limited government" meant minimizing taxes, while "freedom of enterprise" meant climate change denial, the ideological paradigm of Big Oil.

It took more than two decades, but when the Supreme Court ruled in the case *Citizens United v Federal Election Commission* that corporations were persons with first amendment rights, it revoked any limits on how much corporations could spend on political campaigns, so long as they did not directly fund candidates. The court's decision effectively led to Political Action Committees (PACs) that could receive as much money as was offered, so long as the PAC didn't coordinate its actions with a political campaign. And there was more: the court validated the principle that individuals could also give unlimited funding to a PAC(s).

Once the sluice gates were open, how to employ the support of billionaires became paramount. With Obama controlling Washington, the strategy aimed at congressional elections and the control of state gubernatorial offices and state assemblies. It was in the latter assemblies where the new congressional districts would be redrawn following the 2010 census: control the redistricting, and it would be possible to redraw districts to advantage rural and suburban populations, where Conservative supporters lived, and disadvantage urban areas where poorer and ethnic populations lived, likely voters for Democrats. To implement the Redistricting Majority Project, several Koch-supported operatives took over the Republican State Leadership Committee (RSLC), which previously functioned as a catchall bank account for corporations that wanted to influence state laws. All that was needed now, with all limits on funding removed, was to raise the money. By the end of 2010, huge donations were being raised. Tobacco companies Altria and Reynolds gave millions. Walmart contributed millions more, so did the pharmaceutical industry and rich private donors who had attended the Koch conference in 2009. By the end of the year, the RSLC had raised $30 million to fund state elections for governor and state assemblies, while the Democrats had raised only $10 million.[38]

The ploy worked. Consider the following illustration from Wisconsin polling results in 2012. Election data from five of Wisconsin's eight US House districts, seventeen of thirty-three state Senate districts, and fifty-six of ninety-nine state Assembly districts voted Republican for president—although Mitt Romney lost the state as a whole by nearly 7 points.[39] During the midterm elections in 2014, the Kochs spent more than $300 million in support of right-wing candidates. They had great success: nine out of ten of the candidates they helped fund were elected.[40] By the end of 2016, Republicans controlled thirty-two state legislatures to the Democrats twelve; thirty-four states had Republican governors while only fifteen governors were Democrats.

With Obama's second term coming to an end, the Koch-led juggernaut had a chance to take over Washington as well. For the 2016 election, the political war chest accumulated by the Kochs and their narrow circle of billionaire friends reached an unprecedented $889 million, completely dwarfing the scale of money that in the days of Watergate was considered deeply corrupt. The Kochs actually committed more spending to 2016 races than either the Democrats or the Republicans were able to raise.[41] But they had a deep aversion to Donald Trump, so they concentrated on state and congressional campaigns, helping to preserve right-wing congressional Republican seats in key states such as Wisconsin and Texas.

One of the principal claims for electoral democracy is "no taxation without representation." With the Kochs and select conservative billionaires leading the way, that foundation of democracy has been replaced by representation without taxation. It isn't just that billionaires can establish PACs to buy politicians with invisible money. In the USA, it is also about establishing charitable foundations, now numbering more than 100,000, that reroute untaxed money into political campaigns with little if any scrutiny.[42] This has allowed billionaires like the Kochs to claim charitable contributions that reduce their tax bill, while still using their untaxed monies for political purposes by simply rerouting money into so-called charitable foundations.

The USA may lead the way when it comes to corrupting the democratic processes, but Britain, as we know, is not far behind. There as in the USA, the super-rich oligarchs who own the means of communication can employ the full power of modern communication technology to sway public opinion and dictate public perception about what is and what is not "reality." Truth becomes a function of power, power itself becomes truth, and the public interest vanishes into the dim horizon.

As in the USA, the British oligarchy is dominated by rentier capitalists, who support candidates receptive to their deregulating, privatizing, and free trade paradigm. Leading the way in Britain is Rupert Murdoch, the same media mogul who owns Fox News in the USA. Murdoch controls an extensive media empire in Britain that includes Sky television, *The Sun*, the largest tabloid in Britain, and *The Times*, the establishment newspaper. Despite Murdoch's considerable political leverage through the media he controls, he is not British, he was not born in Britain, and he doesn't live in Britain. Moreover, Murdoch's media empire holding company, News Corps, was found, when Tony Blair was Prime Minister, to have paid almost nothing in taxes dating back to the late 1980s. The tax sums that were paid were so meager that a task force consisting of representatives from Australia, Canada, the UK, and the USA was formed to investigate why. When fear of a backlash from Murdoch and his media stalwarts emerged, the investigation was dropped, despite the fact that a study of 101 subsidiaries of News Corps over a period of eleven years concluded that profits of $1.4 billion had hardly been taxed at all.[43]

Had Britain been a democracy in a meaningful sense, Murdoch would not have been protected by any political party, let alone *New Labor*. But he was hardly the only billionaire who had managed to ingratiate himself with Third Way New Labor. Despite the assurances of Chancellor Gordon Brown that he would not grant tax relief to millionaires (and billionaires) who shifted income and profits to offshore tax havens, he was not interested in holding the super-rich accountable. The UK's fifty-four billionaires in the year 2006 had an estimated income of £126 billion. Income tax liabilities should have been about £50 billion: in fact they were estimated to be £14.7, about 0.14% of what they should have been.[44]

Even under New Labor, the British oligarchy was thriving. The power of money and media combined was simply irresistible and corrupting. As Guy Standing has reminded us, no political party in Britain has won a general election since 1974 without the support of Rupert Murdoch and his media empire. Even after several of Murdoch's employees and associates were convicted of illegally hacking mobile phones and bribing police officers, Murdoch was still treated as a quasi-royal by Britain's leading politicians. Andy Coulson, erstwhile editor of the (now defunct) Murdoch-owned tabloid, *News of the World*, was hired by David Cameron as press secretary when Cameron was still in the opposition. Later, Cameron brought Coulson to Downing Street, before the former was forced to resign when he was charged, and later convicted, of phone hacking. And when Tony Blair became the leader of Labor in 1994, he traveled to Australia to reassure Murdoch that Labor would not be a threat to the interests of Murdoch.[45]

In the UK, Conservative Party campaigns are routinely funded by billionaire oligarchs and by multinational financial corporations, most of which pay little if any taxes in Britain. Prior to the 2015 general election, the hedge fund, Caxton Associates played a key role bankrolling the Conservatives campaign: Caxton Associates is registered in the US tax haven of Delaware.[46]

In 2016, the annual Black and White Ball that is used by Conservatives to raise funds was sponsored by Shore Capital, an investment bank registered in Guernsey, another tax haven. The wife of the chairman, who donated £500,000 to the Tories, had helped to organize earlier balls as well. In fact, the Black and White Ball was a veritable gold mine for Conservatives, a happy hunting ground for the super-rich. In 2014, the ball was attended by guests whose estimated wealth was more than £22 billion. A year later, some twenty-seven of the fifty-nine wealthiest hedge fund managers listed on the *Sunday Times* Rich List had donated more than £19 million to the campaign chest of the Conservatives. The world of finance and the Conservative Party were so tight that Michael Farmer, a hedge fund manager who had contributed more than £6.5 million to the Tories, was made co-treasurer of the party and given a peerage.[47]

The sums given by hedge funds were large enough to be corrupting, and they showed how much influence money could buy. The investment turned out to be a golden egg. In 2013, after the Conservatives had already reaped millions in donations from hedge fund managers, Chancellor George Osborne abolished a stamp duty reserve tax on investment funds, returning the favor of the hedge funds that had supported the Tories. The tax savings paid by hedge funds was an estimated £147 million, a figure that swamped the sums acknowledged above. Had donations of the Conservatives been considered an investment, then the return was impressive.[48] From the point of view of the public and the public good, the whole affair was simply a swindle, evidence of a new oligarchy, and a republic of the super-rich.

New Monopoly Rent Seekers

When George W. Bush entered the White House as president, he inherited a budget surplus of 2.4% of gross domestic product (GDP). Within 4 years, he turned that into a deficit of 3.6%, an almost unprecedented turnaround in such a short space of time. How was he able to squander so much public treasure in such a brief period? Between 2002 and 2005, agricultural subsidies doubled. Tax expenditures, mostly a system of subsidies and preferences embedded in the tax code, increased by more than 25%. And tax breaks for the president's friends in the oil and gas industry increased by billions more dollars.[49]

Since 2008, as President Bush was exiting office, more and more sectors of the economy have been dominated by giants: Goldman Sachs, Citibank, JPMorgan-Chase, Google, Amazon, Facebook, Microsoft, and Apple are household names. These companies have taken disproportionate percentages of market share, buying out potential rivals, or squeezing them out, creating near monopolies in the process. And as the economic power of the few has been established, so has the free market been corrupted: monopoly or duopoly or oligopoly is bound to produce less competition and be less entrepreneurial. Robert Reich has provided the evidence. As the giants have solidified their economic power, the number of new firms entering the market in the USA has declined from well over 14% in 1978 to just over 8% in 2011. Meanwhile, the number of firms exiting has remained relatively stable, from just above 10% in 1978 to just under 10% in 2011.[50] Much of what has happened in the USA and the UK, as well, is because of the failure to enforce anti-trust laws sufficiently, or the unwillingness to pass new laws regulating industry: in a word, the capturing of political parties by rent-seeking corporate super-rich, leading to the withering of democracy.

The telecommunications industry, with just a few leaders like Comcast, is no exception. The USA has some of the highest broadband prices among developed countries, but it is the leader in some of the slowest speeds, features that seemed to become permanent by 2016. As Robert Reich has pointed out, the average peak Internet connection speed in America is 40% slower than in Hong Kong or South Korea. The reason the costs are so high and the service so poor is that most Americans have to rely on local cable monopolies if they want to connect to Internet. The USA lags behind Sweden, Estonia, Hong Kong, Japan, and almost all developed countries in fiber connections, placing it twenty-eighth worldwide in speed of Internet access and twenty-third in terms of cost.[51] Even Russia, despite its lagging technology, has faster Internet speeds at a cost of about $10 per month.[52]

The slow speeds and high costs of cable service in the USA are because of monopoly or near monopoly conditions. In other words, limited or no competition; anything but a competitive market. Once again, it does not have to be this way. All the inhabitants of Stockholm have high-speed service for $28 per month. This happened only because Stockholm built fiber lines and then leased them out to private operators. The result was intense competition, low prices, and universal coverage.

The city quickly recovered its costs and has been bringing in millions of dollars in revenue for itself.[53] All this happened because Stockholm blocked monopoly, but still allowed a free market: in fact, it *established* a free market.

The only reason that American cities are not doing the same as Stockholm is that cable companies have barrels of cash they use to buy political influence. The result is virtual monopoly, not competition. Armies of lobbyists and lawyers are employed to make sure that cities don't rebel. Again, Robert Reich:

> [Cable companies] have successfully pushed twenty states to enact laws prohibiting cities from laying fiber cables. In 2011, John Malone, chairman of Liberty Global, the largest cable company in the world, admitted that when it comes to high-capacity data connections in the United States, 'Cable's pretty much a monopoly now'. Indeed, by 2014 more than 80 percent of Americans had no choice but to rely on one single cable company for high-capacity wired data connections to the Internet. Since none of the cable companies face real competition, they have no incentive to invest in fiber networks or even to pass along to consumers the lower prices their large scale makes possible.[54]

Chattanooga has avoided the monopolistic practices of industry by building its own high-speed, efficient, fiber-optic network. But Comcast, which enjoys a virtual monopoly in some markets, sued Chattanooga's utility company twice by 2014 and was promoting a well-oiled PR campaign to discredit the city-owned and managed service.[55] Meanwhile, nineteen states have imposed significant obstacles to communities that might want to follow the Chattanooga example, while several states, Missouri, Nevada, and Texas, have enacted outright bans on community owned and operated cable and high-speed fiber-optic networks.[56]

Telecommunication companies are intent mostly on eliminating competition. The best way to do that is to buy influence, which means once again the diminishing of democracy. To assure this, they have utilized an army of lobbyists, who mostly lobby the Federal Communication Commission (FCC), which oversees the telecommunication industry, or they target members of Congress who sit on relevant committees, including the Senate Subcommittee on Communication, Technology, and the Internet, and the House Subcommittee on Communications and Technology. As noted by the Center for Responsive Politics in 2014, eighteen people had both lobbied for Comcast and spent time in the public sector. Of those, twelve were registered lobbyists for Comcast, with five of them having spent time at the FCC. It was a case once again of the revolving door syndrome. The most flagrant illustration of this was Meredith Baker. She was an advocate of the industry before she was appointed to the FCC in 2009. She remained a member of the FCC for almost two years, but then cut her four-year term short to become Comcast's senior vice president of government affairs.[57]

Baker, who said she saw no conflict of interest, made a transition from FCC leadership to industry that was hardly unprecedented. Michael Powell, chairman of the FCC between 1997 and 2005, became the CEO of the National Cable and Telecommunications Association (NCTA), an industry group, in 2011. And Jonathan Adelson, an FCC commissioner between 2002 and 2009, became the CEO of PCIA, the Wireless Infrastructure Association, in 2012.[58]

According to the Center for Responsive Politics, two years after Michael Powell became CEO at NCTA, the NCTA spent $19.6 million lobbying in Washington. Between the years 2006 and 2016, it spent at least $12 million annually just lobbying Congress.[59] In the 2014 election cycle, Democrats and Republicans each received more than $8 million in campaign contributions from the NCTA.[60]

One of the principal objectives of cable companies like Comcast, aside from maintaining monopolies, has been a long-term objective to soften or eliminate net neutrality, which, currently, lawfully enforces a free and open network. Cable companies want to eliminate net neutrality because they could then dictate access and price. Should net neutrality be abolished—and Donald Trump and his administration support its abolition—then Internet as known today will disappear, replaced by unprecedented rent-seeking opportunities in which various companies will have to pay to play.[61]

The fossil fuel energy sector provides another illustration of welfare for the rich, though leaders of this industry praise themselves for providing the world's energy needs. Unfortunately, the gains of this industry, which siphons off billions in taxpayer-funded subsidies around the world, mostly because it is granted monopolistic rights to extract energy from the ground, establish not only monopoly privileges, but also its unseemly share of government largesse means much less for energy renewables. The cost of subsidizing fossil fuel companies everywhere is not only dangerous to our health, it is robbing people around the globe of their treasure. Globally, in 2013, according to the International Energy Agency, fossil fuel companies reaped $550 billion in subsidies. In its annual *World Energy Outlook*, the agency reported that oil, gas, and coal received four times more subsidies than renewable energy sources solar, wind, and biofuels, which globally were given subsidies of $120 billion.[62] Of the $550 billion worldwide subsidies for fossil fuels, US taxpayers underwrote $21 billion.[63]

The UK has done even worse. It is alone among G7 nations in increasing fossil fuel subsidies, although the Coalition government had pledged to phase them out. Back in 2015 in the UK, production subsidies of about $9 billion helped underwrite fossil fuel companies—mostly foreign owned, while an additional $5.6 billion subsidized fossil fuel production abroad, including in Russia, Saudi Arabia, and China. Additionally, Chancellor George Osborne announced early in 2015 that taxpayers would underwrite new tax breaks for North Sea oil and gas production that would cost about $2.5 billion by 2020.[64]

Damning as these figures are, the International Monetary Fund (IMF) says that global subsidies are much higher if you factor in the cost of environmental damage: about $4.9 trillion (6.5% of global GDP) in 2013 and about $5.3 trillion (6.5% of global GDP) in 2015. That meant significant rises in global pollution caused by fossil fuel use and damage from that use. These much higher figures are more realistic because they factor in fiscal, environmental, and human welfare impacts—for example, health costs, damage to water systems, toxicity caused by extraction, and rising ocean acidity—the carbon imprint globally.[65]

In 2011, Graeme Maxton weighed in on the energy controversy. He noted that annually the world economy was growing by $1.5 trillion, but every year the carbon imprint, global damage to the environment, was rising by $4.5 trillion. How did he explain this? The damage caused by fossil fuel use was three times greater than the wealth that was added if the damage was priced into the cost of consuming dirty energy.[66]

The figures of Graeme Maxton and the IMF suggest a much higher cost to the world economy, to human health, and to the environment, because of enduring reliance on non-renewable energy. They also suggest that the cost of maintaining the energy super-rich is not only expensive, it is dangerous. But here again the ultra-wealthy have used leverage and money to acquire power: Rex Tillerson, CEO of Exxon, has become Secretary of State in the USA, despite no experience in diplomacy, and despite Exxon contracts with Russia and President Putin, even while there remains suspicion that Russia tampered with the US election process. While the vast majority of scientists are admonishing us to reduce carbon pollution, both the USA and the UK are blithely racing in the other direction. Not only has the USA elected a global warming denier as president, Donald Trump has put Scott Pruitt in charge of the Environmental Protection Agency, an agency he has sought to abolish! The British do have a carbon tax, but they have largely failed to provide incentives for innovation in non-renewable energy.

Welfare for the energy rich has been a continuing fixture in American politics and is part of the revolving door syndrome that has come to characterize crony (rentier) capitalism in the USA. There are no shortages of illustrations. A Shell petrochemical refinery in Pennsylvania was offered a state subsidy of $1.6 billion in 2012, the same year the company made a profit of $26.8 billion. The lucrative deal was helped along by the then Republican governor, Tom Corbett, who received more than $1 million in campaign contributions from the oil and gas industry. ExxonMobil's upgrades at its Baton Rouge, Louisiana refinery—the second largest in the USA—benefited from $119 million in state subsidies starting in 2011, a year that the company made a $41 billion in profit. Bobby Jindal, the Republican governor of Louisiana, expressed pride that he had attracted so much new investment to Louisiana, but more than $1 million between 2003 and 2013 went directly to the governor to help him run his political campaigns. And in Ohio, a jobs subsidy plan worth $78 million was granted to Marathon Petroleum beginning in 2011, a year in which the company made $2.4 billion profit.[67]

The US oil and gas industry has spent millions on lobbying to maintain concessions, subsidies, and tax deferments. In 2016, the industry spent more than $119 million just lobbying Congress. Between 2008 and 2015, it spent more than $143 million annually just in lobbying. In 2009, it spent almost $180 million.[68] In 2016, the super-rich in the oil and gas sector pumped $107 million into Republican presidential super PACs, more than half of that money going to Senator Ted Cruz, best known for his denial of climate change.[69] Not only did the industry rack up undeserved rents and corrupt democracy, it cast as much suspicion as possible on climate change and the scientists who observed and reported it.

Measuring the exact cost of the super-rich running the fossil fuel energy industry is difficult because it is not easily captured by a metric like GDP, which does not measure the cost of the carbon imprint on the environment. GDP, for example, does not indicate the costs to the environment, nor does it assess the sustainability of the growth that occurs.

When resources like gas and oil are extracted from the ground, the wealth of a country is diminished, unless it is reinvested above ground in human or physical capital. This, however, is not what happens. The result, Joseph Stiglitz tells us, is that

> Our price system is flawed, because it doesn't reflect accurately the scarcity of many of these environmental resources.... When the oil industry pushes for more offshore drilling and simultaneously pushes for laws that free companies from the full consequences of an oil spill, it is, in effect, asking for a public subsidy.... Because the oil and coal companies use their money to influence environmental regulation, we live in a world with more air and water pollution... the costs show up as lower standards of living for ordinary Americans, the benefits as higher profits for the oil and coal companies.[70]

What Stiglitz does not quite say is that the fossil fuel industry is granted a monopoly when it is allowed to extract wealth not only from the ground, but from the public commons, and then to get subsidies while doing it. The result is a massive transfer of wealth from the 99% to the upper echelons of the 1%, which increases its treasure by not being accountable for the carbon imprint it puts into the environment. The relative absence of competition allows the heavily subsidized oil and gas industry to make handsome profits, even if they have declined in a sluggish market. In the year 2013, the top five oil companies—BP, Chevron, ConocoPhillips, ExxonMobil, and Shell—earned $93 billion in profits.[71] A year later, with oil prices sliding, the big five hardly noticed: their profits for 2014 reached $90 billion.[72] For the same year, all public companies involved in extracting, transporting, refining, distributing, and trading in fossil fuels, in the USA and Canada, netted $257 billion.[73] Yet the top twenty fossil fuel energy companies paid an effective tax rate of a little over 11%, though they claimed a much higher rate. What was the difference? Almost 90% of owed federal taxes were deferred, which meant that virtually all resources extracted outside the USA went untaxed: proving once again that the energy super-rich are expensive.[74] And they don't need to be competitive, not when they have the kind of political clout we have already observed.

Some countries don't think the 99% have a moral obligation to support the super-rich. They think that what is in the ground should belong to the commons, to all citizens of a country, and not just a wealthy elite.

Norway is one of the countries where oil has mostly remained publicly owned. Since the first discoveries of oil in 1969 in the North Sea Basin, Norway has produced about forty billion barrels of oil equivalence. Britain, which shares the North Sea Basin hydrocarbons roughly equally, has produced about 42.8 billion barrels of oil equivalence, a number that is close to Norwegian production. This means that Norway has been as productive as Britain, producing hydrocarbons at a rate comparable to British production. But the comparison ends there. The difference is that oil in the UK is privately owned and exploited, meaning that profits are held privately. Since 1986, when the British controlled part of the North Sea Basin was privatized, the UK government has received a revenue stream only through taxation.[75]

Norway has taken a fundamentally different approach. More than 50% of its hydrocarbon production in the North Sea comes through Statoil—in which the state has a majority stake—while remaining hydrocarbon assets are owned completely by Norway through the State Direct Financial Interest. Although Norway has direct ownership of most of the oil industry, and imposes a heavy tax on the private sector of the industry, it is just as productive as Britain, which has wholly privatized North Sea oil, and yet Norway delivers more revenues (by far) to its citizens while still attracting investment.

The results show just how much rent is collected—or wealth is extracted—by the British oil elite. Between 1971 and 2015, the UK government generated $470 billion in revenues from its North Sea Basin, while the Norwegian government generated $1197 billion from its own North Sea petroleum reserves. The discrepancy in Norway's favor is enormous: these figures suggest that privatizing British oil in the 1980s—which only brought a sum of about $1.6 billion dollars to Treasury then—costs the British taxpayer about $730 billion over a period of around 44 years: an enormous subsidy for the rich who cashed in on what had been the commons.[76]

Unlike the British experience, Norway has used its oil revenues to establish the Oil Fund, the largest sovereign fund in the world, which in May 2016 stood at $819 billion. Had Norway followed the example of the UK, there would be no publicly owned sovereign fund, but a transfer of Norwegian oil wealth into a newly minted Norwegian energy elite.

Add up the enormous sums transferred to private oil-production companies in Britain, the loss of tax revenues in the USA because oil companies defer taxation indefinitely—or forever, add tax incentives for exploration, subsidies given by the USA and UK governments to oil and gas companies by not pricing in environmental damage, and the incalculable cost of the damage to Earth and health, and what emerges is a different calculus than the one submitted by the energy industry. Compound that by the vastly unequal investment in fossil fuels at the expense of renewable energy sources, something like 400% greater, and you begin to get a sense of how costly it is to maintain the super-rich who run the energy sector.

The question that goes begging is: Why don't the British do as the Norwegians do? The answer is even proclaimed in the Conservative Party's manifesto, which outlines a plan to "lead international action against climate change" but immediately pledges to ensure oil and gas plays a "critical role" in UK energy provision.[77]

Critical role, indeed, helped along by generous donations to political parties from the oil and gas industry. Since Theresa May became Prime Minister, top oil executives have donated more than £390,000 to the Conservative Party. Among the highest donors is Ayman Asfari, CEO of Petrofac, a Jersey-registered oil and gas firm: he has contributed £90,000. Mr. Asfari is a Syrian-born businessman who has been questioned about bribery, corruption, and money laundering at his company.[78]

Ian Taylor, CEO at the world's largest oil trader, Vitol, has personally contributed £47,000 to the Conservatives since Theresa May became the head of the Conservatives, adding to the hundreds of thousands he had previously donated. A former Vitol partner, Matthew Ferry donated £124,000 to the Tories just between 2016 and 2017. After he left Vitol, he established his own investment company, which invests in the oil and gas sector. Another pay-to-play figure is Russian-born Alexander Temerko, formerly deputy-chairman of the Yukos Oil Company in Russia, who became a British citizen in 2011. He has donated another £63,800 to the Conservative Party.[79] The British may be behind their American counterparts for excess and for the sums they contribute, but the results are much the same: a captive political party dependent on donations from the super-rich, and not responsive to the electorate. Another episode in the corruption of democracy, another example of pay-to-play politics, and yet another illustration of sometimes foreign-born executives with murky pasts leveraging large sums of money with invisible origins to capture rents through political influence.

Conclusion

With political parties under the influence of the new oligarchs and obedient to the interests of global corporations, with the deliberate promotion of doubt and the proliferation of fake news, with the increasing inequality between Wall Street and Main Street, and with much of the media controlled by the super-rich, disillusionment with conventional politics and parties was inevitable. Donald Trump may be totally unfit to be president, yet he intuitively noticed what Hillary Clinton and the Democrats never acknowledged: the pain of Main Street, and the unfair accumulation of riches and influence of Wall Street. Offering simplistic cures, and mixing utter falsehoods (Muslims and immigrants are the main problem, and tax breaks for the rich will help everybody) with grains of truth (most people have not experienced recovery from the Great Recession, and the elites are the problem—excluding Trump), making it unclear where truth ends and falsehood begins, Trump was able to capitalize on the deep despair of many if not most Americans.

Corruption of politics and parties has become almost universal. Governments cannot be democratic when political parties are funded by billionaires who benefit from tax havens and deferments, and who lobby incessantly for deregulation of the industries they control. As the Panama Papers noted, at least seventy-two former or current heads of state or government have benefited from tax havens.[80] If reform is to come, despite the occasional maverick politician like Bernie Sanders or perhaps Jeremy Corbyn, it seems unlikely it will come from traditional political parties, certainly not in the USA or Britain.

Notes

1. Facundo Alvaredo, Thomas B. Atkinson, Thomas Piketty, and Emmanuel Saez, "The Top 1 Percent in International and Historical Perspective," *Journal of Economic Perspectives* 27, no. 3 (Summer 2013): 4–6. http://pubs.aeaweb.org/doi/pdfplus/10.1257/jep.27.3.3.
2. Guy Standing, *The Corruption of Capitalism: Why Rentiers Thrive and Work Does Not Pay* (London: Biteback Publishing, 2016), 2–4. See also Rana Foroohar, *Makers and Takers: How Wall Street Destroyed Main Street* (New York: Crown Business, 2017), for an incisive analysis of rentier capitalism, blaming its beneficiaries' predation for social and economic inequality *and* retarded economic growth.

3. Dorothy Power, Gerald Epstein, and Matthew Abrena, "Trends in the Rentier Income Share in OECD Countries, 1960–2000" (Political Economy Research Institute Working Paper 58A, University of Massachusetts, Amherst, 2003), online at http://scholarworks.umass.edu/cgi/viewcontent.cgi?article=1045&context=peri_workingpapers. See also Arjun Jayadev and Gerald Epstein, "The Correlates of Rentier Returns in OECD Countries" (Working Paper Series No. 123, Political Economy Research Institute, University of Massachusetts, Amherst, 2007), 4–9, at https://www.peri.umass.edu/fileadmin/pdf/working_papers/working_papers_101-150/WP123.pdf.
4. Standing, *Corruption of Capitalism*, 23–24.
5. Power, *Trends in Rentier Income*, 49, Figure IV.1.1; Standing, *Corruption of Capitalism*, 24.
6. Ibid. Also, Power, *Trends in Rentier Income*, 49, Figure IV.1.1. See especially E. Goldberg, E. Wibbels, and E. Mvukiyehe, "Lessons from Strange Cases: Democracy, Development, and the Resource Curse in the US States," *Comparative Political Studies* 41 (2008): 477–514.
7. Standing, *Corruption of Capitalism*, 243.
8. Ibid., 244.
9. Ibid., and Jack Lawrence Luzkow, *The Great Forgetting: The Past, Present and Future of Social Democracy and the Welfare State* (Manchester: Manchester University Press, 2015), 53–54.
10. Marion Fourcade, "The Construction of a Global Profession: The Transnationalization of Economics," *American Journal of Sociology* 112, no. 1 (2006): 181; Standing, *Corruption of Capitalism*, 245–46.
11. Milton and Rose D. Friedman, *Two Lucky People: Memoirs* (Chicago, IL: University of Chicago Press, 1998), 594; Luzkow, *The Great Forgetting*, 85. For the Free Trade Paradigm, John Weeks, *Economics of the 1%: How Mainstream Economics Serves the Rich, Obscures Reality and Distorts Policy* (London: Anthem Press, 2014). See also Foroohar, *Makers and Takers*, 90–111.
12. Standing, *Corruption of Capitalism*, 7.
13. Ibid., 9.
14. Graham Readfearn, "Research Reveals Almost All Climate Science Denial Books Linked to Conservative Think Tanks," *Desmogblog*, March 20, 2013.
15. Brad Johnson, "CATO's Pat Michael's Admits That 40 Percent of Funding Comes From Big Oil," *Think Progress*, https://thinkprogress.org/catos-pat-michaels-admits-40-percent-of-funding-comes-from-big-oil-9db8d728a494/.
16. Ian Sample, "Scientists Offered Cash to Dispute Climate Study," *Guardian*, February 2, 2007; see the United Nations, "Climate Change

2007: Synthesis Report" (New York: United Nations Intergovernmental Report on Climate Change, 2007), https://www.ipcc.ch/pdf/assessment-report/ar4/syr/ar4_syr.pdf.
17. Michael R. Strain, "Seattle Do-Gooders Just Shot Themselves in the Foot," American Enterprise Institute, June 7, 2014, at http://www.aei.org/publication/seattle-do-gooders-just-shot-themselves-in-the-foot/; Peter J. Wallison, "The Case for Repealing Dodd-Frank," American Enterprise Institute, November 26, 2013, http://www.aei.org/publication/the-case-for-repealing-dodd-frank/.
18. Jane Mayer, *Dark Money: The Hidden History of the Billionaires Behind the Rise of the Radical Right* (New York: Doubleday, 2016), 4, 65–66.
19. See the list of members for the annual meeting in 2015, http://www.businessinsider.com/list-of-ceos-and-politicians-invited-to-2015-bilderberg-conference-in-austria-2015-6.
20. Standing, *Corruption of Capitalism*, 248–49.
21. Ibid., 249; see also "Meet the Carlyle Group," at http://www.hereinreality.com/carlyle.html#.WZijmTOZMcg.
22. Luzkow, *The Great Forgetting*, 86–94.
23. Ibid., 84; see especially Jeff Faux, *The Global Class War: How America's Bipartisan Elite Lost Our Future—And What It Will Take to Win It Back* (New York: Wiley, 2006), 47.
24. Simon Johnson and James Kwak, *13 Bankers: The Wall Street Takeover and the Next Financial Meltdown* (New York: Vintage, 2011).
25. Standing, *Corruption of Capitalism*, 262.
26. Luzkow, *Great Forgetting*.
27. Standing, *Corruption of Democracy*, 255, see Footnote 13 for Chapter 7.
28. Ibid., 254–55.
29. Ibid., 255–56.
30. Mayer, *Dark Money*, 9–10.
31. Ibid., 2.
32. Ibid., 27–29.
33. Ibid., 12–13.
34. Ibid. See also Chrystia Freeland, *Plutocrats: The Rise of the New Global Super-Rich and the Fall of Everybody Else* (New York: Penguin Books, 2013), 3.
35. Mayer, *Dark Money*, 14.
36. Ibid., 14–15.
37. See the statement of purpose at citizensunited.org.
38. Mayer, *Dark Money*, 243.
39. Craig Gilbert, "GOP Redistricting Leaves Its Mark on 2012 Election," *Milwaukee Wisconsin Journal Sentinel*, December 10, 2012, at http://archive.jsonline.com/blogs/news/182754381.html.

40. Andy Kroll, "2014: The Year of Koch," *Mother Jones*, November 6, 2014, at http://www.motherjones.com/politics/2014???/11/koch-steyer-senate-elections-rove-big-money/.
41. Nicholas Confessore, "Koch Brothers' Budget of $889 Million for 2016 is On Par With Both Parties' Spending," *New York Times*, January 26, 2015; Isaac Chotiner, "Are the Kochs Really Sitting This One Out?," *Slate*, May 31, 2016, an interview with Jane Mayer, at http://www.slate.com/articles/news_and_politics/interrogation/2016/05/how_charles_and_david_koch_will_wield_their_power_in_the_2016_race.html; see also Mayer, *Dark Money*, 8, and 143–44, for earlier campaign finance abuses.
42. Standing, *The Corruption of Capitalism*, 258.
43. Stewart Lansley, *Rich Britain: The Rise and Rise of the New Super-Wealthy* (London: Politico's, 2006), 187.
44. Eric Shaw, *Losing Labour's Soul: New Labour and the Blair Government, 1997–2007* (London: Routledge, 2007), 56.
45. Standing, *Corruption of Capitalism*, 257–58.
46. Daniel Boffey, "The Super-Rich Helping to Plan a Glamorous Tory Fundraiser," *Guardian*, February 7, 2015.
47. Standing, *Corruption of Capitalism*, 259.
48. Ibid., 260.
49. Joseph Stiglitz, *The Great Divide: Unequal Societies and What We Can Do About Them* (New York: W. W. Norton & Co., 2015), especially "The Economic Consequences of Mr. Bush," 30–31.
50. Robert B. Reich, *Saving Capitalism: For the Many, Not the Few* (New York: Alfred A. Knopf, 2015), 30–31, especially figure 1: The U.S. Economy Has Become Less Entrepreneurial Over Time.
51. Ibid., 31–32
52. This is based on personal experience. The cost for efficient and reliable Wi-Fi Internet is about $10 per month in Moscow.
53. Reich, *Saving Capitalism*, 32.
54. Ibid.
55. Ibid.
56. David Morris, "To Save the Internet We Need to Own the Means of Distribution," *The Huffington Post*, June 28, 2014, online at http://www.huffingtonpost.com/david-morris/internet-net-neutrality_b_5226232.html.
57. Robbie Feinberg, *The Comcast-FCC Revolving Door*, *Open Secrets Blog* (Washington, DC: The Center for Responsive Politics, 2014), at https://www.opensecrets.org/news/2014???/04/the-comcast-fcc-revolving-door/.
58. Ibid.
59. Center for Responsive Politics, Database, https://www.opensecrets.org/lobby/clientsum.php?id=D000022131&year=2012.

60. Sarah Zhang, "How Much Money Big Cable Gave the Politicians Who Oversee the Internet," https://gizmodo.com/how-much-money-big-cable-gave-the-politicians-who-overs-1657002442. All figures based on Center for Responsive Politics, opensecrets.org.
61. Nikhil Reddy, "Net Neutrality in 2017," *Huffington Post*, August 23, 2017, http://www.huffingtonpost.com/entry/net-neutrality-in-2017-what-you-should-know_us_599debf0e4b06d67e334fa94.
62. Damian Carrington and Harry Davies, "US Taxpayers Subsidizing the World's Biggest Fossil Fuel Companies," *Guardian*, May 12, 2015; see also Alex Morales, "Fossil Fuels with $550 billion Subsidies Hurt Renewables," *Bloomberg*, November 12, 2014, online at https://www.bloomberg.com/news/articles/2014-11-12/fossil-fuels-with-550-billion-in-subsidy-hurt-renewables; International Energy Agency, *World Energy Outlook 2014* (Paris: International Energy Agency, 2014), online at http://www.iea.org/bookshop/477-World_Energy_Outlook_2014.
63. Oil Change International, "Fossil Fuel Subsidies Overview," at http://priceofoil.org/fossil-fuel-subsidies/.
64. Damian Carrington, "UK Becomes Only G7 Country to Increase Fossil Fuel Subsidies," *Guardian*, November 12, 2015.
65. David Coady, Ian Parry, Louis Sears, and Baoping Shang, "How Large are Global Energy Subsidies" (IMF Working Paper, IMF, Washington, DC, 2015), at https://www.imf.org/external/pubs/ft/wp/2015/wp15105.pdf.
66. Graeme Maxton, *The End of Progress: How Modern Economics Has Failed Us* (Singapore: Wiley, 2011), 1.
67. Carrington, "UK Fossil Fuel Subsidies," *Guardian*, November 12, 2015.
68. Center for Responsive Politics, "Oil and Gas Industry Profile: Summary 2017" (Washington, DC: Center for Responsive Politics, 2017), at https://www.opensecrets.org/lobby/indusclient.php?id=E01.
69. Suzanne Goldenberg and Helena Bengtsson, "Oil and Gas Industry Has Pumped Millions into Republican Campaigns," *Guardian*, March 3, 2016.
70. Joseph E. Stiglitz, *The Price of Inequality: How Today's Divided Society Endangers Our Future* (New York: W. W. Norton & Company, 2013), 123–24.
71. Daniel J. Weiss and Miranda Peterson, "With Only $93 Billion in Profits, the Big Five Oil Companies Demand to Keep Tax Breaks" (Washington, DC: Center for American Progress, February, 2014), at https://www.americanprogress.org/issues/green/news/2014/02/10/83879/with-only-93-billion-in-profits-the-big-five-oil-companies-demand-to-keep-tax-breaks/.

72. Danielle Baussan and Miranda Peterson, "Sliding Oil Prices Still Yield a $90 Billion for Big Oil" (Washington, DC: Center for American Progress, February, 2015), at https://www.americanprogress.org/issues/green/news/2015/02/03/105935/sliding-oil-prices-still-yield-90-billion-2014-for-big-oil/.
73. Oil Change International, "Profits for Oil, Gas and Coal Companies Operating in the US and Canada" (Washington, DC: Oil Change International, May 2015), online at http://priceofoil.org/profits-oil-gas-coal-companies-operating-u-s-canada/.
74. Taxpayers for Common Sense, *Effective Tax Rates for Oil and Gas Companies: Cashing in on Special Treatment* (Washington, DC: Taxpayers for Common Sense, July, 2014), 3–5, at http://www.taxpayer.net/images/uploads/downloads/TCS_ETR_Report.pdf.
75. David Manley and Keith Myers, "Did the UK Miss Out on 400 Billion Worth of Oil Revenue" (London: National Resource Governance Institute, 5 October 2015), online at http://www.resourcegovernance.org/blog/did-uk-miss-out-£400-billion-worth-oil-revenue.
76. Ibid.
77. Ben Chapman, "Conservatives Pledge 'Unprecedented' Support for Fossil Fuels After Receiving Almost £400,000 from Oil Bosses," *Independent*, May 23, 2017.
78. Ibid.
79. Ibid.
80. Standing, *Corruption of Capitalism*, 278.

Bibliography

Alvaredo, Facundo, Thomas B. Atkinson, Thomas Piketty, and Emmanuel Saez. "The Top 1 Percent in International and Historical Perspective." *Journal of Economic Perspectives* 27, no. 3 (Summer 2013): 3–20. http://pubs.aeaweb.org/doi/pdfplus/10.1257/jep.27.3.3.

Baussan, Danielle, and Miranda Peterson. "Sliding Oil Prices Still Yield a $90 Billion for Big Oil." Washington, DC: Center for American Progress, February, 2015. At https://www.americanprogress.org/issues/green/news/2015/02/03/105935/sliding-oil-prices-still-yield-90-billion-2014-for-big-oil/.

Boffey, Daniel. "The Super-Rich Helping to Plan a Glamorous Tory Fundraiser." *Guardian*, February 7, 2015.

Carrington, Damian, and Harry Davies. "US Taxpayers Subsidizing the World's Biggest Fossil Fuel Companies." *Guardian*, May 12, 2015.

Center for Responsive Politics. Database. At https://www.opensecrets.org/lobby/clientsum.php?id=D000022131&year=2012.

Center for Responsive Politics. "Oil and Gas Industry Profile: Summary 2017." Washington, DC: Center for Responsive Politics, 2017. At https://www.opensecrets.org/lobby/indusclient.php?id=E01.

Chapman, Ben. "Conservatives Pledge 'Unprecedented' Support for Fossil Fuels After Receiving Almost £400,000 From Oil Bosses." *Independent*, May 23, 2017.

Chotiner, Isaac. "Are the Kochs Really Sitting This One Out?" *Slate*, May 31, 2016. An interview with Jane Mayer. At http://www.slate.com/articles/news_and_politics/interrogation/2016/05/how_charles_and_david_koch_will_wield_their_power_in_the_2016_race.html.

Coady, David, Ian Parry, Louis Sears, and Baoping Shang. "How Large are Global Energy Subsidies." IMF Working Paper, IMF, Washington, DC, 2015. https://www.Imf.org/external/pubs/ft/wp/2015/wp15105.pdf.

Confessore, Nicholas. "Koch Brothers' Budget of $889 Million for 2016 is on Par With Both Parties' Spending." *New York Times*, January 26, 2015.

Faux, Jeff. *The Global Class War: How America's Bipartisan Elite Lost Our Future—And What It Will Take to Win It Back* (New York: Wiley, 2006).

Feinberg, Robbie. *The Comcast-FCC Revolving Door*, *Open Secrets Blog* (Washington, DC: The Center for Responsive Politics, 2014). At https://www.opensecrets.org/news/2014/04/the-comcast-fcc-revolving-door/.

Foroohar, Rana. *Makers and Takers: How Wall Street Destroyed Main Street* (New York: Crown Business, 2017).

Fourcade, Marion. "The Construction of a Global Profession: The Transnationalization of Economics." *American Journal of Sociology* 112, no. 1 (2006): 145–94.

Freeland, Chrystia. *Plutocrats: The Rise of the New Global Super-Rich and the Fall of Everybody Else* (New York: Penguin Books, 2013).

Friedman, Milton, and Rose D. *Two Lucky People: Memoirs* (Chicago, IL: University of Chicago Press, 1998).

Gilbert, Craig. "GOP Redistricting Leaves Its Mark On 2012 Election." *Milwaukee Wisconsin Journal Sentinel*, December 10, 2012. At http://archive.jsonline.com/blogs/news/182754381.html.

Goldberg, E., E. Wibbels, and E. Mvukiyehe. "Lessons from Strange Cases: Democracy, Development, and the Resource Curse in the US States." *Comparative Political Studies* 41 (2008): 477–514.

Goldenberg, Suzanne, and Helena Bengsten. "Oil and Gas Industry Has Pumped Millions into Republican Campaigns." *Guardian*, March 3, 2016.

International Energy Agency. *World Energy Outlook 2014*. Paris: International Energy Agency, 2014. Online at http://www.iea.org/bookshop/477-World_Energy_Outlook_2014.

Jayadev, Arjun, and Gerald Epstein. "The Correlates of Rentier Returns in OECD Countries." Working Paper Series, no. 123, Political Economy Research Institute, University of Massachusetts, Amherst, MA, 2007, 4–9. At https://www.peri.umass.edu/fileadmin/pdf/working_papers/working_papers_101-150/WP123.pdf.

Johnson, Brad. "CATO's Pat Michael's admits that 40 percent of Funding Comes From Big Oil." *Think Progress*. https://thinkprogress.org/catos-pat-michaels-admits-40-percent-of-funding-comes-from-big-oil-9db8d728a494/.

Johnson, Simon, and James Kwak. *13 Bankers: The Wall Street Takeover and the Next Financial Meltdown*. New York: Vintage, 2011.

Kroll, Andy. "2014: The Year of Koch." *Mother Jones*, November 6, 2014. At http://www.motherjones.com/politics/2014/11/koch-steyer-senate-elections-rove-big-money/.

Lansley, Stewart. *Rich Britain: The Rise and Rise of the New Super-Wealthy*. London: Politico's, 2006.

Luzkow, Jack Lawrence. *The Great Forgetting: The Past, Present and Future of Social Democracy and the Welfare State*. Manchester: Manchester University Press, 2015.

Manley, David, and Keith Myers. "Did the UK Miss Out on 400 Billion Worth of Oil Revenue." London: National Resource Governance Institute, October 5, 2015, http://www.resourcegovernance.org/blog/did-uk-miss-out-£400-billion-worth-oil-revenue.

Maxton, Graeme. *The End of Progress: How Modern Economics Has Failed Us*. Singapore: Wiley, 2011.

Mayer, Jane. *Dark Money: The Hidden History of the Billionaires Behind the Rise of the Right*. New York: Doubleday, 2016.

"Meet the Carlyle Group." At http://www.hereinreality.com/.carlyle.html#.WZijmTOZMcg.

Morales, Alex. "Fossil Fuels with $550 Billion Subsidies Hurt Renewables." *Bloomberg*, November 12, 2014. Online at https://www.bloomberg.com/news/articles/2014-11-12/fossil-fuels-with-550-billion-in-subsidy-hurt-renewables.

Morris, David. "To Save the Internet We Need to Own the Means of Distribution." *Huffington Post*, June 28, 2014. Online at http://www.huffingtonpost.com/david-morris/internet-net-neutrality_b_5226232.html.

Oil Change International. "Profits for Oil, Gas and Coal Companies Operating in the US and Canada." Washington DC: Oil Change International, May 2015. Online at http://priceofoil.org/profits-oil-gas-coal-companies-operating-u-s-canada/.

Power, Dorothy, Gerald Epstein, and Matthew Abrena. "Trends in the Rentier Income Share in OECD Countries, 1960–2000." Political Economy Research Institute Working Paper 58A, University of Massachusetts,

Amherst, 2003. At http://scholarworks.umass.edu/cgi/viewcontent.cgi?article=1045&context=peri_workingpapers.
Readfearn, Graham. "Research Reveals Almost All Climate Science Denial Books Linked to Conservative Think Tanks." *Desmogblog*, March 20, 2013.
Reddy, Nikhil. "Net Neutrality in 2017." *Huffington Post*, August 23, 2017. http://www.huffingtonpost.com/entry/net-neutrality-in-2017-what-you-should-know_us_599debf0e4b06d67e334fa94.
Reich, Robert B. *Saving Capitalism: For the Many, Not the Few*. New York: Alfred A. Knopf, 2015.
Sample, Ian. "Scientists Offered Cash to Dispute Climate Study." *Guardian*, February 2, 2007.
Shaw, Eric. *Losing Labour's Soul: New Labour and the Blair Government, 1997–2007*. London: Routledge, 2007.
Standing, Guy. *The Corruption of Capitalism: Why Rentiers Thrive and Work Does Not Pay*. London: Biteback Publishing, 2016.
Stiglitz, Joseph. *The Great Divide: Unequal Societies and What We Can Do About Them*. New York: W. W. Norton, 2015.
Stiglitz, Joseph E. *The Price of Inequality: How Today's Divided Society Endangers Our Future*. New York: W. W. Norton, 2013.
Strain, Michael R. "Seattle Do-Gooders Just Shot Themselves in the Foot." American Enterprise Institute, June 7, 2014. At http://www.aei.org/publication/seattle-do-gooders-just-shot-themselves-in-the-foot/.
Taxpayers for Common Sense. *Effective Tax Rates for Oil and Gas Companies: Cashing in on Special Treatment*. Washington, DC: Taxpayers for Common Sense, July, 2014. At http://www.taxpayer.net/images/uploads/downloads/TCS_ETR_Report.pdf.
United Nations. "Climate Change 2007: Synthesis Report." New York: United Nations Intergovernmental Report on Climate Change, 2007. https://www.ipcc.ch/pdf/assessment-report/ar4/syr/ar4_syr.pdf.
Wallison, Peter J. "The Case for Repealing Dodd-Frank." American Enterprise Institute, November 26, 2013. http://www.aei.org/publication/the-case-for-repealing-dodd-frank.
Weeks, John. *Economics of the 1%: How Mainstream Economics Serves the Rich, Obscures Reality and Distorts Policy*. London: Anthem Press, 2014.
Weiss, Daniel J., and Miranda Peterson. "With Only $93 Billion in Profits, the Big Five Oil Companies Demand to Keep Tax Breaks." Washington, DC: Center for American Progress, February, 2014. At https://www.americanprogress.org/issues/green/news/2014/02/10/83879/with-only-93-billion-in-profits-the-big-five-oil-companies-demand-to-keep-tax-breaks/.
Zhang, Sarah. "How Much Money Big Cable Gave the Politicians Who Oversee the Internet." At https://gizmodo.com/how-much-money-big-cable-gave-the-politicians-who-overs-1657002442.

CHAPTER 3

The Rise and Rise of Wall Street and the City of London

Introduction

In 1998, Lawrence Summers, deputy secretary in the Clinton Treasury, who would later serve as director of the National Economic Council and President Obama's chief economist, became concerned about the efforts of Brooksley Born, director of the Commodity Futures Trading Commission (CFTC), to regulate derivatives. Director Born, not a Washington insider, believed that derivatives were little more than bets, and usually huge bets that could not be covered if the bet was lost. Not to regulate them could lead to a catastrophe.

Summers believed otherwise, and he had the backing of Wall Street and of many government luminaries as well. With their support, he made a now legendary phone call to Born to pressure her to back off from regulation. "I have 13 bankers in my office," he said, "and they say if you go forward with this you will cause the worst financial crisis since World War II."[1]

Deregulating Banks

"Growing inequality," insists Danny Dorling, "is the result of market failure."[2] Joseph Stiglitz has argued much the same, blaming excessive financialization, unregulated derivatives, unchecked speculation, and government guarantees (bailouts), for rigging markets in favor of big finance: "Excessive financialization — which helps explain Britain's

J. L. Luzkow, *Monopoly Restored*,
https://doi.org/10.1007/978-3-319-93994-0_3

dubious status as the second-most-unequal country, after the United States, among the world's most advanced economies — also helps explain the soaring inequality."[3]

Perhaps the lowest levels of moral depravity, as Stiglitz further insinuated, have been practiced by investment banks. These banks, which were designated as "too big to fail" in the wake of the financial crisis of 2007, after they had "failed" and were bailed out, were a clear demonstration, if one were needed, of how inequality was "planned," not the result of chance or simply the market distributing wealth according to ability. It was widely known that banks, prior to the meltdown of 2007–2008, had mismanaged risk and allocated capital in ways that were to hurt many millions. It was also widely known, and not only by economists, that the bonus system then emerging among the large investment banks provided large incentives to take risks—or to cheat as some came to call it. Securitization, that mystical device that required Ph.D. physicists to at least partially understand the new forms that capital was taking, which were supposed to manage risk by simply spreading it widely, provided incentives to mortgage lenders to weaken standards, leading to excessive borrowing. Securitization simply made it possible to lend the same money over and over again, with the added device of sub-prime loans—low-interest loans that would later reset at higher rates that were often unaffordable. The result was that millions of families were lured into the low-interest mortgage market. Eventually, the mortgage bubble caused by an overleveraged market, which pushed the price of homes up beyond all realistic values, was bound to create a bubble that had to burst.

Business has long argued that government is on its back, and that a free market is the best and the fairest way to grow prosperity. But business leaders know that government is required to make a market. Government sets the rules, passes the laws, and enforces them. Government grants patents or denies them. Government decides who has access to a market and at what cost. Government enters into trade agreements or rejects them; it sets customs duties or abolishes them. Government enforces contracts and establishes the rules governing them. Government regulates or deregulates commodity markets and stock exchanges. Government licenses companies to do business and sets the standards for compliance. Government can give away its research, as it has done to pharmaceutical companies fairly routinely, and it can lease vast tracts of forest or oil fields on terms that are virtual giveaways.

Government also makes the rules that govern banks. As a result, the banking and financial sector has become outlandishly prominent and wealthy not only because of its ability to attract talent, but also because of its ability to dismantle, influence, or control regulatory bodies. Business, and especially the banking and financial sector, has sought and achieved legislation that has allowed—and sometimes even promoted and helped to subsidize—banks to speculate in risky securities like derivatives, with minimal government oversight. And government has mostly failed to invoke anti-trust laws, allowing a few banks to become large enough to virtually suppress competition, extract huge sums of money from the real economy, and minimize regulation.

Government can also preserve usury laws or nullify them. Until 1978, usury laws protected consumers against the rapacity of lenders. But that same year the Supreme Court effectively eliminated usury laws by ruling that national banks were at leisure to apply the interest rates of the states where they had their headquarters to all other states where they did business. Three states, Delaware, Nevada, and South Dakota, which had already pushed to abolish usury laws, understood at once the revolutionary implications of the court's judgment. So did banks like Citibank, which had strenuously advocated ending limits on credit card interest rates. The decision of the Supreme Court meant that a bank like Citibank could relocate to South Dakota, with virtually no limits on what it could charge its customers there, and then export South Dakota's rate to any state they pleased, even if that state had its own usury law. In effect, no more usury laws and no more cap on interest rates for credit cards. The new banking environment was so hospitable, courtesy of the Supreme Court, that other banks would soon head to South Dakota, or Delaware or Nevada, where they could begin promoting their credit cards, more or less at the interest rate of their choice. Soon, mortgage lending followed suit, including the infamous sub-prime loans that were central to the mortgage crisis meltdown of 2008.[4] The warning of the Supreme Court to put some kind of restrictions on interest rates, which was also part of its ruling in 1978, was not heeded by Congress. Once again, government regulation gave way to "self-indulgence, irresponsibility, and imprudence," as David Brooks would put it decades later.[5] Rather than prudence and fairness, banks were at leisure to enrich themselves with impunity, using the new rules to prey upon the foolish and unsophisticated.

It was not always that way. In fact, all Christian nations, which profess themselves to ardently embrace the strictures of biblical moral codes, have routinely invoked the rhetoric of the New Testament: "Sell all that thou hast and distribute unto the poor, for it is easier for a camel to go through the eye of a needle than for a rich man to enter the kingdom of God."[6] Jesus held humanity to a high standard, advising believers in the Kingdom of God to sacrifice for the needy. Yet in today's creed of greed, the advice of Jesus has been entirely turned on its head and inverted: the rich make gains at the expense of the poor (and the not so poor), though not without often accusing the impoverished that they are poor because of their greed and indolence.

Abolishing usury laws and scrapping legal limits on interest rates were a stunning reversal of Christian compassion. It was just as stunning an apologia for the greed of the super-rich who are always preaching that the unlimited wealth of the few is sure to benefit those who are relatively deprived. It was also to overlook the reason for much borrowing: divorce, unemployment, catastrophic health costs, and stagnating wages. In a country like the USA, which still denies universal healthcare and promises to continue doing so in the wake of the elections of 2016, where wages have stagnated since 1973, actually falling below 1973 wages when adjusted for inflation as late as 2016 for much of the population, where 17% of the nation has fallen into poverty and with millions more at risk—figures that are comparable in the UK—and where unequal education in both the UK and the USA makes folly of the claim of "equal opportunity," Congress would have done better to mandate universal, free, and equal education and embrace universal healthcare.

Instead, Congress ignored the warning of the Supreme Court. As David Cay Johnston put it: "In place of rules that protect the vulnerable, the innumerate, and the foolish, our government … set forth onerous new rules that reward those who prey on the poor."[7] Once we prosecuted loan sharks, after 1978 they could charge any interest rate they pleased with relative impunity. Lenders could charge rates and even impose penalties that only a generation earlier had been obscene and illegal.

Another institution that thrived in the wake of the 1978 ruling was the payday loan. With no caps whatsoever on interest rates, and with many workers unable to last between paydays without short-term borrowing, the payday loan emerged as a "solution." But this made the situation of workers even more precarious: interest rates on these loans could rise meteorically, especially if there was a late payment, to over 100%. There were after all no caps.

The abolition of usury laws produced the inevitable result. Over the next three decades or so, one American family in seven sought relief from debt and creditors. As Elizabeth Warren, then at Harvard Law School, and her associates found, the vast majority of those seeking relief did so not to game the system but because of job loss and major medical problems. The same study found that more than 50% of personal bankruptcies were because of medical debt. The chaos of the Great Recession also boosted personal bankruptcies, more than 1.41 million were declared in 2009 alone as many people lost their jobs and homes: because of the overall economy to be sure, but also because they were overloaded with personal debt acquired well before the Great Recession.[8]

What many people found out when resorting to bankruptcy was that they had less protection than rich people. When Wall Street got into trouble, the government preached that they had to be bailed out or the world's financial system would be at risk. Moreover, laws protect the rich who run the corporations through limited liability and also because of the ease with which they can shed debt by invoking bankruptcy laws. Wall Street therefore has an out, and government is there presiding over the ruins just in case, as it did in 2008–2009.

Consumer credit card debt, however, as it rose in the wake of the virtual elimination of usury laws, could not be so easily discharged, especially after another bankruptcy iteration of 2005. In that law, passed after the credit card industry had spent nearly $100 million lobbying for it for almost a decade, Americans found many barriers discouraging them from filing for bankruptcy, precisely what the credit card industry had lobbied for. Under Section 101 of the Bankruptcy Abuse Prevention and Consumer Protection Act of 2005, bankruptcy courts could unilaterally—or urged by a "party of interest"—dismiss "complete liquidation" of debt. Under Section 102, the standard for "substantial abuse" was lowered to "simple abuse."[9] The net effect was to make personal bankruptcy more difficult to obtain by far, discouraging up to 20% of potential filers. Once again, legal protection was afforded to the rich, but not to those who needed it most. As for the effective nullification of usury laws that had been a major contributing factor to bankruptcy, these remained as they had been for decades. The fresh start that was supposed to be mandated by constitutional provisions on bankruptcy had been effectively shelved, putting the jobless and the sick at the mercy of their creditors.

One of the very rich who didn't need a fresh start—he was protected by bankruptcy laws because of his membership in the financial elite—was none other than Donald Trump. When he opened Trump Plaza for business in Atlantic City in 1984, he celebrated his investment as the "finest" building in Atlantic City and possibly the nation. As Robert Reich tells the story, "Thirty years later, the Trump Plaza folded, leaving some one thousand employees without jobs. Trump, meanwhile, was on Twitter claiming he had 'nothing to do with Atlantic City' and praising himself for his 'great timing' in getting out of the investment."[10]

The super-rich don't have to worry about bankruptcy because they are protected by limited liability and bankruptcy laws. But borrow from the banks and financial institutions of the super-rich and they will remind you that you have a legal obligation to honor your debt since you had the privilege of borrowing from them. Never mind that the burden of risk has been shifted away from the banks to the consumer, which was the intended consequence of abolishing the usury laws to begin with, and never mind also that usury laws were not restored later when banks could borrow much more cheaply themselves.

Look closely at the financial and mortgage meltdown of 2007–2008 and you will find weakening safeguards going back for decades that led to increased speculation and unmanageable risk, much of it shifted onto the most vulnerable. Changes in the rules created the crisis. In the decade of the 1980s, the Securities and Exchange Commission (SEC) diluted and effectively neutered insider-trading rules that had treated company stock buybacks as insider trading. Just as shamefully, when a corporation decided to buy its own shares, this decision did not have to be communicated publicly for thirty days: which might sound like insider trading to those not in on the secret maneuver. Such rule changes encouraged buybacks by corporate executives because this was the technique that inevitably led to a rise in share value: the value of a corporation would be the same, but now it was divided among fewer shares. When this was increasingly linked to CEO and executive pay for performance, it did not require much insight to see the incentive to artificially raise share prices through buybacks.

In the decade of the 1990s, the SEC eliminated complex disclosure requirements regarding communications between shareholders, making it more difficult to litigate insider-trading violations. In 1993, Congress changed the tax code to provide an incentive to companies to pay executives according to their "performance," completing the process begun in the 1980s.[11] The problem was how to measure performance. Many executives decided that rising stock prices were a fair barometer of their managerial skills. So the question then became: how best to raise share prices. The answer seemed clear enough, it had already been giftwrapped by Congress. With minimal disclosure requirements, and with executive income tied directly to share buybacks, the incentive was irresistible. All corporate executives had to do to give themselves an income boost was to use company cash to buy their own shares. The inevitable rise in share price was a windfall for the corporate super-rich. They could unload their shares at however much their price inflated.

But there was also an implicit tax break in all this or rather a new kind of tax evasion. Bill Clinton had sought to cap executive earned income. But the new form of income enrichment came in the form of much lower taxed capital gains, which fell to 21.2% in Clinton's last years in the White House and subsequently were lowered to 21% or lower in subsequent years, until rising to 25% in the latter years of Obama's presidency. By comparison, the top bracket for earned income remained fairly steady, at 39.6%.[12]

Executives found the loophole, shifting more and more of their income to lower-taxed capital gains and away from higher-taxed payroll income. As a result there was little or no relation to performance, executive compensation exploded upwards regardless of the trajectory of their companies. In the meantime, executives' rising incomes would only be subject to much lower capital gains taxes, which in turn elevated tax bills for everybody else.

These rules changes effectively put the fox in charge of the chicken coop. But they did not occur in a vacuum; on the contrary, they were part of the new deregulation creed. Deregulation was the official mantra in Washington as it was in London and had been around since the Reagan ideologues of the 1980s and the Thatcherites of the same decade. Milton Friedman, himself, the guru of free market and government nonintervention policies, had shamelessly argued that insider trading should be legal: rules curtailing it were too intrusive, he said. Friedman's argument was too much even for the *Financial Times*, not a paragon of government-regulated markets, in a 2010 editorial:

> These arguments completely fail to justify what amounts to corporate corruption. If executives— and the bankers, consultants and lawyers who advise them—are permitted to profit from inside information in this way, it makes a mockery of fairness and undermines the legitimacy of financial markets.[13]

Alan Greenspan, chairman of the Federal Reserve Bank (FED) agreed with Friedman, not the *Financial Times.* Greenspan had an obsessive distrust of regulation, even of government. He believed in self-discipline: regulation, he insisted, only disrupted the normal functioning of the markets. He was also an acolyte of Ann Rand, who believed that every government inevitably tilted toward the Soviet model and in any case regulation was superfluous. She argued that corporations had an interest in sound products and virtuous behavior and could regulate themselves. In Rand's view, government was less virtuous and more burdensome. Greenspan, however, was bovinely optimistic about the benefits that accrued to the deregulation of banking, avowedly defending the rules changes we have cited above:

> The use of a growing array of derivatives and the related application of more sophisticated methods for measuring and managing risk are key factors underpinning the enhanced resilience of our largest financial institutions. ... As a result, not only have individual financial institutions become less vulnerable to shocks from underlying risk factors, but also the financial system as a whole has become more resilient.[14]

Greenspan apparently had suffered a serious lapse of memory. It had only been a few years since the savings and loan fiasco, when customers' savings had been looted by executives such as Charles Keating, who had been reimbursed at a cost of $256 billion to the taxpayer. Greenspan also insisted that like-minded deregulators be inserted into other slots in Washington: men like Christopher Cox, for example, who was appointed head of the SEC in 2005. Cox was an ideologue in the truest sense, so extreme in deregulating that he was watched by the USA's Government Accountability Office (GAO). It concluded that Cox had consistently disrupted investigations of stock manipulation, weakened enforcement, and minimized fines.[15] SEC fines and penalties fell 84% during his tenure.[16]

There was one man who understood the need for greater prudence in regulating the finance industry, Arthur Levitt, Jr., who was appointed chairman of the SEC by Bill Clinton. Levitt was not a foolish mongoose type like Greenspan. Having run the American Stock Exchange for years, he understood the dangers and also the potential solutions to the pervasive greed of Wall Street. He knew that competition thrived only when paired with prudent regulation. Levitt had learned that accounting firms were negligent watchmen because they had an incentive to ignore the deceit on Wall Street. The reason was obvious: they had a lucrative consulting business with the same firms they were auditing, a disincentive for effective oversight and a conflict of interest that should have set off a high-decibel alarm. Levitt had a simple proposal: prohibit auditors from consulting with the same firm they were auditing, freeing the accounting firms to make full disclosure. As George R. Tyler summarized Levitt's solution: "Rather than being paid to overlook problems, they [accounting firms] would be paid to spotlight firms mispricing risk, holding inadequate reserves, or hiding liabilities on off-balance-sheet-affiliates."[17]

Levitt's solution made sense too many, why not use market expertise to make markets more efficient and fair: full disclosure, in other words, by incentivizing legitimate audits. One might go further: why resort to a market solution when the government could change other rules like imposing criminal charges for committing fraud or hiring more government auditors? But Levitt never got the support he needed for his sensible proposal, least of all from Greenspan. And accounting firms, standing to lose many millions in consulting fees, were among those lobbying against anything sensible if opposed to the interests of the super-rich.

The Repeal of Glass–Steagall

Bill Clinton promoted himself as a kind of populist president. Nevertheless, he also pursued many policies that were concessions to Wall Street, not Main Street. He was committed to reducing the federal budget deficit largely as a gift to Wall Street bond traders, who prosper when government buys back its debt. Hence, he raised taxes but then slashed the federal budget, getting rid of Aid to Dependent Children altogether. Clinton also did his best to dismantle many of the financial regulations devised by Franklin Delano Roosevelt to control the excesses of Wall Street. In 1994, Clinton and the Democrats supported the Interstate Banking and Branching Efficiency Act, effectively eliminating all restrictions on interstate banking, making it possible for the birth of the mega-banks. In 1999, Clinton pushed for what amounted to a revolution in banking, the repeal of the Glass–Steagall Act, which had separated commercial and investment banking since 1933.

It is widely believed—though disputed—that the latter act, the repeal of Glass–Steagall in November 1999, was responsible for the Great

Recession meltdown of 2008–2009. Though the repeal was not the only factor in the eventual collapse of the banking and financial industry, it was at the least a huge gift to the financial industry and an example of rent-seeking of monumental significance. The repeal of Glass–Steagall, the result of a sustained $300 million lobbying effort by the financial services industry—led by Citibank—was spearheaded in Congress by Senator Phil Gramm. Glass–Steagall had, since 1933, separated commercial banks, which lend money, from investment banks, which underwrite the sale of bonds and equities. One of the main purposes of Glass–Steagall had been to prevent conflicts of interest. Without a firewall between investment and commercial banks, as Joseph Stiglitz has noted, an investment bank would be tempted to pressure a commercial bank, if it had one, to lend money to any company whose shares had been issued by the former.[18] The possibility of fraud was obvious since investment banks had an incentive to support the commercial banks they had merged with by keeping them afloat.

But there were other important consequences of the repeal of Glass–Steagall, notably the transformation of a whole culture and understanding of the purpose of banking. Commercial banks are managers of people's money, not high-risk adventurers speculating with the money of depositors. They are supposed to lend money for mortgages and to business entrepreneurs, and to minimize risk. It was because of this limit on risk, and the avowed purpose to avoid it, that the government agreed to guarantee commercial banks against failure. Armed with government backing, the public could be assured that its deposits would not be at risk and that banks were solid and safe.

Investment banks, however, have an entirely different function. They have historically managed the money of wealthy people who can sustain losses and therefore tolerate higher risks as the cost of greater (potential) returns. When investment and commercial banks came together, the new culture inevitably favored investment banks. They now had access to other people's money as they never had before.[19] Moreover, once investment banks became "banks," they also had access to the Treasury window, normally a privilege accorded only to commercial banks. And as banks they also had the assurances that commercial banks had. Government would be there to bail them out if their bets went bad. The same assurances that applied to commercial now applied to investment banks. By law, the taxpayer was committed to save speculating millionaires and billionaires.

Bank Deregulation Continues: Derivatives and Beyond

Under President Clinton the deregulation religion of the Republicans became the mantra of the Democrats, also, almost exactly in tandem with what was happening in the UK, first under Margaret Thatcher and John Major of the Tories, and then Tony Blair and Gordon Brown of Labor. In 2000, Clinton failed to oppose the Commodity Futures Modernization Act, which prevented the CFTC from regulating over-the-counter derivative contracts, including Collateralized Debt Obligations (CDO) and Credit Default Swaps (CDS). The former provided an opportunity for investment banks to put together complicated securities that were highly risky and then to offload them to institutional buyers looking for high returns. Alternatively, investment banks could keep CDSs on their own balance sheets as a hedge: CDSs were in effect insurance policies that paid off if CDOs went south. It seemed a foolproof scheme, but it was the deregulated derivative market that was one of the chief factors in the eventual meltdown of the US financial system.

An obscure provision in the Commodity Futures Modernization Act stipulated that no regulator could regulate or touch derivatives regardless of the peril to the economy. And peril there was. A leading cause—if not *the leading cause*—of the credit crisis in 2007–2008 was uncertainty over insurance company American International Group's (AIG) losses, which it suffered from issuing CDSs, which insured losses from other kinds of derivatives, especially CDOs that were mortgage-backed securities, typically based on fragile sub-prime loans. AIG's bet was that it would never have to redeem the CDSs it had issued.

Its judgment was faulty, as was later demonstrated when the mortgage market collapsed, along with the insured derivatives, the CDOs. Given collapse, the financial and legal entanglements were impossible to unravel. From a financial point of view, AIG clearly had to default. But this would have a multiplier effect. Banks had purchased CDOs knowing they were risky, but they had hedged these bets by buying CDSs, which allowed them to accept the risk of one derivative by buying the other. From a legal point of view, this was a nightmare. Lynn A. Stout explains why:

> The leading cause of the credit crisis was widespread uncertainty over insurance giant AIG's losses speculating in credit default swaps (CDS), a kind of derivative bet that particular issuers won't default on their bond

> obligations. Because AIG was part of an enormous and poorly-understood web of CDS bets and counter-bets among the world's largest banks, investment funds, and insurance companies, when AIG collapsed, many of these firms worried they too might soon be bankrupt. Only a massive $180 billion government-funded bailout of AIG prevented the system from imploding.[20]

It doesn't matter if AIG eventually paid the money back. The point is that CDS derivatives were just bets. The banks that made them were not required to have an insurable interest to purchase a CDS. Many just bought a CDS because they knew that if the mortgage market collapsed, banks holding CDSs stood to gain hundreds of millions or even billions of dollars. Others who bought CDO derivatives bought the insurance policy (CDS) because it minimized risk, or even eliminated it. When the government decided that contracts had to be made good, or the house of cards would collapse, it honored the derivatives (CDS) contracts, earning immense profits for the speculating banks.

But that was not the end of government welfare for the super-rich. The same provision that prevented regulation of the derivatives market also gave derivatives claims seniority in the event of bankruptcy. If a bank collapsed, claims on the derivatives would be paid off before workers, suppliers, or even other creditors could make a claim: it didn't matter if the derivatives had caused the bankruptcy of a company to begin with. When AIG collapsed and the government anteed up $180 billion of taxpayer money, it was acting to help make whole the contracts held by companies like Goldman Sachs.[21]

In April of 2004, with George W. Bush in the White House, yet another step down the path of deregulation was taken, indicating that Wall Street had seats at the highest levels of government. The SEC, at a meeting that was widely overlooked and tragically ignored, made a decision to allow big investment banks to increase their debt-to-capital ratio (from 12:1 to 30:1, or higher) so they could buy mortgage-backed securities.[22] This inevitably inflated the housing bubble in the process, ramping up investment bank leverage considerably and fueling even further the notoriously fragile sub-prime mortgages that were the bases of the securities. Most neutral observers would have caught the deceit, but the SEC argued otherwise. It proffered the virtues of self-regulation and the argument that the banks could regulate themselves. Self-regulation was a myth; at the least it ignored the truths about human nature, although it would clearly be imprudent when speculation offered the possibility of unlimited riches: especially when the rules indicated that the government would bail out any and all institutions that were "too big to fail," especially when the rules allowed institutions to shift risk to taxpayers, pension funds, mutual funds, and institutional buyers of securities, all of them interested in the payoffs that seemed so inevitable, unaware, or deceived that they were buying securities that were high risk, much higher risk than was publicly acknowledged or admitted.

The decade of the 1990s was one of the most corrupt decades on record in the financial sector. Riding the dot.com boom, investment banks routinely issued buy advisements to investors for companies that they were lending to and that they were helping to bring public. The boom lasted for more than a decade. The fees and commissions for the brokerage companies were almost incalculable, driving up the stock prices of the investment banks as well, which also had income implications for the CEOs benefiting from the escalation by cashing in stock options. Even this corner of finance was corrupted as Initial Public Offerings (IPOs) were routinely kept lower than their real value so they would obtain (likely) large increases following their initial sale. This was an enormous gift to the executives and others who were granted allocations of an IPO, and it also generated kickbacks to those organizing the sale.

Jeff Madrick followed all this in detail. Though he acknowledged that the losses borne by investors due to the activities of the 1990s and early 2000s were difficult to calculate, he estimated that the losses on money invested in high-tech companies, especially the dot.coms and the telecom industry, amounted to a sum running to nearly $3 trillion. The collapse of Enron, WorldCom, Global Crossing, and Tyco and Adelphia, all of which went bankrupt, came to another trillion dollars. A portion of the sums was the winnings made during the speculative boom, but a large percentage of this money had been kept out of productive activity. Had it been invested more productively, fewer jobs might have been lost, and the manufacturing sector might not have suffered the precipitous losses that would occur later in the next decade.[23]

Misrepresentation by investment banks as to the real value of many of the dot.coms and the stocks in the telecom industry led to accelerated speculation and to large amounts of wasted investment. Speculation and overinvestment in telecoms were significant and often based on outright deception. The overselling of this industry alone, according to Madrick's estimation, led to a minimum of $100–150 billion in superfluous investment. Far greater sums of money were wasted on the purchase of these overinflated companies' shares.[24]

The practices of outright deception—keeping debt off balance sheets, inflating profits for personal gain—were widely documented by Attorney General Elliot Spitzer in New York in the years following the turn of the century. When his investigations ended, he concluded that deceitful investment practices were widespread. The SEC, NASDAQ (NASD), and the New York Stock Exchange, with Spitzer in the lead, got ten firms to agree to a settlement for their deceptions: the sum was $1.4 billion. Citigroup, led by Sandy Weill, paid the largest fine, $400 million. Moreover, the SEC separately charged Citigroup for helping Enron and Dynegy inflate their profits and underreport their debt. Citigroup, in July 2003, admitted culpability for its Enron and Dynegy activities and paid $101 million and $19 million respectively for those transgressions. A class action suit by WorldCom investors cost Citigroup another $2.6 billion in May 2004, and suits brought by Enron shareholders cost Citigroup $2 billion when it was settled in June 2005. Despite these losses, Citigroup earned $16 billion in 2002 and could easily afford the fines. As for Sandy Weill, he was personally worth somewhere between $1.5 and $2 billion in 2002, hardly a sum that seemed a proper punishment for the losses sustained by so many of the public victimized by his company.[25]

The fines and litigation losses paid by Citigroup and other investment banks were slight, especially when measured against the kickbacks and payoffs that had contributed so much to the stock market and dot.com bubble in the late 1990s and early 2000s. Following the 2000 crash, nearly all the many thousands of IPOs that had made a fortune for Wall Street in the late 1990s had fallen below their initial offering prices. Of the surviving companies, many were close to bankruptcy. Of those that had survived, half were selling for less than a dollar a share. The founder of Vanguard Funds, John Bogle, summed it up best when he estimated that the CEOs and top executives of both established companies and those recently taken public had earned more than $1 trillion when they sold their shares during the bull market of the late 1990s. He concluded further that fees and commission payments to investment banks, brokers, and mutual funds totaled at least another $2.275 trillion. Bogle then raised an interesting question: "If the winners raked in what we roughly can estimate as at least $2.275 trillion, who lost all the money? The losers of course were those who bought the stocks and who paid the intermediation fees ... the great American public."[26]

Americans were told that they were buying shares of great value, the proof was in the ratings system that told them so. But Americans were never told that the raters were beholden to the financial houses that provided them with so much lucrative business. Bankers in America were no longer in the business of lending to clients who wanted to buy homes or other assets. They were now financiers looking for the highest return in the global market, more interested in turning loans into assets that provided permanent income, not in liquidating the loan and shifting the asset to the buyer.

We have already met the man who stood at the helm during the era of deregulation, Alan Greenspan. It was Greenspan who argued that markets worked best when the government got out of the way, even though he knew that without government there was no market. Greenspan was an ideologue, and he really believed that the market did best when deregulated. Reality never discouraged that belief. Just weeks before the fall in 1998 of Long-Term Capital Management (LTCM), the largest hedge fund in the USA, which collapsed because of excessive borrowing, Greenspan argued that hedge funds were effectively regulated by their lenders. Lenders, after all, were rational people, and they would never tolerate dangerous levels of debt to their clients for the simple reason that this was irrational. But Greenspan should have known better. Hedge funds were not regulated. They did not have to disclose their debt or borrowing positions. As a consequence, lenders to LTCM were unaware of the debt the hedge fund held.

In 1999, a year after the collapse of LTCM, Greenspan demonstrated how little he had learned, or understood, when discussing the regulation of financial derivatives with the head of the Commodities Futures Trading Commission. Greenspan argued, against logic and history, that unrestricted derivatives trading would stabilize finance, not cause a collapse of the financial markets. At the turn of the century, after LTCM had gone bust, Greenspan had no idea that the relatively new derivatives market, especially mortgage-backed CDOs, could be a principal source of risky investments in the noughties, the decade of the 2000s. As Jeff Madrick put it in *The Age of Greed*, "It never occurred to him [Greenspan] that investment banks were now creating loans just like the commercial banks he oversaw, but this shadow banking system was not regulated by the one agency designed to make sure US credit was strong, his own."[27]

Greenspan adhered to his low regulation, low-interest, free market philosophy throughout his tenure, despite the mounting signs of endemic crisis. Under Greenspan's lead, banks and financial institutions were freer from government oversight than at any time since the 1920s. Even though the late 1980s and the decade of the 1990s and beyond fell into perpetual crisis, Greenspan saw no reason to adjust his philosophy. This was despite the stock market crash of 1987, the thrift crisis of 1989, the collapse of junk bonds in 1990, the derivatives crisis of 1994, the Asian crisis of 1997, the failure of LCTM in 1998, and the stock market crash of 2000, ending the dot.com bubble that had transferred so much wealth to the high-tech sector of the economy.

What all these crises had in common were speculative binges caused by the stimulating monetary policy of the FED and regulatory neglect. The result was over-speculation based on easy money that encouraged banks and financial institutions to borrow and take on massive debt. In the decade of the 1980s, the takeover movement was based on soaring levels of debt, finally rising to levels that were not manageable and that ultimately led to chaos. In the late 1990s, hedge funds borrowed aggressively at low-interest rates and then sent American capital toward Asia in pursuit of much higher interest rates. The results should have been expected: markets rose irrationally and then virtually collapsed in a wave of defaults caused by excessive interest rates. US technology stocks also rose to irrational levels until the bubble burst. So did housing prices, which rose faster than at any time in modern history as Greenspan kept interest rates low to stimulate the economy after the collapse of the dot.com bubble.[28]

Lost during all these crises, and imperceptible to Greenspan, were the accelerating mountains of debt: consumer debt, business debt, government debt were all rising twice as fast as the nation's income. Nor did Greenspan and other free market, deregulation devotees—including President Bill Clinton and Secretary of Treasury Robert Rubin, and Larry Summers—notice or care that much of the income increases, lagging well behind the nation's spending, was already going to the top 1%, especially the top 0.1%, a trend that would accelerate over the next decade and a half. There could only be one conclusion, though it would take the Great Recession before Greenspan would concede this. Not only had his free market ideology failed, but it had masked the larger truth that deregulation was the cause of one of the greatest transfers of wealth in history. Stimulating the market while deregulating it, providing cheap capital to banks and financial institutions with few restraints on how to employ that capital, allowing unregulated derivatives which encouraged unchecked speculation on new kinds of mortgage-backed securities that were themselves based on poor-quality sub-prime loans, was sure to fail. Once commercial banks and large investment banks were allowed to merge—as they were after the repeal of Glass–Steagall—what was to keep banks from making relatively cheap loans if they could offload those loans onto the investment banks. And why would the latter care if they could offload these same loans by packaging them into mortgage-backed securities—repackaged as CDO derivatives—and then selling them to European banks or to pension funds and other institutional buyers.

The whole point was to shift risk, while avoiding it for the banks. But we know that the banks also hedged against the possible (or probable) collapse of CDOs by purchasing another derivative, the CDS, which could be redeemed if CDOs failed. Knowing in advance that the derivatives they had offloaded to institutional buyers would likely fail when sub-prime loans reset, making loans unaffordable for millions and leading to a wave of defaults, financial institutions snapped up CDSs, as they legally could. The result was catastrophic when sub-prime loans did reset: millions of families lost their homes—14 million and counting—as the escalating cost of sub-prime mortgages put monthly premiums beyond the reach of many ordinary families. Once again, financial institutions, speculating with other people's money—legal because of deregulation—had shifted risk to those who could least afford it, siphoning off billions in wealth for themselves if they had hedged by buying CDSs, or relying on the largesse of the government to bail them out because they were too big to fail.

Of course financial institutions lost, too, consider Lehman Brothers. But this was unique. In the end, Wall Street was saved despite pursuing fraudulent practices. The same could not be said for the millions of homeowners who could not rely on the government for their salvation. With great irony, taxpayers, largely treated with contempt by the big investment banks, ended up saving the institutions that had betrayed them.

The financial elite, however, had other practices and policies that also contributed to the massive transfer of wealth from the middle classes to the super-rich, in a reversal of the Robin Hood narrative. In a word, deregulation was the ticket to massive wealth, and it allowed practices that had failed for generations to be invoked as the way forward in the modern economy. Dani Rodrik, a Harvard economist with a front-row seat, wrote an apt summary in 2011: "The idea that markets are self-regulating received a mortal blow in the recent financial crisis and should be buried once and for all." Speaking about the hypothetical virtues of the so-called free market, he continued:

> Markets require other social institutions to support them. They rely on courts and legal arrangements to enforce property rights and on regulators to rein in abuse and fix market failures. ... In other words, markets do not create, regulate, stabilize, or sustain themselves. The history of capitalism has been a process of learning and relearning this lesson.[29]

Rodrik was hardly alone. Ben Bernanke, as FED chairman, had uttered much the same sentiment a year earlier in 2010. Diagnosing the problem in a speech given in Atlanta, he blamed the deregulation policies of Alan Greenspan, his predecessor, for the Wall Street meltdown of 2008–2009. Speaking bluntly, Bernanke argued that stronger regulation would have been a more effective approach to constraining the housing bubble than an increase in interest rates.[30]

The financial and banking sector succeeded in collecting "rents" or profits because it had a virtual lock on credit cards, mortgages, and securities. Even after the meltdown, even after Dodd–Frank—which tried to rein in excess in the financial industry, credit card companies still charged excessive interest rates. Even after the sub-prime mortgage disaster, mortgage companies and banks could still make sub-prime loans though they had to reduce their leverage. Even after wild speculation by hedge funds, they remained largely unregulated. Even after derivatives almost destroyed the world economy, derivatives were widely used. These were the methods and the devices, but the aim was the same: the conversion of public goods to private gain, the reduction or elimination of competition to create economic advantage, the shifting of risk from the investment banks to everybody else because the former were shielded by rules they helped to write. The banks never could have succeeded except for one thing: deregulation. As Joseph Stiglitz said, it was well known that banks had mismanaged risk, and it was well known that banks had misallocated capital by offering outsized bonuses for jobs "well done." It was widely understood that credit rating agencies had failed to assess risk, and that securitization had provided incentives for mortgage lenders to weaken standards. It was known that banks had engaged in predatory lending:

> But we didn't know the full extent of the moral depravity of the banks, of their willingness to engage in exploitive practices, or their recklessness. … We didn't know of the sloppiness in their record keeping, in their race to write an ever larger number of bad mortgages. And we didn't know the full extent of fraudulent behavior, on the part not just of the banks but of the credit-rating agencies … Competition among rating agencies to provide a high rating had led them to deliberately ignore relevant information that might have yielded a more favorable rating.[31]

The worst problem was that banks knew they were "too big to fail." That was why they had worked so hard to get Glass–Steagall passed in 1999. This legislation tore down the firewall between investment and commercial banks, making it possible for the first time for investment banks to tap free money at Treasury, to which they now had access. That was why they took the risks they did, and they now had the same government guarantee that commercial banks had. And that was where government welfare for bankers came in. The bankers knew that if their bets paid off they would keep the profits, but if they lost the taxpayer would clean up the mess.

Which also prompted Dodd–Frank, the financial sector reform bill of 2010, intended by its authors to rectify the excesses of the bankers. But this reform bill never had much of a chance. It did nothing to solve the "too big to fail" problem. It failed to reverse the growth of banking conglomerates. The government even made some banks merge, giving them greater market power than ever. The one success that Dodd–Frank did have was in limiting the ability of federally insured banks to write derivatives, the same products that led to the collapse of AIG and the unprecedented bailouts of 2008–2009. There was disagreement about the value of derivatives, but a widely shared view was that they never should have been provided by lending institutions or insured by government. Unfortunately, what came next revealed how little the desire for reform impacted on Congress. With language written by Citibank, even this provision was struck down in 2014 and with no Congressional hearings.[32]

"The Best Way to Rob a Bank Is to Own One"[33]

President Reagan put his famous deregulating playbook into action early, unleashing executives to participate in a Gold Rush. In 1982, as one example, he signed the Garn-St. Germain Depository Institutions Act into law, declaring as he did so that the bill was the most important legislation for financial institutions in the previous fifty years. The new legislation, he said, provided a long-term solution for troubled thrift institutions. He concluded that "we had hit the jackpot." This was ironic, but if the pronoun had been changed to "they," the 0.1%, Reagan would have been correct. He had just opened up Fort Knox for the privileged few. Savings and Loan (S&L) executives soon were able to carry off their deregulated treasure without the oversight that might have deprived them of participation in the robbery of their own banks.

Garn-St. Germain stripped away oversight that could have prevented what soon followed: S&L executives making unwise loans to themselves, their wives, and their cronies and allies. The S&Ls, or thrifts as they were ironically called, now had carte blanche to borrow and invest in commercial real estate, junk bonds, and any suitable temptations that pleased them. Edwin Gray, a California Republican who was the director of the Federal Home Loan Bank Board under President Reagan, agreed that self-regulation was culpable, the cause of the neglect which produced the meltdown. He observed that the Reagan White House was full of ideologues, who argued that the best way to solve the problem, any problem, was more deregulation: de facto, this meant fewer bank examiners, allowing for more "wheeling-dealing."[34] Reimbursing customers for deposits that had been looted by S&L executives—like the notorious Charles Keating—in the 1980s eventually cost taxpayers $256 billion (in 2008 dollars). Here, George Tyler noted was a precursor to the Wall Street bubble and meltdown of 2007–2008, which cost the taxpayer the equivalent of 2% of GDP.[35] Eventually, during the financial crisis of 1987, in the wake of the deregulation of the S&Ls, bad loans given to board members and other officers bankrupted 747 institutions. But even this was not enough to prevent the crises that loomed ahead. Regulatory capture, especially in the financial sector, was now the official religion of Washington, which led to the continuing flogging of regulation.[36]

Regulatory capture has meant a revolving door between industry and government. One infamous illustration of this was Wendy Gramm, wife of former Republican Senator Phil Gramm and the chair of the CFTC under President George H. W. Bush in the early 1990s. The CFTC was in a particularly sensitive position because it "regulated" financial derivatives as well as the market for commodities like oil, gold, and cotton. In her capacity as chair, Wendy Gramm led efforts to deregulate energy derivatives, prior to her joining the board of Enron, which netted her a handsome million-dollar payday. It was CFTC deregulation (regulatory capture) that enabled Enron to post spectacular profits prior to its infamous speculative collapse. The officials at Enron certainly knew what they were doing when they brought Wendy Gramm to the board, but it was revealed later that they had other reasons to celebrate. Before she left CFTC as chair, she obtained a promise from one of the chief administrative judges who issued rulings affecting CFTC, and therefore derivatives, that he would always rule against the complainant. Translated, this meant he would adhere to the continuing deregulation of derivatives. The judge, court records revealed, kept his word. Enron, which specialized in energy derivatives, continued its trade, largely in the regulatory shadows. Profits were easy, clients unsuspecting, and deregulation made it easy to shift risk to ignorant investors.[37]

The year 1994 was one of heavy losses for companies speculating in derivatives, but losses were concealed by keeping them off the balance sheets—easy to do because of the deregulating mania. However, the GAO now made a recommendation to regulate them. Jim Leach, at the time the ranking Republican on the House Banking Committee, even demanded regulation. But the ten leading dealers of derivatives, including Citicorp, Goldman Sachs, and Merrill Lynch, blocked the proposed legislation.[38] Derivatives remained as lethal and unregulated as they had always been, providing a clear path for Wall Street to continue its wanton speculation in the shadows.

Irresponsible accounting practices, aggressive and unregulated trading, and the pressure on federal agencies to absent themselves from their oversight role led directly to the Enron debacle, ultimately costing the taxpayer and investors billions of dollars. Formed in 1985 by combining a natural gas and an electricity company, Houston Natural Gas and Internorth, the company was run by Kenneth Lay and Jeffrey Skilling, a Harvard MBA who embraced the company's "innovations"—which would eventually lead to its destruction. Traditionally, energy—oil, natural gas, and electricity—was bought and sold by regional or local companies. Skilling's innovation was to use the new derivatives markets to abolish the physical limits of energy. To succeed, Enron lobbied for the deregulation of electric energy prices, which were normally fixed by state governments. It took a few years, but in 1996 Enron got the consent it wanted. Enron's argument that the deregulation of electricity—oil and gas futures had long been deregulated—would force energy providers to compete and lower costs for consumers led to a new mandate. Local utility companies were now required to transmit the energy of their competitors through their utility lines for a fee if requested by customers.[39]

Skilling would employ the new rules to his considerable advantage, using derivatives to buy and sell energy, which he then sold to local communities. The futures contracts were complicated, but Enron traders were adept, especially since the derivatives used for the financing were used with the expertise and support of Wall Street. The contracts enabled a buyer to place an order in the future at an agreed price in the present, or the seller to arrange a sale in the future at a set price. Using the commodity futures market, Enron promised a town or customer a specified price up to thirty years in the future and then hedged its costs by trading in futures contracts that enabled it to lock in a future price for energy.[40]

The scheme seemed flawless; at least, it appeared so to the Enron executives and their traders. The fact that the objective was fraudulent, based on the manipulation of the market, and the creation of scarcity—to establish near-monopoly conditions that favored Enron, infamously creating rents—did not trouble Skilling and Lay and company. Armed with their deregulation rule, Enron activated its plan. It made the electricity shortage in California in 2000 seem even worse than it actually was by selling electric energy out of state. When the price of electricity in California inflated quickly, Enron sold it back to California at a huge profit—so great, that Enron felt compelled to conceal it.[41]

Accounting firm Arthur Andersen was right there to help them hide their profligate earnings. It simply reduced them by shifting the windfall profits into the future. Enron traders, who apparently thought of their adventures as minor peccadillos at the worst, were seen in a documentary rejoicing over their public swindles—and the profits they produced—while electricity prices in California soared. Countless businesses were shuttered, and untold numbers of households did without electric energy.[42] Enron generated some $3 billion in profits in the first three quarters of 2001, but by the end of the year disaster struck. What brought down Enron, why did the celebration come to an abrupt halt? The answer was the unethical financial schemes that had been created on Wall Street: Enron had an active partnership with firms like Citigroup, which helped facilitate many unwise decisions made by the company. With cheap funds available, Enron invested in oil and natural gas pipelines and energy plants around the globe. It made venture capital investments in high tech. Everything was financed with borrowed money, usually concealed off the balance sheets with the active collaboration of Citigroup, JPMorgan Chase, Merrill Lynch, and other financial companies.[43]

JPMorgan Chase and Citigroup devised what appeared to be ingenious methods to provide financing to Enron. They developed and promoted a device known as a prepay swap, a complex derivative trade that was a loan that never appeared on the accounting books. Citigroup lent almost $4 billion to Enron using these swaps. JPMorgan signed for even more such transactions.[44] Wall Street, seeing a cash cow that would benefit the Street, began to tout Enron stock. And why not? Wall Street banks were now invested in the company directly and stood to make large fortunes in fees, commissions, and interest.

Meanwhile, Enron pressured Wall Street, reminding the Street it had provided hundreds of millions in underwriting and loans to Wall Street banks. Any bank which questioned Enron or lacked enthusiasm, such as Merrill Lynch and Citigroup, found themselves pariahs, punished because Enron started to withhold underwriting business until enthusiasm could be rekindled.[45] The fact that Enron was committing fraud and that Wall Street was willing to conceal that fraud did not seem to register.

The scheme inevitably failed. The reason was that Enron's stock, which was always being artificially pushed up based on misrepresentation of its assets and cooked balance sheets, was used as collateral for its loans. If the stock fell, the value of the collateral fell, and Enron would have to borrow to buy more stock. The higher stock price then enabled Enron to borrow more against the stock. Ultimately, Enron was caught in a vacuous circle. In 2000, Enron claimed $100 billion in sales and $13 billion in earnings. The company's stock price had tripled in three years, to $90 per share in August 2000. Skilling attached high valuations to the company, without supplying the data to warrant his claims. He argued that Enron shares were worth $126. One analyst at Goldman Sachs obliged his projection by saying he expected Enron to reach $110. In October 2001, just prior to the collapse, sixteen of seventeen analysts who followed Enron awarded it with a "buy" or "strong buy." In the same period, Kenneth Lay and Jeff Skilling made a fortune by selling their shares: Skilling alone made $76 million.[46]

When the high-tech boom began to bust in late 2001, many of Enron's investments went south. The $1 billion in losses from partnerships that Enron had entered, losses that had been kept off the books, now surfaced. Enron's stock began to fall, and as it kept falling, Moody's credit rating agency began reassessing its rating of Enron's debt. As Enron shares continued to collapse, its reportable losses rose, putting even more pressure on the tumbling shares. Despite what now looked like a freefall and calamitous fraud, Citigroup and JPMorgan Chase demonstrated that greed had no limits on Wall Street: neither did shamelessness. Both banks offered a massive loan on condition that Enron would give them all of its future underwriting business. Since they had billions on the line, it might be understandable that they wanted to protect against losses. But they attempted to influence the ratings agencies to postpone a downgrading of Enron, a decision that was clearly unethical and fraudulent. Robert Rubin, future Treasury Secretary under Bill Clinton, called a Treasury official and requested a delay, claiming that all financial markets could be jeopardized.[47] His request was denied: Enron stock fell from $3 to a dollar the day of the downgrade.

There were many civil suits brought against Enron, its executives and its supporting banks. Ken Lay had sold his total Enron stock over the years, earning him a nice bit of treasure, $144 million. Andy Fastow, the chief financial officer, had earned $30 million. Fastow made an additional $45 million, at least, from various partnerships he had entered into for Enron. The largest of the civil suits, which was a class action brought by shareholders, recovered $7 billion, a sum that was far less than what Enron employees had been induced to invest in the company. Citigroup paid $2 billion in claims for misleading shareholders, while JPMorgan Chase paid $2.2 billion. The SEC fined JPMorgan and Citigroup $300 million each.[48]

Enron's October 2001 bankruptcy was the largest in US history. The firm had $63.4 billion in assets on its books prior to the bankruptcy: other than what was recovered in litigation, as noted above, shareholders still suffered between $45 and $50 billion in losses just related to fraud. Employees at Enron suffered the most: more than $2 billion in pension funds simply evaporated. When the disappearance of 20,000 jobs is factored in, the losses of workers, investors, and pension holders were almost incalculable, a supreme illustration in the annals of American capitalism, of how Wall Street squandered resources, while attempting to extract as much wealth for itself as possible, in this case from investors and employees.[49]

Monopoly Restored: How Big Banks Became Bigger

There were many tools that the Street had accumulated over several decades that helped banks evade regulatory oversight. These included a long list of favors from Congress that had made possible a shadow banking system, which could largely make up its own rules. This could only have happened in the absence of anti-trust policing, but government not only failed to do this, it even bailed out Wall Street in the aftermath of the financial and mortgage collapses of 2007–2009. Derivatives remained largely unregulated and remained so even after 2008, which only encouraged speculation further. Hedge funds weren't regulated. Debt ceilings were high, encouraging even more speculation. The repeal of Glass–Steagall opened the Treasury window for investment banks, and it tore down the wall between commercial and investment banks, allowing the latter to make bets with other people's money.

Armed with the rules and influence at the highest levels of government, having effectively neutered resistance, while fruitfully inserting itself into power, Wall Street not only survived the 2008 near meltdown, it positively was thriving again by 2014. In that year, Wall Street's five largest banks held 45% of America's total banking assets, almost doubling the 25% that the top five held in 2000. These companies virtually took most companies public, were involved in almost all US mergers and acquisitions—such as private equities—and were involved in many abroad. They were responsible for almost all trading in derivatives and complex financial securities. Wall Street's largest banks provided the largest financial rewards, the biggest bonuses, and attracted some of the smartest people. For thirty-four years, between 1980 and 2014, the financial sector of the economy was not only the fastest growing sector in the USA and in the UK, it was growing six times faster than the US economy overall.[50]

As the financial power of the biggest Wall Street banks grew, so did their political clout. Wall Street became one of the largest contributors to political campaigns, for both Republican and Democratic candidates. In 2008, the Street was fourth among all industry groups supporting candidate Barack Obama and the Democratic National Committee, contributing about $16.6 million to his campaign according to the nonpartisan Center for Responsive Politics.[51] Goldman Sachs employees made more campaign donations to candidate Obama than any other single employee group. In 2012, Wall Street contributions mostly went to Mitt Romney.[52]

Wall Street has supplied key cabinet and other positions within both Republican and Democratic administrations for decades, assuring a symbiotic relationship between the Street and government. Robert Rubin and Henry Paulson Jr. were Treasury secretaries under Bill Clinton and George W. Bush, respectively: each had chaired Goldman Sachs before entering government. Rubin then returned to Wall Street after serving in the Clinton administration. Tim Geithner, who served as Barack Obama's Secretary of the Treasury, was personally chosen by Rubin to be the president of the Federal Reserve of New York before he joined the Obama administration. Lawrence Summers, President Obama's chief economic advisor, head of the National Economic Council, and Obama's favorite for becoming chief of the FED, received hundreds of thousands of dollars in fees from Wall Street firms, some of which were later bailed out in the White House's bank relief programs. Among these were JPMorgan Chase, which gave Summers a $67,500 speakers fee for a February 1, 2008, engagement, later receiving $25 billion in government bailout funds; Citigroup, which paid Summers a speaking fee of $45,000 in March 2008 and another $54,000 in May of 2008, and later received $50 billion of taxpayer relief money; and Goldman Sachs, which paid Mr. Summers a fee of $135,000 for a speech in April 2008 and later accepted a more modest taxpayer relief sum of $10 million.[53] Since it was widely expected that Larry Summers would enter the Obama administration should Obama be elected president, it warranted the conclusion that Summers would be pliant when it came to regulating the world of finance.

The election of Donald Trump, despite his so-called populist rhetoric during the campaign, promised post-election that Wall Street would retain a front row seat to power. Steve Mnuchin, a former partner at Goldman Sachs, was chosen to be Secretary of the Treasury. Steve Bannon, a former Goldman Sachs trader, was anointed the chief White House strategist, though he made a quick exit some eight months later. Wilbur Ross did not serve at Goldman Sachs, but he was well known as an investor who bought, restructured, and sold companies in the world of private equity. As a billionaire in a government of billionaires, Ross became Secretary of Commerce.

The financial community and investment bankers know better than anybody that power matters. Whoever makes policy can transform rules, and rules determine where the money goes. Wall Street has known this for decades, and as it succeeded in manipulating the rules, its fortunes rose accordingly, extracting hundreds of billions from the economy to its advantage, often at the expense of many others. Correspondingly, wealth and income disparities rose to unprecedented and obscene levels, at the same time that power was flowing toward Wall Street. Relative to the rest of the economy, the financial sector became bloated and profitable, though its contributions to the real economy in which most people lived and worked were dubious.

Prior to the crisis of 2008, financial services comprised 7.6% of GDP, declined to 6.6% in 2012, and then began to rise again, climbing to 7.3% in 2014. These figures might seem modest, but in the decade of the 1950s, when the US economy was growing rapidly, financial services constituted less than 3% of GDP. Between 1950 and 1980, financial services comprised between 10 and 20% of corporate profits, rising to 26% by 1989, leveling out in the 1990s, and then catapulting to a significant peak of 46% in 2001 before leveling to an average of 32% in the expansion of the 2000s prior to the Great Recession.[54] As the financial sector rose in prominence, so did its income rise correspondingly, becoming a major driver of the 1% (actually the 0.1%), which increasingly included financiers, bankers, brokers, and hedge fund managers. Between 1979 and 2005, their presence among the 1% surged by 80%, from 7.7 to 13.9%. Their numbers in the top tenth of 1% were even more dramatic, rising from 11% in 1979 to 18% in 2005, accounting for 70% of the growth in the share of national income of the 1%. As Joseph Stiglitz and economists Thomas Phillipon and Ariell Reshef have argued, this is not only significant, it is unprecedented and largely undeserved. It is the transformation of the rules, not just talent or genius, that explains the surging monetary rewards in the financial sector, compared to non-financial and non-farm occupations. Wages and income in the financial sector share a similar U-shape pattern with growth in overall inequality, falling in the wake of the Great Depression until roughly 1980 and rising since. It is this sector's ascendance since 1980 that corresponds statistically to deregulation.[55] And it is here that one finds many if not most of the new class of rentier capitalists.

Rules have mattered more than talent, assuming that there were many talented individuals in finance prior to 1980, and as those rules were made more lax, as regulatory capture became more complete, as Congress became more lenient, as individuals moved more freely between government and industry and back again, so did rent-seeking once again surge without corresponding checks, allowing for the super-extraction of wealth from the real economy and into the treasure of big banks and big finance. It was this, concluded Joseph Stiglitz, that allowed for between 30 and 50% of the gains of the so-called innovators of finance to be accrued largely because of their ability to extract from the real economy without adding anything of corresponding value.[56]

Reduced Anti-trust Enforcement

The reduction in anti-trust enforcement, which seriously began during the Reagan years, gave birth to the banks that were "too big to fail." When combined with deregulation, weak anti-trust enforcement made collusion and corruption all but inevitable. The result has been that industry after industry has consolidated into two or three firms, creating oligopolies in the USA and the UK, and revolving door syndromes between government and industry in both countries. Back in the eighteenth century, Adam Smith had understood that the business community greedily conspires against consumers, employees, and the public interest by minimizing competition, which it did by establishing conditions of monopoly or oligopoly. The result of reduced competition brought about by near monopoly or the elimination of competition was higher prices, less innovation, and a reduced variety of goods. Consumers in contemporary America and Britain might recognize these complaints as their own, despite the market exploits and product variety offered by a few champion corporations like Apple. But firms like Apple and Google also prove the point, they were able to challenge established giants like Microsoft and IBM during the era of what Joseph Schumpeter called "creative destruction." As innovative competitors, they were able to challenge and supersede traditional rivals, but in the process they achieved unprecedented market power.

Anti-trust policy was designed to promote creative destruction by limiting the ability of stagnating companies to metamorphose into cartels that restrict competition and inhibit innovation. Yet, the Reagan administration derailed and dismantled anti-trust regulation by rolling back investigations and prosecutions. The result is what we have: there are 8000 banks in the USA, but the largest 20 now control 90% of the market. It is this concentration of banking and financial power that has led to so much consumer fraud, lifting the caps on consumer credit card interest, tapping into the lucrative payday loan business, issuing exploitative sub-prime mortgages, inventing costly derivatives that have put their buyers at risk, and gaining access to taxpayer money by abolishing Glass–Steagall. David Stockman, who served under President Reagan and had a front row seat at the birth of deregulation, summed it all up in August 2010:

> The trillion dollar conglomerates that inhabit this new financial world are not free enterprises. They are rather wards of the state, extracting billions from the economy with a lot of pointless speculation in stocks, bonds, and derivatives. They could never have survived, much less thrived, if their deposits had not been guaranteed and if they hadn't been able to obtain virtually free money from the FED's discount window to cover their bad bets.[57]

On October 19, 1987, Alan Greenspan, FED chairman, christened the era of "too big to fail" when, in the wake of plummeting Wall Street shares, he cut interest rates sharply, a signal to the banks that the FED was there to save them from their failed speculations. Greenspan's move alerted the banks that they could make bets, and speculate without prudence. Banks knew the FED would bail them out because they were too large to fail. The aim was, henceforth, perpetual life, endless profiteering without risk or, as some Europeans put it, corporate socialism. It did not take long for Wall Street moguls to pay premiums on mid-sized banks, the better to become too big to fail. Mergers were the antidote to bank death; in fact, they were the antidote to any risk at all. Out of the wreckage of mergers came the following configuration: JPMorgan absorbed Washington Mutual, First Chicago, Chase Manhattan, and Bear Stearns, among others. Bank of America acquired Merrill Lynch, Countryside Financial, Continental Bank, as well as BancAmerica, the parent company; and Citigroup, which started as Citicorp, absorbed Travelers Group.

The consolidations that occurred over two decades not only created a gourmand rent-seeking paradise for those who lived on a diet of deregulation, they also meant—or would mean—the loss of many millions of jobs, trillions more losses for investors, and trillion dollars losses for families whose homes were repossessed. In the collapse of the financial and mortgage markets in 2007 and 2008, what became known as the Great Recession, Americans lost nearly $13 trillion dollars in the value of their homes, pensions, and stocks. Several trillion dollars were recovered, but hardly enough to overcome the loss of jobs and the loss of share value. From just before the Great Recession until early 2010, Americans lost about 8.8 million jobs: many of these if not most have never returned.[58]

In a report published in April 2012, the Treasury Department concluded that total lost household wealth in the USA was $19.2 trillion, a figure that seems too colossal to be credible. In fact, it was possibly too low. Better Markets, a financial reform watchdog, estimated household losses at $21.4 trillion, including $7 trillion in real estate, $11 trillion in the stock market decline, and $3.4 trillion in pension funds.[59] The GAO, which estimated household losses at $21 trillion, concluded that the decline in home equity was an extraordinary $9.1 trillion.[60]

In addition to losses in household wealth, there was the precipitous decline of GDP. The GAO calculated GDP loss at $2 trillion because of the Great Recession, a massive loss in output. But it also concluded that the cumulative loss of economic output could be much higher, somewhere between $5.7 and $10 trillion dollars by 2018.[61] It is impossible to calculate how much the loss of 8.8 million jobs attributable to the Great Recession contributed to the decline of GDP—or was a consequence of that decline—but this also can be seen as a massive contribution to the growing inequality that followed.[62] Add to all these calculations the $23 trillion that the USA contributed in government programs and bailouts, and you begin to get an idea of the cost of the Great Recession—and the cost of the Wall Street elite who were most culpable. Minimally, even if one were to halve the figures above, which cannot include the suffering of the forty-six million people living in poverty in 2010, the sum comes to more than $23 trillion dollars to maintain the banking and financial elite, to keep them in their mansions, and to preserve their privileges. Other than the super-rich, not many would think they are worth it.

The Great Bank Robbery in the UK: The City of London

The City in the UK has followed many of the same practices as Wall Street, with many of the same predictable results, and with as little shame. Just as Wall Street really believed that everything done by the banks was good for the USA, and for the economy, so did the City of London argue that Camelot was in the near future for Britain, largely because of the efforts of its financiers.

Sir Mervyn King, the erstwhile governor of the Bank of England between 2003 and 2013, though he rose to a prominent position, had a more humble beginning as the son of a railway porter. Showing early promise, he was admitted to Wolverhampton Grammar School and thereafter entered Cambridge where he studied economics and later became professor of economics at the London School of Economics.

Under the guidance of Sir Mervyn, the Bank of England became critical about the culpability of the City of London. Coming from the industrial heartlands, Sir Mervyn expressed deep sympathy for the manufacturing companies and their workers who had lost everything, without the government doing anything meaningful to help them. He was equally critical of the bankers who were responsible for leading the UK into the abyss of financial and economic ruin, while they were bailed out by the taxpayers, many of whom they had ruined because of their greed and recklessness. Looking nostalgically back to the days when banks were more of a local affair, when bank managers and their clients were more likely to know each other, Sir Mervyn rued the loss of the England of yesterday in an interview with Charles Moore of *The Daily Telegraph*: "There isn't that sense of longer-term relationships. There's a different attitude toward customers. Small and medium firms really notice this: they miss the people they know."[63] In the same interview, Sir Mervyn noted that since the Big Bang of 1986, referring to the deregulation of banking and finance, banks had increasingly speculated with other people's money and increasingly adopted the view that "if it's possible to make money out of gullible or unsuspecting customers, particularly institutional customers, that is perfectly acceptable."[64]

For at least two decades, beginning in the mid-1980s, British governments had bet on the City, ignoring and even encouraging imprudent speculation, and promoting easy credit fueled by lax monetary policies, just like its American counterpart. Whenever the City was challenged, it pointed out that it employed a lot of people and generated great wealth. Ministers bought the logic, though it was hardly true. Light regulation remained the rule, the better to ensure the innovations, they were assured, were certain to follow. Tory and Labor governments alike argued in Brussels and Luxemburg that the dirigisme of European regulations should not be imported into the UK: why worry about traders raking off money mountains anyway since the proceeds could be recycled into higher public spending. As Larry Elliott and Dan Atkinson put it: "It did not register that the only ways City traders could be making such high returns were by ripping off their employers and shareholders, or taking monumental risks."[65]

The City never created nearly as many jobs as it claimed. The only thing that improved was the influence and power of the City, monumentally so between the Big Bang of 1986 and the financial collapse in 2007. It was only in 2007, when the house of cards collapsed, that the ministers understood that the City had been toxic for the country and had caused systemic risk. Lord Adair Turner, the former head of the Confederation of British Business, who became the head of the Financial Services Authority in 2008, whose responsibility in theory was to police the City, ingenuously admitted that the City was "socially useless," in part if not in whole. He confessed he could not draw a line between what was socially useful and what was useless, but the inability to make a distinction could hardly inspire confidence in him as a regulator. Simultaneously, Turner advocated for a financial transaction tax that recalled an earlier proposal by American economist James Tobin back in the 1980s, as a check to unbridled speculation in foreign exchange markets.[66] What could be concluded, he said, was that financial innovation was not "axiomatically beneficial in a social as well as private opportunity sense."[67]

Turner's analysis was at best an understatement. He was more on the mark when he said that much of what was going on in the City, especially after the so-called reform of 1986, was parasitical. The Big Bang that year was partially about the modernization of the City, investing in new computer-driven technology and making it possible to trade electronically. But it was a veritable revolution in the banking and finance industry, opening the doors to widespread predation. It did this by dismantling the separation of investment banking and commercial banking. Where before there had been a wall between advisors and brokers, between deposit banks and investment banks, which mostly speculated in shares, the Big Bang tore the barrier down. This meant that a client could get advice about the market and execute a trade within the same bank. More than a decade before the USA tore down its wall between investment and commercial banking, the British had decided to do the same in the UK.

Inevitably, this proved a boon for investment banks, which now had access to piles of deposits not previously available. The Big Bang may have created a more meritocratic banking system, but it also created a culture that was no longer client based. As Tony Greenham of the New Economics Foundation explained, the investment banks were a transaction-based business: "You change from long-termism to short-termism, from looking after the long-term interests of your client to making the biggest buck out of today's deal."[68]

Looking back at the Big Bang of a quarter century earlier, historian David Kynaston said much the same thing in *The Telegraph*, exposing the dramatic shortcomings of the Big Bang reforms:

> Long-term relationship banking has been replaced by short-term transactional banking, often involving opportunistic financial engineering; the maximization of profits, in pursuit of shareholder value, has meant an increasing reliance on intrinsically risky proprietary trading; and, for the traders, the annual lure of the seven-figure bonus has seen them systematically engaged in ludicrously one-way bets – one-way because they are not personally responsible for the losses ("other people's money"), quite unlike the old City's salutary partnership structure.[69]

Predation was inherent in finance after Big Bang. Bank traders were not held accountable for losses, but were able to reap handsomely when they made winning bets. Under the new regime, traders were being told there were no limits to their speculations, no checks to their greed: advising clients, and then selling them the products they had just promoted, was not deemed morally culpable or a conflict of interest.

Another feature of the Big Bang was that the UK opened up the City for the first time to international banks. This created a precedent for many things: foreign banks were allowed 100% ownership of banks in the UK. The result, as anticipated, was that the City of London became the international home of banking and finance, attracting American banks and foot-free capital from around the globe. Mountains of capital would soon arrive, and as they did so easy credit was everywhere, fueling unprecedented borrowing—and debt: consumer debt, mortgage debt, bank debt. Combined with sub-prime mortgages, home prices surged and debt climbed even higher, especially when sub-prime loans began to reset.

Meanwhile, as in the USA, the UK relied heavily on derivatives to meet escalating demand for credit: derivatives had a way of expanding credit markets beyond the physical limits of the commodities that were the bases of the derivatives securities. And just as in the USA, derivatives were not regulated, and they were part of the shadow banking system. They were therefore invisible, just as the investment banks were gaining access to other people's money following Big Bang. Bankers should have known that the risk was systemic, and that the derivatives market was inherently fragile. It was after all based on sub-prime loans that were bound to become less affordable when they reset. But then why worry when risk was spread to clients such as pension funds, who were buying the risky securities. And why worry when it was so obvious that the government would step in if the bets went south.

Deregulation had other faces as well. One of them was that Britain had no usury laws. It had abolished them by 1854, about 126 years before the USA decided to shelve its usury laws. This was an open invitation to the consumer credit industry, which after Big Bang was open to the world.

Danny Dorling has likened the new arrangements following the Big Bang as a modern tribute system.[70] With no usury laws to put caps on consumer credit, with the repeal of the firewall separating banks that speculated from banks that took deposits and made prudent loans, with sub-prime loans emerging as a suitable instrument for cashing in on the unsophisticated borrower, with cheap credit fueled by lax monetary policies, the City of London was open for business.

Nigel Lawson, Margaret Thatcher's Chancellor of the Exchequer in 1986, when the Big Bang was embraced by government, minced no words about what had caused the global financial crisis of 2007–2012. Speaking on the radio program, *Analysis*, he explained that the global meltdown was an unintended consequence of the Big Bang, admitting that neither he nor anybody else had understood the catastrophic implications of spreading risk (and offloading it onto others). UK investment banks, previously very cautious with what was their own money, had merged with high street banks—the name for commercial or deposit banks in the UK—putting depositors' savings at risk.[71]

Cost of the Great Recession and the Super-Rich in the UK

Several years on from the financial and mortgage debacles and the Great Recession, the Bank of England sought to quantify the damage caused by the City and its profligate waste of money. It found that the cost of giving license to the City of London to make increasingly larger bets with shrinking reserves of capital and liquidity was unsustainable when the market turned against the bankers, which happened when credit froze and the mortgage crisis exposed the high debt levels taken by bankers. At some levels, the direct transfer of wealth following the financial collapse seemed modest: the taxpayer paid a little less than £20 billion in bailouts, or just over 1% of annual GDP, to the Royal Bank of Scotland (RBS) and Lloyds.

The Bank of England, however, applied a different calculus to its estimations. Its analysis looked not at the actual bailout sums, but at the collateral damage to the entire economy, including the cumulative effect going forward. After all, the banks had caused a global recession, well beyond the borders of the UK. Global losses were estimated somewhere between $60 and $200 trillion: losses for the UK economy were put somewhere between £1.8 and £7.4 trillion. In the case of Britain, the higher estimate was five times larger than Britain's annual output, a monumental squandering of wealth, the vast majority of it extracted from the British people who paid the supreme penalty in the loss of homes, bankruptcies, and jobs.[72]

While British banks were being bailed out by the taxpayer in the aftermath of their failed speculations, the latter were finding that there was nobody to save them. In 1998, there had been less than 20,000 bankruptcies in England and Wales: an additional 4901 had accepted Individual Voluntary Agreements (IVA) with creditors, meaning that they agreed to pay some or all of their debts at an agreed timetable in the future. Eleven years later, in 2009, the number of bankruptcies had grown by a multiple of four, to 74,670: the number of IVAs rose an elevated 1100%, to 47,641, which might be taken as an indication that even if the rich had caused the meltdown with their reckless greed, those who were less fortunate were still trying to pay off some or all of their debts.[73]

The rise in bankruptcies was an indication that unemployment rates were climbing. According to the Chartered Institute of Personnel and Development (CIPD), some 1.3 million people were made redundant by the Great Recession. This was the equivalent of 4.4% of people in work prior to 2007. Of those made redundant, about two-thirds were paid 28% less when they returned to work. In many cases, this was because of the difficulty in finding a full-time job, reflected by a rise of 6.2 million in fresh claims for jobseeker's allowance between April 2008 and November 2009, an astonishing figure revealing the depth of suffering in Britain because of the Great Recession.[74] Predictably, the overall poverty rate in Britain reached a peak of almost 19% in 2008, before gradually falling off to about 15.8% in 2013. Just as astonishing and revealing, a third of the people living in the UK experienced poverty at least once between the years 2010 and 2013.[75]

Poverty, joblessness, rising debt, and historically high levels of inequality in the UK could not entirely be attributed to bankers and financiers, yet when they had taken so much for themselves, and then had cost taxpayers so much when the City failed, it seemed obvious except to the high rollers in finance that the more they took, the less there was for everybody else: somebody had to pay for their mistakes and the treasure they extracted from the real economy. So excessive was the damage that Larry Elliott and Dan Atkinson even called it a disease, what economists generally called the Dutch disease. In the UK, the Dutch disease was not caused by the discovery of a natural resource like oil, but rather by the excessive size of the financial sector, which drove up the value of sterling while also skimming off the cream of British universities. What the City accomplished, Elliott and Atkinson argued, was the equivalent of a military coup, in this case a "silent affair … which saw an elite take control of the country and a disproportionate share of its wealth."[76]

As they suggested, the numbers were mind-boggling, though they did not come about by stealth in the middle of the night. Just compare some of the figures. The CEO of Barclays Bank earned a little more than £87,000 in 1980, about 13 times more than what an average worker made in the UK. By 2010, the head at Barclays was paid £4,365,636, the equivalent of 169 times the average wage in the UK. Lloyds Bank was a bit more constrained, perhaps because the bank was almost half-owned by the British taxpayer: the CEO there had to skim by on only £2,572,000, an increase of more than 3141% in three decades. As in the case of Barclays, the CEO at Lloyds in 1980 had made 13 times what the average cashier had made.[77]

Giving undeserved sums to so few who contribute so little is the definition of a tribute, or rentier, economy. It is what happens, as Sir Mervyn

King regretted, when there is an institutional capture of the government machine by a financial elite. This was precisely what occurred in Britain when the financial sector mobilized resistance to regulation, producing a speculative bubble that eventually burst and led to the crash. It is what happens, adds Danny Dorling, when,

> Entire countries have largely become tribute economies where people do very little of any real value but have to perform particularly intricate rituals to justify their existence while growing no crops, making nothing and helping no one. Being a tribute economy does not greatly benefit most citizens of these countries or even most inhabitants of the tribute cities, of which the greatest in the world are London and New York. … It is only a few at the top of these tribute systems who collect many more tithes than they can spend.[78]

At the very top of this pyramid are the financial elite, to whom much of the tribute flows. But when this elite skims so much for itself, it must somehow justify and legitimize its predation. This requires an intellectual corps, which uses its ideological acumen to defend the upper echelons of the banking elite, arguing they are indispensable. But it also requires an army of bankers to do the grunt work: they are the bean counters or those responsible for conducting the actual transactions. They are also the engineers and the sales force who conduct the flows of tribute. They keep tabs on how much has been skimmed. Their collective work is referred to by economists as the transaction costs in coordinating and managing markets. These workers apply the fees for the mutual funds and the commissions for the brokerage houses; they are the accountants who track the money siphoned off by the elites at the top, the legal counsel who help lobby for favorable rules to maintain deregulation. Add all this up and you have what we have become, a transaction economy, or a rentier economy that deeply rewards the financial elite.

In the USA, as early as 1970, 45% of US "productivity" was for transaction costs, more than half of this occurring between firms. Simultaneously, the proportion of sales workers rose from 4% in 1900 to 12% of all employees in 2000.[79] The UK is not far behind, and especially so in the banking and finance sector, the preeminent transaction economy.

One might have supposed that when this sector experienced monumental failure there would have been ambitious reform. This did not happen in the UK any more than in the USA. If there would have been substantive reform, the big banks would have been broken up, solving the "too big to fail" problem. Deposit banks would have been forced to shed their investment bank relationships, eliminating the conflicts of interest that had jeopardized and in many cases destroyed the savings and assets of many households. Banks would have been required to hold much larger capital cushions, as high as 25% of their investments, as advised by economist Barry Eichengreen, instead of the paltry percentage of 3% or less. The result would have been less likelihood of failure and less need for a bailout. Derivatives and complex financial securities could have been banned—or forced to trade on an exchange where they would not be invisible. Finally, and just as importantly, the largest credit rating agencies, Moody's, Standard and Poor's, and Fitch, could have been barred from advising security issuers about the structures of what they were offering, while also rating those same securities. It was this last failure in particular that conveyed significant misinformation to institutional investors like pension funds, resulting in catastrophic breakdown.[80]

The result of these collective failures to reregulate the banking and finance sector is that banks formerly too large to fail are bigger than ever. In 1960, there were sixteen clearing banks (deposit banks–commercial banks in the USA); by 2016, fifteen of these banks were owned by the four big UK banking groups: RBS, Barclays, HSBC, and Lloyds Banking Group. These banks, plus Nationwide and Santander, accounted for almost 80% of UK customer lending and deposits, with much of the growth occurring in the decade prior to 2017, a decade that included the near global financial apocalypse. Altogether, the assets of UK banks are more than 500% of annual UK GDP; three of the four largest banks have, individually, assets greater than the GDP of the UK, more than $7.9 trillion dollars at the end of 2013. The expansion of the UK banking sector since the 1990s—a period coinciding with deregulation and government coddling of the super-rich banking elite—by far exceeds the growth of the financial sector in all other developed countries.[81] And in Britain, the financial sector grew twice as fast as the British economy in the decade prior to the Great Recession.

In 2014, the largest four banks in Britain controlled almost 40% of the UK's banking assets. They were involved in many if not most mergers and acquisitions in the UK and many abroad, and they were involved in the bulk of trading in derivatives in the City. Like their American counterparts, the top four British banks offered the largest financial rewards and attracted the brightest talent. In effect, the top four UK banks stood at the helm of the financial sector of the British economy.

As economic power translated into political power, the banking and financial sector was able to exert political muscle. In the elections of 2010, the financiers of the City of London provided more than 50% of funding received by the Tories, a total of £11.4 million. This compared with £2.7 million that the City gave to the Tories in 2005—the year that David Cameron became the party leader—amounting to 25% of total funding raised that year.[82] In 2015, despite the attempts to legislate finance reform, City support for the Tories was hardly diminished: the number of big City backers of the Conservatives had doubled since 2010. A *Financial Times* analysis showed that eight of the top 20 Tory donors had a City background, accounting for 35% of all party funding. In total, eight City contributors gave £12.2 million.[83]

The City has also provided many of the key personnel for economic positions at the helm of British banking and finance: Nigel Lawson, for example, who served Margaret Thatcher as the Chancellor of the Exchequer between 1983 and 1989. Lawson's father, Ralph Lawson, owned a commodity-trading firm in the City of London and his mother, Joan Elisa Davis, came from a successful family of stockbrokers.[84] In office, Lawson promoted Thatcher's privatization agenda and helped launch the Big Bang of 1986.

Norman Lamont, who served as Chancellor between 1990 and 1993, had previously served at Rothschilds, an investment bank. Following his stint in John Major's Cabinet, he became a director of the hedge fund RAB Capital and Balli Group, a commodities trading house. George Osborne served as Conservative shadow chancellor between 2005 and 2010, and then as Chancellor between 2010 and 2016 after David Cameron became Prime Minister in 2010. His background was not finance, but his father, Sir Peter Osborne, 17th Baronet, was a co-founder of the firm Osborne and Little, fabric and wallpaper designers. And David Cameron, himself, is son of a British stockbroker, Ian Cameron. Theresa May does not have the same pedigree as Cameron, but she worked at the Bank of England for a dozen years prior to entering Parliament. Just as Wall Street and the finance and banking community in the USA has come to dominate the levers of power, and the financial rewards of rent-seeking that power has afforded, the City has done much the same in the UK. The result is an anemic manufacturing sector, unprecedented inequality, and the disappearance of jobs and prosperity for much of what used to be called the working class.

Conclusion

The links between the City of London and the British Tories are more tenuous than those between the Republicans and Wall Street, but they are hardly negligible. Wall Street has had many placemen in the Democratic presidencies of both Presidents Clinton and Obama, whereas City influence on Labor in Britain has been more indirect. But this is an understatement. It has been the avowed policy of all prime ministers since Margaret Thatcher, to place all their bets on finance. Both Tony Blair and Gordon Brown learned their lesson well after some eighteen years of Tory governance: the future was in finance, not manufacturing. Thatcher and John Major and their governments, and Blair and Brown and theirs, all believed that Britain's comparative advantage was in finance and in the City, not in manufacturing. In fact, the steep decline in manufacturing in the UK and the USA was hardly a coincidence or inevitable in the way that it occurred:

> The policies pursued by Ronald Reagan in the US and by Margaret Thatcher in the UK were highly favorable to the financial sector. Each embraced financial and market deregulation and supported a strong currency. The effect was to overvalue the dollar and the British pound sterling respectively, a dream world for bankers but a problem for manufacturing exporters.[85]

We cannot foresee the consequences of Brexit on the City and on the UK. The City will want to hedge against the fall of sterling, and it will certainly move some operations to the continent. But, within the UK, the concentration of economic power in the City is unlikely to be reduced, partly because manufacturing has already been diminished. By 2012–2013, banking and financial services accounted for about 12% of GDP at £144 billion. This has been tempered somewhat by the bank levy introduced by the Tories and George Osborne back in 2010, scheduled to reach as high as £2.8 billion per year through 2020—before diminishing to below £1.0 billion—but these figures pale when juxtaposed with damages caused by the banking and financial sector during the crisis. At a minimum, as we have observed, the Great Recession wrought by the banking and financial sector cost Britain minimally some £1.8 trillion, up to £7.4 trillion. These figures are scandalous, yet the

City has remained largely unapologetic, arguing that bankers and financiers are roughly three times as "productive" as the rest of Britain.[86]

This is a conclusion that demonstrates we have indeed returned to a tribute economy and shamelessly at that. In fact, it is highly unwarranted. Manufacturers make tangible products that consumers can buy and own. Upon purchase, an asset is transferred to the buyer. Finance is different. It is a rent on capital. The borrower has a right to use the capital of a bank or lender, but the borrower must return that capital with a rent. Those who lend the capital will object that they are providing service and they are right. But remember that banks are not lending their money, they are getting their funds from the same taxpayers borrowing from them—via the federal government. Moreover, when governments resort to quantitative easing, they are essentially giving investment banks the right to "create" money by purchasing US treasuries and mortgage bonds from them. That was not only a privilege granted only to big banks in the USA, once again led by the ubiquitous Goldman Sachs, but it gave the same banks the opportunity to charge fees (or rents) to the federal government for the purchase, while being flush with free cash from quantitative easing that could then be used for further speculation.

We should have no illusions. Abolishing usury laws has led to huge rents for the finance and banking sector charged against all borrowers. Deregulating derivatives has led too astronomical rents. Legalizing subprime loans, especially with insufficient lending scrutiny, has produced outsized rents and simultaneously led to the loss of trillions of dollars in assets in the USA. Coddling too big to fail banks has fueled bank speculation, leading to enormous subsidies, or rents, to bail them out. Legalizing derivatives like CDOs that are insurance policies on assets not even held by banks is a form of insanity, and an excessive rent that could easily have been avoided by not honoring derivative contracts.

And then there is perhaps the biggest rent of all: the rent that fell on all of us when the governments in the USA and the UK decided that the future was in finance, not manufacturing. This unwarranted decision—and it was a political decision, *manufacturing could have been protected*—that manufacturing was in the past and not the future was and is a large part of why the USA and the UK de-industrialized as rapidly and as deeply as they did. This was indeed a rent charged against most of us. It not only was a conscious decision to transfer economic and political power to the Street in both countries, it also cost many of us our jobs and homes. We should remember that Germany and Scandinavia did not abandon manufacturing as deeply as in the USA and the UK. We should also remember that economic growth has not been as rapid in the post-industrial era as before. And we should remember that we were much more equal, living in societies that were much fairer, before the era of the rentier in which we live today.

Notes

1. Simon Johnson and James Kwak, *13 Bankers: The Wall Street Takeover and the Next Financial Meltdown* (New York: Vintage, 2011); Louis Uchitelle, "Your Money, Their Pockets," *New York Times*, April 22, 2010.
2. Danny Dorling, *Inequality and the 1 Percent* (London: Verso, 2014), 55.
3. Joseph E. Stiglitz, "Inequality Is a Choice," *New York Times*, October 13, 2013; see also James Galbraith, *Inequality and Instability: A Study of the World Economy Just Before the Great Crisis* (New York: Oxford University Press, 2012).
4. Elizabeth Warren and Amelia Warren Tyagi, *The Two-Income Trap* (Cambridge: Basic Books, 2003), 128–29.
5. David Brooks, "The Bloody Crossroads," *New York Times*, September 8, 2009.
6. The Gospel According to Saint Matthew, 19:21.
7. David Cay Johnston, *Free Lunch: How the Wealthiest Americans Enrich Themselves at Government Expense (and Stick You with the Bill)* (New York: Penguin/Portfolio, 2007), 18.
8. Ibid., 19.
9. Bankruptcy Abuse Prevention and Consumer Protection Act, Public Law 109–8—April 20, 2005, online at https://www.congress.gov/109/plaws/publ8/PLAW-109publ8.pdf.
10. Robert Reich, *Saving Capitalism: For the Many, Not the Few* (New York: Alfred A. Knopf, 2015), 59.
11. Joseph E. Stiglitz, *Rewriting the Rules of the American Economy: An Agenda for Growth and Shared Prosperity* (New York: W. W. Norton, 2016), 52–53.
12. "Federal Tax Rates by Year," at http://federal-tax-rates.insidegov.com.
13. Editors, "Insiders Off Side," *Financial Times*, November 28, 2010.
14. Alan Greenspan, "Corporate Governance," Speech to 2003 Conference on Bank Structure and Competition, Chicago, May 8, 2003, http://www.bis.org/review/r030509a.pdf.

15. George R. Tyler, *What Went Wrong: How the 1% Hijacked the American Middle Class … and What Other Countries Got Right* (Dallas, TX: Benbella Books, Inc., 2013), 81.
16. Zachary A. Goldfarb, "In Cox Years at the SEC, Policies Undercut Action," *Washington Post*, June 1, 2009.
17. Tyler, *What Went Wrong*, 83.
18. Joseph E. Stiglitz, *The Great Divide: Unequal Societies and What We Can Do About Them* (New York: W. W. Norton, 2015), 42.
19. Ibid., 43.
20. Lynn A. Stout, "Why Re-regulating Can Prevent Another Disaster," Harvard Law School Forum on Corporate Governance and Financial Regulation, July 21, 2009, online at https://corpgov.law.harvard.edu/2009/07/21/how-deregulating-derivatives-led-to-disaster/.
21. Joseph E. Stiglitz, *The Price of Inequality: How Today's Divided Society Endangers Our Future* (New York: W. W. Norton, 2013), 61.
22. Bethany McLean, "The Meltdown Explanation That Melts Away," *Reuters*, March 19, 2012, at http://blogs.reuters.com/bethany-mclean/2012/03/19/the-meltdown-explanation-that-melts-away/. McLean makes the point that leverage was very high already by the end of 1998 at all the big banks, up to a ratio of 28:1. The real problem may have been non-enforcement. However, a leverage of 28:1 also drove the housing bubble, driving up prices and interest rates that inevitably led to collapse.
23. Jeff Madrick, *The Age of Greed: The Triumph of Finance and the Decline of America, 1970 to the Present* (New York: Vintage Books, 2011), 349.
24. Ibid.
25. Ibid., 347–49.
26. John Bogle, *The Battle for the Soul of Capitalism* (New Haven, CT: Yale University Press, 2005), 11–12.
27. Madrick, *Age of Greed*, 225.
28. Ibid., 226–27.
29. Dani Rodrik, *The Globalization Paradox* (New York: W. W. Norton, 2011), 237.
30. Catherine Rampell, "Lax Oversight Caused Crisis, Bernanke Says," *New York Times*, January 10, 2010.
31. Stiglitz, *The Great Divide*, 10.
32. Ibid., 16–17.
33. William K. Black, *The Best Way to Rob a Bank Is to Own One: How Corporate Executives and Politicians Looted the S&L Industry*, updated ed. (Austin, TX: University of Texas Press, 2014).
34. Kevin Phillips, *Bad Money: Reckless Finance, Failed Politics, and the Global Crisis of American Capitalism* (New York: Viking, 2008), 41.

35. Tyler, *What Went Wrong*, 80; and Paul Krugman, "Disaster and Denial," *New York Times*, December 14, 2009.
36. Tyler, *What Went Wrong*, 75.
37. Ibid., 74–75; see especially David S. Hilzenrath, "CFTC Judge Says Colleague Issues Biased Rulings," *Washington Post*, October 20, 2010.
38. US General Accounting Office, *Financial Derivatives: Actions Needed to Protect the Financial System* (Washington, DC: GAO, May 1994), online at http://www.gao.gov/assets/160/154342.pdf; also Nomi Prins, *Other People's Money: The Corporate Mugging of America* (New York: The New Press, 2006), 149–50; and Madrick, *Age of Greed*, 335.
39. Frank Partnoy, *Infectious Greed: How Deceit and Risk Corrupted the Financial Markets* (New York: Times Books, 2003), 326–27; Bethany McLean and Peter Elkind, *The Smartest Guys in the Room: The Amazing Rise and Scandalous Fall of Enron* (New York: Penguin, 2003), 270–71, 327–31.
40. Jeff Madrick, *Age of Greed*, 336; David Barzoa, "Former Officials Say Enron Hid Gains During Crisis in California," *New York Times*, June 23, 2002.
41. Ibid.
42. See the documentary by Alex Gibney, *The Smartest Guys in the Room*, based on McLean and Elkind, *The Smartest Guys in the Room*, 270–71, 327–31; many of the details of this story are in Partnoy, *Infectious Greed*, 321–31.
43. Ibid.
44. Madrick, *Age of Greed*, 337.
45. Ibid., 338.
46. Ibid.
47. Mark Lewis, "Rubin Red-Faced Over Enron? Not in the *Times*," *Forbes*, February 11, 2002, online at http://www.forbes.com/2002/02/11/0211rubin.html.
48. Madrick, *Age of Greed*, 340.
49. Kris Axtman, "How Enron Awards Do, or Don't, Trickle Down," *The Christian Science Monitor*, June 20, 2005; online at http://www.csmonitor.com/0620/p02s01-usju.html.
50. Reich, *Saving Capitalism*, 40–41; Thomas M. Hoenig, "Statement by Thomas M. Hoenig, Vice Chairman, FDIC on the Credibility of the 2013 Living Wills Submitted by First Wave Filers," Federal Deposit Insurance Corporation, August 4, 2014, online at https://www.fdic.gov/. The five largest banks are JP Morgan Chase, Goldman Sachs, Bank of America Merrill Lynch, Morgan Stanley, and Citigroup.
51. Center for Responsive Politics, "Contributions to Presidential Candidates, Barack Obama (D): Top Contributors, 2008," online at https://www.opensecrets.org/preso8/indus.php?=2008&cid=N00009638.

52. Reich, *Saving Capitalism*, 41.
53. Sam Stein, "Summers Received Hundreds of Thousands in Speaking Fees from TARP Recipients," *Huffington Post*, May 4, 2009, updated May 25, 2011, online at http://www.huffingtonpost.com/2009/04/03/summers-received-hundreds_n_183058.html.
54. Stiglitz, *Rewriting the Rules of the American Economy*, 42–43.
55. Ibid., 43–44.
56. Ibid., 31.
57. David Stockman, "Four Deformations of the Apocalypse," *New York Times*, December 1, 2010.
58. Christopher J. Goodman and Steven M. Mance, *Employment Loss and the 2007–09 Recession: An Overview* (Washington, DC: Bureau of Labor Statistics, 2011), at https://www.bls.gov/mlr/2011/04/art1full.pdf.
59. US Department of the Treasury, *The Financial Crisis Response in Charts* (Washington, DC: US Department of the Treasury, April 2012), https://www.treasury.gov/resource-center/data-chart-center/Documents/20120413_FinancialCrisisResponse.pdf; Sarah Childress, "How Much Did the Financial Crisis Cost?," *Frontline*, PBS.org, online at http://www.pbs.org/wgbh/frontline/article/how-much-did-the-financial-crisis-cost/. See also Better Markets, "Americans Have Rebuilt Less than Half of Wealth Lost to the Recession, Study Says," June 3, 2013, online at http://www.bettermarkets.com/newsroom/americans-have-rebuilt-less-half-wealth-lost-recession-study-says. The Saint Louis FED estimated lost household wealth at $16 trillion for the Great Recession.
60. US Government Accountability Office, *Financial Regulatory Reform* (Washington: GAO, 2013), 21, http://www.gao.gov/assets/660/651322.pdf.
61. Ibid., 13–17; Congressional Budget Office, *Policies for Increasing Economic Growth and Employment* (Washington, DC: Congressional Budget Office, November 15, 2011), online at https://www.cbo.gov/sites/default/files/112th-congress-2011-2012/reports/11-15-Outlook_Stimulus_Testimony.pdf.
62. Christopher J. Goodman and Steven M. Mance, *Employment Loss and the 2007–09 Recession: An Overview* (Washington, DC: Bureau of Labor Statistics, 2011), online at https://www.bls.gov/mlr/2011/04/art1full.pdf.
63. Charles Moore, "We Presented a Great Depression, but People Have a Right to be Angry," interview with Sir Mervyn King, *The Daily Telegraph*, 4 March 2011; Larry Elliott and Dan Atkinson, *Going South: Why Britain Will Have a Third World Economy By 2014* (London: Palgrave Macmillan, 2012), 78–79.
64. Moore, "We Prevented a Great Depression."

65. Elliott, *Going South*, 80.
66. Interview with Adair Turner, conducted August 27, 2009, by John Gieve, Jonathan Ford, Gillian Tett, and Paul Woolley "How to Tame Global Finance," *Prospect Magazine*, September 2009, online at http://www.prospectmagazine.co.uk/magazine/how-to-tame-global-finance.
67. Adair Turner, speech at Southampton University, September 2011, cited in Elliott, *Going South*, 80.
68. Heather Stewart and Simon Goodley, "Big Bang's Shock Waves Left Us with Today's Big Bust," *Guardian*, October 9, 2011.
69. David Kynaston, "Was the Big Bang Good for the City of London and Britain?," *Telegraph*, October 26, 2011.
70. Danny Dorling, *Injustice: Why Social Inequality Still Persists*, rev. ed. (Bristol: Policy Press, 2015), 298–99.
71. *BBC*, "Glass-Steagall: A Price Worth Paying?" February 10, 2010, online at http://www.bbc.co.uk/radio/player/b00qbxwj.
72. Andrew Haldane, "The $100 Billion Question," comments made at the Institute of Regulation and Risk, Hong Kong, March 2010, online at: www.bankofengland.co.uk/publications/Documents/speeches/2010/speech433.pdf.
73. *Guardian*, "Bankruptcies and Insolvencies Since 1960," November 6, 2009.
74. Office for National Statistics, "UK Labor Market: December 2016," Figure 11: UK unemployment rates (aged 16 and over), 1971 to 2016, online at https://www.ons.gov.uk/employmentandlabourmarket/peopleinwork/employmentandemployeetypes/bulletins/uklabourmarket/dec2016???#unemployment and "Recession Has 'Deep Impact' on Jobs," *BBC News*, January 25, 2010, at http://news.bbc.co.uk/2/hi/business/8477687.stm.
75. Office for National Statistics, "Persistent Poverty in the UK and the EU, 2008–2013," May 20, 2015, at http://webarchives.gov.uk/20160105160709/; see also Mike Brewer, Alissa Goodman, Jonathan Shaw, and Luke Sibieta, *Poverty and Inequality in Britain* (London: The Institute for Fiscal Studies, 2006), at https://www.ifs.org.uk/comms/comm101.pdf.
76. Elliott, *Going South*, 81.
77. Ibid., 81–82.
78. Dorling, *Why Social Inequality Still Persists*, 298.
79. Douglass C. North, "Transaction Costs, Institutions, and Economic Performance" (Occasional Papers no. 30, International Center for Economic Growth, San Francisco, 1992), online at http://pdf.usaid.gov/pdf_docs/PNABM255.pdf; Avner Offer, *The Challenge of Affluence: Self-Control and Well-Being in the United States and Britain Since 1950* (Oxford: Oxford University Press, 2006), 94.

80. Barry Eichengreen, "Time to Get Serious About Bank Reform," *Prospect Magazine*, January 22, 2015, online at http://www.prospectmagazine.co.uk/magazine/time-to-get-serious-about-bank-reform.
81. Richard Davies, Peter Richardson, Valva Katinalte, and Mark Manning "Evolution of the UK Banking System," *Quarterly Bulletin* Q4 (2010): 323–25, online at http://www.bankofengland.co.uk/publications/Documents/quarterlybulletin/qb100407.pdf.
82. Nicholas Watt and Jill Treanor, "Revealed: 50% of Tory Funds Come from City," *Guardian*, February 8, 2011.
83. Elizabeth Rigby, George Parker, and Gavin Jackson, "Number of Big City Backers for Tories Doubles," *Financial Times*, February 4, 2015.
84. Nigel Lawson, *The View from No. 11* (London: Corgi, 1992), 3.
85. Jack Lawrence Luzkow, *The Great Forgetting: The Past, Present and Future of Social Democracy and the Welfare State* (Manchester: Manchester University Press, 2015), 163.
86. UK Parliament, House of Commons Library, "Taxing of Banking-Commons Library Briefing," September 12, 2015, at http://research-briefings.parliament.uk/ResearchBriefingSummary/SN05251; and Alan Tovey, "Financial Services Employee Numbers at Highest Level Since Crisis Hit," *Telegraph*, December 22, 2014.

Bibliography

Axtman, Kris. "How Enron Awards Do, or Don't, Trickle Down." *Christian Science Monitor*, June 20, 2005. http://www.csmonitor.com/0620/p02s01-usju.html.

Bankruptcy Abuse Prevention and Consumer Protection Act, Public law 109–8—April 20, 2005. Online at https://www.congress.gov/109/plaws/publ8/PLAW-109publ8.pdf.

Barzoa, David. "Former Officials Say Enron Hid Gains During Crisis in California." *New York Times*, June 23, 2002.

BBC. "Glass-Steagall: A Price Worth Paying?" February 10, 2010. http://www.bbc.co.uk/radio/player/b00qbxwj.

Black, William K. *The Best Way to Rob a Bank Is to Own One: How Corporate Executives and Politicians Looted the S&L Industry*. Updated ed. Austin: University of Texas Press, 2014.

Bogle, John. *The Battle for the Soul of Capitalism*. New Haven, CT: Yale University Press, 2005.

Brewer, Mike, Alissa Goodman, Jonathan Shaw, and Luke Sibieta. *Poverty and Inequality in Britain*. London: The Institute for Fiscal Studies, 2006. https://www.ifs.org.uk/comms/comm101.pdf.

Brooks, David. "The Bloody Crossroads." *New York Times*. September 8, 2009.

Center for Responsive Politics. "Contributions to Presidential Candidates, Barack Obama (D): Top Contributors, 2008." Online at https://www.opensecrets.org/preso8/indus.php?=2008&cid=N00009638.

Childress, Sarah. "How Much Did the Financial Crisis Cost?" *Frontline*, PBS.org. http://www.pbs.org/wgbh/frontline/article/how-much-did-the-financial-crisis-cost/.

Davies, Richard, Peter Richardson, Valva Katinalte, and Mark Manning. "Evolution of the UK Banking System." *Quarterly Bulletin* Q4 (2010): 321–32. http://www.bankofengland.co.uk/publications/Documents/quarterlybulletin/qb100407.pdf.

Dorling, Danny. *Inequality and the 1 Percent*. London: Verso, 2014.

Dorling, Danny. *Injustice: Why Social Inequality Still Persists*. Rev. ed. Bristol: Policy Press, 2015.

Eichengreen, Barry. "Time to Get Serious About Bank Reform." *Prospect Magazine*, January 22, 2015. http://www.prospectmagazine.co.uk/magazine/time-to-get-serious-about-bank-reform.

Elliott, Larry, and Dan Atkinson. *Going South: Why Britain Will Have a Third World Economy by 2014*. London: Palgrave Macmillan, 2012.

"Federal Tax Rates by Year." http://federal-tax-rates.insidegov.com.

Financial Times. "Insiders Off Side." November 28, 2010.

Galbraith, James. *Inequality and Instability: A Study of the World Economy Just Before the Great Crisis*. New York: Oxford University Press, 2012.

Gieve, John, Jonathan Ford, Gillian Tett, and Paul Woolley. "How to Tame Global Finance." *Prospect Magazine*, September 2009. http://www.prospectmagazine.co.uk/magazine/how-to-tame-global-finance.

Goldfarb, Zachary A. "In Cox Years at the SEC, Policies Undercut Action." *Washington Post*, June 1, 2009.

Goodman, Christopher J., and Steven M. Mance. *Employment Loss and the 2007–09 Recession: An Overview*. Washington, DC: Bureau of Labor Statistics, 2011. https://www.bls.gov/mlr/2011/04/art1full.pdf.

Greenspan, Alan. "Corporate Governance." Speech to 2003 Conference on Bank Structure and Competition, Chicago, May 8, 2003. http://www.bis.org/review/r030509a.pdf.

Guardian. "Bankruptcies and Insolvencies Since 1960." November 6, 2009.

Hilzenrath, David S. "CFTC Judge Says Colleague Issues Biased Rulings." *Washington Post*, October 20, 2010.

Hoenig, Thomas H. "Statement by Thomas M. Hoenig, Vice Chairman, FDIC on the Credibility of the 2013 Living Wills Submitted by First Wave Filers." Federal Deposit Insurance Corporation, August 4, 2014. Online at https://www.fdic.gov/.

Johnson, Simon, and James Kwak. *13 Bankers: The Wall Street Takeover and the Next Financial Meltdown*. New York: Vintage, 2011.

Johnston, David Cay. *Free Lunch: How the Wealthiest Americans Enrich Themselves at Government Expense (and Stick You with the Bill)*. New York: Penguin/Portfolio, 2007.

Krugman, Paul. "Disaster and Denial." *New York Times*, December 14, 2009.

Kynaston, David. "Was the Big Bang Good for the City of London and Britain?" *Telegraph*, October 26, 2011.

Lewis, Mark. "Rubin Red-Faced Over Enron? Not in the *Times*." *Forbes*, February 11, 2002. Online at http://www.forbes.com/2002/02/11/0211rubin.html.

Luzkow, Jack Lawrence. *The Great Forgetting: The Past, Present and Future of Social Democracy and the Welfare State*. Manchester: Manchester University Press, 2015.

Madrick, Jeff. *The Age of Greed: The Triumph of Finance and the Decline of America, 1970 to the Present*. New York: Vintage Books, 2011.

McLean, Bethany. "The Meltdown Explanation That Melts Away." *Reuters*. March 19, 2012. http://blogs.reuters.com/bethany-mclean/2012/03/19/the-meltdown-explanation-that-melts-away/.

McLean, Bethany, and Peter Elkind. *The Smartest Guys in the Room: The Amazing Rise and Scandalous Fall of Enron*. New York: Penguin, 2003.

Moore, Charles. "We Presented a Great Depression, but People Have a Right to Be Angry." Interview with Sir Mervyn King. *Daily Telegraph*, 4 March 2011.

North, Douglas C. "Transaction Costs, Institutions, and Economic Performance." Occasional Papers No. 30, International Center for Economic Growth, San Francisco, 1992. http://pdf.usaid.gov/pdf_docs/PNABM255.pdf.

Offer, Abner. *The Challenge of Affluence: Self-Control and Well-Being in the United States and Britain Since 1950*. Oxford: Oxford University Press, 2006.

Office for National Statistics. "Persistent Poverty in the UK and the EU, 2008–2013." May 20, 2015. http://webarchives.gov.uk/20160105160709/.

Office for National Statistics. "UK Labor Market: December 2016." Figure 11: UK Unemployment Rates (Aged 16 and Over), 1971 to 2016. https://www.ons.gov.uk/employmentandlabourmarket/peopleinwork/employmentandemployeetypes/bulletins/uklabourmarket/dec2016#unemployment.

Partnoy, Frank. *Infectious Greed: How Deceit and Risk Corrupted the Financial Markets*. New York: Times Books, 2003.

Phillips, Kevin. *Bad Money: Reckless Finance, Failed Politics, and the Global Crisis of American Capitalism*. New York: Viking, 2008.

Prins, Nomi. *Other People's Money: The Corporate Mugging of America*. New York: The New Press, 2006.

Rampell, Catherine. "Lax Oversight Caused Crisis, Bernanke Says." *New York Times*. January 10, 2010.

Reich, Robert. *Saving Capitalism: For the Many, Not the Few*. New York: Alfred A. Knopf, 2015.
Rigby, Elizabeth, George Parker, and Gavin Jackson. "Number of Big City Backers for Tories Doubles." *Financial Times*, February 4, 2015.
Rodrik, Dani. *The Globalization Paradox*. New York: W. W. Norton, 2011.
Stein, Sam. "Summers Received Hundreds of Thousands in Speaking Fees From TARP Recipients." *Huffington Post*, May 4, 2009, updated May 25, 2011. Online at http://www.huffingtonpost.com/2009/04/03/summers-received-hundreds_n_183058.html.
Stewart, Heather, and Simon Goodley. "Big Bang's Shock Waves Left Us with Today's Big Bust." *Guardian*, October 9, 2011.
Stiglitz, Joseph E. "Inequality Is a Choice," *New York Times*, October 13, 2013.
Stiglitz, Joseph E. *Rewriting the Rules of the American Economy: An Agenda for Growth and Shared Prosperity*. New York: W. W. Norton, 2016.
Stiglitz, Joseph E. *The Great Divide: Unequal Societies and What We Can Do About Them*. New York: W. W. Norton, 2015.
Stiglitz, Joseph E. *The Price of Inequality: How Today's Divided Society Endangers Our Future*. New York: W. W. Norton, 2013.
Stockman, David. "Four Deformations of the Apocalypse." *New York Times*. December 1, 2010.
Stout, Lynn A. "Why Re-regulating Can Prevent Another Disaster." Harvard Law School Forum on Corporate Governance and Financial Regulation, July 21, 2009. Online at https://corpgov.law.harvard.edu/2009/07/21/how-deregulating-derivatives-led-to-disaster/.
Tovey, Alan. "Financial Services Employee Numbers at Highest Level Since Crisis Hit." *Telegraph*, December 22, 2014.
Tyler, George R. *What Went Wrong: How the 1% Hijacked the American Middle Class … and What Other Countries Got Right*. Dallas, TX: Benbella Books, Inc., 2013.
Uchitelle, Louis. "Your Money, Their Pockets." *New York Times*, April 22, 2010.
UK Parliament, House of Commons Library. "Taxing of Banking-Commons Library Briefing." September 12, 2015. http://researchbriefings.parliament.uk/ResearchBriefing/Summary/SN05251.
US Congressional Budget Office. *Policies for Increasing Economic Growth and Employment*. Washington, DC: Congressional Budget Office, November 15, 2011. https://www.cbo.gov/sites/default/files/112th-congress-2011-2012/reports/11-15-Outlook_Stimulus_Testimony.pdf.
US Department of the Treasury. *The Financial Crisis Response in Charts*. Washington, DC: US Department of the Treasury, April 2012. https://www.treasury.gov/resource-center/data-chartcenter/Documents/20120413_FinancialCrisisResponse.pdf.

US General Accounting Office. *Financial Derivatives: Actions Needed to Protect the Financial System*. Washington, DC: GAO, May 1994. http://www.gao.gov/assets/160/154342.pdf.

US Government Accounting Office. *Financial Regulatory Reform*. Washington, DC: GAO, 2013. http://www.gao.gov/assets/660/651322.pdf.

Warren, Elizabeth, and Amelia Warren Tyagi. *The Two-Income Trap*. Cambridge: Basic Books, 2003.

Watt, Nicholas, and Jill Treanor. "Revealed: 50% of Tory Funds Come From City." *Guardian*, February 8, 2011.

CHAPTER 4

The Ascendancy of the Corporate Elite

Introduction

Hewlett-Packard had always prided itself on its egalitarianism. All employees were considered, if not as equals, at least on the same "plane." The company believed so strongly in the value of collaboration that it could be credited—or blamed—for giving to corporate America the cubicle workplace, a touch that apparently made employees feel they were part of a caring family or team. So caring, in fact, that the original founders of the company, William Hewlett and David Packard, routinely sent a baby blanket to every employee who gave birth, or sent a silver bowl as a wedding present to newly married employees. Nor was it unusual for Mr. Hewlett and Mr. Packard to join employees for lunch in the company cafeteria.

When Carly Fiorina was brought in as CEO in mid-1999, she wasn't interested in tradition, or the Hewlett-Packard culture. Or in meeting employees in the lunchroom. She was after all a "modern" executive, and her compensation package proved her worth. She was given a $3 million signing bonus and a stock package worth $65 million. She even asked the board to pay the cost of shipping her 52-foot yacht from the East Coast to the San Francisco area. Meanwhile, over the next six years of her tenure, she managed to lay off 30,000 employees, ending, perhaps forever, the caring culture that had been Hewlett-Packard. Her response? Progress has its price.[1] That might have made sense, if only there had been progress.

J. L. Luzkow, *Monopoly Restored*,
https://doi.org/10.1007/978-3-319-93994-0_4

Executives Wanted: No Experience Necessary, Past Non-performance a Plus

Since the 1980s, executive compensation, especially CEO pay, has ballooned while the bottom 80% of Americans have seen their incomes stagnate at best. The disparities are not because of innovations that corporate executives have bestowed upon the larger public, but because of the political favors they have obtained and the rules changes they have themselves helped to engineer.

Beginning with the Reagan era, and especially after 1989 and the virtual collapse of any kind of utopian—or "progressive"—futures, the Left has been in sharp retreat. In the absence, or weakening, of a progressive Left, the Right has been able to challenge the Left on everything it held most sacred: the welfare state and the social contract on which it once stood, civil rights, including universal voting rights, protection of the environment—now under serious challenge from the Trump administration, affordable and universal healthcare *with matching cost controls*, the protection of unions and worker rights, much tighter control of the financial industry, and the reigning in of corporate power.

It is the expansion of corporate power in particular that has produced the extreme inequality of modern America, a result of the concentration of income and wealth grabbed by the super-rich, and the corresponding transfer of political power to the same group of the ultra-wealthy:

> Without the active presence of liberals, there has been little public protest when corporations dismantle much of what was once called the democratic state, or when they decimate the manufacturing sector, or loot the US Treasury, or wage endless imperial wars that are undeclared, unwinnable, and unaffordable. …Americans…might wonder why government reduces taxes on corporations and then allows them to use their expanded profits to invest abroad, exporting jobs along with their investments. Or why government bails out banks and then allows the same banks to use their bailout funds to pay the bonuses of bankers who have just failed.[2]

Part of the answer is that political parties, emphatically so in the USA, have become dependent on corporations to fund them, so that political agendas are routinely set by the corporate class for political campaigns and policies. In 2010, as we know, the Supreme Court in *Citizens United v. Federal Election Commission* gave corporations the right to spend whatever they wanted on political election campaigns: since corporations were people, or citizens, their First Amendment rights could not be abridged. This has helped to transfer considerable market power to corporations, less than a decade after the Supreme Court reached its historic decision, giving corporations license to act with impunity, without serious challenge from the parties they are funding.[3] And as corporations have globalized themselves, for well over three decades, they have been able to act with fewer restraints then ever, avoiding legislative restrictions by shifting everything from profits and production to jobs abroad. The result? Without the regulations that were part of the progressive Left agenda, corporations have exploited, polluted, and repressed, while reaping low-taxed profits around the globe. Does it come as any surprise then that, with minimal government intervention, corporations have abandoned their communities, evaded taxes, impoverished their employees by exporting their jobs, evicted people from their homes, and abandoned the uninsured, even while defending unaffordable for-profit healthcare and deregulated drugs?

Nor does it come as any surprise that corporate executives have used their expanded political and globalized market power to resist the democratization of their corporations, and to boost executive compensation for themselves, using all the tools they have preserved or won in the political arena. In order to shift income and wealth in their direction, corporations and their CEOs have done much more than manipulate tax structures. As we have observed, they have discovered something even better called stock options. These have offered management the prospect of windfalls almost beyond measure, though to take full advantage has required something of a conjuror's trick. To earn them, management has had to improve earnings per share from one quarter to the next: in other words, corporate leaders have concentrated on the short term, ignoring everything learned in business schools about focusing on productivity growth and long-term investment. Put another way, corporate executives have abandoned everything that made the American economy bountiful in the three plus decades following World War II. George Tyler has summed up the new corporate model at the dawn of the Reagan era:

> Instead, to personally strike gold, they needed to spike earnings per share over the next 90 days. The easiest way was to switch corporate outlays from expenses (such as wages and R& D) to share buybacks and risky mergers. For American executives, the long term abruptly crystallized at three months.[4]

During the age of prosperity prior to the mid-1970s, American and British executives were paid modestly, with rare (and sometimes deserved) exceptions. That all changed abruptly. Overnight, beginning with the Reagan era, the highest—and often the sole—priority became the maximization of profit: community and employee goals became secondary at best. In the wake of this shift, profits did rise—as did crises—but they rose much less rapidly than executive compensation. The rewards went predominantly to the top, and they went there regardless of executive performance. Nor was this incidental, it was the result of a flawed philosophy that personal gain based on greed was good for the overall health of a firm and the economy as well. Now the incentive was to concentrate on raising profits based on short-termism, to encourage employee layoffs or part-time employment, to move companies to low-wage states or countries, to employ tax evasion schemes to boost profitability, to acquire other companies to raise market share and corporate revenues, and to use share buybacks to (artificially) raise share value.

As a consequence, the corporate super-rich have artificially boosted their income at the expense of reinvestment and research and development (R&D). They have moved employees into part-time work, or temporary employment, creating a leaner work force and reducing employee benefits. The super-rich have proved indifferent to the communities they have abandoned, often callously disregarding the increase in poverty among the workers who lost their jobs or were reduced to temporary or part-time work. The corporate elite have increasingly displayed a sense of entitlement, arguing that they are the great wealth and job creators, that they pay more than their fair share of taxes, and that they deserve the wealth they have acquired. Acting in a culture in which they often portray greed as a virtue, corporate executives have increasingly behaved like royals surrounded by undeserving sycophants. The result is that the business community has increasingly regarded itself as a celebrity class, attempting to impose narcissistic views of itself onto the public at large.

Since the Reagan era in the USA and the Thatcher era in the UK, CEOs have had almost free reign to choose their own boards. The inevitable result of servile boards has been to reinforce the trend toward short-termism, and this has accelerated the shift toward profit taking within a short one quarter horizon at the expense of most of the stakeholders.

We know from comparisons to corporate boards in Europe—for example in Germany—that board directors of all large corporations must have employee representation. Such boards tend to be contentious, but they are just as often visionary, and among the results of board democratization is a much greater tendency to rein in executive pay, invest in workers for long-term employment, maintain decent wages and benefits, and not resort to shifting as much employment abroad as possible. The result? Long-term benefits for all stakeholders, low rates of unemployment, employee loyalty, and high profitability. Just as important, executives cannot display the same kind of contempt for employees as do American and British firms, which are more concerned with accounting tricks to raise the bottom-line.

American corporations would do well to emulate Europeans. If they did so, hundreds of billions of dollars would not be drained away from employees, investors, and the communities where corporations are housed. Instead, American CEOs and their corporate boards have created incestuous relationships. CEOs appoint their friends, and many of the same CEOs also serve on other boards, ramping up their income even further in the form of outsize compensation packages, outlandish bonuses, mushrooming incomes—all distributed as perpetual Christmas stockings for corporate executives who then go into self-indulgent sprees spending their lavish sums.

There are ample illustrations of US corporate malfeasance. James Westphal, a business professor at the University of Michigan, conducted a survey over 15 years of 350 top firms comprising the S&P stock indices, and found that almost 50% of compensation committee boards members were called friends by their CEOs, and not just acquaintances. He discovered that customized boards tolerated mediocrity or worse in their CEOs. Westphal provided abundant examples. In 2007, Merrill Lynch was bankrupt, and was slated to be sold on the cheap at literally pennies on the dollar, having been driven into bankruptcy by CEO Stanley O'Neal. Inexplicably, the board decided to allow O'Neal to resign, rather than firing him for incompetence. The result? O'Neal was able to cash in $131 million in stock options. Had he been fired, he would have forfeited the gift and spared shareholders the loss.[5]

David Cay Johnston, in *Perfectly Legal*, cited another case involving Eugene M. Isenberg, CEO of Nabors Industries, a large oil-drilling company. Nabors reported sales of $1.3 billion in 2000. Through a combination of stock options and a well-crafted compensation arrangement, Isenberg received $127 million of that cash flow, or roughly 10% of gross revenue.[6]

The case of Craig Dubow is even more infamous. Dubow was CEO of Gannett, a media giant, for six years, ending with his resignation in 2011. It was a good run for Dubow. Following his tenure, he received a golden parachute worth $37.1 million and an additional $16 million in cash during the last two years of his term. Despite these lucrative paydays for Dubow, Gannett performed poorly while he was CEO. Share price fell from $75 when he arrived to $10 at the time of his departure.[7]

Richard Fuld at Lehman Brothers outdid Dubow when it came to executive pay for Lilliputian performance. In 8 years at the helm, he made $484 million before driving his company into bankruptcy. In his last year, even as he was leading his company into the corporate wilderness, he earned about $45 million.[8]

Merrill Lynch may have outdone Fuld. In September of 2008, the company admitted that it couldn't pay its bills anymore. But, just before it ended its final quarter of business in 2008, Merrill Lynch gave out nearly $4 billion in executive compensation bonuses. This was especially intriguing given that CEO John Thain continued to press for a lucrative golden parachute for himself, although he admitted that Merrill had lost $15 billion just in the last quarter of 2008—the same quarter as the outsized bonuses—and $27 billion for the year.[9]

But even Thain's outsized ego seems small when compared to the titanic ambition and deceit of Angelo Mozilo at Countrywide Financial. During five years between 2001 and 2006, he made his company the number one mortgage lender in the USA, but this created a problem for his imperial adventures. His empire was based on the proverbial subprime loans and the flinty derivatives that were based on them. Mozilo came to the head of his class as he had wanted, but everything was based on borrowing and just when the mortgage market was collapsing. The result? He made almost half a billion dollars for himself, but the company was turned into a slag-heap, losing 91% of its value before being sold off. Asked for his comments afterward, after the destruction of many lives and loss of homes, the unrepentant Mozilo said he had no regrets.[10]

Maurice R. Greenberg also was a standout in the department of not-so-creative destruction, presiding over American International Group (AIG) as it declined in value by 98%. This did not stop him, however, from siphoning off more than $130 million in executive compensation for himself.[11] As we know, AIG was saved by President Obama.

No matter the metric, the rise of executive pay in the USA is unjustified. Executive pay has increased much more rapidly than indices such as sales, profits, and returns to shareholders. Former Labor Secretary under Bill Clinton, Robert Reich has provided this shocking revelation: "By 2006, CEOs were earning, on average, eight times as much per corporate dollar of corporate profits as they did in the 1980s."[12] Such disparities point to one of the chief reasons for inequalities in income and wealth: executive pay is largely the result not of extraordinary ability but of personal stealth and market failure.

Economist Kevin Murphy has confirmed the lack of correspondence between compensation and performance in a study evaluating the pay-for-performance of the twenty-five top earning CEOs between 2000 and 2010. He concluded that there was little if any relationship after analyzing shareholder returns. Pay was utterly random. Only five of the CEOs he studied headed companies that outperformed the Dow Jones stock index. And four of these CEOs, one each at Countrywide, Capital One, and Cendant, ran firms whose shareholders lost money during their tenure.[13] But the greatest losers were not on the list. Michael Dell enriched himself by $454 million while shareholders lost 66% of their value; Richard Fuld of Lehman Brothers, whom we have met, received $484 million for the honor of driving Lehman into bankruptcy in 2008.[14]

CEOs, Boards of Directors and Their Incestuous Relationships

Board members covet their relationships with CEOs and corporations because of the many benefits and the pay. George Tyler has demonstrated just how lucrative it can be to serve as a corporate board member. In 2008, the median compensation for non-executive board members of Fortune 500 companies was $199,949.[15] This figure is even more impressive if one remembers that this was the year of the financial meltdown, a period when many Americans were driven into bankruptcy, lost their homes, and often their jobs.

Corporate America continued to thrive, nevertheless. In fact, while Americans suffered from the worst economy in decades, board directors were hardly noticing a ripple. They reaped, but not what they sowed. Board members generally escaped punishment or fines even in cases of clear corporate malfeasance and corruption. Between 1980 and 2006, there were only thirteen instances when outside directors had to settle suits using their own money. When directors were punished, often the punishment was mild. According to John Gillespie and David Zweig, in *Money for Nothing*, Enron directors paid only 10% of prior net gains when selling Enron stock. In other words, they retained 90% of the net earnings while presiding over the destruction of Enron and while Enron employees were losing their pensions.[16]

Moreover, former Enron directors seemed more or less unaffected by their Enron connection. Four served on other boards, one became a professor at Stanford, and another became president of Brunel University in London. And then there was Wendy Gramm. She landed at George Mason University at the Mercatus Center, where she was supported in part by the Koch brothers, despite their avowed declaration that there should be punishment for market failures.[17]

Boards of directors are anything but independent. They are routinely staffed by members who are obligated to the CEO, as in the case of Murdoch industries. Or they are staffed by celebrities who lack financial expertise and are unlikely to challenge corporate executive leadership, even if that is their desire. The result is that boards regularly endorse lush compensation packages. Unsurprisingly, as Harvard law Professor Lucian Bebchuk and Economist Jesse Fried have argued, boards are manipulated by CEOs because they set the compensation for the CEO.[18] The result is that boards tend to ignore performance, which all too often they are indifferent toward or incapable of judging—other than by watching the ticker tape or share price of the day. Instead of providing a conscience, or at least sound judgment, they become a kind of club whose major purpose is building the resume and income of the CEO and his or her own "cabinet." The fussy *Financial Times* has agreed with this conclusion, judging that executive compensation packages are the result of clubby remuneration committees and concluding that the members of such clubs should be "slung out on the street."[19] Richard Posner, a conservative federal appeals judge made the same point in 2008: "Executive compensation in large publicly traded firms often is excessive because of the feeble incentives of boards of directors to police compensation."[20]

Since the 1980s, CEO pay in the USA has become pathologically and disingenuously inflated, hardly consistent with pay-for-performance, or else many executives would work for nothing or even pay their companies just for the privilege of being the CEO. Among the reasons? Stock options and bonuses that have brought windfalls outrageously out of synch with performance. Once again we see the convergence of corporate behavior and rent-seeking or, as Joseph Stiglitz has referred to it, "America's Socialism for the Rich."[21] Columnist John Kay of the *Financial Times* expressed it well in November 2009 as he looked back on the recent financial collapse:

> America has a new generation of rent-seekers. The modern equivalents of castles on the Rhine are first-class lounges and corporate jets. Their occupants are investment bankers and corporate executives. ... The scale of corporate rent-seeking activities by business and personal rent-seeking by senior individuals in business and finance has increased sharply. The outcome can be seen in the growth of Capitol Hill lobbying and the crowded restaurants of Brussels; in the structure of industries such as pharmaceuticals, media, defense equipment, and, of course, financial services; and in the explosion of executive remuneration.[22]

The use of stock options is one of the major causes of accelerating executive remuneration. Such windfalls are another form of rent-seeking: they extract value without any corresponding creation of new wealth. Executives have the option of purchasing stocks at well below the market price, which during the boom 1990s was an incentive to boost the value of share prices even further to take advantage of free money. Moreover, when options were exercised the earnings were not taxed at income tax rates but as capital gains, a considerable advantage because this tax was capped at 15% during the George W. Bush era, and today, 2018, it is capped at 20%, well below the highest marginal rate for income taxes in 2018 at 39.6% (37% after passage of the Tax Cuts and Jobs Act).

Executive gain has often meant losses for everybody else: for shareholders because when executive stock options are exercised they dilute share value for all other share owners, and total options can be up to 20% of outstanding stock. Consumers lose also since business expenses such as premiums for executives can be passed along to the ultimate users. And then companies deduct executive remuneration from their earnings, lowering their profits and the corporate taxes they pay (detailed from the corporate side in Chapter 6).

For executives, especially the CEOs, the lure is irresistible: high compensation, low taxes, and all the benefits that are part of the corporate executive lifestyle. How critical have the stock options been as a component of CEO compensation? For the period 2003–2008, many of the top executives received bonuses in stock options that would have embarrassed Scrooge. Charles Schwab, as head of his eponymously named company, was paid $19.4 million while the chief at Charles Schwab, but earned $797.2 million from stock sale proceeds on options that he exercised. Angelo Mozilo, whom we have met, earned $92 million in regular income, but $378.5 million in stock sale earnings, a multiple of about 4 to 1. Richard Fuld reveals a similar story, earning $45.2 million in conventional earned income, but an additional sum of $139.3 million from his options. And finally Maurice Isenberg, who was paid $17.5 million income by AIG, but received a whopping addition of $115.2 million from stock options, a significant gift for failing and having to be bailed out by the taxpayer.[23]

None of these earnings packages could have been realized without the outright complicity of boards of directors. Directors and the CEOs of the companies they oversaw had an incestuous relationship which is easy to explain: they were a mutual admiration society because of the remuneration that they afforded to each other, making it easier to reap what had never been sowed. Robert Reich has put it bluntly:

> Directors are amply paid for the three or four times a year they meet and naturally want to remain in the good graces of their top executives. Being a board member is the best part-time job in America. In 2012, the average compensation for a board member at an S&P 500 company was $251,000. In addition, boards consist of other CEOs who have considerable interest in ensuring their compatriots are paid generously. To advise on executive pay, boards typically hire people called "compensation consultants," whose actual roles are more akin to that of the oldest profession in the world. Such consultants typically establish benchmarks based on the pay of other CEOs, whose boards typically hire them for the same purpose. Since all boards want to demonstrate to their CEO as well as to analysts on Wall Street their willingness to pay generously for the very best, pay packages ratchet upward annually in the faux competition, conducted and directed by CEOs for CEOs, in the interest of CEOs.[24]

It hardly needs to be added that under the provisions of corporate law in the USA, shareholders have only an advisory role deciding the compensation for a CEO. Dodd–Frank financial legislation gives shareholders a say on pay, but the votes are not binding. Again, Robert Reich gives an illustration of this unfortunate gap in corporate law—which of course could be easily revised in Congress if it had the will to do so. Billionaire Larry Ellison, back in 2013, was granted a pay package valued at $78.4 million by Oracle's board. The sum was so absurd that shareholders rejected it. The rejection, however, was ignored by the board because it was, after all, controlled by Ellison. Had Oracle been in Australia, notes Reich, the outcome would probably have been different. That is because shareholders there have the right to force an entire corporate board to stand for reelection if 25% or more of a firm's shareholders vote against a CEO pay plan two years in a row.[25]

The Rise and Rise of Corporate Executive Pay

Members of corporate boards play the leading role in doling out generous rewards to CEOs, and the most significant tool in their toolbox remains the stock option. Granting this concession to CEOs provides incentives for them to pump up a firm's shares and then to cash out following the rise in value. And here again, despite Dodd–Frank and the desire to rein in executive compensation, stock options granted to CEOs and others have continued to escalate, remaining a significant form of corporate expenditure.

Corporate executives have become expert at boosting share prices. They use company earnings or borrow additional money for share buybacks, reducing the number of outstanding stock owned by the public, inevitably raising the price of the remaining shares. William Lazonick, a professor of economics and director of the Center for Industrial Competitiveness at the University of Massachusetts-Lowell, using SEC data, has done the math. Between 2001 and 2013, corporate expenditures on share buybacks of companies in the Standard & Poor's 500 Index accounted for outlays of $3.6 trillion dollars.[26] By law, corporations are required to announce publicly when they have approved buybacks, and the amount as well, but they are not required to disclose when they are actually entering the market to do so. The result is that buybacks are purchased anonymously, leading, routinely, to rising stock prices without investor knowledge that the cause may be the buybacks. There is a hitch in all this: CEOs can legally use their insider knowledge when buybacks will occur and exercise their stock options to coincide with the rise in share price.[27]

This will sound like insider trading too many and therefore illegal. But the deceit goes even deeper than that. David Cay Johnston noticed that executives had an uncanny ability to have options awarded to them on days when the stock price was at its lowest point during each period: "The timing was too perfect to be possible were the rules being followed."[28] Johnston had sniffed the deceptive practice: perfect timing such as he discovered was unlikely to be random. It wasn't. Corporations had not aborted the rules, they had found a legal way to simply avoid them by backdating to a time of low or lower price. Or alternatively, they resorted to the equally pernicious insider practice of pricing options on days when adverse corporate performance was scheduled to be released to the public.[29]

All this might sound like fraud and illicit stock manipulation to advantage CEOs and other executives. And for almost five decades, the SEC agreed. It believed that stock buybacks could lead readily to stock manipulation, which was why it required companies to disclose the volume of their buybacks and prevented them from repurchasing more than 15% in a single day—though that was hardly a significant deterrence. But even this was too much for Wall Street. In 1982, under President Reagan, the chairman of the SEC, John Shad, removed even these minor hindrances. Henceforth, corporations were free to manipulate the prices of their shares, and insider trading was unshackled to the advantage of corporate executives.

A decade later, the rules changed even more to the advantage of illicit corporate behavior. What was formerly fraudulent now became a virtue. In 1991, top executives with insider knowledge of the timing of their company's stock buybacks were permitted to exercise their stock options with public disclosure. And then in 1993 came a fateful decision by the Clinton administration allowing companies to deduct executive pay in excess of $1 million from the company's taxable income—as long as that income was linked to executive performance, i.e., derived from stock options and bonuses connected to share prices. In this way, as rules changed to the benefit of corporations and their top executives, remuneration skyrocketed, abetted by the government's benevolent attitude toward Big Business.[30] But the huge wealth legally diverted toward the corporate super-rich had to come from somewhere. And indeed it did. It came directly out of the shareholders' pockets, taxpayers who picked up the tab of reduced corporate taxes, employees who lost their jobs (not because of China), and workers who didn't get needed job retraining, or who received no gains in wages. Neither globalization, nor automation accounted for all these changes, but rules changes favoring the rich atop the corporate ladder created windfalls at the expense of wage bills, employment, and R&D, the better to raise share price and lift CEO compensation. Again, it was something for nothing, a modern version of rentier capitalism.

The new corporate model ultimately proved costly for employees, sometimes fatal, but it has also been a disaster for many corporations as well, which would have been much better off had they invested more in R&D and in their employees, as Germany has routinely done. IBM perfectly illustrates the lesson, and it has suffered the consequences. In 2014, Andrew Ross Sorkin, of the *New York Times*, explained how and why:

> Since 2000, IBM spent some $108 billion on its own shares, according to its most recent annual report. It also paid out $30 billion in dividends. To help finance this share-buying spree, IBM loaded up on debt. While the company spent $138 billion on its shares and dividend payments, it spent just $59 billion on its own business through capital expenditures and $32 billion on acquisitions.[31]

IBM had not always followed such laggard practices. Once upon a time, it had been committed to providing lifelong employment and long-term investments in technologies of the future. This dramatically changed in the 1990s when IBM shifted its priorities. It began laying off employees, scrimping on research, borrowing heavily, and using its cash to buy back shares. Robert Reich has pointed out that between 2000 and 2013 IBM spent $108 billion in share buybacks, raising share prices even as revenues went—and remained—flat.[32]

Meanwhile, this practice continued. Between 2005 and 2013, IBM spent $125 billion on buybacks and $32 billion on dividends, more than its capital spending and R&D combined in the same period.[33] Inevitably, IBM's stock began its proverbial slide, while its US work force, once in the range of 150,000, was roughly cut in half. Many of those jobs have gone abroad, so globalization has taken its toll. But much of what has undermined IBM in the USA has been its corporate strategy to subsidize its senior executives and top shareholders at the expense of workers and innovation.

Karen Brettell, David Gaffen, and David Rohde have documented similar practices at Hewlett-Packard (HP).

> When Carly Fiorina started at Hewlett-Packard Co in July 1999, one of her first acts as chief executive officer was to start buying back the company's shares. By the time she was ousted in 2005, HP had snapped up $14 billion of its stock, more than its $12 billion in profits during that time. Her successor, Mark Hurd, spent even more on buybacks during his five years in charge – $43 billion, compared to profits of $36 billion. Following him, Leo Apotheker bought back $10 billion in shares before his 11-month tenure ended in 2011. The three CEOs, over the span of a dozen years, followed a strategy that has become the norm for many big companies during the past two decades: large stock buybacks to make use of cash, coupled with acquisitions to lift revenue. All those buybacks put lots of money in the hands of shareholders. How well they served HP in the long term isn't clear. HP hasn't had a blockbuster product in years. It has been slow to make a mark in more profitable software and services businesses. In its core businesses, revenue and margins have been contracting.[34]

William Lazonick has characterized the practices of HP as self-destructive: "HP was the poster child of an innovative enterprise that retained profits and reinvested in the productive capabilities of employees. Since 1999, however, it has been destroying itself by downsizing its labor force and distributing its profits to shareholders."[35] Indeed, "downsizing" HP's labor force was an understatement. Between CEOs Meg Whitman and Carly Fiorina, HP laid off 80,000 workers in the wake of what was called "restructuring," but which ultimately was what paid for the greed and extraction of wealth by the ascendant few. The failure to innovate, the high volume of extracted wealth from the corporation, ultimately fueled the failure of HP. The gains of the CEOs and top executives and high-end shareholders were paid for by the most vulnerable and least compensated in yet another advance of the rentier economy.

There were of course exceptions, but what we have seen was also typical of the corporate culture that began to emerge in the 1980s. And that culture was destructive. The windfalls that were being routinely given to CEOs and their teams were contingent on constantly improving earnings per share from one quarter to the next. Long-term investment, R&D, and the focus on productivity growth were replaced by new corporate strategies. American executives, their total earnings now tied to share price more than ever, were motivated—supported by their boards of directors—to receive their gold bricks in share buybacks and mergers, the former a dilution of value to other shareholders, the latter a method to exponentially boost gain for executives while shifting the tax burden to others lower on the totem pole: altogether another example of extraction of wealth and rent-seeking by the super-rich.

Prior to the Reagan era in the USA and the Thatcher era in the UK, executive pay had been stable for decades, and senior executives earned about thirty times the multiple of the average pay of their employees. But with Reagan and Thatcher, with their advocacy for letting the market set the wages, and their removal of any lingering commitment to social democratic values, as well as their hostility to organized labor, all obstacles for accelerating executive pay were removed. By 2000, the sea change in senior executive remuneration had contributed to the burgeoning inequality gaps that have become all too common. Top management pay escalated to more than 300 times average employee wages. George Tyler noticed that it became typical for a handful of executives at larger firms to each average $5 million in annual pay, including bonuses and stock options.[36]

Well after the financial and housing market crash of 2007–2008, executives and their minions had not been shamed, nor had legislation curbed their insatiable appetites for wealth. The AFL-CIO released data in 2014 showing that American CEOs in 2013 earned an average of $11.7 million—an eye-popping 331 times the average worker's $35,293. This was down from 2012s 354-to-1 CEO-to-worker pay ratio, but the multiple more than doubled when compared to minimum wage workers; the average CEO in 2013 out-earned this group by a multiple of 774.[37] Gillespie and Zweig, cited above, noted that CEOs were receiving 10% of all corporate profits, a staggering percentage considering that corporate executives in earlier eras were no doubt just as creative and productive, but earning far less than the income of rock stars.[38] Executives argue that they are creative and innovative, and in any case, they have to play by the same rules as everybody else. But we have already seen that they set the rules.

In other democracies, executive pay has not risen to the obscene levels of the USA. In the UK, which comes closest to emulating the USA in executive compensation, CEOs at the largest 100 firms on the UK stock exchange (FTSE 100) earned 88 times the average wage of their employees in 2009.[39] In Japan, in 2008, the top fourteen executives at Mitsubishi, Japan's largest bank, received $8.1 million altogether, a sum that pales when compared to the pay scales of their American counterparts.[40] A Harvard Law study showed that American CEO pay packages were not only undeserved, but were well beyond what counterparts received everywhere else. This study found that American CEOs at large firms averaged $12.3 million, which contrasted with $5.9 million in Germany, $3.8 million in the UK, $3.4 million in Sweden, and $2.5 million in Norway.[41] Generally, Scandinavian countries grant their executives much less compensation, though hardly pauperizing them, by maintaining democratized boards of directors. The result is greater commitment to employees, reasonably low unemployment rates, and much greater benefit levels, including government determination to keep people who want jobs in employment.

Outlandish executive remuneration in the USA strongly suggests a disconnection between executive pay and performance. The same is true for Britain. The British Institute of Directors, hardly a proletarian organization, back in 2011 argued that business in the UK was "significantly damaged" in the view of the public because of undeserved pay packages hardly earned by performance, though average CEO pay at $3.8 million was less than 30% of what was taken in the USA.[42]

During my brief stint as a "banker" or investment counselor at UBS investment bank, some of the counselors were ingenuous enough to realize and to admit that they had little idea of where the market was heading. But that didn't stop them from making somewhat educated guesses dressed up as science, not opinion. Others had degrees in economics and were more self-confident: the result was sometimes better, even in the flat year of 2002. The degreed felt they had something of value, and therefore, when they made good commissions, they believed the earnings were merited because they brought value to the client. But when the client lost, the reasoning was that it was the fault of the market, not the advice of the investment broker. Whether the client won or lost, the broker still made money in fees and commissions: he never participated in losses, but could and often did take a percentage of the winnings. UBS itself participated in the deception, granting the title of vice president to every broker it hired. This was merely cosmetic, but somewhere there was the conviction that a title of vice president would be more convincing for UBS' clientele.

Robert Reich was on the mark when he reminded us in *Saving Capitalism* of the "meritocratic myth," the belief that executives making excessive earnings were worth their outsized incomes and wealth. In fact, as Reich demonstrates, much of the wealth taken in finance was based on insider trading. Reich cited the case of Steven A, Cohen, who in 2013 earned $2.3 billion. During Cohen's twenty years at the helm of SAC Capital Advisors, he reaped a fortune estimated at about $11 billion. Was he really worth that sum of money other than in the most tautological sense that he must have been worth that sum if he had earned it? The Justice Department didn't think so, and it subsequently filed a criminal complaint, noting that under Cohen's leadership insider trading was "substantial, pervasive and on a scale without precedent in the hedge fund industry."[43]

Had Cohen and SAC Capital not cheated and gamed the system, and had insider trading been discovered and prosecuted earlier, investor confidence would have waned, returns would have diminished, and Cohen's wealth, $11 billion, would have been much reduced. As it turned out, Cohen was fined $1.8 billion, meaning that he had succeeded in gaming the system after all. But there was one thing that could not be said for Cohen: he was hardly worth the $11 billion or the $9.2 billion he was allowed to retain. He had committed fraud, yet was richly awarded for it. He had amassed a huge pile of money, but he had not contributed anything of value to the real economy. In siphoning money, he was parasitical, and he had found the means—legal or not—to extract the wealth that others had produced, with no moral claim to that wealth. Had the rules been different, had insider trading been banned, and had that ban been enforced, Cohen's wealth would have been vastly diminished.

Private Equity: Stealing Wealth by Firing Workers—The New "Flexible Labor Force"

The last three plus decades in both the USA and the UK, beginning with the Reagan and Thatcher eras, have seen the emergence of strident managerial capitalism fueled by short-termism, artificially raising share price to enrich the corporate elite. But this has come at the expense of many and ultimately of corporations themselves. That is because this era has produced corporate mergers, and these have been value destroying for a number of reasons. Corporations that acquire other companies have too often done so in order to boost revenues by buying the assets that produce them. This strategy, however, means an increase in debt, which in turn has led to reducing what should have been regarded as the main assets of every company engaged in competitive capitalism: research

R&D and investment in human capital—or the employees of a given company. Put in perspective, to make short-term gains that are likely to produce rising overall earnings and share prices, too many corporations have sacrificed R&D, the necessary investment in innovation which made them successful in the first place, and any serious commitment to their employees and long-term employment.

Welcome to the wonderful world of private equity and corporate mergers. Borrow large sums of money, acquire a company, sell off its assets to pay off the loan, fire thousands of workers to give yourself operating capital, use mostly flexible labor to avoid benefits, and flip the company that is now operating in the black at an enormous profit: or simply keep it if it brings enough revenue.

Seems like an exaggeration? Not at all, it is part of the ethic of modern corporate capitalism: to balance new debt incurred in acquisition, shed workers, and reduce capital investment. But look at the subtle and not so subtle risks: the more mergers, the less competition, and the less competition, the less competitive a company is bound to be. From the point of view of workers, this whole new era of capitalism has meant a disaster. Companies have less need for them, treat them as an expendable commodity, see them as an unfortunate and unnecessary expense, and convert them from important contributors of knowledge to part-time or contract workers, replaceable and easy to shed.

But what of the viewpoint of private equity corporations and companies engaging in takeovers and mergers that they are engaged in "creative destruction," making the economy overall much stronger by restructuring failing companies and eliminating redundancies? An important study by economists Ulrike Malmendier, Enrico Moretti, and Florian Peters examined all contested US mergers between 1985 and 2009 where at least two suitors vied to acquire a company. The results were startling. The researchers found that, following the mergers, the losers—those whose bids had failed—outperformed the "winners" by roughly 50% in the three years following the merger. This was an enormous penalty for "success," but the reason for the striking underperformance was clear to the researchers: it was the debt taken on to effect the merger. It was because of that debt and the high leverage it signified, that expenses had to be cut elsewhere in order to manage the new obligation.[44] Economists Jeffrey S. Harrison and Derek K. Oler came too much the same conclusion. The inevitable consequence of mergers was a rise in debt leverage and a corresponding reduction in the work force, replete with layoffs, conversion to more part-time jobs, and growing indifference to both the communities where companies were located and the effect that downsizing the workforce would have on them. Harrison and Oler examined 3000 mergers and found that leverage had risen on average 45%, steep enough to lead to dramatic paring of "risk" elsewhere. This meant cutting spending on R&D and wages.[45] Not surprisingly, somebody had to pay for the cost of mergers and the handsome executive rewards that were the objectives of the mergers. Typically, that meant that jobs were lost and workers were out of luck.

Some firms remain dinosaurs that need restructuring. That is part of the narrative: mergers and/or acquisitions can also revive a company by making it more efficient, more competitive, and less capital starved, enabling necessary changes. Certainly redundancies can be eliminated. And nobody can deny the impact of technology and innovation, as well as globalization. But many American corporations, in particular, including private equity firms, have shed workers, reduced R&D, and concentrated on short-term strategies in order to pump up earnings, without creating anything of corresponding value.

Since the 1980s, there has been a sea change in mergers and hostile takeovers, initially enabled by Reagan and not subsequently reversed. Ironically, government changed the rules that made piles of cash available for mergers and acquisitions. But the transformation was also promoted by corporate interests and Wall Street and was embraced by Congress as far back as 1974. In that year, Congress enacted the Employee Retirement Income Security Act at the urging of pension funds, insurance companies, and the Street, which, prior to that act, could only invest in high-grade, conservative corporate, and government bonds. This was transformed by the 1974 act, which allowed pension funds and insurance companies to invest their portfolios in the stock market. Overnight this provided mountains of fresh funds made available to Wall Street. In 1982, Congress went further along the same path, when it authorized savings and loan banks—at that time the pillar for home mortgages—to invest their deposits in any number of financial products, including junk bonds and their equivalent high risk securities, all of them promising high, and sometimes spectacular—and irresistible—gains. The temptation proved to be too great: when many of these banks went under, the taxpayer lost some $124 billion.[46]

Conclusion

Wall Street and corporate America, and the City and corporate Britain, abetted by the Washington and London political elites, have cleared the way for "creative destruction," the absorption of "less efficient and tenable" companies to make the overall economy more competitive. Driven by insatiable greed, they created a perfect storm for what would come in 2007–2008, the last hurrah for many in the middle classes and the working classes of both countries, who paid the ultimate price in the loss of homes, health, and jobs. For such workers, creative destruction meant massive unemployment, followed by work forces ever more flexible, ever more contingent, ever more at risk, increasingly without unions to protect them, or politicians to legislate for them. But for private equity companies and corporations with mountains of pension money newly available, it was a new era of acquisitive, rentier capitalism and its executive beneficiaries.

Notes

1. Gary Rivlin and John Markoff, "Tossing Out a Chief Executive," *New York Times*, February 14, 2005.
2. Jack Lawrence Luzkow, *The Great Forgetting: The Past, Present and Future of Social Democracy and the Welfare State* (Manchester: Manchester University Press, 2015), 133.
3. Ibid., 136.
4. George R. Tyler, *What Went Wrong: How the 1% Hijacked the American Middle Class...And What Other Countries Got Right* (Dallas, TX: Benbella Books, 2013), 132–33.
5. Heather Landy, "Executives Took, But the Directors Gave," *New York Times*, April 5, 2009.
6. David Cay Johnston, *Perfectly Legal: The Covert Campaign to Rig Our Tax System to Benefit the Super Rich—And Cheat Everybody Else* (New York: Penguin/Portfolio, 2003), 250.
7. David Carr, "Why Not Occupy Newsrooms?" *New York Times*, October 23, 2011.
8. Nicholas Kristof, OP-ED, "Need a Job? $17,000 an Hour. No Success Required," *New York Times*, September 17, 2008.
9. Andrew Sorkin, "Thain Speaks Out in Defense of Himself," *New York Times*, January 26, 2009.

10. Mark Maremont, John Hechinger, and Maurice Tamman. "Before the Bust, These CEOs Took Money Off the Table," *The Wall Street Journal*, November 20, 2008; "Executive Incentives." See chart, "Executive Incentives," comparing executive performance and compensation.
11. Ibid.
12. Rober Reich, *Supercapitalism: The Transformation of Business, Democracy and Everyday Life* (New York: Alfred A. Knopf, 2007), 108.
13. Tyler, *What Went Wrong*, 137.
14. Ibid.; See also Kevin Murphy, "Pay, Politics and the Financial Crisis," *Economics and the Financial Crisis*. Russell Sage, 2012.
15. Tyler, *What Went Wrong*, 129.
16. John Gillespie and David Zweig, *Money for Nothing: How the Failure of Corporate Boards Is Ruining America and Costing the US Trillions* (New York: Free Press, 2010), 35.
17. Steven M. Davidoff, "On Boards, Little Cause of Anxiety," *New York Times*, August 3, 2011.
18. Lucian A. Bebchuk and Jesse M. Fried, "Tackling the Managerial Power Problem," *Pathways*, Stanford University Center for Poverty and Inequality, Summer 2010, online at http://inequality.stanford.edu/sites/default/files/summer_2010.pdf.
19. Editors, "Executive Pay," *Financial Times*, February 7, 2010.
20. Adam Liptak, "Justices to Weigh in on Corporate Culture and Its Paychecks," *New York Times*, August 18, 2009.
21. Joseph E. Stiglitz, *The Great Divide: Unequal Societies and What We Can Do About Them* (New York: W. W. Norton, 2015), 192–95.
22. John Kay, "Powerful Interests Are Trying to Control the Market," *Financial Times*, November 10, 2009.
23. Maremont et al., "Before the Bust."
24. Robert B. Reich, *Saving Capitalism: For the Many, Not the Few* (New York: Alfred A. Knopf, 2015), 99.
25. Ibid., 99–100.
26. William Lazonick, *Taking Stock: Why Executive Pay Results in an Unstable and Inequitable Economy* (New York: Roosevelt Institute, June 5, 2014), 5, at http://www.theairnet.org/v3/backbone/uploads/2014/08/Lazonick_Executive_Pay_White_Paper_Roosevelt_Institute.pdf.
27. Reich, *Saving Capitalism*, 101.
28. David Cay Johnston, *Free Lunch: How the Wealthiest Americans Enrich Themselves at Government Expense—And Stick You With the Bill* (New York: Portfolio/Penguin, 2008), 263.
29. Peter Lattman, "Prosecutions in Backdating Scandal Bring Mixed Results," *New York Times*, November 12, 2010.

30. Reich, *Saving Capitalism*, 101; Steven Balsam, *Taxes and Executive Compensation*, Briefing Paper #344 (Washington, DC: Economic Policy Institute, August 4, 2012), online at http://www.epi.org/publication/taxes-executive-compensation/.
31. Andrew Ross Sorkin, "The Truth Hidden by IBM's Buyback," *New York Times*, October 20, 2014.
32. Reich, *Saving Capitalism*, 102.
33. Karen Brettell, David Gaffen, and David Rohde, "As Stock Buybacks Reach Historic Levels, Signs That Corporate America Is Undermining Itself," *Reuters*, November 16, 2015, online at http://www.reuters.com/investigates/special-report/usa-buybacks-cannibalized/.
34. Ibid.
35. Ibid.
36. Tyler, *What Went Wrong*, 133.
37. Kathryn Dill, "Report: CEOs Earn 331 Times as Much as Average Workers, 774 Times as Much as Minimum Wage Earners," *Forbes Magazine*, April 15, 2014.
38. Gillespie, *Money for Nothing*, 35.
39. Richard Lambert, "Blueprint to Put Bosses' Pay in Order," *Financial Times*, November 4, 2011.
40. Ian Verrender, "Running to Save Their Executive Bacon—Alas It May Be Too Late," *Sydney Morning Herald*, October 15, 2011, online at http://www.smh.com.au/business/running-to-save-their-executive-bacon--alas-it-may-be-too-late-20111014-1loyo.html?deviceType=text.
41. Roberto A. Ferdman, "The Pay Gap Between CEOs and Workers Is Much Worse Than You Think," *Washington Post*, September 25, 2014.
42. Kate Burgess, "More Calls for Reform of Executives' Pay," *Financial Times*, November 27, 2011.
43. Cited by Robert Reich, *Saving Capitalism*, 90.
44. Ulrike Malmendier, Enrico Moretti, and Florian Peters, *Winning by Losing: Evidence on the Long-Run Effects of Mergers*, Working Paper 18024 (Cambridge, MA: National Bureau of Economic Research, 2016), at http://emlab.berkeley.edu/~moretti/mergers.pdf.
45. Jeffrey S. Harrison and Derek K. Oler, "The Influence of Debt on Acquisition Performance," *Academy of Management Journal*, Presented at Academy of Management Annual Meeting Proceedings, August 2008, online at https://doi.org/10.5465/ambpp.2008.337168, 34; see also Tyler, *What Went Wrong*, 143.
46. Reich, *Saving Capitalism*, 120–21; see also Timothy Curry and Lynn Shibut, "The Cost of the Savings and Loan Crisis: Truth and Consequences," *FDIC Banking Review* 13, no. 2 (2000): 26–35.

Bibliography

Balsam, Steven. *Taxes and Executive Compensation.* Briefing Paper #344, Economic Policy Institute, Washington, DC, August 4, 2012. Online at http://www.epi.org/publication/taxes-executive-compensation/.

Bebchuk, Lucian A., and Jesse M. Fried. "Tackling the Managerial Power Problem." *Pathways.* Stanford University Center for Poverty and Inequality, Summer 2010. Online at http://inequality.stanford.edu/sites/default/files/summer_2010.pdf.

Brettell, Karen, David Gaffen, and David Rohde. "As Stock Buybacks Reach Historic Levels, Signs That Corporate America Is Undermining Itself." *Reuters,* November 16, 2015. Online at http://www.reuters.com/investigates/special-report/usa-buybacks-cannibalized/.

Burgess, Kate. "More Calls for Reform of Executives' Pay." *Financial Times,* November 27, 2011.

Carr, David. "Why Not Occupy Newsrooms?" *New York Times,* October 23, 2011.

Curry, Timothy, and Lynn Shibut, "The Cost of the Savings and Loan Crisis: Truth and Consequences." *FDIC Banking Review* 13, no. 2 (2000): 26–35.

Davidoff, Steven M. "On Boards, Little Cause of Anxiety." *New York Times,* August 3, 2011.

Dill, Kathryn. "Report: CEOs Earn 331 Times as Much as Average Workers, 774 Times as Much as Minimum Wage Earners." *Forbes Magazine,* April 15, 2014.

Ferdman, Roberto A. "The Pay Gap Between CEOs and Workers Is Much Worse Than You Think." *Washington Post,* September 25, 2014.

Financial Times. "Executive Pay," February 7, 2010.

Gillespie, John, and David Zweig. *Money for Nothing: How the Failure of Corporate Boards Is Ruining America and Costing the US Trillions.* New York: Free Press, 2010.

Harrison, Jeffrey S., and Derek K. Oler. "The Influence of Debt on Acquisition Performance." *Academy of Management Journal.* Academy of Management Annual Meeting Proceedings, August 2008. Online at https://doi.org/10.5465/ambpp.2008.33716834.

Johnston, David Cay. *Free Lunch: How the Wealthiest Americans Enrich Themselves at Government Expense—And Stick You With the Bill.* New York: Penguin/Portfolio, 2008.

Johnston, David Cay. *Perfectly Legal: The Covert Campaign to Rig Our Tax System to Benefit the Super Rich—And Cheat Everybody Else.* New York: Penguin/Portfolio, 2003.

Kay, John. "Powerful Interests Are Trying to Control the Market." *Financial Times,* November 10, 2009.

Kristof, Nicholas. OP-ED, "Need a Job? $17,000 an Hour. No Success Required." *New York Times*, September 17, 2008.

Lambert, Richard. "Blueprint to Put Bosses' Pay in Order." *Financial Times*, November 4, 2011.

Landy, Heather. "Executives Took, But the Directors Gave." *New York Times*, April 5, 2009.

Lattman, Peter. "Prosecutions in Backdating Scandal Bring Mixed Results." *New York Times*, November 12, 2010.

Lazonick, William. *Taking Stock: Why Executive Pay Results in an Unstable and Inequitable Economy*. New York: Roosevelt Institute, June 5, 2014. At http://www.theairnet.org/v3/backbone/uploads/2014/08/Lazonick_Executive_Pay_White_Paper_Roosevelt_Institute.pdf.

Liptak, Adam. "Justices to Weigh in on Corporate Culture and Its Paychecks." *New York Times*, August 18, 2009.

Luzkow, Jack Lawrence. *The Great Forgetting: The Past, Present and Future of Social Democracy and the Welfare State*. Manchester: Manchester University Press, 2015.

Malmendier, Ulrike, Enrico Moretti, and Florian Peters. *Winning by Losing: Evidence on the Long-Run Effects of Mergers*. Working Paper 18024. Cambridge, MA: National Bureau of Economic Research, 2016. At http://emlab.berkeley.edu/~moretti/mergers.pdf.

Maremont, Mark, John Hechinger, and Maurice Tamman. "Before the Bust, These CEOs Took Money Off the Table." *The Wall Street Journal*, November 20, 2008.

Murphy, Kevin. "Pay, Politics and the Financial Crisis." *Economics and the Financial Crisis* (Russell Sage, 2012). Online at https://www.russellsage.org/sites/all/files/Rethinking-Finance/Murphy.PayPoliticsCrisis%202-16-12.pdf.

Reich, Robert B. *Saving Capitalism: For the Many, Not the Few*. New York: Alfred A. Knopf, 2015.

Reich, Robert B. *Supercapitalism: The Transformation of Business, Democracy and Everyday Life*. New York: Alfred A. Knopf, 2007.

Rivlin, Gary, and John Markoff. "Tossing Out a Chief Executive." *New York Times*, February 14, 2005.

Sorkin, Andrew Ross. "Thain Speaks Out in Defense of Himself." *New York Times*, January 26, 2009.

Sorkin, Andrew Ross. "The Truth Hidden by IBM's Buyback." *New York Times*, October 20, 2014.

Stiglitz, Joseph E. *The Great Divide: Unequal Societies and What We Can Do About Them*. New York: W. W. Norton, 2015.

Tyler, George R. *What Went Wrong: How the 1% Hijacked the American Middle Class…And What Other Countries Got Right.* Dallas, TX: Benbella Books, 2013.
Verrender, Ian. "Running to Save Their Executive Bacon—Alas It May Be Too Late." *Sydney Morning Herald*, October 15, 2011. Online at http://www.smh.com.au/business/running-to-save-their-executive-bacon--alas-it-may-be-too-late-20111014-1loyo.html?deviceType=text.
Wall Street Journal. "Executive Incentives." November 20, 2008.

CHAPTER 5

The Decline of Main Street and the Middle Class

Introduction

Shortly after mid-year in 2016, BHS (British Home Stores) Department Stores collapsed after almost ninety years, causing 11,000 workers to lose their jobs. In what was the biggest failure in the retail industry in Britain since the collapse of Woolworths in 2008, administrators to BHS made the call to wind down the business and close its 163 shops. But the liquidation of BHS put increasing pressure on Sir Philip Green, well known as the retailer who owned Top Shops, and Dominic Chappell, former owners of BHS, who had left it with a £571 pension deficit.[1]

Why the pension deficit? During his ownership of BHS, which he purchased in 2000, Green and other investors collected more than £580 million in dividends, rent and interest payments. Eventually, hoping to avoid responsibility for the pension deficit, Green sold off BHS for £1, to Chappells consortium, Retail Acquisitions. Chappell then collected millions more in salaries and management fees. Eventually, Green agreed to pay £363 into a revised pension scheme under pressure from Parliament. But it was too late to save BHS—and its 11,000 employees—which had been starved of investment money for improvements since Green had acquired it.[2]

J. L. Luzkow, *Monopoly Restored*,
https://doi.org/10.1007/978-3-319-93994-0_5

Neoliberalism, Reaganism, Thatcherism and the Decline of Workers and Wages

The vast and growing inequalities and inequities in income and wealth in the USA and UK are not accidents of history. They flow directly from policies adopted in the 1980s by the administration of Ronald Reagan in the USA and Margaret Thatcher in Britain. These policies, deregulation, privatization, low-tax regimes, and suppression (or bypassing) of unions, which are still embraced by many "neoliberal" economists, have led us into a long period of stagnation and worse, yet they still remain orthodox economic strategies in both the USA and the UK, and they have had wide influence in Europe as well. Despite the reigning orthodoxy, Reaganomics has not been kind to most Americans or citizens of the UK. The decades since the 1980s have seen serious income erosion for the vast majority, the return of poverty at rates unsustainable if democracy is to thrive, low productivity, and wages that have not kept up with productivity rates. During the period sometimes called the Golden Age in the USA, between 1947 and into the mid-1970s, productivity, measured as total output divided by total labor hours, grew an impressive 2.8% per year, slumping during the decade of the 70s, before dipping to 1.9% between the mid-1970s and 2011.[3]

Although productivity dropped modestly in the 1970s, it was ample enough for both profits and wages to rise. But that was not what happened. Average wages went flat or declined and remained stagnant for decades in the USA and the UK. So where did the gains go if not to wages for the majority of people? Virtually, all gains went directly to the top, into corporate profits and personal incomes at the heights of the income scale. The divide was precipitous. Economists Emmanuel Saez and Thomas Piketty have demonstrated that a meager 5% of income earners exceeded the rate of inflation during the years of the Reagan presidency between 1981 and 1989, and those earnings were received disproportionately by the top 1% of earners.[4] This was the beginning of what has now become endemic.

Rentier Capitalism: How the Corporate Super-Rich Plundered Everybody Else

Waves of corporate mergers and corporate raiding transformed America and Britain, between 1980 and 2010. What followed was mass "redundancy," permanent layoffs of millions of employees, the hollowing out of the middle class, and the decimation of the working class. What emerged was a marginalized population living on the edge without secure employment or a hopeful future, without equal access to education, healthcare, or affordable housing, pushed aside by the modern multinational corporation.

During the decade of the 1970s, there were only thirteen hostile takeovers of companies valued at more than $1 billion in the USA. But in the decade that followed, between 1979 and 1989, there were more than 2000 leveraged buyouts backed by financial entrepreneurs, each valued at more than $250 million.[5]

One of the most dramatic illustrations of the merger mania and the slash and burn ideology was Jack Welch at GE. He became CEO in 1981 and in two decades grew the company from $14 billion to $400 billion, much of it by emasculating payrolls, slashing more than 100,000 jobs during his tenure. Welch was not unique. IBM, between 1985 and 1993, managed to slim its workforce by 180,000 workers, almost half of its entire workforce. Citigroup, after its management coups and multi-mergers and acquisitions, laid off 60,000 workers in November 2008. And AT&T eliminated 40,000 jobs in January 1996 to create more shareholder value.[6] It should not have come as a shock that as mergers and acquisitions became more routine in the corporate world, the fortunes of CEOs rose, reaching the unprecedented pay packages that we have already observed. Did corporations become more efficient in the wake of new acquisitions? Productivity certainly rose, but almost all increases in profits went straight to the top. The net result was stagnation or worse for much if not most of the workforce, as economists Josh Bevins and Lawrence Mishel have documented:

> Since 1973, hourly compensation of the vast majority of American workers has not risen in line with economy-wide productivity. In fact, hourly compensation has almost stopped rising *at all*. Net productivity grew 72.2 percent between 1973 and 2014. Yet inflation-adjusted hourly compensation of the median worker rose just 8.7 percent, or 0.20 percent annually, over this same period, with essentially all of the growth occurring between 1995 and 2002.[7]

Translated, this meant that workers' pay did not keep up with productivity: even worse, many ordinary workers lost jobs—many permanently—or had to accept brutal paycuts that were degrading and that failed to maintain modest standards of living. Workers lost bargaining power, unions were demoralized, and communities were abandoned.

What was true in the USA was just as true for the UK, where the same kinds of rising productivity and corresponding rise in poverty and despair were increasingly evident post-2008. In 2012, almost 30% of the British population fell below the minimum living standard set by society as a whole, a figure that had doubled since 1983. According to Stewart Lansley and Joanna Mack, 10% of British households lived in a damp home, a thirty-year high. The population that could not afford to heat their home adequately had trebled since the 1990s, rising from 3 to 9%. And a startling 28% of the British population reported skimping on meals occasionally, a figure up from 13% in 1983.[8] As Lansley and Stewart bluntly put it:

> The reality for people on low incomes today is one of a constant struggle to get by, of endless worry about how to pay the next bill, of parents cutting back for themselves to prioritise the kids, and of young people left with few hopes for the future. Person after person tells a similar story: 'I only tend to eat one meal a day and that does me, 'cos I like to make sure I've got enough for my children'; 'I try to keep the heating on for a couple of hours and then turn it off – I'm afraid of the bill coming in, to tell you the God's truth'.[9]

What Lansley and Stewart observed was not a temporary catastrophe because of the financial credit crisis of 2007, or the mortgage crisis that followed in 2008–2009, but a long-term trend coinciding with the increasing greed and predation of the corporate class, the super-rich. It begs credulity to believe or to argue that as Britain became twice as rich in the three decades between 1983 and 2013, and poverty rates doubled, the cause was anything other than direct exploitation, predation led by the financial sector—home mortgages especially—a so-called flexible labor market allowing corporations to freely shed jobs, a full-fledged assault on labor unions, the only reliable defense of the working class, and corporate practices abandoning any commitment to employees in favor of temporary and contract labor.[10] Beginning with Reaganism in the 1980s, and Thatcherism during the same decade, labor unions came under direct assault from government, labor markets became far more regulated ("flexible"), finance was substantively deregulated, manufacturing plummeted, and government no longer acted as a steering mechanism. As for the working classes in the USA and the UK, the new stance of governments in both nations meant that they were on their own, increasingly abandoned by their governments and their employers.

Class Struggle: How Income Gushes Up and Trickles Down

If the super-rich created jobs in proportion to the growth of their wealth, then employment opportunities in the USA and the UK would be virtually unlimited. That, however, is not what has been happening. If one discounts part-time and contract employment, then the US rate of unemployment remained in mid-2016, at a minimum of 10%. Instead, it is in Germany, where the wealthiest 1% receives roughly half as much income as their US counterparts, that unemployment declined to twenty-year lows at 4.5% (March 2016). Critics will point out that Germany has no minimum wage law and many jobs are insecure. But this picture is false. German workers have more rights and more job security than workers in the USA and the UK. German workers have representation on the boards of large corporations, unions are much better protected, the wealthiest 1% pay much higher taxes, and the result is that this group works more effectively for the good of everybody, presenting less of an obstacle to the rights of workers than their counterparts in the USA and the UK.

It is widely forgotten today that both the USA and the UK were much more equal in the decades following World War II, and that greater income and wealth parity did not harm economic growth. On the contrary, equality and affluence grew together, far more robustly than in the decades following 1970, which increasingly embraced the ideology of the corporate elite: that nations prosper more in eras of increasing inequality. By 2015, as the 1% in the USA cornered almost 45% of the financial wealth, productivity growth had declined to 0.7% while GDP growth was about 1.9%.[11] How to account for this? The increasing predation of the super-rich: the shredding of the social contract, the suppression of unions, the evasion of taxes (as we will see in this chapter), the establishment of monopolies, and the vast expansion of undeserved government subsidies granted to the super-rich and their corporations. How to sum this up? An extortionate rigging of markets by the corporate elite to diminish or eliminate competition, to weaken the legal protection of workers and their unions, and to establish monopolies: in a word, rentier capitalism.

Rigging the high end to extract wealth was one way to concentrate it in the hands of the super-rich. But suppressing the minimum wage at the low end has also contributed to the growth in inequality. Had the

National Minimum Wage in Britain kept pace with FTSE (Financial Times Stock Exchange) top 100 CEO salaries since 1999, it would have stood at £18.89 in 2013, rather than the £6.19 where it was.[12] Even the adjustment in early 2016 to £7.20 was well shy of a decent living standard. The minimum wage in the USA has likewise been stagnant: the federal minimum wage in 1971, adjusted to 2012 dollars, was $8.89, significantly higher than the minimum wage of 2012 at $7.25—and still $7.25 in 2017![13] This was so low that several states enacted a higher minimum wage, notably California, which adopted a $10 per hour standard at the beginning of 2016.

The Case of Apple: Jobs Creation?

Today more than 70 million iPhones are made each year. Around 30 million iPads and fifty-nine million other products are sold by Apple annually. How many iPhones and iPads are made in the USA? Zero! So what does Apple under Tim Cook have to say about this? It is not the responsibility of Apple to provide jobs, that is the task of government.

What Tim Cook does not say is how much Apple owes to the government. He omits to mention that it is not the hedge funds, not the private equity funds, but the federal government that is mostly responsible for the innovations used in Apple's original technology and productive assets. The government is responsible for the bulk of technologies that make smartphones smart, including touch screens, GPS, voice activation, and even the Internet. What the government—and the taxpayer—has not reaped are the profits.[14] The bulk of those have gone to the same army of rent-seekers, the world of finance capital, and the owners of intellectual property rights, cashing in on the golden egg originally laid by the public.

How profitable is Apple? A few years ago Apple made more than $400,000 profit per employee and more than $18 billion in profit in one quarter! That was better than Goldman Sachs, Exxon Mobil, or Google.

So what about jobs? Apple employs about 45,000 workers in the USA. It directly employs about 20,000 overseas. But Apple does hire contractors abroad, and these employ for Apple more than 700,000 workers, who mostly work as engineers, builders, and assemblers. Most of these work in China, for Foxconn, under conditions where there are no independent unions, no labor standards considered fair in the West, and low or no environmental standards. Workers often work twelve-hour shifts in poor or adverse conditions. And what are they paid? Working six days a week, often up to twelve hours a day, they make about $17 per day.[15]

Consider this comparison. In 1960, at General Motors (GM), it took 600,000 workers to make $7.6 billion in today's (2017) dollars. According to John Lanchester, in 2015 Apple directly employed 92,000 globally to produce a profit of $89.9 billion.[16] This is profit after all workers have been paid. So where does the profit go? Not to American workers, obviously not to Chinese workers. It goes to company executives and to shareholders.

Apple executives argue that Apple can't hire Americans because there are not enough middle management or mid-skill level graduates. Yet this is false also. There is something like a dozen universities in Silicon Valley producing many skilled graduates in exactly what is needed by Apple.

So how much would it cost to make iPhones in the USA? According to industry and academic analysts, paying American wages would add up to $65 to each iPhone produced in the USA. Apple would still make a large profit, as it earns several hundreds of dollars per phone in profit.[17]

Unequal Work, Unequal Lives: Why the Middle Class Got Poor and Poorer

Some people continue to defend trickle-down theories, which assume that economic growth, encouraged by a free market, will inevitably succeed in bringing about greater justice and inclusiveness in the world, This opinion, which has never been confirmed by the facts, expresses a crude and naïve trust in the goodness of those wielding economic power and in the sacralized workings of the prevailing economic system. Meanwhile the excluded are still waiting. Pope Francis, 2013[18]

You are the captains of American industry, the titans of Wall Street, and the billionaires who for decades have been the backbone of the Republican Party. You've invested your millions in the GOP in order to get lower taxes, wider tax loopholes, bigger subsidies, more generous bailouts, less regulation, lengthier patents and copyrights and stronger market power allowing you to raise prices, weaken unions and [make] bigger trade deals allowing you to outsource abroad to reduce wages, easier bankruptcy for you but harder bankruptcy for homeowners and student debtors, and judges who will let you engage in insider trading and who won't prosecute you for white-collar crimes. All of which have made you enormously wealthy. Congratulations! Robert Reich[19]

As both Pope Francis and Robert Reich have agreed, we can no longer afford to maintain the rich, not when they are impoverishing us while claiming that we are getting what we deserve: or that we want to be like them if only we had the ability. For those of us who are employed, we are told we should be grateful. If we are in poverty or close to the breadline, we are told we lack the necessary skills. Acquire those and we will get a job that compensates us according to our ability. If those jobs we trained for are exported, we are told that is the global market, and it is irreversible, and in the long run better for all of us: it helps reduce prices and makes for better shopping. If we ask for government assistance, we are told that the government is getting too big and that is the reason our taxes are so high. If we want tax relief, we are reminded by the super-rich that they pay the bulk of taxes, and that they are the ones who deserve tax relief so they can invest and create more jobs. If we argue that we deserve universal and affordable healthcare like they have in Europe, the corporate elite argue that the European system doesn't work, they have long waiting lines, and anyway the government decides who gets surgery and who doesn't. If we want stronger unions to protect our benefits, our jobs, our incomes, and our livelihoods, the ultra rich argue that unions destroyed manufacturing in America and Britain by driving up prices, causing inflation, and leading to outsourcing.

Several decades ago Tony Blair announced that the middle class was everybody. The *Daily Telegraph* in Britain echoed Blair: "We're all middle class now, darling." *The Times* added its own version: "We're all middle class now as social barriers fall away." And the *Daily Mail* added more detail yet: "You might say that there are now three main classes in Britain: a scarily alienated underclass; the new and confident middle class, set free by the Thatcher revolution … and a tiny, and increasingly powerless upper class."[20]

To paraphrase these citations, we have all reached the comfortable middle, we all share in plenitude and goods, in a prosperous future, and we are all more or less equal. Sure, we have the fabulously rich among us, but they have little power, and in any case, there are not so many of them. The point is, the working class and their ilk are disappearing, but so what. Who wants to work in all that dirt and grime anyway. And of the few remnants, they can't be saved anyway. They will soon disappear after their rump sails into oblivion in a fog of opioids.

So it is goodbye to the working class after all, from the point of view of those who stand at the helm. Admittedly, it did used to be easier to define the working class. They were the people who made things, like cars and appliances. They were the miners and dockworkers and makers of steel. They were the line workers who constructed automobiles in Detroit, the steelworkers who worked the forges in Pittsburgh, the coal miners in the midlands of Britain, and the coalfields of West Virginia and Kentucky. Some of these workers ran straight into automation, or energy conservation, or water and air pollution. But many, the majority, ran into ruinous economic policies of successive governments in the UK and the USA, vastly favorable to finance over manufacturing, governments which deregulated finance and the banking industry, governments which deregulated the housing and mortgage market, governments which signed off on trade agreements that forced workers in the UK and the USA to compete with low-wage workers in China and elsewhere. It was governments in America and Britain that were intent on weakening and even sabotaging unions, the best line of defense of workers. It was governments, from Reagan through Clinton and George W. Bush, from Thatcher through Cameron and May, that railed against "welfare queens"—the poor who gamed the system. And it was governments, including those of Gordon Brown and George W. Bush and even Barack Obama, who then saved the bankers and their banks from oblivion because—as we were told—without them the whole world economy would collapse.

The response of Bill Clinton in the decade of the 1990s, and of David Cameron after he became Prime Minister in 2010, was the same. Everybody has an opportunity, the jobs are there, but there are too many people without skills to match the high-tech jobs on offer. Wrong people, right market. Just to prod the intransigent a bit, the Clinton and Cameron administrations did all they could to remove state help-fare programs. Clinton's advice was to become employed: go to college and get the skills that are needed in the market. Cameron's advice was much the same. He explicitly targeted the young who, he might have sincerely believed, preferred to be on the dole rather than gainfully employed. Back in 2013 and several years into his premiership, Cameron cynically opined the following: "Today it is still possible to leave school, sign on, find a flat, start claiming housing benefit and opt for a life on benefits."[21] No doubt that Cameron, himself a millionaire, educated in one of the best private schools—Eton—a descendant of King William IV, and coddled from birth, might have believed that youth preferred a life of poverty: which was why he decided to remove benefits as a kind of assist to get the "recalcitrant" and the "indolent" to seek employment.

Leading a life of privilege, it is perhaps difficult to understand that few people if any want to be on the dole. A life of poverty, or want, is no pleasure: nobody chooses a life of deprivation. Flaunting privilege by lavish lifestyles does little for a sense of a person's dignity standing on the outside. It hardly inspires anybody to watch *Lives of the Rich and Famous* as they teach us how to make an omelet à la française. It could hardly have been warmly received when Cameron and the Tories cancelled most social allowances in 2010, a lifeline that had kept some out of penury and out of the breadline. Cameron's motivation was the exceptionally high numbers of youth that claimed Educational Maintenance Allowances, choosing to study instead of claiming state welfare. The choice of youth was clear and admirable: study instead of living at the expense of neighbors. Had not the Tories in Britain, like both the Republicans and Democrats in the USA, repeatedly counseled youth to study at university, the better to secure a promising future?

Not to know these elementary truths suggests deliberate ignorance, or wrathful contempt, for the classes "below." As anybody should know intuitively, if not from experience, virtually all young people choose work—as Danny Dorling puts it rightly—too a life on the dole. Yet we have to remember that many if not most in the Coalition government in the UK, like the cabinets and principal advisors of Clinton, George W. Bush, Barack Obama, and certainly Donald Trump, are members of that most elite of groups, the super-rich, and therefore by definition live in a millionaire and billionaire bubble. Two-thirds of the Cameron cabinet were millionaires (in British pounds sterling), while most of the rest were among the super-rich as indicated by gross household incomes.[22]

Ross Ferguson of the British Open University, a scholar in criminology, found the youth employment policy of Britain in 2013 so egregiously immoral that he all but called it criminal. He argued that the policy was one that could be expected from a group of millionaires "unashamed by a record of youth non-participation worse than that of almost all twenty-nine Organization for Economic Cooperation and Development (OECD) countries," and intent not on helping youth but on withdrawing "the last remaining welfare rights of young people."[23] As Danny Dorling has added: "Apparently the rich need a lot of money to persuade them to work—but the Coalition wants young people to take any job going, no matter how unsuitable or insecure it might be, even if it is based on a 'zero hours' contract, and no matter how bad the future prospects of that line of work."[24]

For the uninitiated in the British system, "zero hours" contracts are those that only the 1% or the 0.1% could devise for their "lessers." Such contracts are obligatory for those claiming allowance benefits, compelling "workers" who sign them to be available for work without a corresponding obligation by the employer to actually provide hours of work: hence zero hours contracts. British law is suitably hazy here. For example, signing a zero hours contract does not even make you an employee. You remain a contingent, more or less on call, without claim on hours and with no certain pay per hour. You are not actually present at the workplace. Nor does the employer have to grant benefits: "yer on yer own darlin," as some British youths might put it.

Without humane policies that are intended to help youth find suitable employment, the rate of poverty among British youth aged 18–24 has risen, rising even above the Irish rate for comparably aged youth and falling below only Estonia in the European Union (EU), with the highest rate of poverty, and Spain. Cameron's Coalition had argued that since there were still youth coming to Britain to take jobs, then British youth were being too selective. But Nick Hanauer, a successful entrepreneur, put it bluntly—and famously—by pointing out that if it were true that lower taxes for the wealthy and increased wealth for the super wealthy were the keys to job creation, then Britain would be "drowning in jobs."[25] Indeed, Britain is not awash in jobs, so there is little chance of getting people into work when—well—there is no work, and emphatically so for youth.

Equality Trust back in 2014 thought that Hanauer had a point. It calculated that some 1.75 million living-wage jobs could have been created if the richest hundred people in Britain had not seen their wealth increase in only one year by £25 billion—roughly $38 billion in 2014 dollars—and those monies had been used to generate jobs.[26] This could have been done by raising the highest marginal tax rate, which affects the top 1%. Better yet, says Danny Dorling, don't put such vast sums into the pockets of the super-rich to begin with. Instead, let firms pay "their 'top' employees less and employ more younger people alongside them."[27] Does seem to make sense. When the top 1% takes more, there is less for everybody else. Assuming Equality Trust's calculations to be correct, the 1.3 million unemployed youth, plus the 1.2 million underemployed or overqualified—40% of the youth population aged between 16 and 24—might indeed have had their lives turned around by simply revising the tax code and abolishing punitive social policies reminiscent of the Poor Laws—that blame the victim, in this case, youth.

The USA fares no better. There financial wealth has become so concentrated that the bottom 90% may have to perish the thought of ever retiring or sending their children to college. The research of Emmanuel Saez and Gabriel Zucman explains why. According to 2012 figures, four years after the Great Recession, the top 0.1% of American families had as much financial wealth as the bottom 90%. One might wonder, how was it possible to be at the tenth percentile in the USA and still be included in the "bottom" 90% of financial wealth in a country so rich? The answer? The bottom 90% had actually lost a percentage of total financial wealth as the riches of the top 0.1% escalated into the stratosphere. That means that just as in Britain, when the top 1% or top 0.1% takes so much, there is less for everybody else, which means that much of American joblessness is because of the prodigious wealth and income gap.[28]

Like Bill Clinton, David Cameron advocated acquiring needed skills and knowledge to secure employment. But Cameron, like Clinton, kicked the ladder out from those who didn't prefer poverty. In fact, how many would have rejected the Prime Minister's advantages had they been born into a prosperous family. Clinton's origins were more humble, and no doubt his native ability prodigious, but as president he promoted free—not fair—trade, which exposed American workers to low-wage countries around the globe. In fact, this was one of the prime reasons why the USA became a low-wage country and a primary attraction for German employers and others from abroad to set up shop in the USA. When in America, do like the Americans, put factories in right-to-work states, and pay minimal benefits to non-unionized workers.

Like Cameron, later, Clinton did little to protect workers, only giving vague promises that they could participate in the new global marketplace by educating themselves or by accepting lower wages that made them more competitive. He did little to help provide affordable education even as he kicked the ladder away from the working class. As for youth, he simply counseled them to attend college, where they could train for jobs that were coming online in the twenty-first century. But he provided no assurance that even middle-class jobs would be there post-training and degree. On the contrary, the North American Free Trade Agreement (NAFTA) and the entry of China into the World Trade Organization (WTO) in 2001, both of which he endorsed, shifted significant risk toward both the middle class and the working class by making it so much easier to export both jobs and capital from the USA.

By the time the Great Recession arrived, the middle class was already being hollowed out, and the working class—or what was usually taken for the working class, the industrial workers—was disappearing altogether. The standard explanation by most economists, seconded by the super-rich—and they continued to beat this dead horse well after the financial collapse—was that globalization and the technological revolution—innovation—were the culprits. The rich did not mention their own greed, the tax loopholes, the extended patents, the ignoring of anti-trust laws, the weakening of unions, the evisceration of pensions, the large subsidies given to their companies, the outsourcing, and the trade deals that helped them become the 0.1%.

Compassion was out, greed was in. Richard Wilkinson and Kate Pickett demonstrated in *The Spirit Level* and other writings that Americans and their British counterparts were suffering numerous pathologies—drug use, teenage pregnancies, obesity, anxiety—because of the high levels of inequality in both countries. It didn't matter if the poorest—or bottom half—Americans and British had more income and wealth than most people on the planet. What mattered was how they compared to fellow Americans or fellow Britons.[29] That did not convince the corporate super-rich, however. They continued to sniff that the reason for poverty or anxiety or obesity, teenage pregnancy or poor performance in school, for example, was because of indolence, lack of discipline, lack of ability, or all of these together. Nary a one or maybe a few at best ever thought that they were taking too much and giving back too little. Nary a one thought their income too high, or that they didn't deserve the immensity of their wealth. Nary a one ever mentioned the war against unions or even thought that part of their immense wealth was because of the high incomes they had voted for themselves by controlling boards of directors and investing vast sums in share buybacks to inflate the incomes of corporate executives.

Goodbye to the "Middle Class?"

For the three decades following World War II, the average hourly earnings of American workers and their British counterparts rose along with their productivity. Economies grew, families prospered, purchasing power rose, employment stayed mostly full, new investments were made, innovations helped increase productivity even more, and generally the USA and UK both became "middle-class" nations. They also became societies that shared the new fruits of the galloping economies widely, and they were more or less societies that embraced the virtues of collaboration, not class conflict. As a result, wages rose, standards of living improved, and profits escalated: social alienation and gaping inequality did not. Greed was contained as the price of labor peace, good so long as profits kept growing.

In the 1970s, the virtuous circle ended in both Britain and America. By the early 1980s, productivity gains continued as in the previous decades, but wages flattened and median household income ceased growing, when adjusted for inflation. By 2013, the median household was earning less than it did in 1989, a quarter century earlier. The major reason? Job security started to decline and with it the number of working-age Americans and British in jobs. This story was repeated for individual workers paid an hourly wage: average pay in the USA in September 2014 was $20.67. This might have been acceptable to some, but it meant the same purchasing power as workers had in 1979, and even less than January 1973, at $22.41 in 2014 dollars.[30] Of course averages don't tell us enough, they fail to consider those not working, or temps or agency workers, or contract workers.

But clearly something was happening, and it wasn't a good narrative for the millions of workers who had fought the industrial wars and built the unions and achieved a kind of middle-class status denied to their predecessors. The standard explanation—which contains some truth—is that market forces, globalization, technological advances, automation, and robotization made American and British workers less competitive. Jobs were outsourced to workers in Mexico and Asia who were willing to work for far less, or they were done at home by robots and machine tools. In the USA, production was moved to right-to-work states that were much harder to unionize, and even in those states, robots took many of the jobs previously done by workers. The result was the same in all cases. Good-paying, stable jobs were gone, perhaps forever. If somebody wanted to work, he would have to settle for a lower wage and less security. If a worker wanted more pay, or a more secure job, it was necessary to acquire the right skills to match the emerging economy of the digital age.[31] And in the digital age and the information economy, this meant going to college.

But this standard explanation does not tell us why college graduates' median wages have become stagnant or even declined. Back in 2014, the Federal Reserve Bank of New York revealed that the share of recent college graduates working in jobs that typically do not require a college degree had risen to 46%. This was a substantial increase and not likely to comfort parents facing rising tuition costs for their college-age children (though college counselors might not brief them on the future prospects of their college bound progeny).[32]

There are other causes that have hollowed out the middle class while marginalizing the working class. We already know about corporate "downsizing," mergers and acquisitions—promoted by private equity firms that have dismantled hundreds and even thousands of firms, with few anti-trust challenges. The result has been the shedding of hundreds of thousands and even millions of jobs. The argument is always the same. Lower wages make firms more competitive, and the more they are competitive, the more people they can employ. Or this refrain: high wages cause inflation, and inflation wipes out the value of the wealth of the super-rich, a conclusion that they cannot publicize openly.

These arguments are frivolous. Robert Preston, a British journalist and authority on private equity firms and their habit of promoting mergers and acquisitions—which has the unfortunate consequence of making so many of us unemployed—has struck the right chord in his estimation of the value of private equity firms for the vast majority of us. What private equity really does, he notes, is to rob us of our futures, often pitting us against each other. In the long run, private equity firms extract wealth from everybody else by shedding our jobs and squandering our wealth, while adding lavishly too lifestyles of the super-rich, which come at the expense of many if not most of us. Here is Preston in *Who Runs Britain*, speaking of the super-rich and the corporations they run,

> You will be hard-pressed to find in their publications much consideration given to the idea that the growth of the super-wealthy class is contributing to the fragmentation of society. There is much wringing of hands in newspapers about the collapse of the ties that bind us together. Every other page contains an indictment of the anti-social behavior of young people, the putative threat to our way of life from the influx of illegal or legal migrants, the assault on 'Britishness' of those with a different dress code or religious outlook from our own. Which is all very well. But what about our duty to make a proper financial contribution to the society which allows us to prosper? Why is the propensity of the super-wealthy to shelter the great bulk of their income and capital gains from taxation any less reprehensible than other manifestations of disdain for the norms of citizenship?[33]

Preston's larger point was that hedge funds and private equity firms had borrowed cheap money, speculated wildly with it, bought up firms, and squeezed them for short-term profits, almost inevitably by selling off assets and laying off workers. A few entrepreneurs had gamed the system by speculating on people's homes and jobs, and then cashed out, as in casino capitalism.

Then, we have the mega-firms, Apple, Amazon, Facebook, which seem to have few if any limits to their thirst for expansion into new markets. These firms, which might in a previous era have faced anti-trust litigation, have acknowledged minimal social responsibility. They are global businesses: employment, to repeat the words of both Steve Jobs and then Tim Cook, is not their responsibility. So what is the ultimate end of all these multinationals? A workforce that does not work and is replaced by machines and robots? But who will buy all the stuff produced by the machines? Improbably, the corporate culture could create machines that could also consume. But presuming this kind of brave new world, robots will need stomachs to eat, homes to live in, and perhaps ultimately the ability to reproduce themselves?

The Vanished Working Class and the Decline of Unions

The demise of unions has also been part of the hollowing out of Britain and America. This has not been a result of globalization—though that is a part of the story—but of a deliberate policy to draw back concessions made to the working classes over many decades and to ramp up corporate power and monetary rewards for its executives. For want of a better term, this has been part of a concerted class struggle to diminish the political and market power of employees in order to reap higher profits. And it has worked, largely because corporations and government have entered into an alliance that privileges money, an un-virtuous circle that helps extract wealth from the real economy and puts it directly into the pockets of the new corporate brokers.

A half-century ago GM workers on average earned $35.00 an hour in 2017 dollars, far better than the average GM workers in the USA in 2017. Newly employed GM workers are hired in at $14 an hour, a sum less than the minimum wage in Australia. We know that the average autoworker today makes less than half what a comparable autoworker makes in Germany. So what is the difference between past and present in the USA? The autoworkers of the 1950s had a strong union behind them, the United Auto Workers. They had a strong national labor movement behind them: a third of the nation was unionized. And it was because of strong unions that wages were set by collective bargaining, which in turn not only raised wages to decent levels for organized workers, but set higher wages for non-unionized workers as well.[34]

Today in the USA, less than 7% of private sector workers are unionized. Largely because of this, most employers across America do not have to match union contracts. Companies that are unionized are at a competitive disadvantage, resulting in a race to the bottom. American companies routinely offshoring, setting up shop in right-to-work states, recruiting skilled labor from abroad through special skilled-worker visas, or simply pushing for "flexible" labor forces that allow corporations to behave as empires—can unilaterally determine work rules. All of these strategies depress wages, eliminate jobs, and turn the lives of ordinary people into a kind of perpetual free-fall.

In Germany, 18% of the labor force is unionized, low by Scandinavian standards, but unions retain leverage because they are included in the bargaining process and they help establish national standards. Moreover, employees already have representation on works councils, where they can bargain with corporate managers and company boards. And unions have not been targeted as they have been in the USA and UK.

So what are the results? Unlike stagnant wage growth for the multitudes in the USA and in the UK, real average hourly pay in Germany has risen by nearly 30% since 1985. Ironically, the UK has a higher percentage of workers in organized unions than Germany, but this is largely because of public sector unions where union membership is well over 50%. In the private sector, union membership is only 14%, reflecting the decline of manufacturing generally in Britain. The result is low-wage Britain and growing numbers of part-time and temp workers not eligible for union membership.[35]

Scandinavian social democracies, Denmark, Finland, Iceland, Norway, and Sweden, have maintained high-density union membership. With the exception of Norway, with a more than respectable union membership rate above 50%, the other Nordic countries have union membership ranging from just below 70% in Finland and Sweden to 85% in Iceland. This is largely because of social democratic traditions respecting the dignity of labor, governments that have retained social democratic commitments to full (or fuller) employment, government subsidized training, long-term unemployment benefits, universal healthcare, and generous maternity leave. And like Germany, Scandinavia uses works councils and democratic corporate boards to sustain growth and industrial peace. The result is that unions have remained healthy, jobs are relatively protected, and people are reasonably prosperous, protected by their prophylactic states.

In the aftermath of World War II, the USA and the UK also entered into periods of industrial peace and growth. In the USA, in the landmark Treaty of Detroit in 1950, Big Business and Big Labor agreed to share future productivity gains. This meant labor peace in exchange for wages indexed to rising productivity. The result was good: productivity rose and so did wages and benefits. By the mid-1950s, more than 30% of employees in the private sector of the economy belonged to unions.

Even prior to the 1950s, labor had begun to organize, supported by Congress. When Congress passed the National Labor Relations Act in 1935, it guaranteed the right of workers to organize themselves into unions; it also obligated employers to bargain with unions. This was progress and it seemed at last to give workers a voice in setting wages and establishing benefits in the workplace.

So what went wrong? The consequences of globalization and automation to be sure. But again, what was critical was how governments dealt with those consequences, and in America and Britain, they mostly allowed or failed to block the reversal of corporate strategies to serve shareholders and the interests of corporate executives. Risk shifted dramatically to stakeholders, primarily employees and pension holders.

Here is how they did it. With Ronald Reagan in the White House, Milton Friedman's star rose, and he helped add to the shine. He didn't have to exert himself too strenuously to officially enshrine his ideas. It wasn't long before neoliberalism emerged as the mantra in Washington. What did so-called neoliberals believe about unions? They were distortions of the free market. Organized labor power meant strikes, and strikes were not only messy, they meant having to pay wages that were above their "natural" level, though nobody could define what "natural" level meant. And strikes meant inflation, too, as wages went up prices followed, though the cost of the war in Vietnam, the detachment of gold and the dollar in 1972, and the skyrocketing in the price of oil after 1973, following the organization of OPEC, might have suggested other causes of inflation. The argument had little to say about organized manufacturers, such as the National Association of Manufacturers, and why this was not a conspiracy against employees to keep wages low.

Armed with this new philosophy, which was consistent with Reagan's own ideology and penchant for favoring Big Business—he was after all on the payroll of General Electric for years and was their unofficial champion—Reagan fired the nation's air traffic controllers because they had gone on strike. The mass firing was a signal, if one was needed: labor relations in America had just gone through a sea change and not to the advantage of workers.

Corporations and their CEOs now had the opportunity they could only have dreamed about a decade earlier, when Milton Friedman and his acolytes were still having trouble getting past the butler. They could now challenge unions, if that was their problem, and challenge they did. Many insisted on wage concessions as the precondition of job retention. Others moved to right-to-work states, which had laws allowing employees to accept jobs without having to join unions or to pay dues. Even before "globalization," right to work was a misnomer. Actually, it meant the right of corporations to shed workers by moving to low-wage states. In fact, the law that authorized the right to work, Taft-Hartley, was passed in 1947. It created an incentive not to join a union, because a worker could gain all the benefits of unionized workers without paying any of the messy dues. Manufacturers did not flock into right-to-work state initially because they and their workers were mostly in mid-western and northeastern states. But when states that did have right-to-work laws proved profitable alternatives, and the emphasis shifted toward shareholders and CEOs, the attraction was irresistible.[36]

The Growth of the Precarious Classes (Precariat)

Who and what is the "precariat?" It is a condition of modern life in which formerly secure people who had well-paying, sustainable jobs, secure futures, and decent pensions in retirement suddenly inherited a universe in which they became surplus commodities, robbed of their status as humans, reduced to intangible and disappearing jobs, redundant in the British understanding, embarrassments to employers who think of them as unskilled and undeserving. Guy Standing, who coined the term "precariat," tells us that,

> [Its members are] dominated by insecurity, uncertainty, debt and humiliation. They are becoming denizens rather than citizens, losing cultural, civil, political and economic rights built up over generations. The precariat

> is the first class in history expected to endure labor and work at a lower level than the schooling it typically acquires. In an ever more unequal society, its relative deprivation is severe.[37]

The precariat, in other words, are most of us and could become almost all of us, with the exception of the 1%. As the burden of risk has shifted from the super wealthy, it has been assumed by almost everybody else and promises to do so increasingly. The weakening of unions, regulatory capture by Big Business, the shifting of the tax burden as multinational corporations and wealthy individuals find innovative ways to evade and shelter their tax obligations, the continuing predation of Big Finance, and a "flexible" workforce composed of more and more displaced labor (part-time, temp jobs, agency workers, and the so-called self-employed), all converge into what is now increasingly the life-pattern of a majority of people: less work, less satisfying work, less protected work, less jobs for more and more of us, and even fewer good jobs for our youth.

The result, says Guy Standing, is what we have, the pursuit of austerity in the developed world to meet the challenges of fiscal deficits and surging debt, to a significant degree caused by broken tax codes and tax evasion in both the UK and the USA. Unlike some observers, Standing does see globalization as a major factor in creating the precariat, especially following the financial shock of 2008, though he would agree that inequalities are hardly the result only of globalization. Global adjustment, he says, is "pushing the high-income countries down as it pulls the low-income countries up." And this: "Unless the inequalities willfully neglected by most governments in the past two decades are radically redressed, the pain and repercussions could become explosive."[38]

Globalization was never inevitable and, when it arrived, the rules of the global economy still had to be written. And they were, mostly by the most developed countries, backed by the economic philosophy in vogue, neoliberalism, or as one economist put it, "Mother Market," unchallengeable and infallible.[39]

When neoliberalism was widely embraced during the Reagan era and during the Thatcher era, it brought with it the seemingly innocuous phrase, "labor market flexibility," a phrase we have already met. But what exactly did labor market flexibility mean and is it really harmless? It meant above all that labor had to make concessions—demand less in wages and benefits—and then it had to keep making them. It meant giving back gains of the past or corporations would transfer operations abroad where labor and investment costs were lower. Labor market flexibility meant transferring workers to part-time employment, or seasonal work, or just eliminating as many full-time workers as possible by shifting more and more of them into agency employment, or contract work, or temp work, the better to avoid those messy benefits packages. Labor market flexibility meant replacing defined benefit with defined contribution pensions. It was the latter that shifted financial burden from employer to employee. The reason: it is far cheaper to match an employee contribution—usually capped at fairly modest levels—than to guarantee a lifetime income that almost matches the earnings of an employee during his working life.

So what did all this mean? Insecurity for employees and inequality for society, and much more as many British and American employees have found out: inadequate opportunity, diminished job and income security, skill dilution, reduced workplace security against accidents and illness, and less union or representation security, leading in turn to inadequate minimum wages, absence of a collective voice, and enfeeblement of the right to organize and even to form or join a union.

For the precariat, labor market flexibility produces anger, anomie, anxiety, and alienation. There are no ladders of mobility, no sustained sense of status and potential, much segmentation of the labor force caused by flexi-jobs, no material success, no sense of trust, or of deeper meanings associated with relations with others. In sum, the feeling of despair, purposelessness and uselessness, the lack of identity or security, no assured future, and the loss of entitlements, and sense of social contract (or solidarity) such as had formerly been obtained by the traditional working class.[40]

Globalization required a sea change in corporate strategies to maximize earnings and profits, and to establish rules that would prioritize those objectives. Guy Standing explains how this worked: "The objective of economic growth—making us all richer, it was said—was used to justify rolling back fiscal policy as an instrument of progressive redistribution."[41] High direct progressive taxes were rolled back that once were used to provide security for low earners and now "presented as disincentives to labor … and as driving investment and labor abroad. And a reorientation of social protection from social solidarity to dealing with poverty and with people deemed social failures ushering in a trend to means-tested social assistance and from that to 'workfare'."[42] Meanness, greed and opportunity, in other words, took advantage of the global order that corporate leaders now were building. And why not? The incentives and the new technology made it possible for corporate rhetoric to be transformed into something now called globalization: that plus the low-cost, low-wage environment that was there for the picking, and all of this abetted by government policies promoting something called free trade.

Prior to globalization, the labor markets open to trade had about a billion workers. By 2000, as China, India and the former Soviet bloc entered the global economy, another 1.5 billion workers entered global labor markets. All this weakened the bargaining power of labor everywhere. After 2000 everything became even worse, as Vietnam, Cambodia, Thailand, and Bangladesh entered global labor markets. It is not shocking then that the new world economy that emerged gave license to entrepreneurs who won concession after concession, depressing wages, reducing and eliminating benefits, and otherwise no longer valuing employees they could now shed with contempt. Yet even now, it was clear there were other responses, such as we have seen in Germany and Scandinavia, as to how societies and the rules of work engagement were to be conducted. Unfortunately, the UK and the USA both chose the low road, and it does not lead to Shangrila.

Broken Britain and Broken America

Much of the reason the rich have gotten even richer is quite simple. They pay themselves more and tell us they are worth it. And then they shift the burden of taxes onto everybody else. They also have significant political power because of their wealth, giving them leverage in politics, which they use to shape labor laws and put themselves at the helm of government. And while greedily amassing wealth by extracting as much of it as they can, and then calling the deprived insolent and indolent, they have concocted quite a fairy tale.

So how do they do it?

A rather lucrative field for the rich has been people in their twenties, easy to exploit—or to ignore—because they are at the bottom of the heap, they possess little market power, and they are unorganized and inexperienced. In Britain, in the four years between 2008 and 2012, the income of people in their twenties fell about 3% per year, adding up to a 12% total decline in real terms by 2012. But workers under twenty-five were in no position to bargain for more because a fifth of them were out of work at the beginning of 2014. And of those in work, as Danny Dorling explains, "most were working part-time, or on zero-hours contracts, or were on probation, or otherwise without any security. Many were even working for free as interns, under the guise of training or 'work experience'."[43] Needless to say, if the market really were efficient or even adequate, people would not be working for nothing. But free work has become the new norm, including some of the most egregious examples of outright wage theft. And if young people can increasingly be had for nothing, why then hire them and pay them a decent wage?

But it is not just the young who are suffering. At the end of 2013, there were almost 1.5 million people who were working part-time in Britain because they could not find full-time work, the highest mark in a little more than two decades. The rise in part-time work made Britain look better than it was, pushing up the nation's official number of "employed" to thirty million and reducing the number on the dole to just under 2.5 million.[44] But this concealed a larger truth. Fewer people were receiving adequate wages or using the skills and qualifications that they had—though they had acquired their skills based on the advice of the corporate elites, who were simultaneously outsourcing, downsizing, and eliminating jobs even as they preached austerity, a national policy sure to reduce employment wages even further. Moreover, a third of the new jobs were going to foreign nationals.

In Britain, throughout 2013, there was reason for gloom. The UK Labor Force Survey found that a third of working men who were in part-time employment were there only because they could not find a full-time job; for women, the figure was just over an eighth. For people of all ages, the jobs future looked daunting and unlikely to improve. For many Britons, those who governed were perceived as ignorant, cruel, or both. Most likely just indifferent and cruel.[45]

Then, George Osborne hatched a new plan entitled Help to Work, in the autumn of 2013. The new model was based on Denmark, which has a world-class training and work finding program underwritten by government. The difference is that in Denmark the program was supported with conviction, and everybody was all but guaranteed a job. There was more support money because the rich took less for themselves.[46] Denmark was spending 1.3% of GDP on its program to train and employ anybody without work who wanted employment. But, using OECD data, the Work Foundation calculated, in 2013, that the UK spent 0.3% of GDP on similar measures.[47]

Osborne's plan gave little if any indication that he was serious about solving the riddle of good jobs for those who wanted them. Cynically calling Britain's earlier jobs program a success because a quarter of the recipients had received at least three months part-time employment, Cameron announced that the new program would be even better because it mandated compulsory community service helping to feed the elderly, or intensive job training, or simply queuing every day at the employment commission. Some smelled duplicity in all this because the new plan targeted the unemployed who were on government benefit, creating make-work without corresponding pay. Nothing was mentioned about creating meaningful employment, how it would be done, or why compulsory training or unpaid work would improve anybody's future. Nor did Cameron explain why Britain had been spending about a quarter of what Denmark spent as a percentage of GDP on job training and education. As for Osborne, he could have revised the tax code, reined in tax evasion, or reversed austerity instead of punishing those on jobseekers allowance.[48]

The *Mirror* understood this and voiced a widely critical view of Osborne's intervention. Its headline read: "Forced Labor: Conservative Party to Force the Jobless to work for Nothing or Lose Their Dole: The Long-Term Unemployed Are to be Sent Out to Cook for OAPs [Old Age Persons] or Pick Up Litter in the Meanest Welfare Shake-Up Ever."[49] Danny Dorling was right to make his own conclusion: "Forcing people to work for nothing puts the UK in danger of breaking international laws on slavery."[50]

Even that did not deter Chancellor Osborne, who had a knack for squeezing the vulnerable. A millionaire, he praised his Help to Work scheme and then told a Tory Party conference at Manchester in autumn of 2013: "No one will get something for nothing."[51] Not quite nobody, of course: Mr. Osborne was a trust fund baby who had been getting something for nothing his entire life. The new regime, Help to Work, was to begin April 2014, but it was plagued by some with a conscience. They noted that doing community service as a punishment for being out of work demeaned community service itself. But the Scottish Council for Voluntary Organizations went even further, calling Help to Work a twenty-first century version of the workhouse.[52]

In the USA, it was much the same. Mean streets for the poor and the shrinking middle, and massive doses of self-deception, and regulatory capture, even though the rhetoric of the Barack Obama administration was intended to be more comforting. In the end, it was merely rhetoric for millions while Wall Street was bailed out. The US Bureau of Labor Statistics estimated in 2009 that more than thirty million people were working in part-time jobs by necessity, a figure that was more than twice the number of unemployed. The adjusted unemployment rate was actually 18.7%. Work in the USA was becoming more and more tenuous, so much so, that up to 45% of American employees were leaving their jobs annually.[53]

With globalization as backdrop, continued emphasis on outsourcing, dilution of the power of unions and their ability to organize, increasing corporate control of job classification, shedding of benefits, alternative pension schemes that required less support from corporations, low-wage alternatives, private equity mergers and acquisitions that had eliminated tens of thousands of jobs, Big Business made job security and decent compensation for those in work more a relic of the past than a future indignity. Labor market flexibility increased corporate control further over the status and future of workforces. In the auto industry, as jobs were scaled back, workers become like nomads, moving around the country in the USA in search of replacement work. Employment in auto firms declined by three quarters in the USA between 2000 and 2009. Company pensions continued to decline dramatically in the USA, where corporations had been systematically cutting pension obligations for well over a decade. In 2009 alone, more than a third of US firms either cut or eliminated matching payments to 401-k retirement plans. Even the American Association of Retired Persons (AARP), an advocacy group for people aged 50 and above, did that to its own employees.[54]

State pensions were also being cut back. The UK state pension, Guy Standing reported in 2014, was "worth 15 percent of average earnings and declining, and the age of entitlement [was] to rise to 68 from 65. It could rise to 70 or more."[55] The Turner report advised employees to stay in employment longer, the better to have a still modest state pension, something that was intended to halt the rise in means testing. "But unless the basic pension rises, and means testing is reduced, the incentive to save will be enfeebled. [In fact] there is no incentive for low-income earners to save, since if they do they will lose their pension entitlement."[56] The ability to save and to make larger pension contributions of course was limited because of the paucity of incomes, regardless of incentives.

There has been a long-standing tendency for companies in a number of OECD countries, especially the USA and UK, to rely more on wages, while reducing benefits and then to let wages stagnate, especially during recession. In 2009, Ford workers conceded cost of living allowances and lost holiday pay as well, and then scholarships for their children, though wages remained consistent. Ford also participated in occupational dismantling. It reached a collective bargaining agreement with the UAW freezing entry-level wages, introducing a "no-strike clause, and paying current workers a bonus for agreeing to the concessions. GM and Chrysler followed suit in similar agreements."[57] Two years later, Ford negotiated a collective bargaining agreement with the UAW that substantively halved the incoming wages of new hires.[58]

As benefits disappeared and jobs became more tenuous and wages stagnated, unemployment benefits were reduced or made more difficult to get. This was because otherwise many youth would refuse the poor jobs on offer and prefer the dole. The result was that governments generally had to be more coercive, or introduce in-work benefits or earned income tax credits, or simply limit unemployment benefits. As a result, in 2010 some 57% of the unemployed did not qualify for unemployment benefits in the USA. Many who did not qualify dropped out of the labor force, while 67% feared their benefits would run out before they found a job. By 2010, poverty in the USA among the unemployed and underemployed was worse than at any time since the 1930s. There were six registered seekers for every job vacancy.[59] Even after the so-called recovery, in October 2015 some 46.4 million Americans were on food stamps, about one out of seven Americans. By the time US elections rolled around in the fall of 2016, the number of Americans still relying on food stamps stood at 43.6 million. A few years earlier, the USA spent $76 billion just on food stamps, a high cost for social inequality. In real dollars, in 2014, Supplemental Nutrition Assistance Program (SNAP) recipients received on average net incomes of $335 per month, the lowest since 1989.[60]

Thus, a new category was emerging in the workforce: the working poor. As real wages stagnated at best for the vast majority of Americans, as work increasingly disappeared or was converted into part-time, contract, agency, or seasonal work, as more and more Americans were in call centers where jobs were proverbially temporary, or demeaning and low paying, with few benefits and typically non-unionized, as more and more newly generated income went to the 1%, the population of the working poor swelled by one estimate to forty-seven million people in a population of roughly 350 million in the USA. About a fourth of all Americans in work were in jobs with incomes below the poverty line for a family of four. And the downward trend continued even after the Great Recession. For the three years between 2010 and 2013, average incomes for the bottom fifth of the population declined 8%, while average wealth for the same population fell 21%. Oxfam America revealed that more than half the users of food pantries and other charitable food programs in 2013 were in work or members of working families.[61]

Making the problems of unemployment and benefit reduction even worse was the dismantling of the public sector, contributing to the rise in unemployment and the depression of wages generally. The public sector had provided a stable and high social income with employment security. As the rest of the labor market became more flexible, however, the same thing happened to the civil service. The problem began with the privatization, commercialization, and contracting out or outsourcing of what had been government functions or responsibilities. The crisis in 2008 provided a catalyst for this. As public revenues declined, and governments had to bail out the financial sector, public pensions were declared unaffordable and unfair in Britain. When government tried fiscal stimulus packages, quantitative easing, and subsidies, as happened in the USA especially, it mostly bailed out the rich, while adding to the public debt. None of this was the fault of the public sector, but it became a favorite target for budget cuts. And of course governments insisted on the strategy of austerity, which further cut into the public sector and into public sector employment as well.[62]

Wage Theft

> To keep our wages coming in, we have at all times to be polite and welcoming to the very rich, hiding our disgust behind our hand as we open the door to plutocrat X or prince Y and say: 'Ah sir, how very good it is to see you again. I have prepared a warm bath and a hot concubine just as you like them. Pay no attention to the talk of revolution in the kitchen'.
> Ian Jack[63]

In Great Britain, in the years 2010 and 2011, millions of workers either took pay cuts or had to accept shorter hours. In those two years, average public sector pay fell from £16.60 to £15.80 per hour; for the same period, private sector pay went from £15.10 to £13.60. The following two years wages fell again in real terms. After these cuts, the average employee in Britain was earning 15% less than she would have been had wage increases remained the same as in the period prior to 2008. The reduction was dramatic, and lethal: the bottom 95% of British workers had effectively seen their wages reduced by £52 million annually since 2008.[64] The Resolution Foundation concluded, in 2011, that well over 20% of British workers were earning less than a living wage: the vast majority of these were living in poverty, or working at more than one job.[65] And as recently as 2014, according to the Office of National Statistics, the overall poverty rate—measured as less than 60% of median income—stood at 16.8% in the UK.[66] Finally, the Institute for Fiscal Studies, in late 2016, concluded that Britons faced the worst decade for pay in 70 years: according to their projections British workers would earn no more in real wages in 2021 than they earned in 2008, which already set a low benchmark for workers.[67]

But at least these workers were paid something. That was not the case for many others. In the UK—as in the USA—thousands of unemployed workers have been compelled to work without any compensation. The companies using them could legally conceal the number of workers who toiled without pay: this practice was so widespread, it even included a charity like the Salvation Army.[68] When a British judge ruled in 2013 that the Department of Work and Pensions should make public the names of employers using coerced, unpaid labor, the department replied that it was disappointed in the judge. The department indicated it might appeal the decision or simply block it with a ministerial veto. It did not occur to anybody that there was anything inhumane about the practice of coercing labor from the unemployed, many of whom had accepted government benefit because they could not find work.[69]

So when those at the bottom, and throughout the middle, are suffering a decline in income, often being shuffled out of full-time work, or facing declining income even in full-time work, where does the money go? The answer is what we have seen: it is going straight to the top. UK employers, like their US counterparts, had effectively splintered workers, making it more difficult for them to organize, by resorting to temps in a flexible labor force advantaging companies. Temps have precarious lives, precarious jobs, precarious housing, and precarious education. They are the least likely to organize, not an easy task given that they appear in jobs for ten months, or ten days or ten hours, having to compete against each other instead of collectively fighting for decent wages. And the more fragmented the workforce, the less bargaining power they have.

In the USA, even for those fortunate enough to be in gainful employment, wages have been stagnating for more than four decades. The official unemployment rate in March 2016 declined to a new low since the Great Recession of 2008, roughly 4.9%, but the real rate was much higher, 10% according to some, but as high as 17% if workers working part-time, involuntarily, are counted as "employed." Even of those working full-time, many do not have the kinds of better paying jobs they held before 2008. And they are told that those much better jobs, many in manufacturing, are not coming back. In the meantime, it is not just wages that are falling, pension benefits are declining or disappearing altogether while healthcare, despite the Affordable Care Act, is becoming more expensive again after a hiatus of several years.[70] And even the Affordable Care Act is on the verge of extinction following the election of Donald J. Trump.

However, many if not most Americans are learning that there are also the twin crises of wage theft and payroll fraud. Dishonest employers are literally stealing money from their employees by directly cheating them of wages owed or simply not paying their employees at all. Many companies have no compunction at all lying to authorities about even having certain employees, knowing that the latter are often reluctant to make the fraud of their employers public because they fear the reprisals that are bound to follow, including the loss of their jobs.

Wage theft fraud is widespread, and it is robbing workers of billions of dollars annually, a figure that contributes directly to the growing income and wealth gap that have become America. Wage theft is getting worse and more widespread because it is often practiced with impunity. To date, there is little protection coming from a government that has largely withdrawn in the age of deregulation. Wage theft results when workers are not paid all their wages, or they are denied overtime when they have put in extra hours, or when they are denied pay for work they have performed.

Employers committing wage theft range from small businesses to giant multinational corporations and every enterprise in between. Wage theft is pervasive. We know that 60% of nursing homes have stolen wages from their workers.[71] The percentage of wage theft is much higher for non-monitored garment factories. In Los Angeles, almost 90% of such factories have routinely withheld wages due to their workers.[72] Farm workers are among the least protected, so it is no surprise that 25% of tomato producers, 58% of onion producers, and 62% of garlic producers have stolen wages from their employees.[73] In New Orleans, nearly 80% of restaurants have stolen wages from workers. Virtually, all poultry plants have stolen wages from their hourly employees.[74] And construction workers can expect to have shorted paychecks in at least half the construction companies in America.[75]

It is not just small businesses that take advantage of their smaller workforces. Large corporations also feast on their workers. The long list includes many of the best known names among American corporations: Walmart, Tyson (the mega-producer of chickens), FedEx, notorious for squeezing its employees by making them buy their own uniforms, Target, Pulte Homes, and many more.

Wage theft is perhaps most pernicious in stealing from low-wage workers, but it affects many middle-income workers as well: this includes construction workers, nurses, dieticians, writers, and bookkeepers. It affects mid-career as well as young workers. Although flagrant wage theft occurs when immigrant workers are not paid minimum wage or are not paid at all, the largest sums of stolen money come from native-born white and black workers in unpaid overtime.[76]

A report published in 2009, *Broken Laws, Unprotected Workers: Violations of Employment and Labor Laws in America's Cities*, based on a survey of 4387 workers working in low-wage industries in New York, Chicago, and Los Angeles, found that one out of four workers weren't paid the minimum wage. Of those who worked overtime (more than forty hours per week), 76% weren't paid for it. Not only was there almost total disregard for US labor laws, but there was pervasive retaliation when workers complained or attempted to organize.[77] When Kim Bobo first published *Wage Theft in America* in 2009, there were millions of workers having their wages stolen. More than three million were not being paid the minimum wage. Another three million were victims of their employers' payroll theft because employers were regularly lying about the status of their workers, calling them independent contractors when they were, according to American law, regular employees. The result was workers received no health and pension benefits, nor did employers add their contribution to the payroll tax. Millions of more workers were denied overtime pay because their employers wrongfully claimed they were exempt, while millions suffered because their breaks, to which they were legally entitled, were deducted from work time.[78]

The Economic Policy Foundation, a think tank funded by business, has estimated that US companies annually have been stealing $19 billion in unpaid overtime.[79] It is probable that this figure is too low. The Administrative Office of the US Courts has published settlements that suggest wage theft is systemic and worsening. The number of cases litigated because of unfair labor practices has reached epic numbers in recent decades. This is because of persistent and widespread violations of labor laws such as the Fair Labor Standards Act, which covers minimum wage and overtime issues. Under this law, workers are granted the right to sue along with the right to hire private attorneys; workers have used this rule to bring suits in record numbers. In 1990, there were a relatively small number of lawsuits brought against employers, only 1257. In 1995, 1580 cases were filed, and five years later, the number of lawsuits litigating for stolen wages reached 1935. But then the number of suits exploded, quadrupling by 2010.[80] These figures reflect only federal lawsuits and do not include all lawsuits brought under state laws, but the sums are large enough, and widespread enough, that it is not an exaggeration to claim that wage theft is a deliberate ploy to exploit workers who are reluctant to fight back because of the fear of reprisal.

Just a quick summary is sufficient to understand how pervasive wage theft has become. It is not just blue-collar workers or the working poor who are affected, but many professions that require college degrees and specialized knowledge. The Farmers Insurance Exchange, for example, settled in the year 2004 for $200 million, for not paying overtime to 2402 claims adjusters. The State Farm Group settled a year later for $135 million for not paying overtime to 2600 California claims adjusters. Other corporations settling for unpaid overtime were Allstate Corporation, $120 million; Citigroup in 2006, which settled for $98 million for not paying 20,000 brokers; UBS financial services, which settled in 2006 for $89 million for unpaid overtime to 13,000 brokers; and finally, UPS, which settled for $87 million in 2007 for unpaid overtime to 20,000 drivers; and Walmart, which settled in 2010 for $86 million for unpaid overtime and holiday pay.[81]

Walmart's settlement, though large, was only one case brought to trial with Walmart as defendant. That is because Walmart is a classic case of the kind of pressure brought by some corporations to extract as much from employees as possible. The reason? Cutting labor costs helps to realize outsized profits. Walmart has traditionally exerted pressure on its managers to cut costs, and the easiest way to trim them is to steal wages from employees who are vulnerable and who lack union protection; unions do not exist at Walmart because the corporation drastically limits full-time employment so it can restrict benefits and readily avoid unions. Historically, given the complicity of store managers, costs have been reduced by stealing wages at local stores. The senior leadership may not have had a written policy to extract as much work from employees for as little pay as possible, but store managers have understood the implicit expectations and have acted accordingly. The result has been many legal suits and many settlements in addition to those mentioned above. In December 2008, for example, Walmart agreed to settle sixty-three wage and hour lawsuits lodged against it for at least $352 million and no more than $640 million, depending on how many workers would actually claim the money.[82]

These were among the biggest violations and the largest settlement sums, but the total listed above comes out to more than $800 million, and it excludes most of the thousands of lawsuit settlements paid by corporate defendants. But do not conclude that the Obama administration was able to reverse wage theft. In a report published in 2014, the Economic Policy Institute found that wage theft from frontline workers in New York, Chicago, and Los Angeles approached $3 billion annually. It concluded that if the entire USA were canvassed, wage theft likely would reach $50 billion per year.[83]

A study commissioned by the US Department of Labor of minimum wage violations in New York and California in 2011 found that workers were shorted between $1.6 and $2.5 billion for just one year. The Economic Policy Institute has estimated that minimum wage violations annually cost workers between $8.6 and $13.5 billion just for minimum wage fraud.[84]

The most pervasive and perhaps the most egregious violations of workers' rights come in the form of payroll fraud, a practice so widespread that it has become almost invisible. Yet this form of fraud costs billions of dollars in lost revenue to the states, the federal government, and workers. FedEx is notorious for practicing this form of wage theft, which literally extracts income and wealth from its own employees as well as tax revenues not paid to state and federal treasuries. How does FedEx do it? FedEx has built its business empire by reclassifying its workers to the firm's advantage: it calls its 15,000 drivers independent contractors, not the employees they actually are. This means FedEx doesn't have to pay for health benefits, unemployment insurance, retirement accounts, or overtime to anybody designated as "independent." By reclassifying workers, and by shifting many cost burdens to them, FedEx manages to siphon even more in operating expenses, increasing FedEx revenue at the direct expense of its workforce. Some drivers have to purchase a delivery route, which can cost $5000. All drivers have to purchase their own vans and they have to pay for their vehicle's maintenance, which routinely means oil changes, brakes, and transmission and radiator replacements. Employees must pay for FedEx uniforms and decals for their vans, company-mapping software, and for leasing a FedEx scanner for package bar codes. They even have to pay for Department of Transportation inspections and random drug tests required by the company.

Deliberately misclassifying workers as contract workers has obvious advantages for FedEx. Yet this is clearly fraud. FedEx assigns drivers their routes, packages are delivered in FedEx approved trucks, and drivers can only take time off if their replacements are approved by FedEx. The labor practices of FedEx are designed to maximize profits: the more flexible its labor force, the more money that can be extracted from its workers and the more wealth that can be transferred to the senior management of FedEx. Ray Marshall, former Secretary of Labor from 1977 to 1981, has commented that FedEx's tactics go beyond opposition to labor unions:

> These misclassifications … nullify the protections that the US and other advanced democracies have extended to all workers. Wage and hour, anti-discrimination, occupational safety and health, pension protection, and unemployment compensation policies are all designed to protect employees from discriminatory actions by employers, as well as damage that could be done to workers, their families, and the public by unemployment or substandard wages and working conditions.[85]

Payroll fraud involves more than money. When workers get injured, they lose owed wages and often are denied the medical care they should have been entitled too because workers compensation insurance was not paid by the employer. Payroll fraud also means that minimum wage and overtime laws are ignored, as are health and safety laws. This means shifting risk onto workers to the advantage of executives and shareholders of companies. Deliberately underreporting income, inaccurate or deceptive misclassification of employees—reporting they are independent contractors when they are not—has also robbed public coffers of income taxes, payments into Social Security and Medicare, and reduced remittances to unemployment insurance.

Payroll fraud is pervasive. In 2009, the Government Accountability Office published a report on payroll fraud admitting that the national extent of the problem was not known. But it referred to a 2000 Department of Labor study that concluded from 10 to 30% of firms audited in nine states had misclassified employees as independent contractors.[86]

In 2009, the Institute for Public Policy and Social Research at Michigan State University published a report revealing that 30% of employers had some payroll underreporting or inaccurate reporting of employees. But whether much or most of this was intentional or not, the institute believed that the state's unemployment trust fund lost $17 million each year and probably an estimated $20 to $35 million in state income taxes, a serious loss to the public treasury of the state of Michigan.[87] Another study, published in 2010, *The Economic Costs of Employee Misclassification in the State of Indiana*, looked at data from 2007 to 2008 and concluded much the same as what had happened in Michigan. Almost 17% of employees were illegally called independent contractors. The study concluded that employee misclassification had cost the state $36.7 million in unemployment insurance taxes, $147.5 million in unpaid state income taxes, and $24.1 million in workers compensation insurance premiums; local governments also lost $59.9 million in tax revenues.[88] The Washington State Department of Labor and Industries Fraud Prevention and Compliance Program recovered $137.4 million in 2010 alone, a return of $7 for every dollar invested in the program and an example of what government can do if it enforces compliance with the law.[89]

The Annual Report of the New York State Enforcement Task Force on Employee Misclassification, for the year 2009, identified more than 12,300 cases of payroll fraud. It announced that it had recovered more than $4.8 million in unemployment taxes, $1 million in unemployment insurance fraud penalties, $12.5 million in unpaid wages, and over $1.1 million in workers' compensation fines and penalties. In one sweep of 304 businesses, the task force found that in 67% of the businesses it had visited and analyzed, there was evidence of payroll fraud requiring further investigation.[90] The Annual Report of New York enforcers in 2014 found that payroll fraud and misclassification continued unabated: in 2013 alone, more than 24,000 employees were misclassified.[91]

Payroll fraud is not accidental and it is not a disease, it is a deliberate ploy to rob workers of income, it is illegal in thousands of cases, and it is yet another device for shifting income, profits, and wealth up toward the summit where the corporate rich live. Payroll fraud is widespread and it is growing. It is also synonymous with the new so-called sharing economy that threatens to become global, and that is harming workers everywhere. The sharing economy is anything but sharing, except in risk for many of us, from adjuncts teaching college to Uber drivers. Uber, which is estimated to be worth some $40 billion, has only 850 employees (officially). This compares to General Motors which is worth some $60 billion, has 200,000 workers, and pays them somewhere between $18 and $32 per hour, including benefits. Why the enormous gap in the number of employees? Uber uses more than 330,000 drivers—the number climbs about 50,000 per month—who average somewhere between $17 per hour in Los Angeles and $23 per hour in New York.

That might sound like reasonable pay, but Uber doesn't count its drivers as employees. It calls them independent contractors, which means that drivers have to pay for their cars, including their maintenance, insurance, gas, oil changes, tires, and cleaning. When these expenses are subtracted, the hourly pay of Uber drivers is reduced sharply.

But Uber drivers aren't just paid poorly—likely below minimum wage after expenses—they have none of the benefits enjoyed by regular employees: not Social Security, not pension protection, not worker's compensation, not minimum wage protection, not unemployment insurance protection, not employer provided health insurance under the Affordable Care Act, and not car insurance. By classifying Uber drivers as independent contractors, not Uber employees, the company has avoided any and all obligations toward its employees.

This is not an exception. There are millions of agency workers and contract workers in Britain as well, and many millions more in the USA and UK who toil as construction workers, restaurant workers, truck drivers, office technicians, and beauty operators in hair salons, who have also found themselves expendable, actual employees deprived of regular employment status who find themselves vulnerable, alienated, without the resources to litigate, without the support they deserve from government, and with inadequate revenues, who do not come under the protection of labor laws because they are "independent contractors."[92]

So how do companies violate laws with impunity? They avoid putting workers on the payroll to avoid labor law obligations: work is contracted or sub-contracted out, leading to a race to the bottom. Contract workers not only are paid poorly, by accepting contract work they lose their rights as employees. How do companies that use independent contractors and agency workers justify such practices? They argue they are providing more freedom to workers to choose the hours they want to work. There are some workers who do prefer that, but the vast majority would prefer full-time work and full-time benefits. After all, to work at below minimum wage pay, with no benefits, no retirement, no paid healthcare insurance, no paid vacations, no protection against losing a job, no sick pay benefits, is not what corporate chiefs would prefer for themselves. Deprived of the means of subsistence, or of human dignity, or of legal protection, it should occur to some "workers" that they are entering a modern era version of slavery.

The Age of Permanent Temps and Permanent Risk

Corporate executives say that flexible workforces are good for companies and for the economy. If companies are able to shift people into and out of work as needed, corporations are ultimately able to hire more employees. That is the theory, and it has been widely advocated by economists. But it is false. Making more and more of us vulnerable does not mean that most of us are better off. It means the opposite: a life of contingency, a life where economic growth benefits very few, mostly the 1%, at the expense of the rest of us.

Over the last four decades or so, the number of part-time and temporary workers, agency and contract workers, or contingent workers, sometimes described also—dishonestly in too many cases—as independent or self-employed workers, has soared. But flexible workforces are not benevolent things. They make it easier and cheaper for bosses to hire and fire workers, often arbitrarily and without any fear of reprisal from government. Flexible labor markets have coincided with the emergence of the contingent worker, expendable, with no intrinsic value, just another commodity in the process of production. "Flexible workforce" has become synonymous with the death of the secure full-time job. A "temp" can be hired and fired with an hour's notice; he or she can be paid less for doing the same job as a full-time worker. In Britain, there may be as many as 1.5 million temporary workers, virtually all of them having no rights or secure employment. In the USA, there are as many as twenty-seven million people in part-time work, as many as 25% of them working part-time involuntarily.

Linda Tirado, who has been through the cycle of employment, from full-time to part-time work and back again, was moved to write a memoir about her experiences:

> There is something even worse than minimum wage. It's called temp work. I bet that the majority of Americans — unless they've experienced it for themselves — would be shocked to find out that companies regularly hire temps to work full-time hours, but because they hire these workers through temporary work agencies, they have to pay no benefits and offer no job security. To save a buck, companies will regularly hire such workers for years — *years*. And they do it because it's cheaper than hiring labor directly, and they are legally entitled to do so. The laws in this country are so weak that we're actually behind South Korea (!) in temp workers protections. ... You get to work for a company full-time, as anything from a janitor to an attorney, but you don't get any benefits ... They don't guarantee anything ... like raises and promotions. One plant I lived near used to hire a revolving number of temp workers whom they laid off after ninety days — the point at which a temp worker is supposed to get permanent job status. Then after three weeks of unemployment, the plant hired them again.[93]

Agency work, or contract work—temp work—has been thriving in the service sector in both the USA and the UK, but Owen Jones reminds us that it is thriving also in manufacturing, as illustrated by an incident at a car factory near Oxford in 2009. Some 850 temps, many of whom had worked in the factory for years, were fired by Bavarian Motor Works (BMW) with only an hour's notice. Getting rid of temps was the cheapest option for BMW, the company owed them no compensation at all. Humiliated workers, without any recourse to unions or government support, or legal defense, resorted to pelting managers with oranges and apples.[94]

What is equally disturbing is that BMW has had a different attitude toward its employees in Germany. There, BMW retains an active apprenticeship program, a board of directors half of whom are employees, and works councils where employees and managers mutually determine company strategies. So what explains the difference between BMW in Britain and in Germany? In Germany, industrial policies are negotiated between the unions, corporations, and the state. The result is a huge gain for German workers. But in Britain, BMW follows the British rules, and they are stacked against employees.

The Intuit 2020 Report, published in 2010, argued that the Great Recession provided the perfect rationale for employers to continue moving toward a contingent workforce of long-term freelancers, temps, part-time workers, and independent contractors. The report found that roughly between 25 and 30% of the US workforce was already contingent, a trend that was accelerating. Just as ominous, more than 80% of large corporations planned to increase their use of a flexible workforce in coming years. The report projected that US contingent workers would exceed 50% of the workforce by 2020. Traditional full-time, full-benefit jobs would become even harder to find, while so-called self-employment would continue to increase simultaneously. Nor did the report expect government to be more sympathetic. It had done little to protect unions, to invoke anti-trust laws, or to stop corporations from wage theft.[95] If the Intuit Report is correct, workers in the USA of all kinds can expect a life of misery: perpetual low-wage jobs with few if any benefits for those in work. As Owen Jones has put it, "Fellow workers are forced to compete with people who can be hired far more cheaply. Everyone's wages are pushed down as a result. This is the 'race to the bottom' of pay and conditions."[96]

It is not very comforting to know that America is not alone in the race to the bottom. A document entitled *The Shape of Business—The Next Ten Years*, published by the Confederation of British Industry, representing major employers in the UK, argued that the crash of 2008 was a signal and catalyst for a new era in business. The Confederation called for the creation of an ever more pliable "flexiforce," with fewer permanent employees at the core: more temporary workers, workers who could be hired and fired without due cause or explanation, workers who could never unionize. For workers, this would be catastrophic, if it were not already so. But for the insensitive super-rich, the Confederation was offering a "new employment model."[97] This was the future, and there was a survey to confirm it in 2010. It found that nearly nine out of ten businesses would either be maintaining or increasing the use of temporary workers in Britain.[98]

The rise of the part-time worker or the temp is nothing to celebrate, not even for the companies that are shedding full-time workers and full-time benefits, yet Britain and the USA are moving along the same path. Like the USA, more than a quarter of the British workforce works part-time, many are in agency work or are "self-employed," and the percentage is increasing. The Great Recession was actually a great convenience.

It afforded employers a perfect storm to sack workers. But when workers began to return to the workforce, it was not to their old jobs, not to full-time employment, or to full-time benefits, and too often at reduced pay per hour. The trend toward casual labor was noticeable, and it seemed to be accelerating, as had been predicted by the Intuit Report. "Hire-and-fire" was in, and it seemed to be irreversible, a "new employment model."[99]

There were those who defended the new order, Tory MP David Davis, for example. He saw no reason whatsoever why an employee at a department store like Sainsbury would have any less job security than an employee at Ford. "It's the reverse in many ways because they're growing. So I think the hire-and-fire idea—[is] a piece of Old Labor mythology, frankly. The idea that the only good jobs are ones where you have to lift a half-ton weight every day is unmitigated crap."[100]

Strange advice coming from an MP whose grandfather was a member of the Communist Party, who was raised by a single mother, and who once led a hunger march in London. But he was quite wrong about Britain. The hire-and-fire workforce had arrived, and it has provided little solace or security for many millions of British employees. Davis was speaking about the service sector, but we have seen the example of BMW in Britain. When automobile workers are sacked, they become part of the temps workforce economy, usually in the service sector and with many of the same results: insecure jobs, low pay and few if any benefits. In 2008, half of all service sector workers in Britain earned less than £20,000 per year, not something to look forward to if you have a family or if you wouldn't mind having a decent pension to retire on. The Longbridge carmaker, MG Rover, provides another apt illustration of the problems facing the British worker. When it failed and went bankrupt in 2005, 6300 jobs vanished in one stroke. Before the company collapsed, the median annual income of its workforce was £24,000: but the annual median income of the workers in their new jobs in the service sector—some 60% of the total—was only £18,728.[101]

There are of course thriving professions like the legal and medical sectors: doctors and lawyers are always needed. There are numerous professors in both countries. There are architects, engineers, scientists, and mathematicians whose skills and knowledge are indispensable. Or are they? Universities and colleges in the USA are resorting more and more to adjuncts, who have many of the same skills as their full-time colleagues. Half the classes in the USA today taught at university level are taught by adjuncts. Every manufacturing company today needs engineers, so do software companies and computer industries, but China produces hundreds of thousands of engineers, and they are much cheaper and eager to work for American companies with far less security. Lawyers may be difficult to replace, yet some companies are training citizens of other countries in American law: even legal work can be outsourced. And there are a surplus of lawyers, growing numbers cannot secure work in the USA.

Outside these traditional white-collar professions, there are numerous less secure workers in the service sector. Britain has 170,000 hairdressers working in a booming industry. But these employees are among the lowest paid in the country, with a median income for a woman stylist set at less than £12,000.[102] The most rapidly expanding sectors include data processing, security guards, receptionists, nursing home workers, cleaners, caregivers, secretaries, technicians, call center workers, restaurant workers, and salespeople or commercial travelers. What all of these workers have in common is that they are all poorly paid and unprotected, but this is not necessarily because they are unskilled. In a previous era, they would have been in the middling ranks of employees, and they would have been better paid and more secure. They would have had unions to defend their jobs, more progressive public policy that understood the need for and value of unions, and less powerful employers, or perhaps more enlightened employers willing to match productivity gains with increases in employee wages.

None of these preconditions exists today. Unions might still be the largest civil organizations in both Britain and America, but in Britain union membership has declined from 13 million in 1979 to about seven million as of 2018. Only about 14% of private sector workers are in unions, largely because of the demise of manufacturing but also because the difficult-to-organize service sector is almost free of unions altogether.[103]

Union weakness also reflects public policies and laws. Tony Benn has made the claim that they are more restrictive today than a century earlier. Laws passed under Thatcher and not reversed even by Tony Blair and Gordon Brown have made it more difficult to organize unions in the workplace by far. Strikes are vastly more difficult to call. And, as in the case of a dispute between British Airways and its cabin crews, when 80% of the workers voted to strike, based on a 78% turnout, the judge banned the strike anyway. He claimed that the union failed to notify the court that eleven out of 9282 ballots had been spoiled.[104]

It is inherently more difficult to organize unions in retail. There are too many workplaces, employees are too dispersed, and there is a very high turnover of employees. This is either because they are being sacked or because they leave voluntarily due to wage theft, poor pay, few if any benefits, and constant furloughs into temps.[105]

It is much the same in the USA. I have personally witnessed direct exploitation in a vitamin packaging center of Nutrition Headquarters in Southern Illinois at a time when unions still had a stronger presence and were not in such bad odor with conservative policy makers. I was the only male worker, the rest were women. Even the mention of union to my cohorts drew surprised and fearful looks. The reason was clear: the women feared reprisals by the company. And they had good reason, the entire workforce had already been fired and not just once.

Corporations have insisted that manufacturing jobs have gone to China and won't return. They add that jobs that did not go to China have often been replaced by automation in the USA and UK. And the jobs that remain in the USA and UK stay there only because workers have accepted wages that make them "competitive" with the Chinese and workers in other low-wage countries.

But none of these arguments are convincing. As we have seen, BMW can implement policies that exploit its employees in Britain, yet collaborate in greater solidarity with workers in Germany by embracing labor laws and public policies there that preserve jobs at decent wage levels and share the gains of productivity with employees. We remember also the creed of Apple, which sends jobs to low-wage China despite its admission that the iPhone, for example, could be made in the USA at very little additional cost—$65 per unit. In his documentary film, *Inequality for All*, Robert Reich asks where the money goes for each purchase of an iPhone? Not to China: the iPhone is only assembled in China. Most of its value is in components, and they are made in developed countries—which are definitely not low-wage economies—by highly skilled workers. So where does the money go when an iPhone is purchased: 34% goes to Japan, 17% to Germany, and 13% to South Korea. Here is Reich:

> The components Apple's Chinese contractors assemble come from many places around the world with wages as high if not higher than in the United States. More than a third of what you pay for an iPhone ends up in Japan, because that's where some of its most advanced components are

> made. Seventeen percent goes to Germany, whose precision manufacturers pay wages higher than those paid to American manufacturing workers, on average, because German workers are more highly skilled. Thirteen percent comes from South Korea, whose median wage isn't far from our own. Workers in the United States get only about 6 percent of what you pay for an iPhone. It goes to American designers, lawyers, and financiers, as well as Apple's top executives.[106]

America could also produce the components for the iPhone that are currently produced elsewhere. In fact, Corning has done just that, though it lost its contract with Apple temporarily before developing a virtually shatterproof glass that helped regain Apple as a client.

Conclusion

So why aren't there more companies that produce components for high-tech devices, following the example of Japanese, German, and South Korean companies, and Corning in the USA? The answer is there can be, but American technical and engineering expertise will have to improve beyond what it is, and that will require major commitments to an overhaul of the US system of education. And that would mean substantive contributions from corporate USA, which would itself require a reversal of current corporate strategies—on the part of much of corporate America—to evade taxation. Corporations do not want to pay for the educational system that would produce the kind of skilled and well-trained workforce that once characterized the USA, reversing the low-wage country it has become. To reiterate, it is not globalization per se that is destructive of jobs and economy: it is public policy and the power of the corporate world to assert its private interests over the common good. It is what government and corporations do that will determine the kind of work we will all be doing in the future, how much job security we will have, and the benefits we will enjoy. The conclusion is inescapable: either we will have an extractive (rentier) economy—run by a plutocracy, as in the USA and the UK—which benefits almost exclusively the (mostly) corporate super-rich, or we will have an economy which puts us back to work, based on equitable taxes, allowing us to share the gains of what collectively we produce, on a foundation of universal and equal education, with strong public policies that limit corporate power by protecting trade unions and democratizing corporations.

Notes

1. Julia Kollowe, "BHS Collapse: IoD Chief Accuses Sir Philip Green of 'lamentable behaviour'," *Guardian*, June 3, 2016.
2. Ibid.; Sarah Butler, "How Philip Green's Family Made Millions as Value of BHS Plummeted," *Guardian*, April 25, 2016.
3. Bureau of Labor Statistics, Chart 1.1: Productivity Change in non-farm business sector, 1947–2016 (Washington, DC: Bureau of Labor Statistics, 2017), online at http://www.data.bls.gov/cgi-bin/print.pl/lpc/prodybar.htm.
4. Thomas Piketty and Emmanuel Saez, "Income Inequality in the United States, 1913 to 1998," *Quarterly Journal of Economics* 118, no. 1 (2003): 1–39; see also Emmanuel Saez, "Striking it Richer: The Evolution of Top Incomes in the United States," *Pathways*, Stanford Center on Poverty and Inequality (Winter 2008): 6–7, https://inequality.stanford.edu/sites/default/files/media/_media/pdf/pathways/winter_2008/Saez.pdf.
5. Robert B. Reich, *Saving Capitalism: For the Many, Not the Few* (New York: Alfred A. Knopf, 2015), 121.
6. William Lazonick, *Sustainable Prosperity in the New Economy: Business Organization and High-Tech Employment in the United States* (Kalamazoo, MI: W. E. Upjohn Institute for Employment Research, 2009), 85; Edmund L. Andrews, "Job Cuts at AT & T Will Total 40,000, 13% of Its Staff," *New York Times*, January 3, 1996; and Matt Murray, "Why Jack Welch's Leadership Matters to Businesses World-Wide," *Wall Street Journal*, September 5, 2001.
7. Josh Bevins and Lawrence Mishel, "Understanding the Historic Divergence Between Productivity and a Typical Worker's Pay," Briefing Paper #406 (Washington, DC: Economic Policy Institute, September 2, 2015), online at http://www.epi.org/publication/understanding-the-historic-divergence-between-productivity-and-a-typical-workers-pay-why-it-matters-and-why-its-real/.
8. Stewart Lansley and Joanna Mack Stewart, *Breadline Britain: The Rise of Mass Poverty* (London: Oneworld Publications, 2015), ix–x.
9. Ibid.
10. Ibid., ix–xi, and 1–31.
11. Robert Gordon, *The Rise and Fall of American Growth* (Princeton, NJ: Princeton University Press, 2016).
12. One Society, "How National Minimum Wage is Falling Behind Top Pay, and the Damage This Does to Living Standards and the Economy," Briefing (London: One Society, October 1, 2012), at onesociety.helencross.co.uk/wp-content/uploads/2012/09/NMW-briefing-27Sept2012pdf.

13. US Department of Labor, *History of Changes to the Minimum Wage Law* (Washington, DC: US Department of Labor, 2017), online at https://www.dol.gov/whd/minwage/coverage.htm.
14. Rana Foroohar, *Makers and Takers: How Wall Street Destroyed Main Street* (New York: Crown Business, 2017), 123–24; see William Lazonick, Mariana Mazzucato, and Oner Tulum, "Apple's Changing Business Model: What Should the World's Richest Company Do with All Those Profits?" *Accounting Forum* 37, no. 4 (2013): 249–67.
15. Charles Duhigg and Keith Bradsher, "How the US Lost Out on iPhone Work," *The New York Times*, January 21, 2012.
16. John Lanchester, "The Robots are Coming," *London Review of Books*, 37, no. 5, March 5, 2015.
17. Duhigg, "US Lost Out on iPhone Work," *The New York Times*, January 21, 2012.
18. Cited by World Bank, "Ending Poverty Requires More Than Growth, Says WBG," World Bank Group press release, April 11, 2014, online at http://www.worldbank.org/en/news/press-release/2014/04/10/ending-poverty-requires-more-than-growth-says-wbg.
19. Online at http://robertreich.org/post/140181226720/embed.
20. All citations cited in Owen Jones, *Chavs: The Demonization of the Working Class* (London: Verso, 2012), 139.
21. BBC, "David Cameron Suggests Cutting Benefits for Under-25's," *BBC News*, October 2, 2013, online at http://www.bbc.com/news/uk-politics-24369514.
22. Dorling, *Inequality and the 1 percent* (London: Verso, 2014), 66–67; Christopher Hope, "Exclusive: Cabinet is Worth £70 Million," *Telegraph*, May 27, 2012.
23. Ross Ferguson, "Punishing the Young Unemployed" (London: Centre for Crime and Justice Studies, October 15, 2013), online at https://www.crimeandjustice.org.uk/resources/punishing-young-unemployed.
24. Dorling, *Inequality and the 1 percent*, 67–68.
25. Jillian Berman, "Nick Hanauer's TED Talk on Income Inequality Deemed Too 'Political' for Site," *Huffington Post*, 17 May 2012, online at http://www.huffingtonpost.com/2012/05/17/nick-hanauer-ted-talk_n_1524435.html. Hanauer's TED talk can be seen, online at https://www.ted.com/talks/nick_hanauer_beware_fellow_plutocrats_the_pitchforks_are_coming.
26. Equality Trust Press Release, *Wealth Increase of Britain's 100 Richest Would Pay for 1.75 Million Living Wage Jobs* (London: Equality Trust, February 19 2014), online at https://www.equalitytrust.org.uk/wealth-increase-britains-100-richest-would-pay-175-million-living-wage-jobs; Equality Trust, *Richest 1% Has Greater Share of Wealth Than*

Half the UK Population (London: Equality Trust, May 15, 2014), online at https://www.equalitytrust.org.uk/richest-1-has-greater-share-wealth-half-uk-population.
27. Dorling, *Inequality and 1 percent*, 68.
28. Emmanuel Saez and Gabriel Zucman, *Wealth Inequality in the United States Since 2013, Evidence from Capitalized Income Data*, NBER Working Paper 20625 (Cambridge, MA: National Bureau of Economic Research, October 2014), online at http://www.nber.org/papers/w20625.
29. Richard Wilkinson and Kate Pickett, *The Spirit Level: Why Greater Equality Makes Societies Stronger* (New York: Bloomsbury Press, 2009); Richard Wilkinson, *The Impact of Inequality: How to Make Sick Societies Healthier* (New York: The New Press, 2006).
30. Robert Reich, *Saving Capitalism: For the Many, Not the Few* (New York: Alfred A. Knopf, 2015), 115–17.
31. Ibid., 117.
32. Dave Leonhardt, "The German Example," *New York Times*, June 7, 2011; Heidi Shierholz, Alyssa Davis, and Will Kimball, *The Class of 2014: The Weak Economy is Idling Too Many Young Graduates*, Briefing Paper #377 (Washington, DC: Economic Policy Institute, May 1, 2014), online at http://www.epi.org/publication/class-of-2014/; and Jaison R. Abel and Richard Dietz, "Are the Jobs Prospects of Recent College Graduates Improving," *Liberty Street Economics* (New York: Federal Reserve Bank of New York, September 4, 2014), online at http://libertystreeteconomics.newyorkfed.org/2014/09/are-the-job-prospects-of-recent-college-graduates-improving.html.
33. Robert Preston, *Who Runs Britain: … And Who's to Blame for the Economic Mess We're In?* (London: Hodder & Stoughton, Ltd., 2008), 342.
34. Reich, *Saving Capitalism*, 127.
35. For labor union density figures, see Organization for Economic Cooperation and Development, online at https://stats.oecd.org/Index.aspx?DataSetCode=UN_DEN.
36. Reich, *Saving Capitalism*, 131,
37. Guy Standing, *The Precariat: The New Dangerous Class* (London: Bloomsbury Academic, 2014), vii.
38. Ibid., xi.
39. Philip Mirowski, *Never Let a Serious Crisis Go to Waste: How Neoliberalism Survived the Financial Meltdown* (London: Verso, 2013), 176.
40. Standing, *Precariat*, 33–34, 40–41.
41. Ibid., 43.

42. Ibid., 44.
43. Dorling, *Inequality and the 1 percent*, 71.
44. John Hall, "Unemployment at Three-Year Low as Number of Britons in Work Reaches All-Time High of 30 Million," *Independent*, November 13, 2013.
45. Mary O'Hara, *Austerity Bites: A Journey to the Sharp End of Cuts in the UK* (Bristol: Policy Press, University of Bristol, 2014).
46. BBC, "Q&A: What Will 'Help to Work' Mean for Claimants?" *BBC News*, September 30, 2013, at bbc.co.uk; Patrick Wintour and Nicholas Watt, "George Osborne: Jobless Benefit Conditions are 'Tough Love'," *Guardian*, 30 September 2013.
47. OECD Data, "Public Spending on Labor Markets" (Paris: OECD, 2016), online at https://data.oecd.org/socialexp/public-spending-on-labour-markets.htm.
48. BBC, "Q&A," April 28, 2014, online at www.bbc.com/news/business-24330508.
49. J. Beattie, "Forced Labor: Conservative Party to Force the Jobless to work for Nothing or Lose Their Dole," *Mirror*, September 30, 2013; Wintour and Watt, "Jobless Benefit Conditions are 'Tough Love'," *Guardian*, September 30, 2013.
50. Dorling, *Inequality and the 1 percent*, 73; see also Owen Jones *Chavs*, 92–93.
51. Beattie, "Forced Labor," *Mirror*, September 30, 2013.
52. Dorling, *Inequality and the 1 percent*, 73.
53. Standing, *Precariat*, 60–61.
54. Ibid., 71–73.
55. Ibid., 73.
56. Ibid.
57. Ibid., 74.
58. Matthew Dolan, Jeff Bennett, and Mike Ramsay, "Auto Makers Now Import Jobs," *Wall Street Journal*, October 5, 2011.
59. Standing, *Precariat*, 77–79.
60. Alan Bjerga, "Food Stamps Still Feed One in Seven Americans Despite Recovery," *Bloomberg*, February 3, 2016, online at http://www.bloomberg.com/news/articles/2016-02-03/food-stamps-still-feed-one-in-seven-americans-despite-recovery. See also Peter Edelman, *So Rich, So Poor: Why It's So Hard To End Poverty in America* (New York: The New Press, 2012).
61. US Bureau of Labor Statistics, *A Profile of the Working Poor, 2010* (Washington DC: US Bureau of Labor Statistics, March 2012), online at https://www.bls.gov/opub/reports/working-poor/archive/workingpoor_2010.pdf; see also Rebecca Thiess, "The Future of Work:

Trends and Challenges for Low-Wage Workers," Briefing Paper #341 (Washington, DC: Economic Policy Institute, April 27, 2012), online at http://www.epi.org/publication/bp341-future-of-work/; Jesse Bricker et al., "Changes in US Family Finances from 2010 to 2013, Evidence from the Survey of Consumer Finances," *Federal Reserve Bulletin* 100, no. 4 (September 2014): 2–4, 9–12, online at https://www.federalreserve.gov/pubs/bulletin/2014/pdf/scf14.pdf; and also Oxfam America, *From Paycheck to Pantry: Hunger in Working America* (Boston, MA: Oxfam America, 2014), 2–4.

62. Standing, *Precariat*, 86–88.
63. Ian Jack, "It's Shameful the Way Britain Kowtows to the Super-Rich," *Guardian*, March 9, 2013.
64. Katie Allen, "British Workers Suffer Deepest Real Wages Cut Since Records Began, Research Shows," *Guardian*, June 12, 2013.
65. Heather Stewart, "Working for Nothing: the Truth About Low Pay in the UK," *Guardian*, October 2, 2011.
66. Office for National Statistics, "Persistent Poverty in the UK and the EU: 2014" (ONS, May 16, 2016), https://www.ons.gov.uk/peoplepopulationandcommunity/personalandhouseholdfinances/incomeandwealth/articles/persistentpovertyintheukandeu/2014.
67. Gemma Tetlow, "British Workers Face Worst Decade for Pay in 70 Years," *Financial Times*, November 24, 2016.
68. Johnny Void, "Salvation Army Fights Back—Calls Critics of Unpaid Work Offensive," *The Void* (Blog), December 17, 2013, online at https://johnnyvoid.wordpress.com/2013/12/19/charity-slams-osbornes-workfare-these-placements-are-not-voluntary/.
69. Shiv Malik, "Workfare Placements Must Be Made Public, Tribunal Rules," *Guardian*, May 19, 2013.
70. Kim Bobo, *Wage Theft in America* (New York: The New Press, 2011), xi.
71. US Department of Labor, 1999–*2000 Report on Initiatives* (Washington, DC: US Department of Labor, February 2001), 19, online at http://nelp.3cdn.net/a5c00e8d7415a905dd_o4m6ikkkt.pdf.
72. Ibid.
73. Ibid., 24.
74. Ibid., 25.
75. Kim Bobo, Wage *Theft*, 6.
76. Ibid., 6–7.
77. National Employment Law Project, *Broken Laws, Unprotected Workers: Violations of Employment and Labor Laws in America's Cities* (New York: National Employment Law Project, 2009), especially 49–50, online at http://nelp.3cdn.net/e470538bfa5a7e7a46_2um6br7o3.pdf.
78. Bobo, *Wage Theft*, 7.

79. Craig Becker, "A Good Job for Everyone: Fair Labor Standards Act Must Protect Employees in Nation's Growing Service Economy, *Legal Times* 27, no. 36, September 6, 2004; Also Bobo, *Wage Theft*, 7.
80. Ibid., 17.
81. Ibid., 18.
82. Walmart Press Release, *Walmart and Plaintiffs' Counsel Announce Settlement of Most Wage and Hour Class Action Lawsuits Against Company* (Bentonville, Arkansas: Walmart, December 23, 2008), https://corporate.walmart.com/_news_/news-archive/2008/12/23/walmart-plaintiffs-counsel-announce-settlement-of-most-wage-hour-class-action-lawsuits-against-the-company; Bobo, *Wage Theft*, 24.
83. Brady Meixell and Ross Eisenbrey, *An Epidemic of Wage Theft is Costing Workers Hundreds of Millions of Dollars Per Year*, Issue Brief #385 (Washington, DC: Economic Policy Institute, September 11, 2014), online at http://www.epi.org/publication/epidemic-wage-theft-costing-workers-hundreds/.
84. Ross Eisenbrey, *Wage Theft by Employers is Costing Workers Billions of Dollars a Year* (Washington, DC: Economic Policy Institute, February 13, 2015), online at http://www.epi.org/blog/wage-theft-by-employers-is-costing-u-s-workers-billions-of-dollars-a-year/.
85. Cited by American Rights at Work, *Fed Up with FedEx: How FedEx Ground Tramples Workers' Rights and Civil Rights* (Washington, DC: American Rights at Work, 2007), 28, online at http://www.jwj.org/fed-up-with-fedex.
86. US Government Accountability Office, *Employer Misclassification: Improved Coordination Outreach and Targeting Could Better Insure Detection and Prevention* (Washington, DC: Government Accountability Office, GAO-09-717, August 2009), 10, online at http://www.gao.gov/new.items/d09717.pdf; see also Department for Professional Employees, *AFL-CIO Fact Sheet* (Washington, DC: AFL-CIO, 2016), online at http://dpeaflcio.org/wp-content/uploads/Misclassification-of-Employees-2016.pdf; and Kim Bobo, *Wage Theft*, 49–51, who has led me to many of these sources.
87. Dale L. Belman and Richard Block, *Informing the Debate: The Social and Economic Costs of Employee Misclassification in Michigan* (East Lansing, MI: Institute for Public Policy and Social Research, 2009), 2–3, 7, online at http://ippsr.msu.edu/publications/ARMisClass.pdf.
88. James I. Sturgeon and Michael P. Kelsay, *The Economic Costs of Employee Misclassification in the State of Indiana* (Kansas City: Department of Economics, University of Missouri-Kansas City, September 16, 2010), especially for the summary, 4–5, online at http://www.isbctc.org/

Uploads/UploadedFiles/docs/Misclassification_in_Indiana_Full_Study__9-10.pdf.

89. "Washington Fraud-Fighting Program Collects $137 Million," *Claims Journal* (January 19, 2011), online at http://www.claimsjournal.com/news/west/2011/01/19/180251.htm.
90. Patricia Smith and Jennifer Brand, *Annual Report of the Joint Enforcement Task Force on Employee Misclassification* (Albany, NY: Joint Enforcement Taskforce, 2009), 3–4, online at https://www.labor.ny.gov/agencyinfo/PDFs/Misclassification_TaskForce_AnnualRpt_2008.pdf.
91. Peter M. Rivera, *Annual Report of the New York State Enforcement Task Force on Employee Misclassification* (Albany, NY: Joint Enforcement Taskforce, 2014), 1, online at https://www.labor.ny.gov/agencyinfo/PDFs/Misclassification-Task-Force-Report-2-1-2014.pdf.
92. Robert Reich, *Why We're All Becoming Independent Contractors*, February 22, 2015, online at robertreich.org/post/111784272135.
93. Linda Tirado, *Hand to Mouth: Living in Bootstrap America* (New York: Berkley Books, 2014), 12–13.
94. Jones, *Chavs*, 149–50.
95. *Intuit 2020 Report: Twenty Trends That Will Shape the Next Decade, 2010*, online at http-download.intuit.com/http.intuit/CMO/intuit/futureofsmallbusiness/intuit_2020_report.pdf.
96. Jones, *Chavs*, 150.
97. Confederation of British Industry, *The Shape of Business—The Next Ten Years*, November 2009, online at www.cbi.org.uk/shape-of-business.
98. Jones, *Chavs*, 150.
99. Ibid., 151
100. Cited in Jones, *Chavs*, 151.
101. *Regeneration and Renewal*, July 20, 2009, online at www.crpltd.co.uk/index.php/archives/category/regeneration/page/3. In July 2009 Angus Kennedy was a speaker at the fifth Annual Regeneration and Renewal Conference, which took place in Birmingham, online at www.crpltd.co.uk/index.php/archives/category/regeneration/page/3.
102. Simon Rogers, "What Do People Get Paid?" *Guardian*, November 12, 2009.
103. Jones, *Chavs*, 152.
104. Ibid., 153.
105. See comments of Jennie Formby, former general secretary of Unite, Britain's largest union, cited in Jones, *Chavs*, 153.
106. Robert Reich, "The Problem isn't Outsourcing," online at robertreich.org/post/27527895909.

Bibliography

Allen, Katie. "British Workers Suffer Deepest Real Wages Cut Since Records Began, Research Shows." *Guardian*, June 12, 2013.

American Rights at Work. *Fed Up with FedEx: How FedEx Ground Tramples Workers' Rights and Civil Rights.* Washington, DC: American Rights at Work, 2007. http://www.jwj.org/fed-up-with-fedex.

Andrews, Edmund L. "Job Cuts at AT&T Will Total 40,000, 13 Percent of Its Staff." *New York Times*, January 3, 1996.

BBC News. "David Cameron Suggests Cutting Benefits for Under-25s." October 2, 2013. Online at http://www.bbc.com/news/uk-politics-24369514.

BBC News. "Q&A: What Will 'Help to Work' Mean for Claimants?" *BBC News.* September 30, 2013. Online at bbc.co.uk.

BBC News. "Q&A." April 28, 2014, at www.bbc.com/news/business-24330508.

Beattie J. "Forced Labor: Conservative Party to Force the Jobless to Work for Nothing or Lose Their Dole." *Mirror*, September 30, 2013.

Becker, Craig. "A Good Job for Everyone: Fair Labor Standards Act Must Protect Employees in Nation's Growing Service Economy." *Legal Times* 27, no. 36, September 6, 2004.

Belman, Dale L., and Richard Block. *Informing the Debate: The Social and Economic Costs of Employee Misclassification in Michigan.* East Lansing, MI: Institute for Public Policy and Social Research, 2009. http://ippsr.msu.edu/publications/ARMisClass.pdf.

Berman, Jilian. "Nick Hanauer's TED Talk on Income Inequality Deemed Too 'Political' for Site." *Huffington Post*, May 17, 2012. Online at http://www.huffingtonpost.com/2012/05/17/nick-hanauer-ted-talk_n_1524435.html.

Bevins, Josh, and Lawrence Mishel. *Understanding the Historic Divergence Between Productivity and a Typical Worker's Pay.* Briefing Paper #406. Washington, DC: Economic Policy Institute, September 2, 2015. Online at http://www.epi.org/publication/understanding-the-historic-divergence-between-productivity-and-a-typical-workers-pay-why-it-matters-and-why-its-real/.

Bjerga, Alan. "Food Stamps Still Feed One in Seven Americans Despite Recovery." *Bloomberg*, February 3, 2016. Online at http://www.bloomberg.com/news/articles/2016-02-03/food-stamps-still-feed-one-in-seven-americans-despite-recovery.

Bobo, Kim. *Wage Theft in America.* New York: The New Press, 2011.

Bricker, Jesse. "Changes in US Family Finances from 2010 to 2013, Evidence from the Survey of Consumer Finances." *Federal Reserve Bulletin* 100, no. 4, September 2014. Online at https://www.federalreserve.gov/pubs/bulletin/2014/pdf/scf14.pdf.

Bureau of Labor Statistics. Chart 1.1: Productivity Change in Nonfarm Business Sector, 1947–2016. Washington, DC: Bureau of Labor Statistics, 2017. Online at http://www.data.bls.gov/cgi-bin/print.pl/lpc/prodybar.htm.

Butler, Sarah. "How Philip Green's Family Made Millions as Value of BHS Plummeted." *Guardian*, April 25, 2016.

Confederation of British Industry. "*The Shape of Business—The Next Ten Years*," November 2009. www.cbi.org.uk/shape-of-business.

Dolan, Matthew, Jeff Bennett, and Mike Ramsay. "Auto Makers Now Import Jobs." *Wall Street Journal*, October 5, 2011.

Dorling, Danny. *Inequality and the 1 Percent*. London: Verso, 2014.

Duhigg, Charles, and Keith Bradsher. "How the US Lost Out on iPhone Work." *The New York Times*, January 21, 2012.

Edelman, Peter. *So Rich, So Poor: Why It's So Hard To End Poverty in America*. New York: The New Press, 2012.

Eisenbrey, Ross. *Wage Theft by Employers is Costing Workers Billions of Dollars a Year*. Washington, DC: Economic Policy Institute, February 13, 2015. Online at http://www.epi.org/blog/wage-theft-by-employers-is-costing-u-s-workers-billions-of-dollars-a-year/.

Equality Trust. *Richest 1% Has Greater Share of Wealth Than Half the UK Population*. London: Equality Trust, May 15, 2014. Online at https://www.equalitytrust.org.uk/richest-1-has-greater-share-wealth-half-uk-population.

Equality Trust. *Wealth Increase of Britain's 100 Richest Would Pay for 1.75 Million Living Wage Jobs*. Press Release. London: Equality Trust, February 19, 2014. Online at http://www.equalitytrust.org.uk/wealth-increase-britains-100-richest-would-pay-175-million-living-wage-jobs.

Ferguson, Ross. *Punishing the Young Unemployed*. London: Centre for Crime and Justice Studies, October 15, 2013. Online at https://www.crimeandjustice.org.uk/resources/punishing-young-unemployed.

Foroohar, Rana. *Makers and Takers: How Wall Street Destroyed Main Street*. New York: Crown Business, 2017.

Gordon, Robert. *The Rise and Fall of American Growth*. Princeton, NJ: Princeton University Press, 2016.

Hall, John. "Unemployment at Three-Year Low as Number of Britons in Work Reaches All-Time High of 30 Million." *Independent*, November 13, 2013.

Hope, Christopher. "Exclusive: Cabinet is Worth £70 Million." *Telegraph*. May 27, 2012.

Intuit. *Intuit 2020 Report: Twenty Trends That Will Shape the Next Decade, 2010*. http-download.intuit.com/http.intuit/CMO/intuit/futureofsmallbusiness/intuit_2020_report.pdf.

Jack, Ian. "It's Shameful the Way Britain Kowtows to the Super-Rich." *Guardian*, March 9, 2013.

Jones, Owen. *Chavs: The Demonization of the Working Class.* London: Verso, 2012.
Kollowe, Julia. "BHS Collapse: IoD Chief Accuses Sir Philip Green of 'lamentable behaviour'." *Guardian*, June 3, 2016.
Lanchester, John. "The Robots are Coming." *London Review of Books* 37, no. 5 (March 5, 2015).
Lansley, Stewart, and Joanna Mack Stewart. *Breadline Britain: The Rise of Mass Poverty.* London: Oneworld Publications, 2015.
Lazonick, William. *Sustainable Prosperity in the New Economy: Business Organization and High-Tech Employment in the United States.* Kalamazoo, MI: W. E. Upjohn Institute for Employment Research, 2009.
Lazonick, William, Mariana Mazzucato, and Oner Tulum. "Apple's Changing Business Model: What Should the World's Richest Company Do with All Those Profits?" *Accounting Forum* 37, no. 4. (2013): 249–67.
Leonhardt, Dave. "The German Example." *New York Times*, June 7, 2011.
Malik, Shiv. "Workfare Placements Must Be Made Public, Tribunal Rules." *Guardian*, May 19, 2013.
Meixell, Brady, and Ross Eisenbrey. *An Epidemic of Wage Theft is Costing Workers Hundreds of Millions of Dollars Per Year.* Issue Brief #385. Washington, DC: Economic Policy Institute, September 11, 2014. Online at http://www.epi.org/publication/epidemic-wage-theft-costing-workers-hundreds/.
Mirowski, Philip. *Never Let a Serious Crisis Go to Waste: How Neoliberalism Survived the Financial Meltdown.* London: Verso, 2013.
Murray, Matt. "Why Jack Welch's Leadership Matters to Businesses World-Wide." *Wall Street Journal*, September 5, 2001.
National Employment Law Project. *Broken Laws, Unprotected Workers: Violations of Employment and Labor Laws in America's Cities.* New York: National Employment Law Project, 2009. http://nelp.3cdn.net/e470538bfa5a7e7a46_2um6br7o3.pdf.
Office for National Statistics (UK). "Persistent Poverty in the UK and the EU: 2014." London: ONS, May 16, 2016. https://www.ons.gov.uk/peoplepopulationandcommunity/personalandhouseholdfinances/incomeandwealth/articles/persistentpovertyintheukandeu/2014.
O'Hara, Mary. *Austerity Bites: A Journey to the Sharp End of Cuts in the UK.* Bristol: Policy Press, University of Bristol, 2014.
One Society. *How National Minimum Wage is Falling Behind Top Pay, and the Damage This Does to Living Standards and the Economy.* Briefing. London: One Society, October 1, 2012. Online at onesociety.helencross.co.uk/wp-content/uploads/2012/09/NMW-briefing-27Sept2012pdf.
Organization for Economic Cooperation and Development. *Public Spending on Labor Markets.* Paris: OECD, 2016. https://data.oecd.org/socialexp/public-spending-on-labour-markets.htm.
Organization for Economic Cooperation and Development. "Statistics." https://stats.oecd.org/Index.aspx?DataSetCode=UN_DEN.

Oxfam America. *From Paycheck to Pantry: Hunger in Working America*. Boston, MA: Oxfam America, 2014.

Piketty, Thomas, and Emmanuel Saez. "Income Inequality in the United States, 1913 to 1998." *Quarterly Journal of Economics* 118, no. 1 (2003): 1–39.

Preston, Robert. *Who Runs Britain: ... And Who's to Blame for the Economic Mess We're In?* London: Hodder & Stoughton, Ltd., 2008.

Reich, Robert. "The Problem isn't Outsourcing." *robertreich.org* (Blog). robertreich.org/post/27527895909.

Reich, Robert B. *Saving Capitalism: For the Many, Not the Few*. New York: Alfred A. Knopf, 2015.

Robert Reich. "Why We're All Becoming Independent Contractors." *robertreich.org* (Blog), February 22, 2015. robertreich.org/post/111784272135.

Rogers, Simon. "What Do People Get Paid?" *Guardian*, November 12, 2009.

Saez, Emmanuel. "Striking It Richer: The Evolution of Top Incomes in the United States." *Pathways*. The Evolution of Top Incomes in the United States," *Pathways*, Stanford Center on Poverty and Inequality (Winter 2008): 6–7. https://inequality.stanford.edu/sites/default/files/media/_media/pdf/pathways/winter_2008/Saez.pdf.

Saez, Emmanuel, and Gabriel Zucman. *Wealth Inequality in the United States Since 2013, Evidence from Capitalized Income Data*. NBER Working Paper 20625. Cambridge, MA: National Bureau of Economic Research, October 2014. Online at http://www.nber.org/papers/w20625.

Standing, Guy. *The Precariat: The New Dangerous Class*. London: Bloomsbury Academic, 2014.

Stewart, Heather. "Working for Nothing: the Truth About Low Pay in the UK." *Guardian*, October 2, 2011.

Tetlow, Gemma. "British Workers Face Worst Decade for Pay in 70 Years." *Financial Times*, November 24, 2016.

Thiess, Rebecca. *The Future of Work: Trends and Challenges for Low-Wage Workers*. Briefing Paper #341. Washington, DC: Economic Policy Institute, April 27, 2012. http://www.epi.org/publication/bp341-future-of-work/.

Tirado, Linda. *Hand to Mouth: Living in Bootstrap America*. New York: Berkley Books, 2014.

US Bureau of Labor Statistics. *A Profile of the Working Poor, 2010*. Washington, DC: US Bureau of Labor Statistics, March 2012. https://www.bls.gov/opub/reports/working-poor/archive/workingpoor_2010.pdf.

US Department of Labor. *1999–2000 Report on Initiatives*. Washington, DC: US Department of Labor, February 2001. http://nelp.3cdn.net/a5c00e-8d7415a905dd_o4m6ikkkt.pdf.

US Department of Labor. *History of Changes to the Minimum Wage Law*. Washington DC: US Department of Labor, 2017. Online at https://www.dol.gov/whd/minwage/coverage.htm.

US Government Accountability Office. *Employer Misclassification: Improved Coordination Outreach and Targeting Could Better Insure Detection and*

Prevention. Washington, DC: GAO, August 2009. http://www.gao.gov/new.items/d09717.pdf.

Wal-Mart. *Press Release. Walmart and Plaintiffs' Counsel Announce Settlement of Most Wage and Hour Class Action Lawsuits Against Company*. Bentonville, AR: Wal-Mart, December 23, 2008. https://corporate.walmart.com/_news_/news-archive/2008/12/23/walmart-plaintiffs-counsel-announce-settlement-of-most-wage-hour-class-action-lawsuits-against-the-company.

Wilkinson, Richard. *The Impact of Inequality: How to Make Societies Healthier*. New York: The New Press, 2006.

Wilkinson, Richard, and Kate Pickett, *The Spirit Level: Why Greater Equality Makes Societies Stronger*. New York: Bloomsbury Press, 2009.

Wintour, Patrick, and Nicholas Watt, "George Osborne: Jobless Benefit Conditions are 'Tough Love'." *Guardian*, September 30, 2013.

World Bank. "Ending Poverty Requires More Than Growth, Says WBG." World Bank Group press release. April 11, 2014. Online at http://www.worldbank.org/en/news/press-release/2014/04/10/ending-poverty-requires-more-than-growth-says-wbg.

CHAPTER 6

The Politics of Taxes

Introduction

Two years before he became Prime Minister, in July 1995, Tony Blair flew halfway around the world to Australia to improve his relationship with Rupert Murdoch at the latter's News Corporation conference. The gambit apparently worked, Blair was elected with the critical support of Murdoch's *Sun*. Murdoch had to wait several years for a return on his "investment," but it came when Blair launched a passionate attack on Murdoch's critics after Lords passed an anti-Murdoch amendment to the Competition Bill in 1998.[1] Later, Murdoch's News Corporation Investments, his main British holding company, came under investigation by a multi-nation task force for tax evasion. Although the group's profits over a decade, roughly between 1989 and 1999, added up to £1.4 billion ($2.1 billion), it had paid no net British corporation tax, a shocking revelation even by corporate standards.[2]

On the other side of the Atlantic, back in 2011, billionaire Warren Buffett was complaining that he paid too little in taxes. While he and his fellow super-rich were paying about 15% in taxes on their income, his secretary and much of the middle class were in the 15 or 25% brackets. Moreover, the middle class had to pay substantial payroll taxes as well, something the super-rich avoided because most of their wealth was in capital gains earned in the market. But, as Buffett acknowledged, Congress was billionaire-friendly.[3]

J. L. Luzkow, *Monopoly Restored*,
https://doi.org/10.1007/978-3-319-93994-0_6

> When governments set tax rates, they are making decisions about who will prosper and by how much. A government that takes 90 cents out of each dollar above a threshold, as the United States did in the Eisenhower years, is deciding to limit the wealth that people can accumulate from their earnings. Likewise, a government that taxes the poor on their first dollar of wages, as the United States does with the Social Security and Medicare taxes, is deciding to limit or eliminate the ability of those at the bottom of the income ladder to save money and improve their lot in life. The rules that governments set for their tax systems, and the degree to which they enforce them, also affect who prospers. Congress lets business owners, investors and landlords play by one set of rules, which are filled with opportunities to hide income, fabricate deductions and reduce taxes. Congress requires wage earners to operate under another, much harsher set of rules in which every dollar of income from a job a savings account or a stock dividend is reported to the government, and taxes are withheld from each paycheck to make sure wage earners pay in full.[4] (David Cay Johnston)

Taxes: Subsidizing the Super-Rich

The taxation system is the result of public policy, but in recent decades (and months) it has largely become a casino game, played especially well by the super-rich. When David Cay Johnston studied the US tax system in 2003, he concluded that the poor, the middle class, and even the upper middle class were subsidizing the very rich. His conclusions were widely challenged, followed by a consensus that he was essentially correct. What is tragic is that some fifteen years later, what Johnston asserted is today even truer: the tax system has become a lucrative subsidy of the super-rich, enabling them to amass a greater percentage of national wealth than at any time since the Great Depression, in both the USA and the UK.

The super-rich have long insisted that they pay more than their fair share of taxes when all taxes are considered. But this is demonstrably untrue even if we consider only income taxes. At the lower end, a substantial part of the UK and US populations pay little or no income tax, but that is because their income is too low for them to have any income tax obligations. But beyond the lowest income earners, the near poor on up through much of the middle classes still pay more taxes relative to their incomes than the super-rich because in recent years, while income taxes on the super-rich were declining, and much of the income of the top 1% was being shifted to lower taxed capital gains—20% in the USA and 28% in the UK—regressive taxes such as Value Added and National Insurance in the UK, and consumption or sales taxes and payroll taxes in the USA, have escalated. Moreover, the top income tax bracket has stayed relatively low in the USA at 39.6 at percent (37% in 2018 as a result of the Tax Cuts and Jobs Act), a tax rate that applies to anybody who makes $1 million or $100 million. In other words, there is no progressive taxation rate at the upper echelons of the income scale. In the UK the top income tax bracket is 45%, considerably higher than the top capital gains bracket.

Thus, while the super-rich take a burgeoning share of the national income, they have managed over time to reduce or avoid taxes levied on them. The British government collects only 26% of its revenue through income taxes, while Value Added and National Health Insurance account for 35% of British government revenues.[5] In the USA, the federal government collects 46% of its revenues from income taxes, 33% in social insurance or payroll taxes, and less than 11% in corporate income taxes; state and local governments also collect a regressive sales tax, often as high as 10% and in some states levied on food.[6] In the USA and the UK, therefore, the poor and middle classes end up paying more of their modest to meager incomes in taxes—relative to their incomes—because of indirect and regressive taxation, and payroll taxes.

What this means for the populations of both the USA and the UK is that as the divide between the corporate elite super-rich and everybody else widens, as more and more of increasing income goes to the 1–93% in the case of the USA since 2008 if we are to believe Anthony Atkinson—the population overall becomes poorer. As the super-rich become richer, everybody else suffers: as the 0.1% avoids or escapes taxation, everybody else has to pay more taxes.

So how did we get here? How did the tax system become a public lottery? When neoliberalism was embraced by Ronald Reagan's administration, and by Margaret Thatcher's in the UK, this meant the deregulation of markets and privatization of public goods; put bluntly, the end of the state-directed economy and public provisioning. It meant replacing the welfare and developmental state with the lean, mean "competition" state. Translated, this meant that people were on their own.[7] Neoliberalism replaced public provision and social citizenship with trickle down economics and so-called personal responsibility. It revoked the social contract that had been in place for four or more decades. And neoliberalism meant the shedding of taxes by the super-rich (as much as possible), who now argued that taxing their corporations was a double tax. Or that taxes on them were not only unfair—it was after all their money—but were harmful to economic growth, which depended on the capital of the super-rich for investment, the basis for all those jobs. The budgetary deficits that followed from diminishing tax returns from the super-rich also elicited a new response from them: the welfare state, they said, was bankrupting everybody. But we already know that was false: people were increasingly on their own. If they were going to get anything, it had better be from the income they earned.

Given what would be a massive tax giveaway from the Reagan administration onward—with some fillips when Democrats occupied the White House—and given the withdrawal of a protective state, the top 1% (1.3 million households) in the USA have come to own almost half (and still increasing) of the stocks, bonds, cash, and other financial assets of the country. They still pay taxes, of course, large sums, but they have managed to shed a good part of the burden and shift it onto others. In 2000, the wealthiest 1%, households with adjusted gross incomes of more than $313,000, earned almost 21% of all reported income and paid more than 37% of individual federal income taxes, a tidy sum. Yet even in 2000, when all federal taxes are considered, including those on Social Security, gasoline, and alcohol, as well as income and estate taxes, the share paid by the 1% becomes much more modest, dropping to about a fourth of total federal tax revenues, not much above their share of reported income.[8]

But this is only part of the story. The super-rich get much more than their share of government largesse when tax revenues are spent, and they also benefit from the large and growing regressive taxation—sales taxes—which taxes everybody at the same rate, and reduces what the rich pay in taxes as a percentage of the total. When all taxes are counted, and not just federal income taxes, the poor are taxed almost as heavily as the rich, and more heavily than the super-rich. For three or more decades the wealthy elite have shifted more of the tax burden onto others: the less they pay, the more everybody else pays. The ultra wealthy can do this because they have good attorneys who know how to rewrite the tax rules, or to conceal money, or to simply shift money to where it is likely to be taxed least.

Big Business: How It Evades Taxes

All this moves the burden of taxation downward, and it makes the USA and the UK ever more unequal. Consider the US Corporations, as one instance, lowered the portion of their profits that go to federal income taxes from 26 cents on the dollar in 1993 to 22 cents in 1998, although the official federal corporate income tax rate remained unchanged at 35%. For the last quarter of the twentieth century corporate profits grew a third faster than corporate income taxes.[9] Since David Cay Johnston published *Perfectly Legal*, in 2003, it has become commonplace for corporations to move their tax home abroad while keeping company headquarters in the USA. This simple device can eliminate a corporate tax bill in the USA altogether. But the modern corporation does not have to establish a tax home abroad. It can keep its tax home and company headquarters in the USA, and still evade taxation. That is because companies can move intellectual property such as patents, trademarks, and title to the company logo to entities organized in tax havens in far-flung places like Bermuda, the Cayman Islands, Cypress, and Nauru. In fact the list is long, seemingly endless, to where corporations can move and conceal their real income and assets.

How corporations do this is deceptively simple, legal, and lucrative, as long as Congress and government are willing to comply. After assigning intellectual property rights to "entities," corporations then pay royalties for the right to use their own intellectual property. Once this is accomplished they are free to convert taxable profits into tax-deductible payments sent to Bermuda or other tax havens, which impose little if any taxes. Once again David Cay Johnston explains why corporate tax evasion is costly to American citizens, or to British citizens since their corporations follow the same rules:

> You pay for this through higher taxes, reduced services or your rising share of our growing national debt. You also pay for it through incentives in the tax system for companies to build new factories overseas and to reduce employment in America. These trends to lower taxes on wealthy people and on corporations are aided by new rules allowing capital and goods to flow freely around the world, while immigration and employment laws limit any mass movements of workers and ever-tougher rules against union organizing give capital an advantage over labor in setting wages.[10]

What it costs the average citizen is obvious: the tax burden has shifted, and that means there is less revenue that flows into the public treasury, and therefore either government services must be reduced, or taxes increased! And it is now evident where those increases come from. Not the corporations that have just shed their taxes, but the average citizen who must ante up for what has been lost in revenue because of the tax evasion of the super-rich.

Besides moving assets, capital, or jobs abroad to low tax regimes, there are many loopholes corporations can take advantage of at home. A report by Citizens for Tax Justice, published in June 2016, found that 315 Fortune 500 companies used what is called the stock option loophole to avoid, collectively, $64.5 billion in state and federal taxes over a five-year period between 2011 and 2015. The five biggest offenders, also among the largest and most profitable and most recognizable firms because of their vast clienteles and outsized profits, were Facebook, Apple, Google, Goldman Sachs, and JPMorgan Chase.[11]

Robert McIntyre, executive director of Citizens for Tax Justice, explains how this tax loophole works: "Corporations in some cases give executives millions in stock options and then they ask taxpayers to help pick up the tab by taking tax deductions."[12] Most big companies grant privileges allowing CEOs and senior management an option to buy a company's stock at a favorable price and time determined by the company. To help executives maximize gain, a company typically selects a time in the past when the price was low. Executives—and others—can then exercise their option in the future whenever the price is higher: the executive pockets the difference as "compensation." When executives exercise these "stock options," corporations can legally take a tax deduction for the difference between what the employees pay for the stock and what it is "worth," the higher price at the time of the exercised option, although it costs nothing for a corporation to grant the option. Since taxpayers do not get to vote on executive compensation, they don't have the right to decide on the real worth of executives. They cannot even veto the "subsidies" since by law, without the intervention of Congress, companies get to decide on the worth of their executive leadership. Facebook, one of the biggest users of this tax loophole, managed to reduce its federal and state tax bill between 2011 and 2015, by 70%.[13]

Counting executive compensation in any form as a company expense is shameful but it is legal, which is why it is practiced by so many corporations. But there are other techniques that companies can use to commit "legal fraud," and the tax savings quickly add up. Oxfam America has concluded that corporate tax evasion costs the American taxpayer $111 billion annually, a figure so astonishing that it hardly seems credible.[14] Yet even this amount seems small when compared to other forms of tax evasion.

Tax Havens: How Taxpayers Unwittingly Subsidize Big Business

So how do corporations avoid paying their share of taxes? One of the more insidious methods is called "earnings stripping." This is a device whereby a subsidiary in a high tax country like the USA or the UK borrows from a subsidiary in a low tax country, enabling the parent company to pay artificially high interest rates to itself. For the global company everything nets out, profits on one side match losses on the other. No real business activity has occurred, but the company's global tax bill has been reduced accordingly.

The corporate tax avoidance that is most costly to taxpayers is called a tax inversion, which occurs when a company renounces its US "citizenship" by buying a foreign subsidiary in a low tax country—or jurisdiction—where it then reincorporates. In many cases nothing changes about the actual business, the new "inverted" company retains its headquarters in the USA and still conducts business there as always, enjoying all the advantages of the US market without the tax obligations. This practice is so obviously a ploy, that when Pfizer attempted to merge with Allergan—which was registered in Ireland, a tax haven because of low corporate taxes—in early 2016, to radically reduce its tax burden in the USA, the Obama administration moved to block Pfizer. Treasury issued a new set of rules mandating that Allergan shareholders had to own 40% of the combined company for Pfizer to get the full benefit of the inversion, a criterion they could not meet. And that was the end of the merger, but only a single instance and a lonely success for government.

Elsewhere, the story is similar: profits have disappeared where actual economic activity is occurring—only to reappear in tax havens. In 2012, according to US Internal Revenue Service (IRS) figures, US companies reported $104 billion in profits in Bermuda, though this figure hardly represented real economic activity there, where sales accounted for only 0.3% of total global sales for the same companies and the share of total number of employees or wage costs was no more than 0.02%: the profits however represented 1884% of Bermuda's GDP.[15]

Bermuda is just one tax haven, there are many more around the globe that multinationals are using to shelter profits. US corporations as a whole have reported that 43% of their earnings come from five tax haven jurisdictions, although these same countries accounted for only 4% of the companies' foreign workforces and 7% of their foreign investment.[16] In 2012, alone, US corporations shifted somewhere between $500 and $700 billion in profits from countries where actual economic activities took place to countries with lower effective tax rates.[17] The new alignment meant that about 25% of US multinationals' reported total gross profits were transferred offshore, away from where the profits were earned.[18]

For over three decades the share of US corporate use of tax havens has been escalating. According to University of California economist Gabriel Zucman, tax haven use has increased tenfold since the mid-1980s.[19] Tax havens have only one use, to dodge taxes and to boost profits. It is not just immoral; however, it is also lethal, one of the chief causes of inequality, and not only in the USA and the UK. Tax dodging by multinational corporations benefits only the rich and the politically powerful and it comes at the expense of everybody other than the richest elite. This small plutocracy, which always complains about Big Government, employs a vast army of lobbyists, insuring that the same companies are the largest beneficiaries of taxpayer-funded support.[20]

A 2016 report by Oxfam America based on the fifty largest public US corporations documented just how cozy the relationship between Big Business and government has become. It showed how political influence could be rewarding in the form of loans, bailouts, grants, and even tolerance for if not outright support of the corporate use of tax havens. Between 2008 and 2014, the fifty largest US companies received $27 in federal loans, loan guarantees, and bailouts for every dollar they paid in federal taxes. Most of that money was paid back, but that did not save the millions of families that lost their homes and the millions of individuals who lost their jobs because of the financial collapse caused by many of the same companies.[21]

Between 2008 and 2014, these same fifty largest companies spent about $2.6 billion on lobbying. The return was good; they received almost $4 trillion in federal loans, loan guarantees, and bailouts—on terms that were not available to anybody but these corporations. The top fifty earned almost $4 trillion in profits between 2008 and 2014, very profitable years for them in the aftermath of the Great Recession, yet they used offshore tax havens to lower their overall tax rate to 26.5%—according to Oxfam—well below the federal statutory tax rate of 35% and below average levels paid in other developed countries.[22]

But even these figures overstated what US corporations paid in corporate taxes. When one subtracts what was paid to states, localities, and especially foreign governments, then effective federal corporate tax rates in the USA came to only 10% of gross profits, a sum that may easily be much lower since disclosure rules are weak, to the advantage of multinationals that can shift earnings to foreign jurisdictions without fear of reprisal.[23] A study in 2014 by the Citizens for Tax Justice, based on five years of data, concluded that Fortune 500 companies paid an effective corporate federal tax rate of only 19.4%, slightly above half the 35% US statutory rate.[24] But even accepting Oxfam's higher effective corporate tax rate of 26.7%, Oxfam concluded that companies underpaid taxes by $337 billion between 2008 and 2014, a period when the US federal government was underwriting corporate losses in the trillions of dollars and making taxpayer money available north of $10 trillion dollars in federal loans, loan guarantees and federal bailout programs.[25] Economist Kimberley A. Clausing has argued that corporate profit shifting cost the taxpayer between $77 and $111 billion annually prior to 2012, and rising thereafter.[26]

The statutory federal corporate tax rate in the USA, in 2017, stood at 35% on all profits no matter where they were earned around the globe. But these taxes were only owed after money earned abroad had been repatriated back to the USA. At the end of 2017, more than $2.5 trillion dollars were held abroad, where they were reported by corporations as "permanently invested," and therefore untaxed. But do not conclude that corporations had no access to profits being held abroad. They could still access that money by borrowing in the USA without paying any taxes simply by using offshore assets as collateral.[27] And since the interest on borrowed money was tax deductible, borrowing was essentially free. Even when the Tax Cuts and Jobs Act was passed, reducing the maximum corporate tax rate to 21%, that was hardly an incentive to repatriate corporate profits to the USA. Not when corporations were paying few if any corporate income taxes.

Tax Havens, Offshore Subsidiaries, and Lobbyists

Globalization is not the cause of corporate tax evasion, but it makes it much easier for corporations to reduce tax obligations or to evade them altogether. But concealing money and profits abroad where they are taxed at lower rates—much lower in most cases, under 5%—is made possible because of public policies which enable multinationals to shift profits abroad without fear of litigation at home. It is the rules which govern globalization that are the problem and large companies have the legal expertise to help craft those rules, and the political clout to defend them.

In 1986, Congress amended a law that had been designed to prevent corporate cash hoarding offshore. With the passage that year of the so-called Tax Reform Act, there were no more obstacles: corporations could hold unlimited amounts of untaxed earnings offshore with complete impunity, regardless of where those earnings—and ultimately profits—were made. It was a veritable gold rush, only now the mining was underwritten by the federal government and, ultimately, the taxpayer.[28] By 2016, Fortune 500 companies collectively were hoarding more than $2 trillion offshore in "subsidiaries" predictably and typically located in tax havens, where they remained legally invisible, or "hidden," from federal tax claims.[29] Since US law does not require corporations to have any physical presence in offshore locations like the Caymans other than a post office box, often the so-called offshore subsidiary retains a US billing address. A single small office building in the Caymans has served as the registered address for 18,857 companies.[30]

The British have the same kind of reporting system as the USA, and with many of the same results. It really doesn't matter much whether Labor or the Tories are at Number 10 Downing Street. Consider Labor under Tony Blair and Gordon Brown. The Blair Government feared jeopardizing the status of the UK as a favored destination for inward investment, so there was a disincentive to use taxation as a means of social reform and redistribution in favor of the sort of people who normally vote Labor. The result was inevitable. In the absence of restraint, corporate tax avoidance ballooned. It has been calculated that the UK was losing—well into the Blair government's tenure—somewhere between £97 and £150 billion per year in corporate tax receipts. As late as 2014 there had been little if any tax reform. According to tax expert Richard Murphy, the UK tax gap that year was £114 billion and still rising.[31]

Consider the illustration of Rupert Murdoch's media empire, News Corporation, which paid almost nothing in taxes from the late 1980s. When a task force composed of representatives from Australia, the UK, the USA, and Canada, investigated why News Corporation paid so little in taxes, fear of Murdoch's reprisals led to the investigation being dropped. News Corporation consisted of a web of some 800 subsidiaries, many of them registered offshore. A study of 101 subsidiaries of its UK holding company for an eleven-year period concluded that profits of £1.4 billion were virtually untouched by corporate taxes.[32] Richard Branson's Virgin empire and Philip Green's Arcadia Group similarly avoided—or vastly reduced—tax liabilities by making astute use of tax havens. The Labor Government, despite Chancellor of the Exchequer Gordon Brown's assurances that he would not permit tax relief to millionaires shifting incomes and profits to offshore havens like Jersey and the Cayman Islands, seemed uninterested in holding the super wealthy accountable, though it could easily have done so.[33] Without insisting on restraints on tax havens and forcing public scrutiny and accountability, the UK's Blair and Brown actively courted the support of the super wealthy, though this came at a considerable cost to Labor's social support and the people of Britain. The UK's 54 billionaires in the year 2006 had an estimated income of £126 billion. Income tax liabilities should have been about £50 billion. In fact, they were about £14.7 million, or roughly 0.14% of what legally they should have been.[34] Here is how Eric Shaw summed it up:

> None of this was accidental or unintended: the new thinking of New Labor was intentionally creating a business friendly culture that it claimed vital to wealth creation, and this meant making the UK attractive for foreign investors by maintaining a low tax regime. Accordingly, two years after reducing staff overseeing corporate tax avoidance, and in response to Big Business, Treasury projected a sea change that would make tax officials less obstructive to potential investors in the UK. Chancellor Brown announced that henceforth he wanted a system that exhibited greater trust in companies and that was more responsive to the needs of business.[35]

Brown was responsive to business as promised: the UK was successful in helping the rich to avoid taxation. Things were hardly different in the USA. When the US Senate launched an investigation in 2008 of twenty-seven large multinationals with large amounts of cash theoretically "trapped" offshore, it found that more than half of that wealth was already invested in US banks, bonds, and other assets.[36]

In the USA, because of weak disclosure rules, some 1600 subsidiaries revealed by the top fifty Fortune 500 companies to the Securities Exchange Commission (SEC), represents a relatively small number of the total subsidiaries used as offshore repositories. The reason is that the SEC requires companies only to disclose "significant subsidiaries," wherever the investment in the subsidiary is more than 10% of the total consolidated assets, or the income from the subsidiary exceeds 10% of the corporation's total (global) consolidated income.[37]

Since there is no limit to the number of subsidiaries that a corporation can establish, it seems credible (inevitable) that they could distribute assets in havens as widely as needed to meet such minimal standards of compliance. In fact, in 2014 the four largest US financial institutions collectively disclosed 1858 subsidiaries to the SEC, but much larger numbers were disclosed to the Federal Reserve Bank (FED) because it required fuller disclosure. The FED was notified that the same four finance corporations actually were using 10,688 subsidiaries to house their offshore assets.[38]

One might conclude that the FED has relatively full information because of its set of rules. But this is not the case either. Most large companies are not required to disclose their foreign subsidiaries to the FED. The result is a vast web of legal concealment, purchased at a bargain price when one compares money spent on lobbying to maintain weak reporting rules of assets held offshore, and low effective tax rates.

The magnitude of tax breaks for wealthy corporations and their executives is enough to shame a Mafia don. But not so the Fortune 500 companies that have bought political muscle by sustained investments in federal lobbying. Each member of Congress is trailed by an average of twenty-one lobbyists at a cost of $6 million in spending each year to influence the votes of that congressman.[39] That is a huge sum, but it has been worth it for the companies spending all that money on lobbyists. Oxfam America has summed up the figures:

> The top 50 companies spent roughly $2.7 billion on lobbying from 2008 – 2014. That means for every $1 they invested in shaping federal policy through lobbying, they received $130 in tax breaks and more than $4000 in federal loans, loan guarantees and bailouts.[40]

The more companies spend on lobbying, the less they spend on taxes. Some of the large investment banks like Citigroup, which had to be bailed out during the great financial crisis of 2007–2008, didn't pay any taxes because of heavy losses incurred. But many other headline companies received tax breaks based on declared profits. Google, for example, received just under $17.2 billion in tax breaks for the period 2008–2014, paying an effective tax rate of 20.2%. But it held $47.4 billion offshore in two declared subsidiaries, and this money was not subject to taxation until it was repatriated to the USA, if ever. Apple, Inc., for the same period, showed $231 billion in profits, and self-reportedly paid a total tax of almost $60 billion, for an effective tax rate of 25.9%. However, as we shall see below, it received tax breaks worth more than $21 billion and held more than $181 billion untaxed or "deferred" offshore in three declared subsidiaries.[41]

Tax dodging may help the balance sheets of corporations and improve the value of company shares, but it is costly to the average taxpayer who is subsidizing the tax breaks of multinationals. Losing up to $111 billion each year in corporate tax revenues means less money available for investment in education, infrastructure, research and development (R&D), less revenue to create jobs or to spend on poverty reduction programs. It also means, inevitably, regressive taxes to replace revenues lost to corporate tax dodging, and this in turn means higher taxes on the dwindling means of middle-class families, and especially on the poor and near poor, who also have to pay escalating sales taxes—caught in the vice of company tax evasion.

In the last sixty years, in the USA, the share of government revenues supported by corporations has dropped by two-thirds. In fiscal year 2014, the US federal government collected $320.7 billion in corporate income taxes, which was 10.6% of the federal government's total revenue. This sounds like a lot, and it is, but consider that corporations paid 32% of total government revenues in 1952. The difference is not accidental, it is the result of deliberate policy choices that are bought and paid for by large corporations, or special interests that have the clout to reduce their tax bill, too the discernible disadvantage of tax payers who have bailed out too many financial institutions.[42]

This easily can be demonstrated by a quick glance at payroll taxes—a regressive tax supporting Social Security and Medicare, levied at 15.3% of all earned income on all employees up to a cap of $118,500—in the

USA, and what percentage they have contributed to total federal revenues. In 1950, the share of payroll taxes in total federal revenues was something just below 10%, a modest figure that reflected a higher share of taxes borne by companies. But during and after the Great Recession, payroll taxes as a percentage of revenue for the federal government rose above 40%, and then stubbornly persisted at levels just below 40%.[43]

Put in larger perspective, corporate tax evasion and lower rates of corporate taxation, not only enriches those who are already wealthy, it makes the rest of us much poorer. It is yet another means by which the corporate super-rich is subsidized by everybody else, one more example of how wealth is moved north toward the ultra wealthy. Oxfam America estimates that the annual $111 billion lost to corporate tax evasion could have lifted 60% of all poor children in the USA out of poverty or, alternatively, created an additional 620,000 jobs rebuilding the crumbling infrastructure in the USA.[44]

It is this narrative that helps to explain why globalization has not lifted all boats. Today, 60% of the world's trade occurs inside multinationals, but it is these same companies doing much if not most of the tax avoidance. With few if any restraints from their governments, large corporations cut or avoid taxes by shifting money between jurisdictions, creating artificial paper trails. Multinationals send profits into tax-free havens, and they move costs into high-tax countries. At the same time, these maneuvers do not appear in corporate annual reports. Under current accounting rules, corporations can bundle their results, consolidating them into one figure from a number of countries, whether profits, debt, or tax payments. A company can show its profits coming from Africa, but there is no way to know which countries they came from. In this way, trillions of dollars can and do disappear. No citizen in a country can actually know what a company does, he cannot even know if a company really operates in his country, what it does, and how profitable it is.[45]

Today, about half of world trade assets pass through tax havens. Over half of all bank assets, and a third of foreign direct investment by multinationals are routed offshore. "Some 85% of international banking and bond issuance takes place in the so-called Euromarkets, a stateless offshore zone ..."[46] Almost every multinational uses tax havens and the largest users by far are on Wall Street.

In 2008, the Government Accountability Office (GAO) reported that two-thirds of American and foreign companies doing business in the USA avoided income tax obligations to the federal government between 1998 and 2005, although corporate sales totaled $2.5 trillion for the same period. Studies soon afterward suggested the problem was only getting worse.[47] Offshoring concealed trillions in cash, was lowering government revenues everywhere, and was making markets inefficient by increasing government revenue deficits and decreasing transparency, while shifting new tax burdens onto the middle and poorer parts of the population. The result was increasing social inequality and increasing social pathologies, everything from disease to crime. As journalist Nicholas Shaxson put it, "wealth [was] transferred from poor taxpayers to rich shareholders," without anybody producing a better product, not even a better banana.[48]

Tax havens essentially amount to government subsidies, made worse by the fact that the tax burden is shifted back to those with less wealth and less able to afford payment of taxes. The use of tax havens dramatically reduces economic efficiency. Again, Nicholas Shaxson explains why: "Companies and capital migrate not to where they are most productive but to where they can get the best tax break. There is nothing 'efficient' about any of this."[49] When the British Virgin Islands, with fewer than 25,000 inhabitants, hosts more then 800,000 companies, or when greater than 40% of all foreign direct investment into India comes from Mauritius, it seems obvious enough that the greatest beneficiaries are the companies hiding assets in the British Virgin Islands and Mauritius, which benefit from non-taxation in their home countries, as well as non-taxation in these islands: the result is double non-taxation.[50]

Tax havens are so pervasive and so widely used by the British—and by Americans—that Nicholas Shaxson has persuasively argued they represent a reconstituted British Empire. In fact, the British Empire never disappeared; its governance was simply taken over by the banks from the British government. If Shaxson is correct, then the great liberal order that was reconstituted after WW II, the Open Society and the era of humanism going back to the Enlightenment, might not be so liberal after all. Here are some data to ponder. The Cayman Islands, a leftover from the colonial days, and a British Overseas Territory today, hosts more than 80,000 registered companies, three quarters of the world's hedge funds, and has $1.3 trillion in registered deposits. Though possibly sheltering more money than any other tax haven, the Caymans are only one among many in a vast network of tax havens, many of them British or formerly British. These include the Bahamas, Dubai, Gibraltar, Hong Kong, Ireland, Singapore, and even the Turks and Caicos Islands.[51]

While the British elite uses the offshore system to move money around the globe, enjoying the benefits of double non-taxation, the USA top 0.1%, the corporate elite, does much the same, often using the same British network to evade US tax levies. A GAO report in December 2008 found that Citigroup had 427 tax haven subsidiaries, of which 290 were in the British network. Morgan Stanley had 273 offshore subsidiaries, of which 220 were in the British network; and News Corporation had 152, of which 140 were in the British zone.[52]

Speaking of the new imperialism, and of the former but now reconstituted British Empire, consisting of former colonies in India, Africa and elsewhere, here is Nicholas Shaxson again:

> But what Britain has done ... is to retain a large degree of control of the vast flows of wealth in and out of these places, under the table. Illicit capital flight from Africa, for example, flows mostly into the modern British spiderweb, to be managed in London. In both the French and the British systems, powerful interest groups in the old colonial powers have built secret financial relationships with the local elites, creating global alliances with each other against the ordinary citizens of these poor countries—and against their *own* citizens too.[53]

We already know that the USA roughly parallels Britain. The US network is the stepchild of the war in Vietnam, when the USA faced massive debts and financial and banking interests became critical to help cover the enormous deficits that followed. The collapse of the post-WW II financial order in the 1970s, the detaching of the dollar from gold, and the end of capital exchange controls—the birth of foot-fancy capital—permitted massive capital flight to wherever money could command the highest interest rate, and at the same time be subjected to low tax regimes eager to borrow the cash troves suddenly on offer. Sound familiar? Welcome to the open era of tax havens, capital flight, and non-taxation of the owners of piles of global wealth, all representing the $100 billion plus per annum escaping the public treasury in the USA via tax havens. As we know, the era of the tax haven has been, in the UK and the USA, the era of lower economic growth, recurring economic crises, stagnation or worse for most Americans and most citizens living in the British Isles, while wealth at the top of the pyramid soars. In sum, the free flight of capital toward lower tax regimes and higher interest rates has given a free pass to the owners of immense wealth not bound by national boundaries or by public interest and the common good.

Apple Incorporated: The High Art Tax Avoidance

Apple Incorporated says that it pays 26% corporate taxes in the USA. Apple also insists that it pays all of its taxes to Ireland—where it has subsidiaries—which has a 12.5% corporate tax rate, as opposed to the 35% statutory corporate income tax rate in the USA. But the European Union (EU) denies Apple is a good citizen. It says Apple has cheated for years, resulting in an effective corporate tax rate for Apple of only 0.005% in Ireland, back in 2014.

So who is right? Certainly not Apple, which has benefited from a tax deal it made with Ireland that the EU says is illegal, not to mention unethical, even by the low standards of corporate behavior. So how did Apple get away with it and win the gold medal for tax evasion, for which it has yet to apologize after being slapped with a €14.5 billion tax bill? Apple devised a method well known to multinational corporations. It created two subsidiaries in Ireland, Apple Operations International (AOI) and Apple Sales International (ASI), which together effectively owned most of Apple's intellectual property (IP). Those companies then licensed Apple's IP to other global subsidiaries, which earned their income from licensing agreements. That meant that when an Apple iPhone was sold in China, Apple's Chinese subsidiary would transfer profits to the Irish company holding the rights to the IP: in this case that meant primarily AOI. Under international laws, Apple did not have to disclose the percentage of the iPhone sale subject to IP licensing fees but, as Robert Willens, a Columbia Business School professor has lamented, the profit earned on the sale in China was then shifted to the Irish subsidiary.[54]

That is the point when Apple's side agreement with the Irish government was implemented, which also triggered the European Commission's disagreement with Apple. This was because when Apple brought its IP profits to Ireland via licensing agreements, the EU insisted Apple should be taxed at the already low Irish corporate tax rate of 12.5%. But Apple resorted to an old accounting trick, whose legality was challenged by the EU. Under a murky side agreement with Ireland, the vast majority of Apple's profits were remitted to its "head office"—otherwise known as AOI—which had no address anywhere, a kind of "virtual" global company that was not physically located in any country and was not subject to taxes anywhere, including Ireland and the USA. Apple responded to EU objections, arguing that the head office had legitimately earned profits that were tax exempt and, moreover, Ireland was a sovereign country that could make whatever tax arrangements it wished with Apple. The head office, since it did not have an Irish address, or any address, could hardly be taxed by Ireland.[55]

This was too much for the EU and the European Commission to accept, and anyway had not Lord Keynes and others declared decades earlier that the only reason to establish a company in a tax haven was to escape taxes. Well, it certainly seemed self-evident to everybody except Apple and other corporations that had been on tax holiday, and that is what the European Commission sniffed as well. Apple was simply engaging in what had been around for a while, transfer pricing—another term for tax evasion, and the EU wasn't going to take it any more:

> Transfer pricing refers in this context to the prices charged for commercial transactions between various parts of the same corporate group, in particular prices set for goods sold or services provided by one subsidiary of a corporate group to another subsidiary of that same group. The prices set for those transactions and the resulting amounts calculated on the basis of those prices contribute to increase the profits of one subsidiary and decrease the profits of the other subsidiary for tax purposes, and therefore contribute to determine the taxable basis of both entities. Transfer pricing thus also concerns profit allocation between different parts of the same corporate group.[56]

The head office, the European Commission concluded, was a ruse. It existed only on paper and was created for the sole purpose of tax evasion. Apple's argument that it paid low, almost nil taxes, in exchange for investing in and creating thousands of jobs in Ireland, was dismissed. The EU pointed out that AOI had no employees in its home office in Ireland—not to mention an address or actual premises that any real employees might actually have inhabited. The most that the head office had was a board of directors that met occasionally. The head office was a fraudulent device to minimize or avoid taxation by claiming it was not a tax resident anywhere, including Ireland. The European Commission concluded that the side arrangement between Apple and Ireland was void, and therefore Apple owed the EU some €13 billion in back taxes.[57]

The case made by the European Commission was based on revelations in 2013 stemming from US Senate public hearings and illustrated how Apple had successfully been able to evade corporate taxes. In 2011, Apple recorded profits of €16 billion through its home office in Ireland.

Under a ruling by the Irish authority only about €50 million of that was considered taxable in Ireland. That left a considerable sum of €15.95 billion untaxed. This meant that Apple paid less than €10 million in corporate taxes in Ireland in 2011, an effective rate of about 0.05% on its overall profits for the same year, a sum considerably less than the (already low) Irish statutory rate of 12.5%, which would have created a tax bill of €1.45 billion for 2011 alone.[58] In subsequent years, Apple's—and the home office's—profits climbed still higher, but because of the agreement between Apple and Ireland—taxable profits in Ireland did not rise. Apple's effective tax rate paid to Ireland actually decreased to 0.005% in 2014.

How did the EU counter this? It said that only Apple's subsidiary, ASI, which had an actual address in Ireland, had the capacity to generate income from Apple products, so only this subsidiary should have been able to record profits in Ireland.[59] An investigation by a US Senate subcommittee, led by Senators Carl Levin and John McCain, concluded much the same. Senators Levin and McCain used the term "unusual" in describing Apple's tactic of shifting substantial sums of money to offshore entities that were not declared tax residents of any jurisdiction. The memorandum they published explained further:

> In 1980, Apple created Apple Operations International, which acts as its primary offshore holding company but has not declared tax residency in any jurisdiction. Despite reporting net income of $30 billion over the four-year period 2009 to 2012, Apple Operations International paid no corporate income tax to any national government during that period.[60]

This was only the beginning of tax evasion, however. The Senate Memorandum also showed how Apple transferred economic rights to its IP through cost sharing agreements to two offshore affiliates in Ireland, as we already have seen. Here is how the Senate Subcommittee explained the labyrinth created by Apple:

> Apple Sales International buys Apple's finished products from a manufacturer in China, re-sells them at a substantial markup to other Apple affiliates, and retains the resulting profits. Over a four-year period from 2009 to 2012, this arrangement facilitated the shift of about $74 billion away from the United States to an offshore entity with allegedly no tax residency and which may have paid little or no income taxes to any national

> government on the vast bulk of those funds. Additionally … Apple makes use of multiple US tax loopholes to defer paying US taxes on $44 billion of offshore income, or more than $10 billion of offshore income per year. As a result, Apple has continued to build up its offshore cash holdings which now exceed $102 billion.[61]

The Senate Memorandum provided a graphic illustration of just how little Apple was paying in corporate taxes globally. In the years 2009–2011, pretax earnings were $38 billion, but the total paid in taxes was a miniscule $21 million, or a tax rate of 0.06%, a figure that is consistent with what we have observed above. The inevitable conclusion, which was reached by the Senate investigation, was that Ireland was providing a tax haven for Apple, helping it to "legally" shed almost all tax obligations.[62]

Some critics have called this cheating. Here is why. AOI is a holding company and is the ultimate owner of most of Apple's offshore entities. Coincidentally, Apple, Inc. directly owns 97% of AOI and holds the remaining shares indirectly. AOI was incorporated by Apple as early as 1980, though Apple, according to the Senate investigation, claimed it was unable to locate historical records explaining why it had incorporated in Ireland to begin with. What was known was that AOI shared a mailing address with several other Apple affiliates in Cork, Ireland, but AOI had no physical presence there or at any other address. Moreover, between 1980 and 2013, when the Senate conducted its investigation, AOI had no employees in Cork. In fact it had no employees anywhere. Yet AOI accounted for 30% of Apple's net revenues worldwide, despite having no address, or building, or employees. AOI also did not have a tax residency, or a tax home, which explains why, between 2009 and 2011, it paid no taxes at all. Notified in summer of 2016 that Apple was in arrears on its taxes to the EU by some €13 billion, CEO Tim Cook expressed astonishment and anger. After all, how could Apple or its subsidiaries owe taxes to Ireland when AOI was not a tax resident of Ireland? Easy to see why he is the CEO, isn't it? But not for the EU, which insisted that Ireland did not have the right to reach side agreements with Apple, Inc., or AOI to all but abolish any tax liability in Ireland. The EU was finally ready to litigate.[63]

But if the EU was willing to go to court to recoup corporate taxes from Apple, the USA meekly succumbed to the logic of CEO Tim Cook. The US administration even managed to defend Apple: how could the EU claim back taxes if Apple's AOI had no employees, no address and nothing tangible to sell in Ireland? Good question, right? But then how could it be that Apple also had no profits?

Though the USA was conveniently angry with the EU, there must have been other reasons as well. Indeed, it turns out there were. The USA was accepting statements made by Apple itself. The company had consistently reported compliance with a high tax rate in the USA, something around 26%. Not state taxes, because Apple, Inc., are registered in the state of Nevada, which has no state corporate tax. So the 26% reported by Apple was for federal taxes. The reality is that the company has probably paid more like 2 or 3% in federal taxes, despite its claims otherwise. Under current US tax laws, American corporations can defer paying taxes on foreign made profits until those sums are repatriated back to the USA. When Apple says it is paying 26% tax rates, it is declaring the rate it would likely pay should it bring its profits to the USA. But it can defer those taxes forever, or at least until Congress declares a tax holiday, as it did in 2005 when it agreed to tax corporations at a 5.25 tax rate on repatriated profits.[64]

Apple is not alone, as we have noted above. In late 2016, there were some $2.1 trillion in corporate profits in offshore tax-deferred accounts, a cash hoard that was held by 358 large US companies in 7622 subsidiaries. That means that the practice of tax deferral by parking vast sums of money abroad is widespread, a convenient dodge for US global corporations in their race to the bottom. Besides Apple, Cisco, Google, Microsoft, Oracle, and Pfizer, among others, keep large cash piles out of reach until they can get Congress to give them a pass or a tax holiday.[65]

Of the several trillions of dollars held abroad, thirty corporations hold about 67% of that cash. This means that even if the already discounted tax rate of 26%, which Apple claims to be paying in taxes, were collected on all corporations, the US Treasury would be about $520 billion richer, a sum that could both help alleviate the tax burden of many Americans, and also literally transform US education, or rebuild infrastructure, or promote the greening of America. Or even the *re-industrialization of America*. Again, it's communism (or rentier capitalism) for the rich and unfriendly capitalism for the rest of us, signifying another massive transfer of income and wealth from us to the super-rich.

The Great Tax Shift from the Rich to the Rest: Individual Income Taxes

The major shift over the last four decades, from the mid-1970s to 2016, has been to tilt the burden of taxation ever more to the "south" despite the cries of the rich and their assertions that they are paying too much in taxes. If you believe it is easy being rich, just think about the problems maintaining multiple residences around the world, paying off large veterinary bills, higher tuition for your children at private schools, and the selfish demands of the middle classes and working classes who demand higher taxes on millionaires and billionaires.

A glance at the top 400 families in the USA shows a shift in the membership of this exclusive club. But it also reveals that the super-rich—or those in this exclusive coterie—have actually reduced their income tax bill as a percentage of their total income. That is because Congress, which is beholden to the corporate elite, the 0.1%, has smiled at the good fortunes of the super-rich as long as benevolence comes the way of Capitol Hill.

The great tax shift began when Ronald Reagan was president, when he enjoyed a partnership with the Democrats in 1983. When the Republicans won the House in 1993, the shift accelerated, and soon was showing up in the official statistics. In 2003, the IRS reported returns for the 400 highest income Americans for the years 1992–2000, the years of the Clinton administration and the stock market bubble, disclosing that the minimum needed to make the list more than tripled, rising from $24.4 million to $86.6 million. The list of course had changed, only 21 taxpayers made the list every year—signifying the rise of some fortunes because of the hi-tech bubble.[66]

Still, even if a few names had changed, the top was rich indeed. The top 400 taxpayers in the year 2000 received 1.1% of all the income in America, more than double the 0.5% share of the top 400 in 1992. The average income of the group in 2000 was almost $174 million, nearly quadrupling the $46.8 million average in 1992. The rich, especially the super-rich, were getting even richer, and there seemed to be no limit. Yet the share of their income going to federal income taxes actually was shrinking. The top 400 paid an average of $38.6 million each in federal income taxes in 2000, some 22.2 cents on the dollar, down from the 26.4 cents on the dollar paid in 1992 and 29.9% in 1995, when it peaked. How did this compare nationally? The tax liability of the 400 was only notionally above the overall federal tax burden of 15.3 cents on each dollar of income. During the eight years of the Clinton administration, the income tax burden for the average American rose about 18%, but for the super-rich it actually fell 16% even as their incomes were rising spectacularly.[67]

So what made this possible? The answer is Congress, which in all its benevolence promoted a tax cut for the rich in 1997, though it was widely represented by Congress and the media as a tax cut for the middle classes. Among the tax cuts that year was a sharp reduction in the tax rate on long-term capital gains, which happened coincidentally to be the source of two-thirds of the incomes of the top 400—and much the same for the entire top 1%. The capital gains tax—levied on stocks, bonds, precious metals, and properties—was reduced from 29.19 to 21.19%.[68] Another law in 1997 featured an item that was good news for tax cheats, those who might otherwise have been on the 400 list had they reported their full income. Previously, the IRS had been able to find tax evaders whose reported income seemed too little to warrant their lifestyles. This had forced some to conceal their wealth, resorting to lavish lifestyles abroad, where they might be more difficult to detect. The new law specified that the IRS could no longer follow the trail, for example, if a middling income did not seem consistent with private jets and million dollar junkets and flashing trinkets. Congress had ruled that the IRS could no longer audit the rich just because of their lifestyles. This moved Lee Shepperd, a tax lawyer specialist who critiqued tax law for *Tax Notes*, to quip that the law "should be called the mobsters and drug dealers tax relief act of 1997."[69]

The super-rich still thought they deserved more, and Congress, ever pliant, agreed. After all, the rich were smarter, more creative, and job providers, and anyway weren't they still paying more than their fair share of income taxes? President George W. Bush thought so. He understood the problems of the rich, being a multi-millionaire himself. The first round of tax cuts in 2001 lowered the top 400's share of income going to taxes even further, slipping to about 21% of income, and then in the subsequent tax reduction of 2003, to 17.5 cents on the dollar, not much more than the average paid by all Americans as a percentage of their income. What had made this reduction possible? Yet another decline in capital gains taxes to about 15%, complementing the reduction of the highest marginal individual tax rate from 39.6 to 35%. In just a matter of a little more than a half-decade, the rich became richer than ever, primarily by reducing capital gains taxes on stocks, bonds, and property, where most of the assets of the rich were held. The Reagan years were profitable, the Clinton years lucrative, but the George W. Bush years were a real boon for the upper reaches of the wealthy in America.[70]

How the UK Super-Rich Evade Taxes

When the Coalition government under David Cameron came to office in 2010 in the UK, it shared much of the worldview that had characterized several decades of American policy makers: lower taxes on the rich so they would conceal less of their money, giving them an incentive to come clean by declaring more of their real earnings and leading to more revenue for government. This bit of snazzy Robin Hood logic might have fooled the rich themselves, maybe they believed their own rhetoric, but capping the top income tax rate at 45%, as the British did in 2013, did not convince the International Monetary Fund (IMF) that the British were doing the right thing. Or Danny Dorling, either, who countered that "the alternative to putting the young into debt was to tax the rich."[71] He advised much more than 45%. In fact the IMF advocated 60% as the optimum figure, anything above that would be a disincentive to growth, and an incentive to conceal income, and would also lead to a further shift of income toward capital gains, which are taxed much lower. But the rich think that 45% is outrageous, after all it is their money, why should they pay any taxes at all on what they earned, as one MP, Douglas Carswell, told *Guardian* journalist Owen Jones in an interview.[72]

But the UK did not have to wait for David Cameron to find a Prime Minister who idolized the rich: they had Margaret Thatcher decades before Cameron came to office. Under Thatcher wealth was glorified, while those who didn't have it quite obviously didn't deserve it: "I believe the person who is prepared to work hardest should get the greatest awards and keep them after tax, that we should back the workers and not the shirkers."[73]

Had Mrs. Thatcher really backed the workers, the UK might have turned out quite differently, but the shirking rich were about to receive unprecedented tax breaks. And for the first time in generations, the government threw as much money as it could in the direction of the wealthy elite, especially the men of the City. In Thatcher's first budget, the top bracket taxes of 83% on earned income and the 98% top bracket imposed on unearned income—capital gains—were reduced to 60%, while corporation taxes were slashed to 35%. Within a decade, in 1988, the chancellor at the time, Nigel Lawson, cut the top rate of earned income tax to 40%.[74]

Geoffrey Howe, who served as Foreign Secretary for much of the 1980s, thought this the right thing to do. He believed the tax structure had to be changed to provide incentives to business, though he was honest enough to admit that he did not know the impact that cutting taxes on the rich would have on everybody else, though it seemed self-evident this would increase inequality in Britain dramatically. But Howe was correct when he observed that chances the super-rich would make money had been dramatically improved.[75]

Reducing direct taxes on the rich meant revenues would have to be found somewhere else. "So they put up VAT, a tax on consumer goods," explains Owen Jones. "The poorer you are, the more of your income goes on VAT."[76] This was class war, unburdening the top 1%, and especially the top 0.1%, so they could make money, and paying for it by taxing those who could afford it least. Toward the end of the reign of the Tories, in 1996, the richest 10% of families with three children were more than £21,000 a year richer than when Thatcher came to power.[77] Income for each married couple in the top decile boomed upward some 65%: their taxes fell from over a half of their income to just over a third.[78] For almost everybody else, the bottom 90%, taxes on average went from 31.1% of their income in 1979 to 37.2% by the end of 1996. The real income of the poorest tenth in Britain virtually collapsed, declining 20% after housing costs.[79]

The top income tax rate was raised to 50% in 2010, but when the Coalition government of David Cameron came to power, this was apparently too much to tolerate. Instead of raising taxes on the rich in order to bring the budget into balance, as virtually all rich countries had done—with the exception of the USA, which had also lowered the highest income tax rate when George Bush was president—Cameron cut top income tax rates to 45%. The reason? The rich would conceal less of their wealth and more taxes would be collected. Cameron could not understand why the top 1% should be taxed to give benefits to the poor anyway. The cure for all those welfare cheats was to cut their benefits: that was sure to create an incentive to work. This then was Cameron's solution for all those shirkers: reduce benefits for the poorer sections of society so the rich could take more, a lot more. The cost of maintaining the rich meant less for everybody else, a lot less. As Danny Dorling put it: "When the 1% takes more there is less for the rest. In the UK the cuts required to preserve the position and wealth of the 1% are taking £19 billion a year out of the economy. The alternative to many of the cuts is to tax the 1% more, along with a few others at the top of society, at the same rate as the 1% are taxed in more equitable countries."[80]

But we have already seen that Cameron did precisely the opposite, he lowered the top marginal income tax rate to 45%. This made him even more of a miser than Margaret Thatcher. In the early 1980s, when she introduced a mild form of austerity, she raised 50p for every 50p that she cut in government spending. Cameron did quite the opposite, raising 17p for every 83p that Chancellor George Osborne cut, and what he did raise was mostly through VAT, a highly regressive tax that made the poor even poorer.

By contrast, in countries that are much more equal, and where states do not shift risk away from the elite rich and toward everybody else, top tax rates were well above what Cameron had instituted in the UK: 75% in France, 57% in Sweden, 55% in Denmark, 52% in Spain, and 50% in Austria, Belgium, Japan, and the Netherlands. And for those countries at 50%, the top rate kicked in somewhat below the sum of £50,000.[81] Again, Britain was not so palatable if you were not born into privilege: the lower 45% top income tax rate only was applied when £150,000 was reached.

To pay for the reduced top tax rate on the 1%, and the high-income threshold, Cameron had to find money somewhere. He did: it came from those who could afford it least. Of the £19 billion cut from public spending, a little less than a quarter came from incapacity benefit for the disabled, a sum that had just barely kept many out of poverty. Another quarter reflected cuts in tax credits that had formerly kept many working class families out of poverty. Another half billion pounds were removed from housing benefit, making the poor even poorer.[82] Simultaneously, while the rich continued to live high on the hog, as wealth again concentrated at the top, English hospitals were reporting a rise in cases of malnutrition, up from 3161 in 2008–2009 to 5499 in 2012–2013. The link between reduced benefits and the rise of hunger was manifest, but the super-rich saw it otherwise. Some blamed the poor for being hungry, as if poverty was the result of shirkers who enjoyed being deprived.[83] Implicit in this opinion was that the poor did not deserve to eat.

The Super-Rich Should Not Pay Taxes on Their Money!

Aside from the smugness of the 1% (and especially the 0.1%), there are good reasons not only to raise taxes on the super-rich, but also to tax them at a rate above 45%. That is because anything lower has only led to rent-seeking—extracting wealth from the real economy, not to growth in GDP or the economy overall, in both the UK and the USA. This seems to contradict the logic of neoliberalism. In fact, based on exhaustive data, Emmanuel Saez and Thomas Piketty have showed that the incentive for rent-seeking rises as top tax rates are cut. But they found something else even more disconcerting: increases in top 1% incomes come at the expense of the 99%! As Saez and Piketty discovered, top-rate cuts stimulated rent-seeking among the super-rich, but did not contribute to "*overall economic growth.*" Their data confirmed what we all intuitively know. There has been no positive correlation between cuts in top tax rates and real GDP-per-capita growth since the 1970s. The USA and the UK both made large cuts in top income tax rates—both were in the 70% range in the 1970s, falling below 40% during the Reagan and Thatcher years, and staying low thereafter—but neither country grew significantly faster than Germany and Denmark which did not reduce top income tax rates below 50% for Germany and 60% for Denmark.[84] What did Piketty and Saez advise as the optimal top income tax rate? Something like 80%! Or a return to the past, when the income tax rates in the 1970s in the USA and UK actually seemed to work best for almost all of us—all except the 1%.

The super-rich have become rich not because they are gifted but because they are able to reduce taxes on themselves (as well as to extract rents), which means that taxes rise for everybody else. That is simple math, not false theory, and it is the result mostly of policy. The wealth of the super-rich as a group has doubled over the last four or five decades (since about 1975), and a primary reason is their taxes have been lowered or simply evaded. Both top income tax and capital gains taxes in the USA and the UK have moved south, and the chief beneficiaries have been the super-rich: the lower the top tax bracket, and the higher the income threshold—where the top bracket kicks in—the greater the benefit for the 1% and even more so for the 0.1%.

We should not presume that the ultra wealthy feel shame when they evade paying taxes. They really believe the capital they have is "earned," the result of greater ability, not the shedding of public obligation. The rich think it obvious that the poor envy them, but lack the ability of their affluent countrymen. Matthew Sinclair of the Tax Payers Alliance, a British think tank, certainly thinks so, and said as much in 2013:

> The idea that capital income is 'unearned' is beneath contempt. You earn the returns on investment by working, delaying gratification and saving. The argument that an inheritance is unearned (so that we can take what we like in Inheritance Tax) is just as weak: someone earned the money.[85]

According to Roman Krznaric, between 1 and 2% of people are not naturally empathic.[86] Apparently, Matthew Sinclair is one of those lacking empathy. Danny Dorling has expanded on the same point:

> This small group find it enormously difficult to understand how other people feel or to appreciate a different point of view. ... It is hard to become rich if you are not primarily looking out for yourself. Those who amass fortunes manage to do so partly because they don't like sharing and see themselves as something special, as more careful with money, as being worth more than others.[87]

Sharing is for others, and is anyway a kind of weakness, for which the strong and the deserving have no use. The implication is that the rich and the super-rich have had enough of sharing with the croppers beneath them.

Tax Relief for the Super-Rich? Raise Taxes on Everybody Else

Government needs revenues and they come primarily from taxes. The solution of the super-rich is to cut government spending, and lower taxes on them. Their argument is that government spends too much on the poor anyway, so why not reduce or even eliminate welfare programs providing government assistance to the clods? Shouldn't the poor do more to help themselves anyway? And wasn't this what Bill Clinton did when he eliminated cash grants for poor single mothers with children in 1996? In the years that followed, the US economy thrived, and the unemployment rolls declined. Reducing welfare is good for the poor, they then have to work instead of relying on the dole, which the rich argue is supported by their taxes. And why should the rich pay for student tuition for the middling sorts when students could borrow under various loan programs—often provided by the super-rich?

The argument can be inverted. The history of taxation on individuals has shown that the rich elite has managed to shed the burden of taxes quite well, in both the USA and the UK. In the USA, for example, the top income tax bracket under President Obama rose to 39.6%, a slight elevation from the George W. Bush era, but significantly lower than the period between 1933 and the late 1980s under President Reagan. During the 1950s under Dwight Eisenhower, the highest marginal tax rate actually reached 91%, and Eisenhower even preached against the greed of the rich as justification for taxing them at that rate. We know that the top marginal rate in Britain stands at 45% in 2018, slightly higher than in the USA, but significantly lower than the pre-Thatcher era when it was more than 70%.

But when we consider what the rich pay in capital gains taxes and factor that into the tax bill on the 1%, we find that this elite, and especially the top 0.1%, have managed to reduce their personal tax rates to the lowest point since the 1920s. Paul Krugman, relying on data from *The Economic Report of the President*, has shown that the top 0.1% of taxpayers in the USA have been able to reduce their tax bill, combining income and capital gains taxes, from slightly over 50% in 1960 to slightly below 30% in 2010.[88] And since we know that the sums of money held by the 0.1% abroad in tax havens have escalated, we can be confident that the real personal tax on the rich is much lower: they have the means to conceal their wealth because much of it does not come from income, which is easier for the IRS to trace. And while the tax bill for the super-rich has declined, even for what we can measure, it has actually gone up for the middle 20% of the American population, from about 14% of all income in 1960 to 20% in 2010.[89]

It didn't used to be this way. In 1913, following the adoption of the Sixteenth Amendment, the federal government in the USA began taxing incomes, gifts and estates. But these taxes came with an explicit promise: the basic means of sustaining life for the majority would not be taxed, the tax regime applied only to the economic elite. Those with surplus incomes would bear the burden of taxation. Originally, the idea was to tax capital more heavily than income from wages, it was considered morally offensive to take more money earned by hard work than money made by clipping coupons, or capital gains such as dividends and equities in the stock market. The levy of taxes to pay for World War I was called a "conscription" of money to pay for the conscription of soldiers into the army, both were considered necessary and fair.[90]

Two principles were applied. The first was that taxes should be based on the ability to pay. And the second was that paying taxes based on capital gains, and wealth, as opposed to income, was actually a patriotic act and should be considered a moral as well as a legal obligation. The estate tax and the gift tax, which applied to wealth, were expanded, while the income tax was applied to a larger, but still minute fraction of Americans.

A little more than a generation later, several decades after the Second World War, the promise that only surplus incomes would be taxed was abandoned. Though only a minority of people were taxed during World War II, the war helped change the political understanding of what could be taxed, and by how much. Politicians understood the immense power, and the expanding uses of tax monies. When the war ended, Democrats, supported by many Republicans, expanded the income tax until it applied to most Americans and to most of what they earned. The new tax-based revenues were used to pay for the Korean conflict, and to build-up the military, but also to support education, build highways and finance advances in technology.[91]

During the fifties and sixties, Congress did nothing as inflation eroded the value of exemptions for taxpayers, who now found themselves in higher brackets, which meant paying higher shares of their income in taxes. As this system became less tenable by the 1970s, tax shelters began to flourish. No longer just the province of the rich, they were now marketed to doctors, dentists, attorneys and many others, proving to be more a drag on the economy overall rather than a benefit. Meanwhile inflation, combined with an end to growth in real wages beginning in 1973, continued to push people into higher income tax brackets even as their take-home pay was stagnating.

Throughout the decade of the 1970s, and into the new century, government continued to grow, fueled by military spending on the war in Vietnam, increased local and state expenditures on public education, professionalization of police departments, and welfare spending on the poor and those unable or unwilling to work. Simultaneously, as government obligations increased, both domestically and internationally, Washington explicitly embraced a policy allowing the richest Americans to pay a smaller percentage of their income in taxes, to defer more of their taxes, and to report a growing part of their income as capital gains, which was taxed at a much lower rate. At the same time Congress began to collect more taxes from the middle classes to compensate what was lost from the higher tax rates where the 1% lived.

The Democrats were not unwilling collaborators in the tax sea change. In 1983, when they controlled Congress, they voted to raise Social Security taxes. Where it had been a pay-as-you-go system, taxpayers were now required to pay 50% more than the retirement and disability program's immediate costs. The purpose of this was to build a trust fund that would pay benefits for more than three decades into the future.[92]

But one cannot surmise from this that tax monies were locked away in a trust fund that would finance Social Security benefits. On the contrary, that is not how the super-rich think. Nor was it the policy of those on Capitol Hill, many of whom owed their office to the 1%, and even more so to the 0.1%. Instead, the new Social Security payroll tax monies were spent to finance tax cuts for the elite super-rich, a process that began in 1981.

A decade and a half later, in 1997, with Republicans controlling Congress, taxation of the middle classes was expanded when the income tax system was modified again. Though the changes were hardly reported in the media, they represented a substantial shift in the tax burden, away from the super-rich and toward everybody else. Then the initial Bush tax cuts in 2001, as we have seen, represented a giant subsidy of the 1% by the middle and upper middle classes, especially for the upper tenth of 1%, the richest 130,000 taxpayers in the USA. This was exactly the reverse of how the tax cuts were represented, as a gift to middling taxpayers, the result of so-called trickle down economics. By any metric this was false. According to Center on Budget and Policy Priorities' (CBPP) figures, based on Congressional Budget Office (CBO) estimates, the Bush tax cuts were a major driver of federal deficits—a legacy that is likely to continue for two decades or more because 82% of the Bush tax cuts were made permanent in 2010, when they were renewed by Congress.[93]

The estimates of the CBPP and the CBO actually understated the real cost to the middle and upper middle class taxpayers. That is partly because of the (additional) cost of the wars in Afghanistan and Iraq, for the years 2001–2008, at $673 billion. Never mind that the war in Iraq was a war of choice, and that it also was a war declared by the corporate super-rich, some of whom were direct beneficiaries. But this figure, which is itself a conservative estimation, omits mention of how the war was financed. Certainly not by the super-rich: they had a tax gift thanks to the Bush administration. If one adds the total deficit caused by the Bush tax gifts for the years 2001–2008, the sum comes to $1.955 trillion. Part of that is for the so-called relief for the middling taxpayers. But the top 1% took fully 30% of the tax relief and that means they were taxed almost $600 billion less than they would have been, had George Bush not reduced their tax obligation. That means also that for the year 2009, when the part of the Bush tax cuts in the federal deficit was $371 billion, the 1% accounted for more than $110 billion, or 30%, of that deficit.[94]

But if you want a more accurate accounting of what the ultra rich and their acolytes are costing the USA, then you have to add the following costs: the war in Iraq, a war of choice, which continues to have an overhang cost of $150–$200 billion per year through 2019; the economic recovery measures taken after the Great Recession of 2008, largely caused by greedy banks and their penchant for gambling in derivatives, at a cost minimally of several trillions of dollars, mostly in 2009–2010; and the Great Recession itself, to a great extent caused by bank deregulation in 1999 and the sub-prime loan fiasco—also the instruments and policies of the 0.1%—creating federal budget deficits since that have consistently been around 25% of the total budget because of shortfalls in the economy and in revenues. In sum, the super-rich are expensive, their privileges cost the majority of us in treasure, and the costs are enduring. When one simply adds the sums presented here, the conclusion is staggering. The super-rich do not add to our wealth, they extract it as best they can, often with the complicity of the government, compounded always by the unfair tax system.

Inheritance and Wealth Taxes: How the Super-Rich Became Shirkers

In Britain, what historically had made the super-rich safe and more secure was simply that they were less wealthy. Inheritance tax was low a century ago, but was introduced by Parliament, itself composed of the rich, to help protect the wealth of the nation, a large part of which belonged to MPs in Parliament.

Inheritance taxes were simply unavoidable, they were needed to help pay government war debts, which, as Danny Dorling reminds us, were because of wars started by the ultra-wealthy. “The First World War began as an argument within an aristocracy and European royal family that simply could not imagine its consequences.”[95] One could extend the illustrations almost indefinitely. The American intervention in Vietnam was largely a quarrel between factions of the super-rich over how much to extend US hegemony. The second war in Iraq was a conflict of choice by the corporate elite nervous about the future of oil supplies and revenues. The result in both cases was massive debt, but much of this debt, as we have seen, fell on the shoulders of the middle classes, at roughly the same time as the collapse of the dot.com bubble in 2002, followed a half-decade later by the Great Recession. The super-rich prefer that others pay for the wars they start.

In Britain, back in 1894, Death Duties had a maximum rate of 8%. In 1914, with the commencement of WW I, they became Estate Duty, which had a maximum rate of 20%, rising to 40% in 1939 and 80% in 1949. The reason for the high figure in 1949 was that in 1945 the first government—perhaps in British history—not consisting of rich men came to power. But the precedent had been established. Death Duties became Capital Transfer Tax in 1975, with a maximum rate of 75%, falling to 60% in 1984. In 1985, it was renamed again, and became more prosaically known as the Inheritance Tax. In 1988 the Inheritance Tax was capped at 40%, where it stands today.[96]

So why were inheritance taxes reduced after 1970? Because the super-rich gained increasing control over political parties, and because they could afford to employ teams of lobbyists who had influence in the centers of power. In the USA and the UK, the super-rich paid a growing percentage of their money to protect, well, their money. Their assets were growing well into the 90s, but so was their ability to reduce their tax bill.

In the 1980s, income taxes were reduced dramatically in the USA. The UK, always admiring its American cousin, followed suit. We know the result: unprecedented income and wealth inequality, and then the Great Recession. Many economists in the USA and the UK did not agree that there was any correlation between inequality and the collapse, and thought there was even less connection between reduced tax bills on corporations and the super-rich, and inequality. But at least one country,

Ireland, where the crash in 2008 was devastating, believed that the reckless behavior of the 1% had led directly to the disaster of the Great Recession. In just five years, between 1995 and 2000, the 1% doubled their share of the national income. No doubt they thought they deserved it.[97]

Many others among the Irish did not agree. In 2013, a wealth tax was proposed that was to be levied on everybody living in Ireland with assets greater than €1 million. Into 2014 the Irish had not levied the wealth tax, but the Irish government did increase the capital gains tax, up to 33% maximum in 2012, and a domicile levy of €200,000 on anybody with property whose worth was greater than €5 million.[98]

The original suggestion in Ireland was that the 1% should be subject to an annual wealth tax rate equal to 0.6% of their wealth. Most developed countries currently levy taxes on income—including capital gains. By comparison, less than 1% is levied directly on wealth across the Organization for Economic Cooperation and Development (OECD), although tax on interest accrued is a minor wealth tax in current use.[99] However, during 2013, a wealth tax that would have been European-wide was proposed, though it was not implemented.[100] The German government, in 2014, subsequently proposed that debtor countries like Ireland should impose a wealth tax more firmly, an emergency capital levy as the Germans put it in a monthly report.[101]

A quarter century earlier, in 1990, half of all OECD countries had a net wealth tax, but by 2000, only a decade later, that number had declined to a third of OECD nations, and since then the number has fallen even further: Finland, Iceland, Luxembourg, Spain, and Sweden, all abandoned their wealth taxes after 2006. However, given the fiscal emergencies that occurred in 2007 and afterward, Iceland, Ireland, and Spain, decided to reintroduce wealth taxes to cope with their financial emergencies.[102] The results demonstrated just how significant an impact wealth taxes could have on inequality (and economic growth) when such a tax is imposed. In Iceland, for example, a wealth tax of 1.5% on net assets exceeding 100 million kroner ($950,000) for married couples was adopted in 2010 for four years. As a result, the disposable income of the 1% virtually collapsed in one year, dropping from 20 to 10% of all income, but by 2014 Iceland's growth was rising by 5% GDP annually.[103]

Spain reintroduced a wealth tax in 2012, levied between 0.2 and 2.5% of global net income for residents. By 2015 the Spanish economy was growing fairly robustly, reaching 3.2 GDP growth that year.[104] The conclusion? Wealth could be taxed without hurting economic growth overall. In a word, wealth taxes were fair, helped reduce inequality, and had a positive impact on GDP.

According to economists Thomas Piketty and Anthony Emmanuel Saez, intermittently levying a wealth tax of 1% on wealth exceeding $20 million would make the US economy both more equitable and more efficient. In other words, more equality would produce more demand, more spending, and ultimately more jobs. They concluded that for the year 2012 a wealth tax of 1% would have raised $80 billion; over a decade it would raise more than $1 trillion.[105]

The very mention of a wealth tax, or an inheritance tax, makes the ultra wealthy tremble with fear. Just hint at a mansion tax—as Ed Miliband, the erstwhile head of the Labor Party, did—and the 1% go into shock: how will they pay for the butler and the driver? Yet, as we learn from Skandia, a global wealth management business, many of the very richest, the multi-millionaires, inherited their wealth. In a survey conducted in 2012, based on 1503 of their super-rich clients, Skandia found that 436 lived in the UK, of whom 94% were British. Despite their extreme wealth, more than 20% said they were no wealthier than their parents and 31% said they had become millionaires before they reached thirty. Of those who had started their own businesses, the majority had done so before they were twenty-five, mostly with the help of their parents.[106] As we have seen repeatedly, the rich and the super-rich often do not get rich through their own efforts, but once they have acquired their wealth they are very adept at defending and preserving it.[107]

So much so that the super-rich in both America and Britain now behave like emergent aristocracies. The new barons do not profit from land—at least not in the old ways—nor from coal nor railways nor even steel mills, over which their predecessors had once held monopolies, but rather from new kinds of wealth, often new kinds of monopolies or results of rent-seeking. These include inheriting copyrights or shares in drug patents or pharmaceutical firms.[108]

But there are other ways of protecting privileges and assets, as Jairo Lugo-Ocando has demonstrated. "Many keep their fortunes by simply avoiding paying taxes, using loopholes created by legislators who are re-elected with that same money they help to evade. In reality, most wealth in the world is the product of inequality and it stays in the same hands thanks to the systems that reinforce that inequality."[109]

Lugo-Ocando's larger point is that much of the wealth of the super-rich in the UK belongs to families whose original treasure can be traced back to slavery or violence, while more recent arrivals come from countries where much of the wealth was illicit at best, based on violence, insider access, or theft.[110]

It may be true that the target of taxation has moved away from inheritance, away from "taxing the dead."[111] Inheritance tax is relatively easy to avoid because the rich can transfer a large amount of their wealth while they are still alive, especially if they are able to transfer it more than seven years in advance of their death. But then there is the danger that nobody knows when he will die. Alternatively, there is always the option of concealing wealth abroad.

In the early 1990s there was a possibility that Inheritance Taxes (IHT) in the UK would be entirely abolished. In October of 1991, the Prime Minister, John Major, even proposed the abolition of IHT at a Conservative Party Conference, though he did not then take action. In July 1995, however, at Prime Minister's Questions, Major was challenged by Tony Blair on this question. Major reaffirmed that he wished to abolish IHT and capital gains taxes, but only when it was "appropriate." Apparently the appropriate moment had not yet arrived, though the Tories did manage to raise the threshold, the point at which the estate tax would begin.[112]

Labor governed for more than a decade between 1997 and 2010. That stopped the campaign for abolition, though Labor did not seek to raise the IHT either. In July 2007, however, the campaign to abolish IHT was resumed by the Institute of Directors, the flagship organization representing corporations and entrepreneurs of Britain, which published a research paper advocating the total abolition of IHT because it hindered economic growth:

> IHT … taxes all wealth, even if it represents income or gains that have already been taxed. And a great deal of wealth will have been taxed already, at the time when it was generated by previous owners or by the present owner. The fact that IHT taxes all wealth means that it is a significant brake on the accumulation of private wealth.[113]

This was slightly disingenuous, IHT does not tax all wealth, so it could hardly be a double tax. Moreover, wealth can be put into trust in the UK, which means that it ceases to belong to the grantor and belongs to the trustee. The tax break is explicit, the valuation of the trust is established at the death of the grantor, not the date the trust is created. That means the beneficiary of the trust will not be liable to pay taxes on the cost basis—the original purchase price—of the assets inherited, only on the value of the assets at the point of inheritance or the time of death of the grantor. The prior appreciation of the assets is not taxed. But the Directors' report also ignores the other dodges: namely, the offshoring of assets, which can escape taxation entirely, and the 50–100% exemption on inherited business property—depending on the kind of business asset(s) inherited.

Chancellor Osborne was especially sympathetic to the problems of the rich, and so he worked on future tax planning for them by lowering inheritance taxes. Currently the threshold is £325,000 for an individual and twice that for a couple, before inheritance tax liability begins. But in 2020 the threshold will move up, an estate valued up to £500,000 for an individual and £1 million for a couple will incur no inheritance or estate tax. Beyond these thresholds, IHT stands at 40%, not counting the exemptions mentioned above.

In the tax year 2013–2014 the inheritance tax raised £3.4 billion, and was forecast to raise £4.2 billion in 2015–2016. It was estimated also that tax was paid on 28,000 estates in 2013–2014, representing 4.9% of all deaths. Taxes raised in 2013–2014 were a significant amount of money, but consider what the impact of the new threshold—£1 million—will be when it begins in 2020. The Conservative Opposition had proposed the £1 million inheritance tax threshold back in 2008–2009, which, at the time was estimated to cost Treasury £3.1 billion. When you add up all the dodges, you begin to get the thinking of the Tories. Many continue to believe that IHT should be abolished altogether.[114] For British Conservatives and the 1%, taxes are regarded more than ever as a voluntary sort of thing, wasteful at best, while relief for the growing legions of the near poor is being slashed as the Coalition government preaches from above about the indolence of the undeserving.

The campaign for abolition of estate or inheritance taxes may have slowed in Britain, but it has accelerated in the USA. Republicans, energized by the quixotic Donald Trump, have tried to tell the American public that enriching the rich further by abolishing taxes on their estates, will be a good thing for everybody. Especially for the super-rich, of course, who would not have to conceal so much wealth or hire so many attorneys to create tax-avoiding trusts.

In the USA, inheritance taxes or death duties were levied in the nineteenth century to help pay for wars and to add needed government revenues. An estate tax levied in 1916 was mostly about raising revenues, not redistribution. It did not intend to redress the concentration of wealth that had already been notable prior to World War I. The idea of redistribution fell to Franklin Delano Roosevelt, who addressed death duties head on: "The transmission from generation to generation of vast fortunes by will, inheritance or gift is not consistent with the ideals and sentiments of the American people." This was an understatement at best. Whatever Roosevelt's intention to make Americans more equal, and to raise inheritance taxes, the wealthiest 1%, and especially the wealthiest 0.1%, managed to minimize their inheritance tax liabilities. So much so, that generations later Gary Cohn, Donald Trump's chief economic advisor, uttered words quite different than Roosevelt's advisements, pointing out that "only morons pay the estate tax."[115] Since we assume that there were and are few rich morons, we can conclude that the super-rich have rarely if ever paid estate taxes.

But in that case why try to abolish them? Seems like an honest question, doesn't it? Well, Paul Ryan has argued, abolishing death duties would create jobs. And Trump has trumpeted that abolishing the estate tax would save millions of small companies and hard-working farmers from utter ruin. Somehow, he managed to add, making the rich even richer would also make the USA much more competitive. And Representative Kevin Brady has echoed Trump by claiming that estate tax relief would help untold numbers of family businesses, including those run by minorities and women.[116]

From these nuggets we might conclude that tax relief for the ultra rich is for the benefit of all those shirkers beneath the 1%. But not according to the Center for Budget and Policy Priorities, which argues that the super-rich have already received relief. A lot of relief. In fact, by 2017 the inheritance tax had already been substantially whittled down from previous levels of taxation. In 2001, with George W. Bush in the White House, estate taxes applied to inheritances above $650,000. But following changes in 2001, the exemption rose to $5.49 million for an individual and that figure doubled for a couple to $10.98 million.[117]

But even that is not enough relief for the super-rich, they want to keep every penny in the family in perpetuity. They argue for abolition of all estate duties, as do Ryan and Trump, because the inheritance tax is a "double tax." And unfair too, it penalizes a bloke for dying.

In fact, more than half of the biggest estates consist mostly of capital gains on stocks that have never been taxed because they have never been sold, it takes a sale to trigger the tax. Moreover, the current estate tax exempts the first $10.98 million from taxation, so the actual tax rate averages out to 17%, considerably below the top statutory rate of 40%.[118]

Does the estate tax cause great suffering for small businesses, minorities, and women? Only two out of every thousand American who die owe any estate taxes. Only the wealthiest 0.2 Americans pay any estate taxes. This translates as only eighty small businesses and farms that will pay any estate taxes in 2017. That means that small businesses, including those run by minorities and women are virtually unaffected by inheritance taxes. Estates that do owe taxes pay on average only a sixth of their value, and much of that is on capital gains that were never taxed, as we know. But even this overstates the case. There remain loopholes that the super-rich are good at squeezing through, such as (perpetual) trusts that savvy lawyers use to help them avoid taxes should they find themselves above the exemption.

Finally, what about jobs? It is very likely that abolishing the estate tax won't empty the food stamp rolls. That is because there is no guarantee there will be more saving, or that less money will be spent on imports. What is certain, according to the Joint Committee on Taxation, is that the government would be deprived of some $269 billion over a decade if the estate tax is abolished.[119]

But all this has become quite beside the point. The Tax Cuts and Jobs Act doubles the exemption on estate taxes. And in 2024, the new law establishes that estate taxes, or "Death Duties," will end altogether, expending inequality to new and unprecedented heights.

Conclusion

Taxes are not the entire explanation for the maldistribution of wealth in the UK and the USA. But the coincidence between shifting tax burdens south and the low growth of GDP is neither accidental nor negligible. And this should not be a surprise. Vast inequality means the concentration of wealth in the hands of a diminishing group of the privileged, which has spent considerable effort evading taxes on that wealth. For everybody else this has meant less revenue for everything from education to infrastructure, from job creation to investment in renewable energy. Tax inequity is not just unfair, it destroys economic growth, robbing many people of their futures. Moreover, it rewards the super-rich, who need tax breaks least. And it vastly shifts income toward those who need it least.

Tax inequity also means that those reaping the benefits from tax shedding will be disposed to use part of their gains to lobby for even more tax breaks. Or more tax avoidance. They will be able to use political muscle to prevent reform. They will be able to preserve tax havens. They will resist levying taxes on corporate profits where they are earned. They will avoid the banning of tax inversions. They will stymie efforts to levy wealth taxes, even though this is one of the best ways to combat inequality, and to restore social equality, social peace, and ultimately democratic institutions. If social equity is to be restored, the long-standing shift of the tax burden away from the super-rich and toward everybody else will have to be reversed. No income should be privileged as capital gains taxes, inheritance taxes should be substantially raised, wealth taxes should be imposed, there should be no tax holidays, and corporate taxes should not be deferred until they can be diminished or abolished.

In a press release filed back in 2014, Oxfam GB noted that Britain in the twenty-first century was a deeply divided nation because the people at the very top had never had it better, while millions of families were struggling just to survive. As growing numbers of Britons were showing up at food banks run by charities, "the highest earners in the UK have had the biggest tax cuts of any country in the world."[120] To be sure, as Oxfam was quick to note, some of the inequality gap was because low paid workers had seen their wages stagnate for decades, while the pay and bonuses of the super-rich had ballooned.[121] But, as Oxfam added, tax inequities ranked high as one of the reasons for growing inequality. By Oxfam estimates, tax evasion, by companies and individuals, was costing the UK economy about £35 billion every year. Of that amount, according to Oxfam, at least £5.2 billion a year was being evaded by elite rich individuals hiding wealth in tax havens.[122]

The implication is clear: inadequate or low taxation, and successful tax evasion, have contributed significantly to increased and dangerous levels of social inequality, and this is true for both the USA and the UK. In the USA, using data for 2010, Edward Nathan Wolff found that the bottom 40% of households were unable to get out of debt, with debts averaging $14,000 non-home wealth per household. By comparison the middle 20% had wealth averaging only $12,200 per household—a full quarter less than in 1983. The next 20% had $100,700 per household; and the top 20% $1.7 million each on average, almost double what this group had in 1983 in real terms. No matter the measurement used, the bottom half of Americans were essentially drowning in debt, with negligible or negative wealth.[123]

Britain has been much the same, no matter the metric. In 2012 the top tenth wealthiest people in the UK were almost 500 times richer than the bottom tenth. But in the top tenth the richest 1% had an increasing share: the very richest were moving away from the merely wealthy.[124] Oxfam's "A Tale of Two Britains," provided the illustration. It found that the richest five households in Britain had more money than the bottom 12.6 million people—almost the same as the number of people living below the poverty line in the UK. Oxfam's advice to the Coalition government run by Cameron was to start raising revenues from those who could afford it, "by clamping down on companies and individuals who avoid paying their fair share of tax" instead of cutting the benefits of those at the margins or in the depths of poverty.[125]

Notes

1. Fran Abrams and Anthony Bevins, "Murdoch's Courtship of Blair Finally Pays Off," *Independent*, February 11, 1998.
2. *Economist*, "Rupert Laid Bare," March 18, 1999, www.economist.com/node/319862.
3. Warren Buffett, "Stop Coddling the Super-Rich," *New York Times*, August 14, 2011.
4. David Cay Johnston, *Perfectly Legal: The Covert Campaign to Rig Our Tax System to Benefit the Super Rich and Cheat Everybody Else* (New York: Penguin, 2003), 12.
5. Danny Dorling, *Inequality and the 1 Percent* (London: Verso, 2014), 20.
6. Tax Policy Center, "Briefing Book" (Washington, DC: Urban Institute and Brookings Institution, 2016), online at http://www.taxpolicycenter.org/briefing-book/what-are-sources-revenue-federal-government-0.
7. Nancy Fraser, *Fortunes of Feminism: From State-Managed Capitalism to Neoliberal Crisis* (London: Verso, 2013), 218.
8. Johnston, *Perfectly Legal*, 13.
9. Ibid., 14.
10. Ibid.
11. Citizens for Tax Justice, News Release, "New Report Finds 315 Fortune 500 Companies Used 'Stock Option Loophole' to Collectively Avoid

$64.5 Billion in State and Federal Taxes," June 9, 2016; for the full report, see online at http://ctj.org/ctjreports/2016/06/fortune_500_corporations_used_stock_option_loophole_to_avoid_646_billion_over_the_past_five_years.php.

12. Ibid.
13. Ibid.
14. Kimberly A. Clausing, "The Effect of Profit Shifting on the Corporate Tax Base in the United States and Beyond," *National Tax Journal* 69, no. 4 (December 2016): 905, https://doi.org/10.17310/ntj.2016.4.09. Gabriel Zucman concludes that corporate tax evasion actually is closer to $140 billion annually in the USA.
15. Oxfam America, *Broken at the Top: How America's Dysfunctional Tax System Costs Billions in Corporate Tax Dodging* (Boston, MA: Oxfam America, April 14, 2016), 3–4, online at https://www.oxfamamerica.org/static/media/files/Broken_at_the_Top_FINAL_EMBARGOED_4.12.2016.pdf.
16. Robert McIntyre, *Offshore Shell Games, 2015: The Use of Offshore Tax Havens by Fortune 500 Companies* (Washington, DC: Citizens For Tax Justice, October 2015), 5, online at http://ctj.org/ctjreports/2015/10/offshore_shell_games_2015.php#.VuMbX-ZXo8I.
17. Francis Weyzig, *Still Broken: Governments Must Do More to Fix the International Corporate Tax System* (Boston, MA: Oxfam America, November 2015), http://www.oxfamamerica.org/static/media/files/still-broken-corporate-tax-101115-embargo-en.pdf.
18. Ibid.
19. Gabriel Zucman, "Taxing Across Borders: Tracking Personal Wealth and Corporate Profits," *Journal of Economic Perspectives* 28, no. 4 (Fall 2014): 121–48, online at gabriel-zucman.eu/files/Zucman2014JEP.pdf.
20. *Broken at the Top*, 1.
21. Ibid., 2.
22. Ibid.
23. Ibid., 7.
24. Robert S. McIntyre, Matthew Gardner, and Richard Phillips, *The Sorry State of Corporate Taxes* (Washington, DC: Citizens for Tax Justice, Institute on Taxation and Economic Policy, February 2014), http://www.ctj.org/corporatetaxdodgers/sorrystateofcorptaxes.pdf.
25. *Broken at the Top*, 6–7.
26. Clausing, "The Effect of Profit Shifting," 905.
27. *Broken at the Top*, 3.
28. Ibid., 7.
29. Robert McIntyre, Richard Phillips, and Phineas Baxandall, *Offshore Shell Games 2015: The Use of Offshore Tax Havens by Fortune 500 Companies*

(Washington, DC: Citizens for Tax Justice, October 2015), 1–3, 7–10, online at http://ctj.org/pdf/offshoreshell2015.pdf; and *Broken at the Top*, 8.
30. US Government Accountability Office, *Cayman Islands: Business and Tax Advantages Attract U.S. Persons and Enforcement Challenges Exist*, GAO-08-778 (Washington, DC: GAO, July 24, 2008), 2–3, online at http://www.gao.gov/products/GAO-08-778.
31. Richard Murphy, "The Tax Gap Is 119.4 Billion and Rising," *Tax Research Blog*, September 22, 2014, online at http://www.taxresearch.org.uk/Blog/2014/09/22/new-report-the-tax-gap-is-119-4-billion-and-rising/.
32. Stewart Lansley, *Rich Britain: The Rise and Rise of the New Super-Wealthy* (London: Politico, 2006), 187.
33. Jack Lawrence Luzkow, *The Great Forgetting: The Past, Present and Future of Social Democracy and the Welfare State* (Manchester: Manchester University Press, 2015), 132.
34. Eric Shaw, *Losing Labour's Soul: New Labour and the Blair Government* (London: Routledge, 2007), 56.
35. Luzkow, *Great Forgetting*, 124; for background see Shaw, *Losing Labour's Soul*, 56–57.
36. General Accountability Office, *Cayman Islands: Business and Tax Advantages*, 2–6.
37. *Broken at the Top*, 8.
38. Stephanie Fontana, "A Hidden Network of Hidden Wealth," *Oxfam America Blog*, January 11, 2016, online at http://politicsofpoverty.oxfamamerica.org/2016/01/a-hidden-network-of-hidden-wealth/.
39. Centre for Responsive Politics, "Lobbying Spending Database," https://www.opensecrets.org/lobby/.
40. *Broken at the Top*, 8.
41. Ibid., 18–19.
42. Drew DeSilver, "High-Income Americans Pay Most Income Taxes, But Enough to Be 'Fair'?" Pew Research Center, March 24, 2015, online at http://www.pewresearch.org/fact-tank/2015/03/24/high-income-americans-pay-most-income-taxes-but-enough-to-be-fair/; see also Leonard E. Burman, "Taxes and Inequality," Tax Policy Center, March 20, 2014, online at http://www.taxpolicycenter.org/publications/taxes-and-inequality/full.
43. *Broken at the Top*, 10.
44. Ibid.; See also Children's Defense Fund, "Ending Child Poverty Now," online at http://www.childrensdefense.org/library/PovertyReport/EndingChildPovertyNow.html; and Lukas Brun, *Infrastructure Investment Creates American Jobs* (Durham, NC: Duke University,

Center on Globalization, Governance, and Competitiveness, October 2014), https://s.bsd.net/aamweb/main/page/file/9d937012edb-12326c4_7vm62z7l5.pdf.
45. Nicholas Shaxson, *Treasure Islands: Uncovering the Damage of Offshore Banking and Tax Havens* (New York: Palgrave Macmillan, 2011), 221–22.
46. Ibid., 11.
47. Senator Carl Levin, News Release, "Dorgan and Levin Release Study Showing Majority of Corporations Pay No Federal Income Tax," August 12, 2008, see summary of this at Andrew Ross Sorkin, "Most US Corporations Pay No Income Tax," *New York Times*, August 13, 2008. See Martin A. Sullivan, "Testimony Before Congress, the Committee on Ways and Means in the House of Representatives," *Tax Analysts*, July 22, 2010, online at http://s3.amazonaws.com/zanran_storage/house.gov/ContentPages/114151771.pdf.
48. Shaxson, *Treasure Islands*, 15–16.
49. Ibid., 16.
50. Ibid.
51. Ibid., 17–18.
52. US Government Accountability Office, *Large U.S. Corporations and Federal Contractors with Subsidiaries in Jurisdictions Listed as Tax Havens or Financial Privacy Jurisdictions*, GAO-09-157 (Washington, DC: GAO, December 18, 2008), see highlights online at http://www.gao.gov/products/GAO-09-157.
53. Shaxson, *Islands*, 20.
54. Harriet Taylor, "How Apple Managed to Pay a 0.005 Tax Rate in 2014," *CNBC*, August 30, 2016, online at http://www.cnbc.com/2016/08/30/how-apples-irish-subsidiaries-paid-a-0005-percent-tax-rate-in-2014.html.
55. Ibid.; and Kate Benner, "Fact-Checking Apple's Claims on EU Tax Ruling," *New York Times*, August 30, 2016.
56. European Commission Letter to Apple, *Alleged Aid to Apple* (Brussels: European Commission, June 11, 2014), 3, online at http://ec.europa.eu/competition/state_aid/cases/253200/253200_1582634_87_2.pdf.
57. Ibid.; see also Taylor, "How Apple Managed to Pay a 0.005 Tax Rate in 2014."
58. Ibid.
59. Ibid.; Senators Carl Levin and John McCain, The Permanent Subcommittee on Investigations of the US Senate, "Memorandum: Offshore Profit Shifting and the U.S. Tax Code-Part II (Apple Inc.), Exhibit 1A," May 21, 2013, 3–5, online at https://www.hsgac.senate.gov/download/?id=cde3652b-da4e-4ee1-b841-aead48177dc4.

60. Ibid., 17.
61. Ibid.
62. Ibid., 21.
63. Ibid., 21–23.
64. Editorial Board, "Apple, Congress and the Missing Taxes," *New York Times*, August 30, 2016.
65. Ibid.; "US Companies Holding $2.1 Trillion Offshore Profits," *CNBC*, October 6, 2015, online at http://www.cnbc.com/2015/10/06/us-companies-holding-21-trillion-offshore-profits.html; and also Citizens for Tax Justice, "$2.1 Trillion Profits Held Offshore: A Comparison of International Tax Proposals," July 14, 2015, online at http://ctj.org/ctjreports/2015/07/21_trillion_in_corporate_profits_held_offshore_a_comparison_of_international_tax_proposals.php#.V967umX0iFI.
66. Johnston, *Perfectly Legal*, 17–18.
67. Ibid., 18.
68. Tax Foundation, "Federal Capital Gains Taxes," online at https://files.taxfoundation.org/legacy/docs/cap_gains_1988-2013.pdf.
69. Cited in Johnston, *Perfectly Legal*, 19.
70. Ibid.
71. Danny Dorling, *Inequality and the 1 Percent* (London: Verso, 2014), 151.
72. Douglas Carswell, Interviewed by Owen Jones, "Owen Jones Meets Douglas Carswell," *youtube.com*, July 22, 2015, online at youtube.com.
73. Cited by Owen Jones, *Chavs: The Demonization of the Working Class* (London: Verso, 2011), 62.
74. Patrick Wintour, "George Osborne Poised to Slash Top Tax Rate from 50p to 40p," *Guardian*, March 15, 2012. This was a reversion to the 40% rate adopted by Lawson in 1988.
75. Jones, *Chavs*, 62–63. Indeed they were, but not for the working classes.
76. Ibid., 63.
77. Mary Shaw, Daniel Dorling, David Gordon, and George Davey Smith, *The Widening Gap: Health Inequalities and Policy in Britain* (Bristol: Policy Press, 1999), 147.
78. Earl A. Reitan, *The Thatcher Revolution: Margaret Thatcher, John Major, Tony Blair and the Transformation of Modern Britain, 1979–2001* (Lanham, MD: Rowman and Littlefield, 2003), 77.
79. Eric J. Evans, *Thatcher and Thatcherism*, 2nd edition (London: Routledge, 2004), 138–39. The bottom tenth saw their wealth nearly halved. Also, Stewart Lansley, *Life in the Middle: The Untold Story of Britain's Average Earners*, Touchstone Pamphle No. 6 (London: TUC, 2009), 14–15, https://www.tuc.org.uk/sites/default/files/documents/lifeinthemiddle.pdf.

80. Dorling, *Inequality and the 1 Percent*, 76–77.
81. Kim Willsher, "Will France's Supertax Spark 'Patriotism' or a 'Brain Drain'?" *Guardian*, September 14, 2012.
82. Dorling, *Inequality and the 1 Percent*, 78–79.
83. Ibid., 76.
84. Emmanuel Saez and Thomas Piketty, "Why the 1 Percent Should Pay Tax at 80 Percent," *Guardian*, October 24, 2013; Emmanuel Saez and Thomas Piketty, "Income Inequality in the United States, 1913–1998," *Quarterly Journal of Economics* 118 (February 2003): 1–39.
85. Matthew Sinclair, "Why No Conservative Should Support a Mansion Tax," *Spectator*, February 18, 2013, online at http://blogs.spectator.co.uk/2013/02/why-no-conservative-should-support-a-mansion-tax/.
86. Roman Krznaric, *Empathy: A Handbook for Revolution* (London: Rider Books, 2014).
87. Dorling, *Inequality and the 1 Percent*, 89.
88. Paul Krugman, "The Long-Run History of Taxes on the Rich," *New York Times*, July 12, 2012.
89. Ibid.
90. Johnston, *Perfectly Legal*, 19.
91. Ibid., 19–20.
92. Ibid., 20–21.
93. Zachary Goldfarb, "The Legacy of the Bush Tax Cuts in Four Charts," *Washington Post*, January 2, 2013; see also Thomas L. Hungerford, "US Library of Congress, Congressional Research Service," *Taxes and the Economy: An Economic Analysis of the Top Tax Rates Since 1945* (Washington, DC: Congressional Research Service, September 14, 2012), online at https://www.dpcc.senate.gov/files/documents/CRSTaxesandtheEconomy%20Top%20Rates.pdf; and Kathy Ruffing and Joel Friedman, *Economic Downturn and Legacy of Bush Policies Continue to Drive Large Deficits: Economic Recovery Measures, Financial Rescues Have Only Temporary Impact* (Washington, DC: Center on Budget and Policy Priorities, February 28, 2013), 1–2, online at http://www.cbpp.org/research/economic-downturn-and-legacy-of-bush-policies-continue-to-drive-large-deficits.
94. Goldfarb, "The Legacy of the Bush Tax Cuts"; also Ruffing and Friedman, *Economic Downturn and Legacy of Bush Policies*; and Hungerford, *Economic Analysis of the Top Tax Rates Since 1945*.
95. Dorling, *Inequality and the 1 percent*, 118.
96. Sarah Butler, "Inheritance Tax: A Brief History of Death Duties," *Guardian*, April 10, 2016.
97. Rory O'Farrell, "Irish Inequality During the 20th Century," *Progressive Economy Blog*, September 23, 2010, online at http://tasceconomists.blogspot.com/2010/09/irish-inequality-during-20th-century.html.

98. "ITI—Tax Credits, Reliefs and Rates for the Tax Years 2013 and 2014," "Domicile Levy," and "Capital Gains Tax," online at revenue i.e., See http://www.revenue.ie/en/personal-tax-credits-reliefs-and-exemptions/index.aspx and http://www.revenue.ie/en/tax/cgt/leaflets/cgt2.html.
99. Thomas McDonnell, *Wealth Tax: Options for Its Implementation in the Republic of Ireland*, National Economic Research Institute, Paper No. 6 (Dublin: NERI, September 2013), 13–26, online at http://www.tasc.ie/download/pdf/tasc_neri_wealth_tax_tom_mcdonnell.pdf.
100. Thomas Piketty, "Should We Make the Richest Pay to Meet Fiscal Adjustment Needs?" in S. Princen and G. Mouree eds., *The Role of Tax Policy in Times of Fiscal Consolidation*, Economic Papers 502 (Brussels: European Commission, August 2013), online at http://piketty.pse.ens.fr/files/PikettyEC2013.pdf.
101. Jeevan Vasagar and Peter Spiegel, "Bundesbank Proposes Wealth Tax for EU States Facing Bankruptcy," *Financial Times*, January 27, 2014.
102. McDonnell, *Wealth Tax*, 20–23.
103. Anthony B. Atkinson and Salvatore Morelli, *Chartbook of Economic Inequality: 25 Countries 1911–2010*, INET Research Note 15 (New York: Institute for New Economic Thinking, 2012), online at https://www.ineteconomics.org/uploads/papers/ChartbookofEconomic-Inequality.pdf.
104. Ibid.
105. Thomas Piketty and Emmanuel Saez, "A Theory of Optimal Inheritance Taxation," *Econometrica* 81, no. 5 (September 2013): 1851–86. https://doi.org/10.3982/ecta10712.
106. Dorling, *Inequality and the 1 Percent*, 122.
107. Ibid.
108. Dorling, *Inequality and the 1 Percent*, 125.
109. Jairo Lugo-Ocando as cited by Danny Dorling, *Inequality and the 1 Percent*, 125; see Jairo Lugo-Ocando, *Blaming the Victim: How Global Journalism Fails Those in Poverty* (London: Pluto Press, 2014), describing how the rich create or preserve inequality by employing their wealth.
110. Dorling, *Inequality and the 1 Percent*, 211, note 103.
111. Ibid., 125.
112. UK House of Commons, Briefing Paper, "Inheritance Tax," Number 00093, September 29, 2015, online at researchbriefings.files.parliament.uk/documents/SN00093/SN00093.pdf.
113. Ibid., 8.
114. Ibid., 3–4.
115. Editorial Board, "Only Morons Pay the Estate Tax," *New York Times*, November 17, 2017.
116. Ibid.

117. Chye-Ching Huang and Chloe Cho, *Ten Facts You Should Know About the Federal Estate Tax* (Washington, DC: Center on Budget and Policy Priorities, October 30, 2017), 1, online at https://www.cbpp.org/sites/default/files/atoms/files/1-8-15tax.pdf.
118. Ibid. 2.
119. Ibid., 2–7.
120. Oxfam GB, "A Tale of Two Britains," *Oxfam Media Briefing* (London: Oxfam, March 17, 2014), online at http://policy-practice.oxfam.org.uk/publications/a-tale-of-two-britains-inequality-in-the-uk-314152.
121. Ibid.
122. Ibid.
123. Edward Nathan Wolff, *The Asset Price Meltdown and the Wealth of the Middle Class*, Occasional Paper (New York: Russell Sage Foundation and Brown University, 2013), 1–10, Figs. 3, 4, and Table 1, online at https://s4.ad.brown.edu/Projects/Diversity/Data/Report/report05012013.pdf.
124. Heather Stewart, "Almost Half of Britain's Private Wealth Owned by Top 10 Percent of Households," *Guardian*, December 18, 2015; see also Stewart Lansley, *Britain's Livelihood Crisis*, Touchstone Pamphlet No. 10 (London: Trades Union Congress, 2011, online at https://www.tuc.org.uk/sites/default/files/tuc-19639-f0.pdf; and Patrick Collinson, "Richest 10 Percent of UK Households Own 40 Percent of Wealth, ONS Says," *Guardian*, December 3, 2012. The *Guardian* found that the top decile was 950 times wealthier than the bottom decile, basing its figures on the Office of National Statistics. The Institute for Fiscal Studies reported that in the year 2012 the top decile of households owned more than 50% of financial wealth in the UK, online at https://www.ifs.org.uk/publications/8239.
125. Oxfam GB, "A Tale of Two Britains."

Bibliography

Abrams, Fran, and Anthony Bevins. "Murdoch's Courtship of Blair Finally Pays Off." *Independent*, February 11, 1998.

Atkinson, Anthony B., and Salvatore Morelli. *Chartbook of Economic Inequality: 25 Countries 1911–2010*. New York: Institute for New Economic Thinking, 2012. https://www.ineteconomics.org/uploads/papers/ChartbookofEconomic-Inequality.pdf.

Benner, Kate. "Fact-Checking Apple's Claims on EU Tax Ruling." *New York Times*, August 30, 2016.

Buffett, Warren. "Stop Coddling the Super-Rich." *New York Times*, August 14, 2011.

Burman, Leonard E. "Taxes and Inequality." *Tax Policy Center*, March 20, 2014. http://www.taxpolicycenter.org/publications/taxes-and-inequality/full.
Butler, Sarah. "Inheritance Tax: A Brief History of Death Duties." *Guardian*, April 10, 2016.
Carswell, Douglas. Interviewed by Owen Jones. "Owen Jones Meets Douglas Carswell." *youtube.com*, July 22, 2015. Online at youtube.com.
Children's Defense Fund. "Ending Child Poverty Now." http://www.childrensdefense.org/library/PovertyReport/EndingChildPovertyNow.html.
Citizens for Tax Justice. "New Report Finds 315 Fortune 500 Companies Used 'Stock Option Loophole' to Collectively Avoid $64.5 Billion in State and Federal Taxes," June 9, 2016. http://ctj.org/ctjreports/2016/06/fortune_500_corporations_used_stock_optionLoopholeto_avoid_646_billion_over_the_past_five_years or https://doi.org/10.17310/ntj.2016.4.09.
Citizens for Tax Justice. "$2.1 Trillion Profits Held Offshore: A Comparison of International Tax Proposals," July 14, 2015. Online at http://ctj.org/ctjreports/2015/07/21_trillion_in_corporate_profits_held_offshore_a_comparison_of_international_tax_proposals.php#.V967umX0iFI.
Clausing, Kimberly A. "The Effect of Profit Shifting on the Corporate Tax Base in the United States and Beyond." *National Tax Journal* 69, no. 4 (December 2016): 905–34. https://doi.org/10.17310/ntj.2016.4.09.
CNBC. "US Companies Holding $2.1 Trillion Offshore Profits," October 6, 2015. http://www.cnbc.com/2015/10/06/us-companies-holding-21-trillion-offshore-profits.html.
Collinson, Patrick. "Richest 10 Percent of UK Households Own 40 Percent of Wealth, ONS Says." *Guardian*, December 3, 2012.
DeSilver, Drew. "High-Income Americans Pay Most Income Taxes, But Enough to Be 'Fair'?" Pew Research Center, March 24, 2015. http://www.pewresearch.org/fact-tank/2015/03/24/high-income-americans-pay-most-income-taxes-but-enough-to-be-fair/.
Dorling, Danny. *Inequality and the 1 Percent*. London: Verso, 2014.
Economist. "Rupert Laid Bare," March 18, 1999. www.economist.com/node/319862.
Editorial Board. "Apple, Congress and the Missing Taxes." *New York Times*, August 30, 2016.
European Commission. *Alleged Aid to Apple*. Brussels: European Commission, June 11, 2014. Online at http://ec.europa.eu/competition/state_aid/cases/253200/253200_1582634_87_2.pdf.
Evans, Eric J. *Thatcher and Thatcherism*, 2nd edition. London: Routledge, 2004.
Fontana, Stephanie. "A Hidden Network of Hidden Wealth." *Oxfam America Blog*, January 11, 2016. http://politicsofpoverty.oxfamamerica.org/2016/01/a-hidden-network-of-hidden-wealth/.

Fraser, Nancy. *Fortunes of Feminism: From State-Managed Capitalism to Neoliberal Crisis*. London: Verso, 2013.

Goldfarb, Zachary. "The Legacy of the Bush Tax Cuts in Four Charts." *Washington Post*, January 2, 2013.

Huang, Chye-Ching, and Chloe Cho. *Ten Facts You Should Know About the Federal Estate Tax*. Washington, DC: Center on Budget and Policy Priorities, October 30, 2017. Online at https://www.cbpp.org/sites/default/files/atoms/files/1-8-15tax.pdf.

Hungerford, Thomas L. *Taxes and the Economy: An Economic Analysis of the Top Tax Rates Since 1945*. Washington, DC: Congressional Research Service, September 14, 2012. https://www.dpcc.senate.gov/files/documents/CRSTaxesandtheEconomy%20Top%20Rates.pdf.

Johnston, David Cay. *Perfectly Legal: The Covert Campaign to Rig Our Tax System to Benefit the Super Rich and Cheat Everybody Else*. New York: Penguin, 2003.

Jones, Owen. *Chavs: The Demonization of the Working Class*. London: Verso, 2011.

Krugman, Paul. "The Long-Run History of Taxes on the Rich." *New York Times*, July 12, 2012.

Krznaric, Roman. *Empathy: A Handbook for Revolution*. London: Rider Books, 2014.

Lansley, Stewart. *Britain's Livelihood Crisis*. Touchstone Pamphlet No. 10. London: Trades Union Congress, 2011. https://www.tuc.org.uk/sites/default/files/tuc-19639-f0.pdf.

Lansley, Stewart. *Life in the Middle: The Untold Story of Britain's Average Earners*. Touchstone Pamphlet No. 6. London: TUC, 2009. https://www.tuc.org.uk/sites/default/files/documents/lifeinthemiddle.pdf.

Lansley, Stewart. *Rich Britain: The Rise and Rise of the New Super-Wealthy*. London: Politico, 2006.

Levin, Carl, and Senators John McCain. The Permanent Subcommittee on Investigations of the US Senate. "Memorandum: Offshore Profit Shifting and the U. S. Tax Code- Part II (Apple Inc.), Exhibit 1A," May 21, 2013. https://www.hsgac.senate.gov/download/?id=cde3652b-da4e-4ee1-b841-aead48177dc4.

Luzkow, Jack Lawrence. *The Great Forgetting: The Past, Present and Future of Social Democracy and the Welfare State*. Manchester: Manchester University Press, 2015.

Lugo-Ocando, Jairo. *Blaming the Victim: How Global Journalism Fails Those in Poverty*. London: Pluto Press, 2014.

McDonnell, Thomas. *Wealth Tax: Options for Its Implementation in the Republic of Ireland*. National Economic Research Institute, Paper No. 6. Dublin: NERI, September 2013, 13–26. Online at http://www.tasc.ie/download/pdf/tasc_neri_wealth_tax_tom_mcdonnell.pdf.

McIntyre, Robert. *Offshore Shell Games, 2015: The Use of Offshore Tax Havens by Fortune 500 Companies*. Washington, DC: Citizens For Tax Justice, October 2015. Online at http://ctj.org/ctjreports/2015/10/offshore_shell_games_2015.php#.VuMbX-ZXo8I.

McIntyre, Robert S., Matthew Gardner, and Richard Phillips. *The Sorry State of Corporate Taxes*. Washington, DC: Citizens for Tax Justice, Institute on Taxation and Economic Policy, February 2014. http://www.ctj.org/corporatetaxdodgers/sorrystateofcorptaxes.pdf.

Murphy, Richard. "The Tax Gap is 119.4 Billion and Rising." *Tax Research Blog*, September 22, 2014. http://www.taxresearch.org.uk/Blog/2014/09/22/new-report-the-tax-gap-is-119–4-billion-and-rising/.

O'Farrell, Rory. "Irish Inequality During the 20th Century." *Progressive Economy Blog*, September 23, 2010. Online at http://tasceconomists.blogspot.com/2010/09/irish-inequality-during-20th-century.html.

Oxfam America. *Broken at the Top: How America's Dysfunctional Tax System Costs Billions in Corporate Tax Dodging*. Boston, MA: Oxfam America, April 14, 2016. https://www.oxfamamerica.org/static/media/files/Broken_at_the_Top_FINAL_EMBARGOED_4.12.2016.pdf.

Oxfam GB. "A Tale of Two Britains." *Oxfam Media Briefing*. London: Oxfam, March 17, 2014. http://policy-practice.oxfam.org.uk/publications/a-tale-of-two-britains-inequality-in-the-uk-314152.

Piketty, Thomas. "Should We Make the Richest Pay to Meet Fiscal Adjustment Needs?" In Sebastiaan Princen and G. Mouree, eds., *The Role of Tax Policy in Times of Fiscal Consolidation*, Economic Papers 502. Brussels: European Commission, August 2013. http://piketty.pse.ens.fr/files/PikettyEC2013.pdf.

Piketty, Thomas, and Emmanuel Saez. "A Theory of Optimal Inheritance Taxation." *Econometrica* 81, no. 5 (September 2013): 1851–86. https://doi.org/10.3982/ecta10712.

Reitan, Earl A. *The Thatcher Revolution: Margaret Thatcher, John Major, Tony Blair and the Transformation of Modern Britain, 1979–2001*. Lanham, MD: Rowman and Littlefield, 2003.

Saez, Emmanuel, and Thomas Piketty. "Income Inequality in the United States, 1913–1998." *Quarterly Journal of Economics* 118 (February 2003): 1–39.

Saez, Emmanuel, and Thomas Piketty. "Why the 1 Percent Should Pay Tax at 80 Percent." *Guardian*, October 24, 2013.

Shaw, Eric. *Losing Labour's Soul: New Labour and the Blair Government*. London: Routledge, 2007.

Shaw, Mary, Daniel Dorling, David Gordon, and George Davey Smith. *The Widening Gap: Health Inequalities and Policy in Britain*. Bristol: Policy Press, 1999.

Shaxson, Nicholas. *Treasure Islands: Uncovering the Damage of Offshore Banking and Tax Havens*. New York: Palgrave Macmillan, 2011.

Sinclair, Matthew. "Why No Conservative Should Support a Mansion Tax." *Spectator*, February 18, 2013. http://blogs.spectator.co.uk/2013/02/why-no-conservative-should-support-a-mansion-tax/.

Sorkin, Andrew Ross. "Most US Corporations Pay No Income Tax." *New York Times*, August 13, 2008.

Stewart, Heather. "Almost Half of Britain's Private Wealth Owned by Top 10 Percent of Households." *Guardian*, December 18, 2015.

Sullivan, Martin A. "Testimony Before Congress, the Committee on Ways and Means in the House of Representatives." *Tax Analysts*, July 22, 2010. http://s3.amazonaws.com/zanran_storage/house.gov/ContentPages/114151771.pdf.

Tax Foundation. "Federal Capital Gains Taxes." https://files.taxfoundation.org/legacy/docs/cap_gains_1988-2013.pdf.

Tax Policy Center. "Briefing Book." Washington, DC: Urban Institute and Brookings Institution, 2016. http://www.taxpolicycenter.org/briefing-book/what-are-sources-revenue-federal-government-0.

Taylor, Harriet. "How Apple Managed to Pay a 0.005 Tax Rate in 2014." *CNBC*, August 30, 2016. http://www.cnbc.com/2016/08/30/how-apples-irish-subsidiaries-paid-a-0005-percent-tax-rate-in-2014.html.

UK House of Commons, Briefing Paper. "Inheritance Tax," September 29, 2015, online at researchbriefings.files.parliament.uk/documents/SN00093/SN00093.pdf.

US Government Accountability Office. *Cayman Islands: Business and Tax Advantages Attract U.S. Persons and Enforcement Challenges Exist.* Washington, DC: GAO, July 24, 2008. http://www.gao.gov/products/GAO-08-778.

US Government Accountability Office. *Large U.S. Corporations and Federal Contractors with Subsidiaries in Jurisdictions Listed as Tax Havens or Financial Privacy Jurisdictions.* Washington, DC: GAO, December 18, 2008. Online at http://www.gao.gov/products/GAO-09-157.

Vasagar, Jeevan, and Peter Spiegel. "Bundesbank Proposes Wealth Tax for EU States Facing Bankruptcy." *Financial Times*, January 27, 2014.

Weyzig, Francis. *Still Broken: Governments Must Do More to Fix the International Corporate Tax System.* Boston, MA: Oxfam America, November 2015. http://www.oxfamamerica.org/static/media/files/still-broken-corporate-tax-101115-embargo-en.pdf.

Willsher, Kim. "Will France's Supertax Spark 'Patriotism' or a 'Brain Drain'?" *Guardian*, September 14, 2012.

Wintour, Patrick. "George Osborne Poised to Slash Top Tax Rate from 50p to 40p." *Guardian*, March 15, 2012.

Wolff, Edward Nathan. *The Asset Price Meltdown and the Wealth of the Middle Class.* Occasional Paper. New York: Russell Sage Foundation and Brown

University, 2013. https://s4.ad.brown.edu/Projects/Diversity/Data/Report/report05012013.pdf.

Zucman, Gabriel. "Taxing Across Borders: Tracking Personal Wealth and Corporate Profits." *Journal of Economic Perspectives* 28, no. 4 (Fall 2014): 121–48. gabriel-zucman.eu/files/Zucman2014JEP.pdf.

CHAPTER 7

The Business of Healthcare

Introduction

In 2009, the Democrats had a once-in-a-generation Democratic Senate supermajority. Yet, as the Senate debated healthcare reform, Sen. Max Baucus (D-Mont.) refused to even consider a single-payer healthcare system in which the government provided universal healthcare. Single-payer had worked well in Canada, and in a number of countries in Europe, including the UK, and some polls in the USA showed that a majority of Americans wanted it in the USA. Yet Baucus, then head of the powerful Senate Finance Committee, refused. He said it was not realistic, and he wanted a healthcare bill that moderate Republicans could support. Eventually, Baucus and the Democrats passed the flawed Affordable Care Act (ACA), the bill that the Republicans have tried to dismantle in 2017–2018. Baucus left the Senate in 2014, but belatedly, he made a reversal and in 2017 endorsed single-payer healthcare. Why the change? He suggested that its time had come.[1] But by then Donald Trump was in the White House and the Republicans controlled Congress. Their time had come first.

How Healthcare Became a Business Instead of a Right

"The problem with American healthcare is not the care," according to Christy Ford Chapin. "It's the insurance."[2] And not just any insurance, but for-profit health insurance. Almost alone among developed

J. L. Luzkow, *Monopoly Restored*,
https://doi.org/10.1007/978-3-319-93994-0_7

nations, the USA has propped up a business model that relies on private for-profit insurers. The result is unequal healthcare in the USA, vastly unequal. American healthcare is unfair, inefficient, inaccessible for many millions, and much more costly than single-payer healthcare systems, such as in the UK, Canada, Denmark, Norway, and Sweden. These countries, largely because they use single payer, in which the government ensures the healthcare of entire populations, and they do not rely on for-profits, have had significantly better outcomes in life expectancy and infant mortality and vastly diminished pathologies such as obesity, teenage pregnancies, and anxiety syndromes. The reason? Healthcare is universal, affordable, and efficient. In the UK, which has experienced at least partial privatization, even under the Labor governments of Tony Blair and Gordon Brown, and the Coalition governments led by David Cameron and Theresa May since 2010, healthcare—though rated the best system in the world by the Commonwealth Fund—has begun to resemble the USA more as pieces of the National Health Service (NHS) have been whittled away and been privatized. The result is less access, lower life expectancy, and greater anxiety (and depression).

So if healthcare in single payer countries is better, more affordable, and universal, why don't we have it in the USA? In the early decades of the twentieth century, the medical marketplace offered a variety of models, before settling on the system in place today. Unions, businesses, consumer cooperatives, and even ethnic mutual aid societies all offered their own versions of organizing and paying for medical care. Physicians also offered a model, something called a prepaid doctor group. Such groups often included a variety of specialists, including general practitioners, surgeons, and obstetricians. These groups worked well, and for several reasons. Their patients received integrated care in one location. And group physicians from across the spectrum of specialties could meet regularly to discuss and review treatment options for chronically ill and hard-to-treat and diagnose patients.[3]

What made this system work was that individuals and families paid a monthly fee to the physician group, not to an insurance company. The system worked because it held down costs. Physicians typically were paid a base salary, plus a percentage of quarterly profits. As a result, they lacked incentive to ration care, which could cost them paying patients, or to provide unnecessary care since they did not reap an additional benefit.[4]

Prepaid doctor groups were both efficient and affordable because virtually all the money that went into healthcare went directly to the physician groups: none of it went to insurers financing medical services. Moreover, doctors had no incentive to provide unneeded services, nor did they need to risk losing patients because physician groups could provide comprehensive care.

So why did doctor groups and healthcare coops fail to be adopted universally? Unfortunately, the American Medical Association (AMA) regarded early healthcare models as a threat. It was politics, not market logic or rational choice theory that positioned for-profit insurance companies as the way to organize medical services. AMA leaders decided in the late 1930s that the best way to protect the professional security of doctors was through insurance companies: these could offer policies that would reimburse doctors for their services. Translated, the AMA believed that it alone should shape the medical market. This belief was rooted not only in the cultural standing of the medical profession, but also in state licensing and medical practice laws that had endowed the AMA with regulatory power. Most observers would have caught the illusion, or the deceit. Once for-profit insurance became the model, it would eventually undermine doctor sovereignty. Missing in all this was assurance of efficient patient care. Here is how Christy Ford Chapin put it:

> For AMA officials, safeguarding physician sovereignty trumped economic efficiency. They therefore created a particular insurance company model: their design required insurers to reimburse the services of individual physicians rather than medical groups; compensate practitioners for each service or procedure provided; and allow doctors to practice medicine as they saw fit, free from supervision or interference. Both physicians and insurers hoped to severely limit health insurance. Doctors feared losing autonomy to third-party financiers. Insurers were troubled by the cost implications of funding physicians who could arbitrarily increase the price and supply of medical services. Meanwhile, the AMA opposed and suppressed all other health care prepayment plans, whether sponsored by businesses, mutual aid societies, consumer organizations, unions, or even physician groups. Professional calculations soon merged with national politics to cement into place the centrality of insurance companies.[5]

The AMA was very successful on multiple fronts. It retained regulatory power for itself, bypassing any state-imposed regulation. It managed to suppress other healthcare plans, whether sponsored by businesses, mutual aid societies, unions, or physician groups. And it institutionalized the model it thought that would best protect the autonomy of doctors: reimbursement of individual doctors for each service or procedure provided. What may not have been so obvious then, but which virtually all health-insured people know today, was that paying physicians for fee-based healthcare would inevitably inflate the number of services and procedures, and that would lead to higher premiums.[6] That is simply common sense, and that is what happened. What was noticeably missing in all this? A so-called free market, or a competitive model that would provide healthcare efficiently and inexpensively. As for universal healthcare, that was a European thing. And it is still being debated in the USA in 2018, long after virtually all developed nations have embraced it.

Although Democrats and Republicans offered numerous healthcare reforms in the 1940s and 1950s, the AMA model endured, to a large extent because of the efforts of the AMA itself. When President Harry Truman proposed a universal healthcare system, apparently hoping to build such a program around prepaid doctor groups, bypassing insurers and the AMA, the latter decided that the best way top keep government out of healthcare, and to keep the AMA in it, was to design a private sector model: the insurance model, that coincidentally was a for-profit model. Motives varied, but doctors preferred to maintain autonomy, a fee-based structure not limited by a fixed salary, and what many believed would be a more comprehensive and generous way to provide healthcare for all population groups. Insurers could see unlimited clients, as long as they could control the fee structure. Predictably, as healthcare was established as a business in which clients shopped around for insured healthcare, medical costs skyrocketed. And since that posed a problem for for-profit insurers, they just as predictably acted to contain costs. They expanded their function from financing medical services to supervising medical care and coordinating the healthcare system. They decided which services and procedures qualified for policy coverage and reimbursement fees for physicians and hospitals. They even shaped medical practices by insisting that healthcare providers follow their treatment blueprints. Once institutional relationships were established between health insurers, physicians, hospitals, and medical societies like the AMA, policymakers would simply act to accommodate that system.[7]

It is this business for-profit model that has persisted in the USA ever since. The predictable result is that healthcare remains very much a casino game or lottery, some seven years after passage of the ACA.

In the USA, healthcare is not a right or an entitlement; it is a market where goods or services are bought just like any other goods or services. The result is that healthcare has become an arena of predation. For-profit health insurers have not only contributed to the fragmentation of the medical marketplace, but also shaped that marketplace by extracting considerable wealth from healthcare. And unlike the NHS in the UK, and all other healthcare systems in developed countries, the USA has never committed to universal healthcare. Healthcare is rationed out according to who can afford it, inevitably reflecting the inequalities that persist throughout the economy. The greater the inequality overall, the more unequally that healthcare is distributed. And there is one other fatal flaw: in single-payer systems, as in Denmark, Sweden, and the UK, government insures everybody: that means a unified administrative system, providing healthcare as a right, and providing it universally.

The NHS has flaws, but that also has much to do with politics. Healthcare in the UK is becoming more unequal but, as we shall see, that has much to do with the partial privatizations beginning with Tony Blair and Gordon Brown and persisting with the Coalition government. It was never the intention to even partially privatize the NHS, or to allocate its services by means testing, when it was founded in 1948. The whole concept, in the wake of World War II, was to establish healthcare as a nonprofit system whose services would provide universal healthcare across the entire population. Partial privatization has been a radical departure from earlier intentions, and the results have only served to make Britain increasingly unequal, simultaneously creating many opportunities for predation.

How the Super-Rich Extort Wealth from Health and Create Inequality

In Europe, Denmark, Finland, France, Germany, Norway, Sweden, Switzerland, and the UK, all have less expensive, more efficient, fairer systems than in the USA. What is the difference? All these European countries have universal-coverage healthcare systems. Many Americans deny these claims, but here is why they are true. In single-payer systems, such as in Canada, Finland, Norway, Sweden, the UK, and Taiwan, the government provides insurance for all citizens and pays all healthcare expenses except for co-pays and coinsurance. This means significant elimination of bureaucratic waste. Instead of many payers and overlapping administrative costs, a unified and universal health insurance system is created. Private for-profit health insurers need an army of actuaries to figure break points in order to be profitable. Universal healthcare systems, where everybody is automatically insured from birth, do not need actuaries. Everybody is automatically covered from birth, and the government is not worried about a profit, only about providing good healthcare. In single-payer systems, where billing is put under one roof, healthcare is automatically centralized, universal, and national. In single-payer systems, the result is much less bureaucratic expense, hence a lower cost per capita as we have seen.[8]

Some developed nations do not use single payer or national health insurance, but rely on what is called mandated insurance that is national and universal. In Germany, which has such a system, this means that health insurance is mandatory for the entire population. Both salaried workers and employees below what is considered a high-income threshold of almost €50,000 (US$66,337 in 2015 dollars) are automatically enrolled into one of the 130 public nonprofit "sickness" funds at the same rate for all members. Payment is made jointly by employer and employee contributions. Provider payment is not decided by the market in Germany, but by complex social bargaining, over which state governments preside. Sickness funds must provide a broad benefit package and cannot refuse membership based on an actuarial basis, which means that coverage is universal. It is also nonprofit, which is how Germany keeps its medical expenditures under control and limits medical inflation. Germans who make above the statutory threshold can still enroll voluntarily, unless they opt for private insurance. Germany's public system includes about 89% of the population. Americans think that German and European medical systems are very expensive in general. But Germans not only have better outcomes, live longer, and have a lower infant mortality rate, they also pay a fixed percentage set at 15.5% of their gross salaried income, which is offset by employer contributions covering almost half of that at 7.3%.

How expensive and how efficient is the German healthcare system? Germany spent 8.7% of GDP on healthcare expenditure in 2011, a little over half of US spending on healthcare for the same year, although Germany has a system of universal healthcare coverage.[9] In 2012, Germany spent $4754 per capita, a little more than half of what the USA spent per capita that year. And despite having universal healthcare,

Germany ranked second overall by a Commonwealth study in 2014 in access, which included costliness of healthcare and timeliness of care, out of the eleven developed nations studied. The USA ranked ninth in access, well behind Germany, despite the mistaken assumption that the USA has a superior healthcare system, one where you do not have to wait long for care. The Commonwealth study says you do, and you will.[10]

The Commonwealth Fund also detailed a number of cost comparisons between Germany, nine other developed nations, and the USA, back in 2015. It published the following: US average cost for heart bypass surgery was $75,345; an appendectomy brought $13,910; an MRI costs $1145, and a CT scan costs an average of $896. Germans having any of these surgeries or tests paid nothing, bills were paid for by the nonprofit insurers who collected payroll tax deductions, of which employers covered almost half. And for those who didn't have an employer, the state had mandated that municipalities had to provide full coverage, the same as for those who were employed.

The French system of healthcare—similar to the German—also provides universal healthcare coverage and uses nonprofit health insurance. Like Germany, it has not charged for surgical procedures such as bypass surgery and appendectomies, nor for medical tests such as the MRI.[11]

So if the healthcare system in the USA is so costly, despite being less effective and efficient, where does the money go and to whom? Much of it goes straight to the super-rich who control the for-profit health insurance companies. Drs. David Himmelstein and Steffie Woolhandler, both professors at the CUNY School of Public Health at Hunter College, have worked out much of the math, including healthcare costs in the USA before and after the ACA was passed into law, comparing these costs with single-payer systems elsewhere, such as Canada and Taiwan. While they note that the ACA is a good thing because it has enrolled twenty-five million into health insurance, they also project prohibitive costs: some $2.757 trillion for private insurance overhead and administration of government health programs between 2014 and 2022. This includes $273.6 billion in new administrative costs attributable to the ACA, but nearly two-thirds of this new overhead—$172.2 billion annually—will go for increased private insurance costs.[12] This is a reference to added bureaucratic waste because many of the dollars put into healthcare through the ACA are filtered through private insurers. As they explain,

> Traditional Medicare runs for 2 percent overhead, somewhat higher than insurance overhead in universal single payer systems like Taiwan's or Canada's. Yet traditional Medicare is a bargain compared to the ACA strategy of filtering most of the new dollars through private insurers and private HMOs that subcontract for much of the new Medicaid coverage. Indeed, dropping the overhead figure from 22.5 percent to traditional Medicare's 2 percent would save $249.3 billion by 2022.[13]

This means that over an eight-year period the government, by filtering public money through private insurers, ACA, and the taxpayer, will be subsidizing private health insurance companies. The result is an overhead of 22.5%, roughly 20% more expensive than if the ACA were a stand-alone program: a program not filtered through private for-profit insurers. Hardly a bargain for the taxpayers, and for those needing healthcare, but a windfall of $172.2 billion per year for private insurers.[14] Granted this is not all profit—there is much bureaucratic waste—but it does represent what amounts to a subsidy given how much cheaper it would be to simply extend Medicare, which would lower overhead by some 20% according to the calculations of Himmelstein and Woolhandler.

As Himmelstein and Woolhandler explain further, Medicaid and other government programs account for $101.4 billion in projected overhead for the years 2014 through 2022. But even here the dollars that are added to administer Medicaid flow predominantly to private Medicaid HMOs, which, by 2022 will account for 59% of total Medicaid administrative costs. It is precisely this subcontracting of Medicaid coverage that has almost doubled its administrative overhead, rising from 5.1% total Medicaid administrative expenses in 1980 to 9.2% in 2015. Altogether, this means $273.6 billion in added insurance overhead or $1375 per newly insured person, about 22.5% of the total federal expenditures for the program.[15]

The vast majority of these sums amount to a giant subsidy for the healthcare super-rich. That is because Medicare historically runs at 2% overhead, which is somewhat higher than single-payer systems such as Canada's and Taiwan's. Yet, traditional Medicare is a bargain compared to the ACA strategy of filtering most new dollars through private insurers and private HMOs, where much of the added Medicaid coverage is contracted. If the 22.5% overhead figure would be lowered to Medicare's historical 2% overhead cost, the savings would equal $249.3 billion by 2022, eliminating a substantial flow of money toward private industry, but a significant savings for healthcare consumers.[16]

Significant as the sums noted above are, a universal single-payer system would reduce both insurers' and providers' overhead substantially, saving $375 billion annually.[17] That would represent savings for medical consumers of more than a trillion dollars every three years, a sum that currently goes to private insurers' and providers' overhead, adding to the wealth of the super-rich. Yet Republicans, led by Paul Ryan, continue to champion a healthcare system that is expensive, inefficient, and inaccessible for large parts of the population.

Keeping a private health insurance system around is bad health. As bloating continues in the for-profit sector, and as profits grow, the health of the nation is increasingly compromised. Bureaucratic waste of $375 billion per year cannot be sustained without helping to boost poverty rates, not to mention poor health. According to a survey taken by the Henry K. Kaiser Family Foundation and the *New York Times*, reported by the *Times* in January 2016, 63% of insured Americans reported using up most or all of their savings because of medical bills, while 42% had taken an extra job or worked additional hours so they could pay their bills, and all this well past adoption of the ACA. Half the population without health insurance reported problems with medical bills, which can only produce anxiety, frustration, and more medical expenses and illness. The Kaiser Foundation study also found that of those people with health insurance, 20% were having problems paying medical bills. Not surprisingly, the situation was worse among the uninsured: half (53%) faced problems with medical bills, which brought the overall percentage of the population having problems with medical expenses to 26%.[18]

Private health insurance administrative bloat accounts for at least $375 billion per annum being siphoned from medical consumers, but this figure still omits profits accrued by the private health insurance sector—profits that not only add to the average medical bill, but represent large sums of wealth transferred from the many to the few, constituting yet another form of rent. United Health Group reported in 2014 that its profit was $10 billion. A year later, despite its claims that the ACA was actually hurting its profits—UnitedHealth Group was considering pulling out of its Medicaid contracts with the government—it posted a handsome profit of $11 billion.[19] Aetna recorded a profit of $2 billion in 2014 and improved that to $2.4 billion in 2015.[20] CIGNA had a similar profit profile, netting a profit $2.1 billion in 2014 and improving a year later to $2.3 billion.[21] Anthem, a primary insurance carrier for and subcontractor with Medicaid, also reported substantial profits, some $815.2 million just in the first quarter of 2015.[22] Insurance companies are not hurting because of the ACA; their profits have in many cases grown, to some extent because the ACA has added millions of new clients. If the results of the above figures are added, and these are only partial at best, profits for the leading insurance for-profit companies amounted to about $18 billion minimally for the year 2015. When added to the bureaucratic waste because of a for-profit health insurance regime, we are already in the neighborhood of $400 billion per annum, a hefty squandering of public wealth and health, but a huge rent or subsidy for the super-rich who run the for-profit health insurance companies. No wonder that health insurance companies spend vast sums lobbying against and publicly denigrating single-payer systems that would eliminate subsidies maintaining their profitable but ineffective, unfair, and expensive health-care model.

The ACA has improved healthcare finances in the USA for many families, but it is not the long-term solution. The cost of medical care remains a financial hardship for significant numbers of families. The percentage of Americans who experienced financial distress because of medical bills has been reduced from a high of 41% in 2012, but it only fell to 35% in 2014, which meant that a third of all Americans were still struggling to pay the cost of medical care. The number of people avoiding medical care because of cost has also fallen, from 43% in 2012, but it still remained high in 2014 at 36%. And of those with health insurance, a third noted that employers and insurance plans were shifting the burden of medical expenses onto the insured, as deductibles, co-pays, and other fees were growing faster than the rate of inflation.[23]

The ACA has reduced the cost of insurance by insuring more than twenty-five million not previously covered, yet we have seen enormous sums of money still flowing away from Americans and toward for-profit insurance companies in the form of waste. The ACA has acted as a conduit for hundreds of billions being wasted by subcontracting with private insurance companies. A study by the federal Consumer Financial Protection Bureau in December 2014 found that medical debt had a significant impact on consumer credit: forty-three million Americans had overdue medical bills on their credit reports. The same report found that about half of all overdue debt on credit reports was because of medical debt. Fifteen million healthcare consumers had only medical debt on their credit reports, which meant that people with good credit under normal circumstances were struggling to pay off their medical bills. Moreover, the report concluded that medical bankruptcy was the leading cause of personal bankruptcy, an indication that the ACA was not efficiently, affordably, and fairly fixing America's failing healthcare system.[24] Finally, *The Huffington Post* reported in 2015—confirming what we have seen—that there were about 1.5 million bankruptcies annually, of which some 62% were medical bankruptcies. Just as startling, the same article reported that 72% of the medical bankruptcies were declared by people who had health insurance.[25]

If one simply compares the subsidies or the cost of maintaining a bloated and inefficient for-profit health insurance system, to the quarter (or higher) of the population struggling with medical bills, it does not require a mathematician to understand that by ending subsidies to for-profits and putting them directly into healthcare, by replacing for-profit health insurance with single payer, the number of Americans facing medical bankruptcy poverty because of private for-profit healthcare would decline dramatically. While the profit margins of private health insurers have been slimmed down to an extent under the ACA—3% is not uncommon—it is nevertheless true that in absolute dollars they have grown considerably. The ACA has added more than twenty million new clients, substantially improving earnings of the for-profits.

But the ACA does not mean that the insured do not worry about medical costs. Back in 2013 about 38% of personal bankruptcies were because of the continuing inflation of medical billings and out-of-pocket expenses, as well as inflating premiums. The result was that many patients were taken into collection: this was one reason that profit margins were slimmed down. But the other side of this was that collection agencies collected more than $20 billion from patients in arrears in 2013 alone. That's another $20 billion wasted down the collection drain and yet another reason that the healthcare system in the USA continues to be broken.[26]

The American healthcare system is one of the chief conduits through which money gushes toward the super-rich. They are the ones with the collection agencies, they own the profits extracted by for-profit private health insurers, and they are the main beneficiaries of the ACA because it continues to subsidize them by not embracing single-payer national health insurance. And as we shall see, the super-rich have also driven policies that keep the price of drugs at historic highs, partially the result of a law that prevents Medicare from using its enormous leverage to negotiate lower drug prices, as is done in all civilized countries.

There is no other explanation for the poor performance of the American healthcare system. Private healthcare insurance remains unaffordable, unfair, and inefficient, but still profitable for insurers. Yet private health insurers also have their complaints to make. Hospitals in the USA, though mostly of the nonprofit sort, have become empires unto themselves. They are veritable profit machines, turning their gains into hefty salaries for their administrations, charging more for the uninsured because they can get away with it, and generally acting as an imperium claiming tax exemptions by retaining their nonprofit status. The result is that they also contribute some members to the elite 1%, while the inflating costs of their services populate the rising numbers of the medically impoverished. Given hospital pricing, it is not a surprise that Americans pay $2.7 trillion per year in medical bills, a figure that is expected to inflate dramatically in the next decade after a hiatus of several years.[27]

The IRS originally granted a tax exempt status to nonprofits if they would restrain executive compensation to market value, and if they agreed to spend 3% of operating revenues taking care of patients unable to pay. Both of these provisions have been largely ignored. Executive base pay or earned income may be limited by law, but hospitals have learned how to provide outsized bonuses and other kinds of income without violating their nonprofit charters. As for patients unable to pay, the 3% figure is miasmic. Inflated hospital costs have boosted need considerably beyond the 3%, raising the number of patients unable to pay, while hospitals routinely charge more for patients who are not insured. There were still well over twenty-five million of these in mid-2016. According to *Forbes Magazine*, "if you count all the sales, property, and income taxes that nonprofit hospitals avoid paying, it would total $20 billion [per annum]."[28] For the healthcare super-rich, this is no less than a subsidy, a rent paid by patients and the communities served by nonprofit hospitals.

If hospitals were serious about reining in costs and servicing the medical needs of their communities, they would lower their prices, using the money they save from their tax exemptions. It is worth noting that 60% of the hospitals in the USA are nonprofits, meaning that the majority of operations and medical procedures in the USA are conducted in them. Yet we know that Americans do not live as long as their British counterparts, who are mostly treated in publicly owned hospitals.

Part of the problem is not the quality of a hospital, but access to it. The USA ranks poorly in access compared to all single-payer countries because of cost and timeliness of medical service. One result is that Americans do not live as long as residents of any single-payer country. Consider the following comparisons between the costs of hospital tests and surgeries in single-payer countries such as Canada, Spain, and New Zealand, and the USA for the year 2013. In Canada, an angiogram was priced at $35, in the USA, on average, it was $914. A hip replacement in Spain cost $7731, but in the USA, it was dramatically higher at $40,364, and an MRI, which was billed at $319 in the Netherlands, was an inflated $1121 in the USA. Finally, a drug comparison: Lipitor in New Zealand was $6 in 2013; in the USA, it was a rent-seeking $124 because it was under patent.[29] There is no apparent reason for these discrepancies, other than greed, as in the USA, supported by a market-based for-profit healthcare system—including so-called nonprofit hospitals. And even if greed is absent, the cost discrepancies represent the difference between profit-fueled medical practice and healthcare treated as a universal public right, which is not only more equitable, but more economical as well.

If the USA adopted the British system today—even when the UK is under assault from the Coalition government—what would that mean? Single payer and mostly public hospitals to begin with. And what would that signify? A saving of about $5000 per capita per annum, universal coverage, longer life expectancy, greater access to medical care, and lower infant mortality. The USA could improve by making its healthcare universal, fair, and efficient. It needs only to extend Medicare to the entire population: automatic enrollment, universal access, cheaper costs, and better care. Here is how David Cay Johnston summed it up in *Free Lunch*, published in 2007 well before the ACA, but prescient in his understanding of healthcare in the USA:

> If health care as a business worked, it would be a success story to embrace. If it resulted in lower costs, more and better care, and longer lives, it would be just what the doctor ordered. The American system provides acute care, trauma care, and access to the highest technology. But by every other objective measure—cost per capita, health status, longevity, costs of paperwork, and economic pollution—the uniquely American approach to health care is a complete failure. We pay more, enjoy shorter lives, and are drowning in infuriating makework, filing claims and making appeals, while distorting the whole economy because one giant component is a commercial activity.[30]

How the British Super-Rich Corrupt Healthcare

The British healthcare system, NHS, has been suffering from creeping privatization since Margaret Thatcher was in power but the decisive plundering of the healthcare commons started with the Blair government in 2007. That was the year that Blair induced NHS hospitals to contract out services.

The result was the scandal of private finance initiative (PFI) hospitals when more than 100 NHS hospital trusts signed deals for private financing in England. Originally conceived by John Major's government, all but one of the PFI contracts were made between 1997 and 2010 by New Labor, which argued that it wanted to shift the cost of projects away from government borrowing requirements. This arrangement worked well, but not for the people of England. By 2016, the trusts were paying £2 billion annually—a sum that was rising—for building and operating new hospitals and renovating old ones. Altogether, the new deals financed £11.8 billion of hospital building, but the hospital trusts will have to repay £79 billion over the twenty-five to thirty years that is the contract life of all deals. In a word, the PFI arrangements meant that the total cost would be more than six times the building cost, far more than if the government had borrowed money directly on behalf of the trusts. Barts Health NHS Trust, which borrowed £1.1 billion, will ultimately pay £4.1 billion, just for the privilege of borrowing from the private sector under PFI.[31]

Meanwhile, many of the holders of PFI debt or equity, that also fund schools, care homes, central and local governments, are investment funds based in tax havens. The largest shareholder of Innisfree, the biggest investor in hospitals other than the NHS, is Jersey-based Coutts & Co. Altogether, indebtedness to financial institutions under PFI was £310 billion in 2016, more than five times the value of the assets created.[32] But don't think that Innisfree is a good citizen paying taxes on earnings. That is the point of being in a tax haven.

Then, there is the misnamed Health and Social Care Act of 2012, which effectively abolished government responsibility for providing a national health service, ending a long-standing legal guarantee that government would provide comprehensive health services. NHS contracts were opened up for limitless privatization. More and more, the people of England would find out that, when it came to their health, *they were on their own.*

Several months after passage of the Health and Social Care Act, in July 2012, the British journal, *New Scientist*, anticipating the negative effects on health and increase in inequality of the new so-called health legislation, concluded that inequality was bad for the health of everybody, at all levels of society. The rich could not insulate themselves by their wealth.[33] Several months later, David Cameron, who was indifferent to the blandishments of the *New Scientist*, and was anyways intent on cutting away benefits for the "bloated" NHS budget, announced that the UK government would no longer assess the effect of its policies on social equality, which he considered to be so much bureaucratic claptrap:

> Let me be very clear. I care about making sure that government policy never marginalizes or discriminates… . I care about making sure we treat people equally. But let's have the courage to say it—caring about these things does not have to mean churning out reams of bureaucratic nonsense… . We don't need all the extra tick-box stuff. So I can tell you today, we are calling time on Equality Impact Assessments. You no longer have to do them if these issues have been properly considered.[34]

What followed was a little more serious than "tick-box stuff." Prime Minister Cameron had just denied any possibility of social impacts on human beings "properly considered," because the standard assessments were to be abandoned as "bureaucratic nonsense."[35]

The Health and Social Care Act passed by Parliament was supported by some members of the House of Lords with declared financial interests in private for-profit healthcare companies.[36] This was a bill effectively embracing the financial interests of the healthcare super-rich. Its intention, despite the remarks of the prime minister, was to divert the flow of NHS money toward the private sector. That was accomplished, but it also proved lethal. Among the many cuts were social care benefits for the elderly, soon followed by an increase in the mortality rates of those dependent on home care. The legislation had real-world knock-on effects; it was another indication of how deadly inequality had become, and how deadly it was for those who could not afford private care. Subsequently, the number of social care recipients in England went from 1,275,000 in 2007–2008, to 928,000 in 2012–2013.[37]

This was part of a concerted drive by the super-rich to divert as much money from the NHS as possible into private healthcare, something that has been historically lucrative for the very wealthy. It was a way of shunting income and wealth toward those who seemed to crave it above all else, while asking others to bear the costs. Private healthcare companies in the UK—which did not fund the education of NHS trained staff—were plucking off the profitable corners, while allowing less lucrative parts to remain within the public sphere.

The Health and Social Care Act of 2012 in Britain had other adverse effects as well. It allowed up to 50% of beds in an English hospital (Scotland and Wales follow different rules) to become private beds, though it was known that the use of hospital rooms is more efficient within the NHS, promising a future crisis in both affordability and access. The act also allowed the advertising of fatty foods to children. Again the super-rich in the private sector were behind this initiative. It was their London companies that bought the advertising. It was in London that there was the greatest concentration of poverty, and it was in London where children were at greatest risk of obesity, between the ages of five and ten.[38]

The Health and Care Act was promised as a measure that would save money. Allegedly, it would also introduce competition into healthcare that would improve the health of the nation. As we know, privatization meant more—much more—not less public debt. And invariably that meant that public health would suffer, especially the health of the poorest. The Child Poverty Action Group was able to show that Coalition government cuts, for the very youngest, meant that an infant born to a low-income family after April 2012 would be about £1500 worse off per year than a sibling born in 2010. That was because of the benefits their parents had lost: £190 Health in Pregnancy grant, a £500 maternity grant, £500 from the Child Trust Fund, and £545 from the baby element of child tax credit, offset by £255 in its child element.[39]

In Glasgow, where health in the UK is at its worst, general practitioners reported that benefit cuts meant greater numbers of patients could not afford to heat their homes, with direct impacts on health and life expectancy. Overall, in the UK, the 1% live at least ten years longer than average, a discrepancy that is repeated in the USA.[40] Men who die in posh areas of London, Kensington, and Chelsea, for example, are on average fourteen years older than men who die in Glasgow. For women the gap is twelve years.[41]

The damage done by the 2012 act was palpable. There was a serious rise in mortality by the summer of 2013. In England and Wales, an additional 23,400 people died in 2012 and early 2013, compared to earlier years—a 5% rise in mortality. Public Health England responded that this was possibly due to the flu. But this was denied by the president of the Faculty of Public Health, Professor John Ashton, who commented that there was little if any evidence that the flu was responsible for the uptick in morbidity. His conclusion? Spending cuts were to blame. Danny Dorling, Tom Hennell, and Martin McKee, all authorities in statistical analysis, have denied that flu caused increased morbidity rates.[42]

When the Tory government came to power in 2010, it announced it would be "supporting the public so they can protect and improve their own health."[43] Translated, however, this meant that the money saved on benefit cuts would go headfirst into private profits. In fact, the new market in commissioning services and outsourcing boomed after the 2012 act, led by Andrew Lansley, Health Secretary between 2010 and 2012.

As Health Secretary, Lansley privatized the NHS helpline, renamed NHA 111. Since it was put out to contract, it has been subjected to withering criticism for poor delivery of services, hardly an anomaly for the outsourcing of NHS England under the Tories. So why do the Tories continue their outsourcing? Not to benefit public health, certainly not to save money, as we have seen. The explanation has to do with the contracting of the renamed NHS 111. The firm winning most NHS 111 contracts was Harmoni, which was subsequently bought by Care UK, whose former chairman, John Nash, had made substantial donations to the Conservatives and even to Lansley's personal office when he was shadow Health Secretary. And just to follow the trail a little further, Care UK is owned by Bridgepoint Capital, which coincidentally employs Alan Milburn, a former UK Labor Health Secretary between 1999 and 2003. It was Milburn who expanded the process of privatization and gave it legs. And finally there is Jim Easton, director of healthcare at Bridgepoint Capital, an erstwhile member of the National Commissioning Board, renamed as NHS England, which awarded the NHS 111 contracts.[44]

In 2015, NHS England announced a new list of approved private suppliers. At the very top of the list was outsourcing giant Capita, which that same year won a four-year contract with NHS England worth £1 billion, making Capita the sole provider of administrative services for GPs, opticians, and dentists. This was despite the fact that it had previously failed to provide adequate services to several local NHS trusts and as a result had its contract terminated less than three years into a seven-year agreement.[45]

The point of all this is that privatization does not work well for the health of England and the UK. It does not save money. It is inefficient and extracts wealth from health, without ostensible benefits for healthcare consumers. It is at best a rent, charged against sick people for the benefit of financial capital and the City. It may be tautological, or self-evident, but money that is drained away by rent-seeking capital is money not spent directly on healthcare for patients, which may also be the explanation for why the UK is already falling from the summit in the ranking of healthcare systems, falling to number thirty, according to The Global Burden of Disease Study 2015, behind all Scandinavian countries, Belgium, France, Germany, Italy, the Netherlands, and Spain.[46]

Privatized Healthcare Is Unhealthy, Expensive, Inefficient, and Unfair

In the USA, healthcare costs are higher than any developed nation, healthcare less efficient and accessible, and the healthcare system more privatized than virtually all developed nations. Danny Dorling has reminded us why medical systems that do not operate on the profit motive, but rather are motivated by well-being, are also the best medicine:

> It is not hard to understand that a medical system that aims to give the best care at the lowest cost, and one in which profit is not allowed, is both likely to do the least harm, and most likely to treat you quickly and appropriately when you actually most need treatment. There are no private accident and emergency wards in the UK; it is not in the interest of private hospitals to provide such facilities, ones where the need is so clear, and the scope for profiteering so low.[47]

This conclusion is borne out by the numbers, and not only in the UK. In the USA, back in 2003, the Bush Medicare expansion—the Medicare Prescription Drug, Improvement, and Modernization Act—led too much higher drug prices in the USA, producing a windfall gain for the drug companies estimated at $50 billion per year or more.[48] This happened because the government was not allowed to use its enormous leverage as the largest consumer of drugs to negotiate lower prices through Medicare, thanks to Congress. This was rent-seeking at best, giving pharmaceutical companies profits far above a normal market return.

Drug pricing is one of the principal reasons that healthcare is so expensive in the USA, where health outcomes are worse than in almost all advanced countries, despite being more costly. But the leading cause of healthcare inflation—and wealth extraction—is for-profit health insurance. Altogether, the USA spends more per capita on healthcare, and more as a percentage of GDP, 16.9%, than almost all rich nations. By comparison, France, with universal healthcare and nonprofit health insurance, spends less than an eighth of GDP at 11.6%, though it has far better outcomes.[49] The USA also spends about two and a half times what the average industrial nation pays for healthcare per capita, an inefficiency that is remarkable since America could easily emulate healthcare systems that are universal, affordable, and more equitable, without the bureaucratic nonsense that continues to characterize the American system several years after the introduction of the ACA.

The US healthcare system is a profit-based, "free-market-based" healthcare system. It has many of the best doctors and hospitals in the world. It is in the vanguard developing the latest technology. Yet by almost all measures the American system is lagging behind most if not all developed nations in many of the metrics that really matter—despite the advances of the ACA, a conclusion that even President Obama has acknowledged. In 2014, the Commonwealth Fund ranked the US healthcare system last of the eleven developed nations that it studied, including Australia, Canada, France, Germany, Netherlands, New Zealand, Norway, Sweden, Switzerland, and the UK.

Comparing quality care, access, efficiency, equity, healthy lives, and cost, the Commonwealth study found that the USA topped the rankings only in cost. The US spent $8508 per capita on healthcare, significantly outspending Switzerland's $5643, which ranked as the second most costly system after the USA. By comparison, the UK spent $3405 per capita for the same year.

As for quality care, the USA scored in the middle, ranked fifth, but the much maligned—in the USA—British system ranked first. As for access, the USA ranked ninth—because of inability to pay—while Switzerland and Germany tied for second. In terms of efficiency, the USA ranked last of the eleven ranked nations, a caveat that the pro-marketers should note: again the UK ranked first, followed by Switzerland, New Zealand, and Norway.

Equity? Dead last for the USA, with Sweden ranked first, followed by the UK and Switzerland tied for second. Finally, a category called healthy lives: the USA again ranked last, France ranked first, meaning that France had the healthiest nation, while the UK foundered in tenth position. The overall rankings reflected the metrics. The USA was ranked as the least effective healthcare system of the eleven nations measured, while the UK was ranked as the first and most effective healthcare system. Sweden and Switzerland were ranked second and third, while Germany and the Netherlands were tied for fifth.[50] The USA also ranked last in preventing deaths from treatable conditions, such as strokes, diabetes, high blood pressure, and certain cancers.[51]

What were the major differences in the healthcare systems compared and analyzed by the Commonwealth Fund? The USA was the most privatized healthcare system by far, practically unique in relying on for-profit health insurance—that is, a vast rent or subsidy—and a (mostly) hands-off policy of drug pricing, allowing a so-called competitive system to determine the cost of drugs. Likewise, the USA practically stands alone in letting the market determine costs of healthcare services. In most developed countries, charges for services provided, as well as drug prices, are negotiated with the government, something easy to do for single-payer countries where insurance is mostly provided by the state.

Damning as the Commonwealth figures are for the US healthcare system, other metrics reported by the Organization for Economic Cooperation and Development (OECD) are even more damning. In 2012, the USA had the highest obesity rates among adults out of sixteen ranked developed nations. Americans also paid more for pharmaceuticals than any of thirty-three measured nations, $1010 per capita per year. And when it came to public expenditure on health, what the state pays for healthcare of Americans, the USA again was last at 47.3% of total health expenditure, well below the OECD average of 72.3% public expenditure on healthcare. That meant more out of pocket expenses for the average American.[52]

To be sure the ACA has modified some of these figures, but healthcare inflation was again accelerating in 2017, not the least because there was little if any control over the cost of drugs which were minimally covered by Medicare. Meanwhile, for-profit insurers, disappointed that they were often losing money by participating in the exchanges set up under the ACA, were withdrawing from the exchanges. They are, after all, for-profits.

Two measures that give an overall view of healthcare systems are life expectancy and infant mortality. Again the US system lags. Americans born in 2016 could expect to live an average of 78.8 years, compared to the UK's 81.2 years. Japanese born the same year could expect to live the longest at 83.7 years, while citizens of France and Sweden could expect 82.4 years. Germany was slightly less at 81 years: what all nations have in common is that their citizens could expect to live a minimum of about two years longer than their American counterparts. It is much the same with infant mortality rates for 2015, a profound embarrassment and shame for the USA. Infant mortality rates per thousand were lowest in Finland and Sweden at two per thousand. Germany and Norway were still low at three per thousand, while Denmark, France, and the UK all recorded two infant deaths per thousand. The USA, once again, lagged significantly; six infants per thousand were dying at birth, still high although a slight improvement over the previous decade.[53]

The UK is increasingly becoming unequal as social benefits are cut and taxes are reduced on the ultra wealthy. British inequality is increasing because of the partial privatization of the NHS, which transfers more medical costs onto patients, who, we know, are being increasingly told to be responsible for their own health. As the British become less equal, it is unlikely their healthcare system will be as equitable and efficient as it has been. And as Britain becomes poorer—especially likely after the exit from the European Union (EU)—as the rate of poverty increases, partially because of the rise in healthcare costs, Britain's top healthcare ranking will be at risk.

At the other end of the spectrum is the USA. With 1% of Americans controlling about 45% of national financial wealth, the USA ranks well ahead of all other countries in concentrating wealth at the top. This means that wealth in the middle, what is owned by the proverbial middle class, is being diminished. The GINI coefficient, which measures the distribution of income throughout society on a scale of 0 to 1—where 0 stands for perfect equality and 1 indicates that all wealth belongs to one person, stood at 0.45 in the USA in 2012, the equivalent of massive reallocation of income upwards. By comparison, Denmark enjoyed a GINI of 0.25, Finland stood at 0.26, Sweden was at 0.275, Germany measured 0.29, France recorded 0.31, and the UK was at 0.35: all these measures were significantly lower than that of the USA.[54]

Moreover, as we might expect, low GINI scores correlated with low poverty rates. While the poverty rate of the USA in 2014 stood at 17.5%, the poverty rates of Denmark, Finland, France, Germany, and Sweden were in a narrow band between Denmark's 5.5% and France's 9%.[55]

When one remembers that health expenditure per capita per annum in these same countries ranges between Finland's $4612 and Sweden's $6808—much lower than the $9403 spent per capita in the USA—and compares these sums with the poor outcomes in the US healthcare system as opposed to other developed nations, several conclusions seem warranted: private, competitive, market-based, for-profit healthcare is expensive, inefficient, unfair, and far short of universal coverage.[56] It is not surprising that as medical inflation continues in the USA, as the cost of healthcare insurance rises even under the ACA, and as wealth and income are concentrated increasingly at the top, the very top, healthcare in the USA could become an unaffordable luxury.

Big Pharma: Getting Drugged by the Super-Rich

A half-decade after the introduction of the ACA, Joseph Stiglitz was still proclaiming that market-based medicine does not work, except for the rich who own and manage the healthcare companies.[57] Several years after Stiglitz warned Americans that healthcare should not be run as a business, and that healthcare in the USA would not improve as long as Americans tolerated a so-called competitive, or for-profit healthcare system, the ACA has made improvements, but not nearly enough to erase all the inefficiencies and shortcomings we have noted above. Some parts of the healthcare system are even worsening. Costs to be sure, access to be sure, but it is especially the inflation of drug prices that distinguishes American healthcare from its counterparts. What has driven the high cost of drugs? One leading cause is the refusal of Congress to allow Medicare to negotiate drug prices with drug producers, a boon for drug companies worth at least $50 billion. It is this fact also that distinguishes the USA from all other developed nations' healthcare systems.[58]

But this is only the beginning. The predation of drug companies in the USA, the industry's ability to extract rents from users of its drugs by minimizing or eliminating competition, by bypassing so-called markets, provides much of the pharmaceutical narrative. For example, government research has figured prominently in many if not most advances in biomedical research. Peter Gøtzsche, in *Deadly Medicines and Organized Crime: How Big Pharma has Corrupted Healthcare*, published in 2013, has shattered the myth that most breakthroughs are the result of industry-funded research. He shows that research for virtually all the basic science-enabling modern medicines has taken place in the nonprofit sector, at universities, research institutes, and government laboratories.[59] A US Congress report published in 2000 provided further confirmation of the government's prominent role in biomedical research: "Of the 21 most important drugs introduced between 1965 and 1992, fifteen were developed using knowledge and techniques from federally funded research."[60] Of these, National Institute of Health (NIH) research led to the development of seven drugs used to treat patients with cancer, AIDS, hypertension, depression, herpes, and anemia.

Other studies have concluded much the same. In 2011, it was reported in the *New England Journal of Medicine* that at least 80% of thirty-five major drugs were based on scientific discoveries made by public sector research institutions.[61] The National Cancer Institute played the lead role in the development of fifty of fifty-eight new cancer drugs approved by the Food and Drug Administration (FDA) between 1955 and 2001.[62] Three of the most important discoveries in the twentieth century—penicillin, insulin, and the polio vaccine—were developed in publicly funded laboratories. The NIH conducted an investigation on the five top-selling drugs in 1995, Zantac (ranitidine, for ulcers), Zovirax (acyclovir, for herpes), Capoten (captopril, for high blood pressure), Vasotec (enalapril, for high blood pressure), and Prozac (fluoxetine, for depression), and found that sixteen of the key seventeen scientific papers leading to the discovery and development of these drugs came from outside the industry.[63]

Between 1998 and 2002, 415 new drugs were approved. Of those, less than a third, 133, were innovative (molecular) entities. The others were modifications of old drugs, and of these only fifty-eight were given what is called priority review. This was a low yield, but over the short duration of five years, the yield actually dropped: in both 2001 and 2002, only seven innovative drugs were approved compared to a high of nineteen in 1999 and sixteen in 1998.[64] The drug industry, despite its claims, has not been so innovative.

Of the seven innovative drugs approved in 2001, five came from Big Pharma. Of the seven innovative drugs approved in 2002, only three came from a drug company, none of which were American. But small as this number was, most of the so-called innovations were what Marcia Angell has called "last-ditch treatments," rarely cures, to be used only when all older drugs had been ineffective.[65] Given this paltry success, it is fair to ask if high prices and high profits are inducements to innovate, or if they are simply the result of greed?

Back in 1998, the journal *Health Affairs* reported that only about 15% of the scientific articles that were cited in patent applications for clinical medicine came from industry research. About 54% came from academic centers, 13% from government and the rest from public and nonprofit institutions. An internal document not published by the NIH revealed similar percentages.[66]

Even in a high-profile disease like AIDS, the initial breakthrough came from public research. The USA spent twice as much on research as all the drug companies combined looking for effective drug therapies to alleviate and cure AIDS, from the time of the discovery of the disease until almost the end of the twentieth century.[67]

Typically, drug companies invest little in biomedical research, including the major breakthroughs in new therapies, despite the clamor heard from pharmaceutical corporations, many leading politicians, and neoliberal economists, that government needs to get out of the way of private enterprise. When there is important publicly funded research, Big Pharma will often—yet another rent—take it over and then sell the drug at an exorbitant price, easy to do since they now have a monopoly, while claiming that they developed the new drug therapy.[68]

If we net out taxpayer subsidies, then drug companies only spend some 1% of their revenues on basic research that is intended to produce new drugs and vaccines. Moreover, if we include pubic spending to develop new drugs and vaccines, the taxpayer actually accounts for 80% of total spending.[69] Investing so little of its own capital in biomedical therapies might seem to go against the best interests of Big Pharma. Yet this is consistent with everything we know about the so-called free market. Rent-seeking comes before public health, despite the claims of industry advertising. Executives are under pressure, some of it self-induced, to show quick returns, helping them to drive up stock prices and typically to push up executive salaries. And why invest those returns in research anyway, if the taxpayer is already there promising subsidies for biomedical therapies?

There are many myths about drug companies and their activities, motives and the effectiveness of their drugs. Some of the claims of Big Pharma have been repeated so often, that they have become widely believed by politicians, the public, and sadly by doctors themselves. Among the leading misconceptions is the belief that drugs are expensive because of the high discovery and development costs. Translated, this means that drug companies charge high premiums because of the expense involved in innovation and bringing new drugs to market. But Raymond Gilmartin, former CEO of Merck, which has ranked as one of the largest drug companies, admitted that high drug prices had little to do with the cost of innovation: "The price of medicines," he confessed, "isn't determined by their research costs."[70] It is rather, as Peter Gøtzsche has expressed it,

> that prices of drugs not only reflect what society is willing to pay but also how good the companies are at keeping competition at bay. Anti-competitive activities are widespread, and price fixing is common. We often hear that it costs $800 million (in 2000 dollars) to bring a new drug to the market, but this is false. It is based on flawed methods, debatable accounting theory and premised on blind faith in confidential information supplied by the drug industry to its economic consultants … who [are] paid by the same industry. The true cost is likely to be below $100 million.[71]

Aside from the accounting tricks that the industry has used to justify expensive drugs, there are numerous flaws with the argument defending high drug costs. As Marcia Angell has said, there is also an implied threat. If you want drug companies to keep developing lifesaving drugs, you should gratefully pay whatever the drug companies say they need to charge.[72] Alan F. Holmer, former president of the industry's trade association, Pharmaceutical Research and Manufacturers of America (PhRMA), confirmed Angell's point when he threatened, during a radio interview in 2002, that putting price controls on the pharmaceutical industry would reduce the R&D of the industry and would do irreparable harm to America's children and millions who had life-threatening conditions.[73]

Holmer's argument has been the industry mantra ever since. But the drug industry has never been transparent. Big Pharma does not make available what it actually spends developing each drug, arguing that such information is proprietary. So there is a permanently sealed black box. Nor is there a clear definition of what R&D includes. Much of it could be marketing costs and so-called education expenses, such as the expense of "educating" doctors. According to the calculations of Marcia Angell and Peter Gøtzsche and others, the actual development cost per drug has consistently been lower than $100 million, despite the industry's claim for the much higher figure of $800 million.[74]

Peter Gøtzsche has documented how drug companies minimize their costs, while reaping enormous profits by patenting scientific advances developed first in university, government or health institute laboratories. And it is not just patenting drugs that has led to windfall profits. Drug companies have long lobbied the US government to restrict competition, which patents help accomplish, and they have not been averse to price fixing, attested to by numerous scandals and a long trail of litigation.[75]

The first AIDS drug, Zidovudine, for example, was synthesized at the Michigan Cancer Foundation in 1964. Burroughs Wellcome spent very little of its own capital to develop the drug, but the company still charged $10,000 per year for one patient in 1987—something it could do because there was no competition. Burroughs knew that desperately ill patients demanded the drug at any cost. In 2003, Abbott increased the price of its AIDS drug, ritonavir, by 400%, though its development had been supported by millions of dollars of taxpayers' money. Abbott caused such outrage among doctors, that hundreds of them decided to boycott all of Abbott's products.[76]

There are many similar examples. Imatinib (Gleevec) is very effective against chronic myeloid leukemia. Novartis synthesized this drug but ignored it until a haematologist's research demonstrated its effectiveness as an anti-leukemia drug. Once again, development costs were minimal, yet Novartis, though it had literally stumbled into this drug, decided to charge $25,000 for a year's treatment in 2002. Taxol, an effective cancer drug, was derived from the bark of the Pacific yew tree and later synthesized by NIH-funded scientists.[77] The drug was then handed over to Bristol-Myers Squibb, which, despite minimal investment, charged between $10,000 and $20,000 for a single year's treatment in 1993. When the patent ran out, the company sued the companies planning to market a cheaper generic.[78] Twenty-nine US states sued Bristol-Myers Squibb for its obvious violation of antitrust laws, but the company knew that under recent legislation it could bring suit and delay the production of generics for thirty months. Bristol-Myers proved to be prescient. While litigation moved along at the pace of a tortoise, the company racked up revenues north of $5 billion. The case of course was settled against Bristol-Myers, but the fine of $135 million was much less than the billions of dollars in additional revenues earned while litigation was pending.[79]

Price fixing occurs in many countries besides the United States, even in Denmark. In 2010 several companies producing generic versions of citalopram—a commonly used antidepressant—withdrew their products from the Danish market, without providing any explanation. The price for the drug suddenly escalated by a factor of twelve, or 1200%: none of the companies still producing the drug offered comment.[80]

Simvastatin, a drug used to lower cholesterol and triglycerides, which was used by 6% of all Danes at one time, was the subject of another scandal in Denmark in 2007, when all companies marketing its generic equivalent raised the price of the 40 mg dose—the most commonly prescribed dosage—by 800%. The drug was also available at a lower dose at about a fifth of the price, but there was a legal problem. Pharmacies were not allowed to sell the lower dosage or to advise patients to take two tablets instead of one. Although the five producers of the drug raised its price to exactly the same level, even to the second decimal, the companies all denied collusion.[81]

Lundbeck, a Danish pharmaceutical company that operates internationally, was taken to court in 2006 by the US Federal Trade Commission, which alleged that the company had taken advantage of a monopoly situation selling a drug for extremely ill infants. Lundbeck had bought a US company, giving it ownership of an older drug, indomethacin, whose price it increased by 1300% after buying it from Merck. In this case there were no development costs at all.[82]

There is no shortage of examples of price gouging in the drug industry, especially when a company is able to establish monopoly control over a drug, as KV Pharmaceutical did in 2011, when it won US government approval to market a drug known as makena. Prior to this approval, for some five decades, obstetricians had routinely used a natural hormone, progesterone, to help prevent premature births. Pharmacies prepared the hormone for doctors at a cost between $10–$20 per injection. This all changed when KV Pharmaceutical won US approval. It soon raised the price of makena to $1500 a dose, an increase of 75–150 times the previous cost. Doctors protested that the high cost would almost certainly lead to more premature births and likely permanently brain-damaged children because women could not afford the elevated cost. Some doctors persisted and announced they were happy to continue getting the cheaper version of the drug from compounding pharmacies. The predictable response from the company was to send cease-and-desist letters to the compounding pharmacies, warning them they could face FDA enforcement actions if they still produced the drug.[83]

In 2015, in the *Harvard Political Review*, Tess Saperstein reported—following a study by the AARP Public Policy Institute—that between

2006 and 2013, the prices of 140 brand-name drugs had increased an average of 113%. This might seem like a modest increase to some, but remember that many of these drugs were not on patent, and anyway the official mantra of drug companies is that they face tough competition, implying that increased prices also reflect increased research costs. But we have already seen a number of examples in which drug companies incur no research costs, and are doing everything they can to eliminate competition by establishing monopolies through patents.[84] The only thing new about escalating prices are the prices themselves, not the drugs, not the costs incurred developing the drugs, not the increased expenses producing them. As Saperstein put it about the outsized profits:

> If the pharmaceutical market were functioning properly, we would expect that prices would gradually drop, since new companies would enter the market and compete with the name-brand companies for business. In reality, the market encountered a roadblock somewhere along the line, and competition to manufacture old medications has dwindled.[85]

Saperstein provided further illustrations of pharmaceutical companies acquiring the rights to a drug from another company and then, with no research expenses incurred, increasing the retail price. In 2013, Horizon Pharmaceuticals purchased the rights to vimovo, a drug therapy that treats osteoarthritis. On the very day that Horizon began selling vimovo, some two months after purchase, it increased the price by almost 600% to just under $960 for sixty tablets. A year later Horizon raised the price again, this time to $1680.[86]

On February 10, 2015, Valeant Pharmaceuticals, a Canadian multinational, bought the rights to Isuprel and Nitropress, two drugs that lower blood pressure. The same day the company raised their list prices by 525 and 212% respectively. According to Valeant, neither of the drugs was improved due to costly investment in lab work and human testing, nor was the manufacture of the medicines made more expensive by shifting it to an expensive new building. The only change was ownership of the drug, the only expense was acquiring it. Other than that, no investment costs, no research costs.[87]

An analysis by Deutsche Bank in 2015 found that drug acquisition and price gouging had become fundamental to Valeant's business strategy. In 2015 alone, Valeant raised the price of 81% of its drugs, according to the bank's study, by an average of 66% (a figure that was disputed by Valeant). But the steepest rises in price were for Glumetza, a diabetes drug whose price shot up 800%, and Zegerid, a drug that treats gastrointestinal problems, whose price was ratcheted up 550% over its original price. Despite the appearance of collusion, or of greed, or of exploitation, or of monopoly and rent-seeking (again), that was not how Valeant saw the suddenly inflated prices of the newly acquired drugs. This was an apt illustration of healthcare rentier capitalism in action. Valeant was just a good player, it claimed, and anyway wasn't this the system that everybody wanted: maximum market freedom: "Our duty is to our shareholders and to maximize the value."[88]

In 2001, Questcor Pharmaceuticals, a small company located in California, bought the rights to Acthar Gel, a medication that was effective in treating infantile spasms, a rare form of childhood epilepsy. A half-century earlier, two researchers at the Mayo clinic were rewarded the Nobel Prize in medicine for their work discovering ACTH, the active ingredient in Acthar. Five decades later, the company that contributed nothing to the discovery and development of the medicine, having acquired the rights to Acthar, raised the cost of a vial from \$40 to \$23,000.[89]

Martin Shkreli provides a recent and egregious example of price gouging. In September 2015, Shkreli, who was then the CEO of Turing Pharmaceuticals, bought the rights to Daraprim (pyrimethamine), a medicine used to treat parasite infections. Shkreli, who was well known as a hedge fund manager, proceeded to hike the cost of the medicine from \$13 to \$750 per dose (\$75,000 for a bottle of a hundred), an increase of 5500%.[90] Here again was an illustration of why drugs need to be regulated. In the absence of any legal restraints, Shkreli raised prices with complete contempt for healthcare consumers simply because he could, though the drug was decades old. He contributed nothing to its development, and once again the only thing that changed about the drug was its ownership.[91]

In 2013, *BBC News* reported that the pharmaceutical industry as a whole earned a profit of about 19%, putting it on a par with the banking industry. Five of the largest pharmaceutical companies earned profits above 20%, with US company Pfizer leading the way at 42%, followed by Hoffman-La Roche, AbbVie, GlaxoSmithKline (GSK), and Eli Lilly, earning profits between 20 and 24%.[92]

In 2012, a hundred leading oncologists from around the globe in an open letter published in the journal *Blood*, called for a reduction in the price of cancer drugs. They complained that of the twelve drugs approved by the FDA for a number of cancer indications in 2012, eleven were priced above $100,000 per year. They noted that drug prices for cancer indications had almost doubled in the previous decade, from an average of $5000 per month to more than $10,000 per month.[93]

Drug companies typically argue that R&D costs can be prohibitive, but their profit margins tell another story. And their narrative is deceptive. Pharmaceutical companies routinely spend more on marketing than they do on R&D, and in some cases the margin is twice as much. Johnson and Johnson, for example, for the year 2012, earned a profit of $13.8 billion, good enough for a 19% profit margin. But this was after accounting for sales and marketing expenses, which were excessively high at $17.5 billion, compared to $8.2 billion for R&D. Pfizer, with a profit of $22 billion, which clocked a 42% profit margin for the same year, spent $6.6 billion on R&D but almost double that amount on sales and marketing at $11.4 billion. Over in the UK, GSK registered similar numbers: it recorded a profit of $8.5 billion and 21%, after spending $5.3 billion on R&D and $9.9 billion on sales and marketing.[94]

There is a reason why drugs in the USA are so much more expensive. The USA is practically the only developed country that does not regulate the drug market. As we have seen in the many instances above, and in many more below, many drugs are expensive because of patents, or because the market is unregulated, or because US government research or funded research can be patented and sold at whatever price the market will bear, or because healthcare in the USA generally is a business. In countries where healthcare is a right, and where the government negotiates and regulates pricing, drugs cost much less. What accounts for the difference? Governments have huge negotiating power, for example, in single-payer countries, where they are the only medical consumer, and therefore any drug priced too high will be excluded from the healthcare market.

Extortion: Me-Too Drugs, or the Same Old Stuff in Different Bottles

There is considerable reason to believe that drug company cost-estimates per-drug development are deliberately falsified, and even extortionate. Big Pharma has argued that exorbitantly high prices are needed to cover high R&D costs, but most of the so-called innovative new drugs come from publicly funded laboratories. Big Pharma has in fact focused more on "me too" drugs—slight variations of existing drugs—and their development (including clinical trials) and marketing.[95]

We have already seen, following the research of Marcia Angell, that of new drugs approved by the FDA between 1998 and 2002, 77% of them were not innovative drugs. If they were not innovative, what were they then? In the words of Dr. Angell,

> Incredibly, they were all me-too drugs—classified by the agency as being no better than drugs already on the market to treat the same condition. Some of these had different chemical compositions from the originals; most did not. But none were considered improvements… . Seventy-seven percent of the pharmaceutical industry's output consisted of leftovers.[96]

There ought to be a law to prevent this kind of abuse, or aggressive rent-seeking, and there is: but it is hardly effective, and that is deliberate. The Bayh–Dole and Stevenson-Wydler Acts, both passed in 1980, and subsequent amendments were adopted to prevent abuses such as price gouging and rank profiteering. The acts specified that in vaguely defined "exceptional circumstances," the NIH could require that research it had supported in medical schools, teaching hospitals, and small biotechnology companies, not be patented but should remain in the public domain. The same was true of intramural research. This meant that the right to patent or license NIH funded research was not a given. Bayh-Dole also required that publicly funded research licensed to drug companies should be made available to the public at reasonable prices. Until 1995, the NIH insisted that drugs resulting from public-private collaboration should bear reasonable costs. The third condition of Bayh-Dole noted that work patented and licensed under terms of that act had to be reported to the NIH, so the institute could track which drugs originated in that way: in other words, drugs developed using government-supported research. If profits were judged excessive, drug companies had to return a portion of the royalties to the government: this was also true of intramural research. Finally, Bayh-Dole stipulated that the government retained the right to use a licensed drug itself, or issue compulsory licenses to other drug companies if the original firm were judged to be profiteering.[97]

Since 1995, given the revolving door syndrome between government and industry, and regulatory capture, safeguard provisions guarding against exploitation have been largely ignored. Drug companies have been allowed to "regulate" themselves, with the result that prices can have no limits: they are whatever the market will bear. But pricing standards are not the only area of predation in the industry. Big Pharma has been allowed to define the meaning of an "effective" drug, and this practice goes back decades.

Pharmaceutical companies do not have to show the FDA that a new drug is better—or even as good—as existing drugs already in use for the same condition. They only have to demonstrate that the new drug is more effective than nothing: comparing new drugs to nothing has been the industry standard since the early 1960s. Even a cursory glance at the FDA website confirms that most new drugs are compared to placebos or sugar pills, not the best current treatment.[98]

As is evident, in comparing new drugs only to placebo-controlled trials, it is possible—and perhaps inevitable—for new drugs to be approved that are worse than drugs already on the market. The relevant law in this case is the Kefauver-Harris Drug Amendment of 1962, which required drug manufacturers to show that new drugs were safe and effective, but failed to say what they should be compared with. This was translated to mean that they need not be compared to anything.

This critical defect in the law has allowed the drug industry to become a "me-too" (copycat) business. If companies had to show that their new drugs were better than older treatments already in use, then the number of copycat drugs would decline considerably.[99] Drug companies would have to engage in real innovation, instead of piggybacking on proven therapies. Instead, many pharmaceutical firms figure out ways to extend the life of a profitable drug about to go off-patent by producing an almost identical drug and shifting users to the new patent. To do this drug companies need only manufacture a drug that is different enough to qualify for a new patent, posing little or no obstacle.

There are many illustrations of this, Nexium for example. Nexium is a heartburn drug made by the British company AstraZeneca that was brought to market in 2001 just as the patent of the company's blockbuster drug, Prilosec, was about to expire. Without a replacement drug, AstraZeneca's finances would have suffered serious losses. With $6 billion in annual sales, Prilosec had once been the top seller globally. When AstraZeneca's patent expired, it would face competition from much lower priced generic brands, and the $6 billion in sales would vanish. So AstraZeneca developed an aggressive plan with multiple strategies, including lawsuits against manufacturers daring to contemplate making cheaper generic drugs. But it also hatched an even more aggressive strategy. The company knew that Prilosec contained an active form of the omeprazole molecule, and possibly an inactive form (isomer) of Prilosec as well. The plan was for AstraZeneca to apply for a new patent based on the active form of the Prilosec molecule, to call it Nexium, and to promote the new therapy as an improvement over Prilosec, and to do all this before the expiration of the patent on Prilosec.[100]

The strategy worked, as did its implementation. Before the patent on Prilosec expired, the FDA approved a patent for Nexium. The company then launched a massive promotion of Nexium, and successfully convinced Prilosec users and their doctors that Nexium was different and better than what it was replacing. In the wake of the campaign, Nexium became the most advertised drug in the USA. And just to make sure that the bait and switch worked, AstraZeneca priced Nexium just below Prilosec. To help make the transition, the company gave discounts to managed care plans and hospitals, provided doctors with free samples, and was brazen enough to offer coupons in newspapers. In 2001 alone, the company invested about a half billion dollars in its campaign, to assure that the new "innovation," the purple pill in the ad campaign, would replace Prilosec. It was not long before AstraZeneca dropped all references to Prilosec, which was meant to vanish from the public memory, even though Prilosec was soon sold over-the-counter for a fraction of the cost of Nexium.[101]

If there are some readers who still promote the magic of the market, they should already be disabused of that notion. But for those who believe that the consumer, or the patient, knows best, it is worth noting how and why AstraZeneca got approval for its "new" drug. Before the drug company could get FDA support, it had to conduct several clinical trials. Some of the trials compared Nexium to placebos. The results were clear, Nexium was better than nothing, satisfying the FDA. But AstraZeneca went further, comparing Nexium to Prilosec in tests for esophageal erosion.[102] The objective was to show that Nexium was not only better than nothing, but that it was better than "something": in this case that "something" was Prilosec.

But to do this was tricky, how could anything not be better than nothing? In other words, how could AstraZeneca make something that was no different than nothing, and still call it something? Yet this is what they did. Instead of comparing equivalent doses of the two therapies, the company used higher doses of Nexium, comparing 20 milligrams and 40 milligrams of Nexium with 20 milligrams of Prilosec. Given these comparisons, Nexium seemed an improvement over the older drug. But this was only marginally true and only in two of the four trials that were conducted. The only surprise, Marcia Angell has observed, was that Nexium didn't do better than it did. What did she think AstraZeneca should have done, if the firm had wanted to serve patients with heartburn? Double the standard dose of Prilosec, allow generic competition, and forget about Nexium.[103] But that would have hurt the profits of AstraZeneca because of the obstinacy of people who refused to pay $4 a pill, and so AstraZeneca turned right when it should have turned left.

Big Pharma and Patent Falsehoods

The drug industry has insisted that it has high research costs—and therefore the rising costs of pills are necessary to protect the public's health. Yet some 80% of the fundamental R&D is done directly by government, the NIH for example, or by publicly funded research at universities and research institutes. In fact, the Bayh–Dole Act of 1980 was passed to explicitly grant access to publicly funded research and then the right to patent products derived from it. But the vast majority of the pharmaceuticals patented by the industry are the same "me-two" products we have described above: they do not represent innovations, but ways for companies to imitate a therapy already developed and brought to market by another company. The result is families of drugs, statins like Lipitor or Crestor, for example, in which each therapy resembles and overlaps the characteristics of a predecessor. The real objective is to patent a slightly altered statin, which can then be marketed under its own brand, allowing a drug company to tap into a lucrative market without doing the preliminary R&D. Clearly, the motive is profit, since the new version adds little to improving drugs already on the market, or to improving the health of the public.

The drug industry is not only subsidized, R&D expenses are fully tax deductible, dollar for dollar. And that does not include all the tax breaks given to drug companies. They enjoy, collectively, tax credits worth billions of dollars, including a 50% credit for costs incurred testing "orphan drugs"—drugs with an expected market of less than 200,000 people. As of 2003, the FDA had listed 221 orphan drugs since the tax credit was adopted in 2000. Despite the tentative market cap, there have been important exceptions granted to industry: Retrovir, the first drug for HIV/AIDS, had a market that was well over 200,000, though it was listed as an orphan drug.[104]

The drug industry has become so super-lucrative that "drug wars" has been redefined. Despite the subsidies given for R&D, the granting of patents for research developed by the USA directly through NIH, or indirectly through university grants, and because drug prices are largely deregulated in the USA, drugs are more expensive than in all developed countries. In almost every case they are much higher. Gleevec, Novartis's breakthrough drug for some types of leukemia and other cancers, was sold in the USA on an annualized basis (in 2013 prices) for as much as $11,007 (much higher for higher dosages), or for as low as $5482, if discounted. In New Zealand the price was $989 and in Canada it was $1141. Nexium, widely prescribed for acid reflux, had an average monthly cost of $215 in the USA—before the patent ended in 2014—but only $23 in the Netherlands. Cymbalta, commonly used as an antidepressant, costs $194 monthly in the USA, but only $46 in England. The list goes on, but several conclusions can be drawn already. The same drugs cost much less outside the USA, and in many cases the differences are a multiple of 10 to 1 or more. The same can be said for tests, for example echocardiograms. The USA charges much more, routinely up to $4000 in mid-2016; the cost in Mexico is about $300 and in Spain it is about $130.[105] Who pockets the difference? The super-rich who own the healthcare companies, the hospitals, clinics, diagnostic centers, and especially drug manufacturers. Certainly not healthcare consumers.

As we have seen, Big Pharma justifies exorbitant prices by citing the high costs of R&D in particular. But the same should be true for other countries as well. The reason that drugs cost much less elsewhere, from Canada to Germany, the Netherlands, and Sweden, is because those countries regulate the price of drugs. In single-payer countries like Canada, Denmark, Sweden and the UK, the government functions as the sole buyer and payer of medical services and therefore has greater leverage. Europeans generally refuse to reimburse drug companies for drugs considered excessive and unjustified, especially when similar drugs are much less expensive and equally or more effective.

While many countries in Europe and Canada set wholesale drug prices, Medicare in the USA is barred from negotiating lower costs despite its considerable bargaining power as a kind of single payer for healthcare consumers above the age of sixty-five. Drug inflation is also explained by the US patent system, which awards patents for a period of twenty years, and then, as we know, routinely grants patents to me-too successors or copycat therapies.

But there has been a relatively new wrinkle in runaway drug prices in recent decades. As Robert Reich and Marcia Angell and many others have noted, the Patent Office and the courts initially ruled that products found in nature could not be patented: this is still the case in India and many other countries. Separating natural products from patents made good medical sense. That was why early vaccines, which used the body's immunity, could not become the private property of drug companies. That is why drug companies hesitated before investing in research necessary to produce new vaccines: without a monopoly, and outsized profits, there was little incentive to invest in research.

Then in the 1990s, the rules changed. New laws granted pharmaceutical companies the right to patent and manufacture vaccines and matter (products) found in nature. The new rules blurred the line—or effectively abolished it—between what was found in nature and what could be transformed into a monopoly protected by a patent. As a result, nature was privatized, effectively allowing Big Pharma to claim what occurred naturally as its own "product." As long as anything could be reproduced in a laboratory, it could be patented. Not only did the increase in patents on vaccines—which boost the body's natural immunity—grow geometrically, some tenfold to more than ten thousand, but vaccine prices also escalated. Pfizer, one of the largest drug companies, led the parade, developing Prevnar 13, a serum based on bacterial strains found in a natural state, which protects against diseases caused by pneumococcal bacteria, from ear infections to pneumonia. Given the new rules, Pfizer obtained a patent and became the only manufacturer. In 2013, it brought in almost $4 billion in sales of Prevnar 13 vaccine.[106]

Put another way, the government, often decried by Conservatives as anti-business, had drafted new rules granting monopolies to drug companies, obviously shifting rising costs of healthcare onto the consumer while protecting the monopoly profits of Big Pharma.[107] Such practices shift risk onto the consumer. They also illustrate how drug companies siphon billions of dollars from the real economy away from consumers to corporations and shareholders.

Big Pharma has demonstrated impressive ingenuity, not so much in developing new drugs but in figuring out ways to extend patents. Many drugs that are lifesaving remain under patent long after the patent has expired. This might seem like a contradiction, but again drug companies have been able to get the rules governing patents changed to suit them. This is because the Patent Office routinely renews patents on the basis of small and often insignificant changes in the original drug. Alterations in a single molecule are considered enough to make a "new drug" patentable.[108]

The financial burdens posed by extending patents, or recognizing a drug as new (and innovative), are not considered by the Patent Office. Alternatively, pharmacies are forbidden to substitute generic versions of a brand-name drug if it has changed in even a minor way. What is at stake is not just a matter of high prices, forcing consumers to go elsewhere. The problem is that often there is nowhere else to go—because of the patent system. The real problem, however, is not only that drug companies reap monopoly profits, but that these profits siphon wealth from the real economy and concentrate it at the top, which is why Americans pay much more for their drugs than do Europeans.

Subsidizing the Super-Rich: Drug Companies as Welfare Kings

The USA and the UK, and everywhere else, would be better off if we all abandoned the idea that we need drug companies. Just consider what we already know. Most of the innovative research and drug innovations have been based on government research or government-supported research at public institutions such as universities. What the industry reports as its research costs is, predominantly, direct advertising to consumers, legal only in New Zealand and the USA among developed countries, providing free drug samples to doctors—knowing they are more likely to prescribe these medications—and organizing conferences, where the industry presents its views as science. There are also clinical trials, with the infamous testing standards we have already discussed: the "new" medication need only be better than nothing.

A report published by the Health Research Group of Public Citizen, in July 2015, provided insights into how American taxpayers unwittingly subsidize the drug industry, often at the expense of their own health, contributing billions of dollars in welfare to an industry committed to profit, not the health and well-being of those who consume their pills and vaccines. Here is how the industry does it. Even after rebates, brand-name drugs cost Medicare 198% of the median costs for the same brand-name drugs for the thirty-one OECD countries. Within the USA, Medicare pays about 73% more than Medicaid and about 80% more than the Veterans Health Administration (VHA) for brand-name drugs. Under current Medicare pricing practices, non-innovative or me-too drugs are routinely priced as much or higher than older, equally effective drugs that are normally cheaper because they are off-patent. The result is that profits are artificially increased, reducing the incentive to develop innovative drugs. By simply allowing Medicare to negotiate drug prices—disallowed by the Medicare Modernization Act (MMA) of 2003—and by applying the same kind of standards as other governments—by refusing to buy brand drugs that are no more effective than older drug therapies that are generics and off-patent—taxpayer contributions to Medicare for drug insurance would be reduced by at least $11 billion per year. Finally, if Medicare could secure the same prices as Medicaid or the VHA, Medicare would save up to $50 billion per year, and more than $100 billion annually in the 2020s. In effect, this represents a substantial subsidy, and therefore an annual welfare payment to Big Pharma.[109]

But this is only the beginning. The Pew Charitable Trusts reported that for the year 2012, pharmaceutical companies spent more than $27 billion on marketing, $24 billion to physicians and $3 billion directly to consumers.[110] Since the industry does not promote generic drugs, but predominantly brand names because of their higher profitability, had there been much better regulation of prices, if Medicare had the right to negotiate the cost of drugs, if drug companies were not allowed to conduct promotion campaigns directly to consumers, and—to repeat—if they could not promote a brand name when there was another equally effective drug, and if pharmaceutical companies were not allowed to "educate" doctors as they now do, much of the $27 billion so-called research costs could be eliminated. If these expenses could not be used to reduce corporate taxes, drug companies would have greater tax liabilities as well.

However, the $27 billion price-tag pales in comparison when we consider what privatizing the drug industry costs us, though how we do the financing of the pharmaceutical industry hardly gathers any attention in public discourse or in the media. Currently, toward the end of 2016, the USA spends about $328 billion per year for prescription drugs. What drives this prohibitive cost? The fact that drugs are not sold in a competitive market, despite what we hear from the drug companies. On the contrary, pharmaceutical companies do everything to avoid competition. That is why they lobby for a patent system, knowing they can gain a monopoly and knowing also that they can patent government research. What drug companies know, but will never publicize, is that if drugs were sold in a truly competitive market, a market that did not include government granted patent monopolies, or rent-seeking gifts, or tax incentives, the drug industry would earn approximately $200 billion less per year. The pharmaceutical industry invests about $25 billion annually into research—much more goes for marketing as we saw—which means that Big Pharma earns about $8 dollars for every dollar it invests in research.[111]

In 2015, Medicare spent about $75 billion on prescription drugs for seniors. In 2016 it spent more than $97 billion. According to the Congressional Budget Office, by 2026 Medicare will spend $195 billion per year on prescription drugs, a rise of more than 100% in just one decade.[112] Paul Ryan and his Republican supporters argue that Medicare will bankrupt the USA because of healthcare inflation. But he is wrong. It isn't Medicare that is the problem. It is Paul Ryan: all he would need to do is to help raise taxes on the 1% to fund Medicare prescription purchases. But there is an even better remedy: regulate the drug companies, allow Medicare to negotiate the cost of prescriptions, and the cost to Medicare and to the taxpayer will be reduced by up to 80%. That could represent a savings of up to $80 billion for 2017, or $160 billion for the year 2026 if only Congress would repeal the law prohibiting Medicare negotiations of drug prices with the industry.[113]

Conclusion

Diminishing competition by routinely granting undeserved patents on drugs, banning Medicare negotiation of drug prices, maintaining a healthcare system using private for-profit healthcare insurance, granting patents on me-too drugs, routinely allowing patent extensions for drugs only a molecule different from predecessors, is expensive. Taking all these devices together, they constitute massive fraud and a giant rent charged against healthcare consumers, those very same taxpayers who are paying the rent.

Americans pay a tidy sum for a healthcare system that is not universally inclusive, that is more expensive per capita than any healthcare system in the developed world, and ranked last by most metrics when compared to healthcare in Canada, France, Germany, Italy, and Scandinavia. Maintaining the elites who control the drug companies, the private for-profit health insurance companies, and the so-called non-profit hospital systems, is expensive: a minimum of a half trillion dollars annually, with the promise of medical inflation looming in the immediate future, especially if the ACA should be amended or abolished by the administration of Donald Trump.

Like most other developed countries, the UK negotiates drug prices with the drug industry, mostly on the basis of what it calls "value-based pricing." This phrase is more than a cliché. It indicates that pricing has a direct relationship to value for the patient and for the NHS. This means that profits must be modest, it also means that for a drug to have value it must be an improvement on what already exists in the market.[114] The NHS keeps drug prices modest because it operates as an exclusive buyer of drugs for all citizens. The result is that the UK pays about a third less for its drugs compared to the USA, providing further evidence that the USA would be far better off adopting a drug regime closer to Britain and Europe, where healthcare is too important to become just another business.[115]

Notes

1. David Weigel, "Max Baucus, Once a Foe of Single-Payer Healthcare, Belatedly Endorses It," *Washington Post*, September 8, 2017.
2. Christy Ford Chapin, "How Did Healthcare Get to Be Such a Mess?" *New York Times*, June 19, 2017.
3. Ibid.
4. Ibid.
5. Christy Ford Chapin, *Ensuring America's Health: The Public Creation of the Corporate Healthcare System* (Cambridge: Cambridge University Press, 2015), 2–3.
6. Ibid.
7. Ibid.
8. David Himmelstein and Steffie Woolhandler, "The Bureaucratic Waste of ACA Quantified: The Post-Launch Problem: The Affordable Care Act's Persistently High Administrative Costs," *Health Affairs Blog* (May 27, 2015), http://healthaffairs.org/blog/2015/05/27/the-post-

launch-problem-the-affordable-care-acts-persistently-high-administrative-costs.

9. Reinhard Bussel and Miriam Blumel, "Germany: Health System in Review," *Health Systems in Transition* 16, no. 2 (2014), online at http://www.euro.who.int/__data/assets/pdf_file/0008/255932/HiT-Germany.pdf?ua=1.
10. Karen Davis, Kristof Stremikis, David Squires, and Cathy Schoen, *Mirror, Mirror on the Wall: How the Performance of the US Healthcare System Compares Internationally* (New York: The Commonwealth Fund, June 2014), online at http://www.commonwealthfund.org/publications/fund-reports/2014/jun/mirror-mirror; see also data.worldbank.org/indicator/SH.XPD.PCAP.
11. David Squires and C. Anderson, *US Healthcare from a Global Perspective: Spending, Use of Services, Prices and Health in 13 Countries* (New York: The Commonwealth Fund, October, 2015), https://www.ncbi.nlm.nih.gov/pubmed/?term=Squires%20D%BAuthor%5D&cauthor=true&cauthor_uid=26591905.
12. Himmelstein, "Bureaucratic Waste of ACA." For the $350 billion per annum figure, see Aliya Jiwani, David Himmelstein, Steffie Woolhandler, and James G. Kahn, "Billing and Insurance-Related Administrative Costs in United States' Healthcare: Synthesis of Micro-Costing Evidence," *BMC Health Services Research*, no. 14 (2014): 1–6, https://bmchealthservres.biomedcentral.com/track/pdf/10.1186/s12913-014-0556-7?site=bmchealthservres.biomedcentral.com.
13. Himmelstein and Woolhandler, "Bureaucratic Waste of ACA."
14. Ibid.
15. Ibid.
16. Ibid.
17. Ibid.
18. Henry K. Kaiser Foundation, News Release, "New Kaiser/New York Times Survey Finds One in Five Working-Age Americans with Health Insurance Report Problems Paying Medical Bills," January 5, 2016, online at http://www.kff.org/health-costs/press-release/new-kaisernew-york-times-survey-finds-one-in-five-working-age-americans-with-health-insurance-report-problems-paying-medical-bills/; see also Liz Hamel, Mira Norton, Karen Pollitz, Larry Levitt, Gary Claxton, and Mollyanne Brodie, *The Burden of Medical Debt: Results from the Kaiser Family Foundation/New York Times Medical Bills Survey* (Kaiser Family Foundation/*New York Times*, January 5, 2016), online at https://kaiserfamilyfoundation.files.wordpress.com/2016/01/8806-the-burden-of-medical-debt-results-from-the-kaiser-family-foundation-new-york-times-medical-bills-survey.pdf.

19. Wendell Porter, "No, Obamacare Is Not Killing the Insurance Industry," *Wendell Porter Blog*, online at https://www.healthinsurance.org/blog/2016/03/01/no-obamacare-isnt-killing-the-insurance-industry/; see also United Health Group, News Release, "United Health Group Reports 2015 Results Highlighted by Continued Strong and Diversified Growth," January 19, 2016, at http://www.unitedhealthgroup.com/investors/~/media/205CB82AC734CBDA8361AA1C1FFA803.ashx.
20. Aetna, News Release, online at https://news.aetna.com/news-releases/aetna-reports-fourth-quarter-and-full-year-2015-results/.
21. CIGNA, News Release, online at http://www.cigna.com/newsroom/news-releases/2016/cigna-reports-strong-2015-results-expects-revenue-and-earnings-growth-in-2016.
22. Anthem, News Release, April 29, 2015, online at http://ir.antheminc.com/phoenix.zhtml?c=130104&p=irol-newsArticle&ID=2041266.
23. Margot Sanger-Katz, "Signs of a Decline in Financial Distress Connected to Medical Bills," *New York Times*, January 15, 2015.
24. Consumer Financial Protection Bureau, press release, "CFPB Spotlights Concerns with Medical Debt Collection and Reporting," December 11, 2014, at http://www.consumerfinance.gov/about-us/newsroom/cfpb-spotlights-concerns-with-medical-debt-collection-and-reporting/; and Elizabeth Rosenthal, "How the High Cost of Medical Care Is Affecting Americans," *New York Times*, December 18, 2014.
25. *Huffington Post*, "Top 10 Reasons People Go Bankrupt," May 24, 2015, online at http://www.huffingtonpost.com/simple-thrifty-living/top-10-reasons-people-go-_b_6887642.html.
26. Olga Khazan, "Why Americans Are Drowning in Medical Debt," *Atlantic Magazine*, October 8, 2014, online at http://www.theatlantic.com/health/archive/2014/10/why-americans-are-drowning-in-medical-debt/381163/.
27. Elisabeth Rosenthal, "Paying Till It Hurts: A Case Study in High Costs, the $2.7 Trillion Medical Bill," *New York Times*, June 1, 2013.
28. David Whelan, "Obamacare Could Cause Nonprofit Hospitals to Lose Their Tax-Exempt Status," *Forbes Magazine*, September 17, 2012, online at http://www.forbes.com/sites/davidwhelan/2012/09/17/obamacare-could-cause-nonprofit-hospitals-to-lose-their-tax-exempt-status-heres-how/#5b379e9217d3.
29. Rosenthal, "The $2.7 Trillion Medical Bill."
30. David Cay Johnston, *Free Lunch: How the Wealthiest Americans Enrich Themselves at Government Expense (and Stick You with the Bill)* (New York: Penguin Group—Portfolio, 2008), 209.
31. Robert Mendick, Laura Donnelly, and Ashley Kirk, "The PFI Hospitals Are Costing NHS £2 Billion Every Year," *Daily Telegraph*, July 18,

2015. See Guy Standing's take on this problem in *The Corruption of Capitalism: Why Rentiers Thrive and Work Does Not Pay* (London: Biteback Publishing, Ltd., 2016), 189–90.
32. Ibid., 190. For background information, J. Owen, "Crippling PFI Deals Leave Britain £222 Billion in Debt," *Independent on Sunday*, April 12, 2015; and The Private Finance Watchdog Initiative, "Meet the Investment Firms That Own Your PFI Funded Schools and Hospitals," *pfeyeblog*, February 18, 2015, https://pfeyeblog.wordpress.com/2015/02/18/meet-the-investment-firms-that-own-your-pfi-funded-public-schools-and-hospitals/.
33. Liz Else, "Inequality: Of Wealth and Health: The Rising Affluence of the 1 Percent May Not only Mean There Is Less for Everyone Else. What Does Inequality Mean for Your Health? Special Report on Inequality," *New Scientist*, July 28, 2012, online at https://www.newscientist.com/article/mg21528752-400-inequality-of-wealth-and-health/.
34. Hélène Mulholland, "David Cameron Axes Equality Assessments in War on 'Red Tape'," *Guardian*, November 19, 2012.
35. Ibid.
36. Danny Dorling, *Inequality and the 1 Percent* (London: Verso, 2014), 132; and Danny Dorling, *In Place of Fear: Narrowing Health Inequalities* (London: Center for Labor and Social Studies (CLASS), May 21, 2013), 11–18, online at http://classonline.org.uk/docs/2013_05_Think_piece_-_In_Place_of_Fear_(Danny_Dorling).pdf. See also Danny Dorling, *Injustice: Why Social Inequality Still Persists*, revised edition (Bristol: Policy, 2015), 319–23.
37. Dorling, *Inequality and the 1 Percent*, 132.
38. Allan Baker, Justine Fitzpatrick, and Bobbie Jacobson, *Capital Concerns: Comparing London's Health Challenges with England's Largest Cities* (London: London Health Observatory, 2012), 7–9, 16–23, online at www.apho.org.uk/resource/view.aspx?RID=118051.
39. Child Poverty Action Group, *Welfare Reform: What It Means for Families at Risk of Poverty* (London: CPAG, 2012), online at http://www.cpag.org.uk/sites/default/files/CPAG_factsheet_the%20cuts_May13.pdf.
40. David Blane and Graham Watt, *GP Experience of the Impact of Austerity on Patients and General Practices in Very Deprived Areas* (Glasgow: Institute of Health and Wellbeing, University of Glasgow, 2012), online at http://www.gla.ac.uk/media/media_232766_en.pdf.
41. *BBC News*, "Life Expectancy Rises Again, ONS Says," October 10, 2011, online at http://www.bbc.com/news/business-15372869.
42. Dorling, *Inequality and 1 Percent*, 134–35, 214, note 17.

43. On the website of Public Health England, January 2017, to define its limited responsibilities, online at www.gov.uk/government/organisations/public-health-england/about.
44. Standing, *Corruption of Capitalism*, 273–74.
45. Crispin Dowler, "Trusts Exit from Capita HR Contract," *Health Service Journal*, June 18, 2014, https://www.hsj.co.uk/finance-and-efficiency/trusts-exodus-from-capita-hr-contract/5072024.article; and Ben Clover, "Three Trusts End Capita HR Contracts," *Health Service Journal*, September 30, 2014, https://www.hsj.co.uk/home/three-trusts-end-capita-hr-contracts/5075278.article.
46. Institute for Health Metrics and Evaluation, "Healthcare Access and Quality Index Based on Mortality from Causes Amenable to Personal Healthcare in 195 Countries and Territories, 1990–2015: A Novel Analysis from the Global Burden of Disease Study 2015," *Lancet* 390, no. 10091 (July 17, 2015): 231–66, http://dx.doi.org/10.1016/S0140-6736(17)30818-8.
47. Dorling, *Why Social Inequality Still Persists*, 442, footnote 40; Dorling's comments are based on the work of Edward Tufte, *Envisioning Information* (Graphics Press, 1990).
48. Dean Baker, *The Savings from an Efficient Medicare Prescription Drug Plan* (Washington, DC: Center for Policy Research, 2006), 3, online at http://cepr.net/documents/efficient_medicareMedicare_2006_01.pdf. According to Baker, Medicare could have saved almost $80 billion per year, $50 billion is closer to the low end! See also Stuart Silverstein, "This is Why Your Drug Prescriptions Cost So Damn Much," *Mother Jones*, October 21, 2016. See the statement by Kirsten Axelson, Vice President of Pfizer, http://www.motherjones.com/politics/2016/10/drug-industry-pharmaceutical-lobbyists-medicareMedicare-part-d-prices. Pfizer was a major lobbyist for denying Medicare the right to negotiate drug prices.
49. Joseph E. Stiglitz, *The Price of Inequality: How Today's Divided Society Endangers Our Future* (New York: W.W. Norton, 2013), 122–23; and IMF World Economic Outlook Database, online at http://www.stiglitz-sen-fitoussi.fr/documents/overview-eng.pdf.
50. Commonwealth Fund, press release, "US Health System Ranks Last Among Eleven Countries in Measures of Access, Equity, Quality, Efficiency, and Healthy Lives," June 16, 2014, online at www.commonwealthfund.org/publications/press-releases/2014/jun/us-health-system-ranks-last.
51. For the full Commonwealth Fund report, see Karen Davis, Kristof Stremikis, David Squires, and Cathy Schoen, *Mirror, Mirror on the Wall: How the Performance of the U. S. Healthcare System Compares*

Internationally (New York: The Commonwealth Fund, June 2014), online at http://www.commonwealthfund.org/~/media/files/publications/fund-report/2014/jun/1755_davis_mirror_mirror_2014.pdf.
52. Commonwealth Fund, "US Health System Ranks Last Among Eleven Countries."
53. These figures are based on OECD, *Country Statistical Profiles: Key Tables from OECD* (Paris: OECD, 2017), online at http://www.oecd-ilibrary.org/docserver/download/191100301e1t013.pdf?expires=1500225822&id=id&accname=guest&checksum=BCB10C83C4267695F3732C35249B3F25.
54. See OECD, "Income Inequality," online at data.oecd.org/inequality/income-inequality.htm.
55. OECD, "Poverty Rates," online at https://data.oecd.org/inequality/poverty-rate.htm#indicator-chart.
56. World Bank, "Health Expenditure Per Capita, 1995–2014," http://data.worldbankorg/indicator/SH.XPD.PCAP.
57. Stiglitz, *The Price of Inequality*, 122.
58. Ibid.
59. Peter C. Gøtzsche, *Deadly Medicines and Organized Crime: How Big Pharma Has Corrupted Healthcare* (Boca Raton, LA: CRC Press and Taylor and Francis Group, 2013), 249–51; Henry Mintzberg, "Patent Nonsense: Evidence Tells of an Industry Out of Social Control," *CMAJ* 175, no. 4 (August 15, 2006): 374, online at https://www.ncbi.nlm.nih.gov/pmc/articles/PMC1534100/.
60. US Senate, Office of the Chairman, Connie Mack, *The Benefits of Medical Research and the Role of the NIH*, May 2000, online at http://www.faseb.org/portals/2/pdfs/opa/2008/nih_research_benefits.pdf.
61. Ashley J. Stevens, Jonathan J. Jensen, and Katrin Wyller, et al., "The Role of Public-Sector Research in the Discovery of Drugs and Vaccines," *New England Journal of Medicine* (February 10, 2011): 535–37, online at http://www.nejm.org/doi/pdf/10.1056/NEJMsa1008268.
62. Merrill Goozner, *The $800 Million Pill: The Truth Behind the Cost of New Drugs* (Berkeley: University of California Press; 2005), 167.
63. Arnold S. Relman and Marcia Angell, "America's Other Drug Problem: How the Drug Industry Distorts Medicine and Politics," *The New Republic 227*, no. 5 (December 2002), 30–33.
64. Marcia Angell, *The Truth About the Drug Companies: How They Deceive Us and What to Do About It* (New York: Random House, 2005), 54–55.
65. Ibid., 56.
66. Ibid., 64–65.
67. Goozner, *The $800 Pill*, 86–87.

68. Ibid., 77–80; Robert Steinbrook, "The NIH Stimulus—The Recovery Act and Biomedical Research," *New England Journal of Medicine* 360 (March 12, 2009), online at http://www.nejm.org/doi/10.1056/NEJMp0900665.
69. Donald W. Light and Joel R. Lexchin, "Pharmaceutical Research and Development: What Do We Get for All That Money?" *BMJ (British Medical Journal)* 345 (August 11, 2012): 22–24, online at http://www.bmj.com/bmj/section-pdf/187604?path=/bmj/345/7869/Analysis.full.pdf.
70. Cited by Gøtzsche, *Deadly Medicines*, 249.
71. Ibid.
72. Angell, *Truth About Drug Companies*, 37.
73. Ibid., 38; and Alan F. Holmer on National Public Radio, "Talk of the Nation," hosted by Juan Williams, January 2, 2001, cited by Public Citizen, *Rx R&D Myths: The Case Against the Drug Industry's R&D "Scare Card,"* Congress Watch (Washington, DC: Public Citizen, July 2001), 1, online at https://www.scribd.com/document/62703342/This-new-Public-Citizen-report-reveals-how-major-U-S-drug-companies-and-their-Washington-D-C-lobby-group-the-Pharmaceutical-Research-and-Manufactu.
74. Angell, *Truth About Drug Companies*, 41–44; Gøtzsche, *Deadly Medicines*, 249.
75. Ibid., 251–52, 265, Gøtzsche, *Deadly Medicines*, 253–54; US Federal Trade Commission, *Generic Drug Entry Prior to Patent Expiration: an FTC Study* (Washington, DC: Federal Trade Commission, July 2002), online at www.ftc.gov.os/2002/07/genericdrugstudy.pdf; and Goozner, *The $800 Million Dollar Pill*, 231–48.
76. Gøtzsche, *Deadly Medicines*, 249.
77. Angell, *Truth About Drug Companies*, 38–39.
78. Gøtzsche, *Deadly Medicines*, 249–50; and Howard Brody, *Hooked: Ethics, the Medical Profession and the Pharmaceutical Industry* (Lanham, MD: Rowman and Littlefield, 2008),76–78.
79. Ibid.
80. Gøtzsche, *Deadly Medicines*, 250.
81. Ibid.
82. Ibid.
83. Ibid.
84. Tess Saperstein, "Medicated Monopolies," *Harvard Political Review* (December 10, 2015), online at http://harvardpolitics.com/covers/medicated-monopolies/.
85. Ibid.

86. Ibid., Jonathan D. Rockoff and Ed Silverman, "Pharmaceutical Companies Buy Rivals' Drugs, Then Jack Up the Prices," *Wall Street Journal*, April 26, 2015, online at http://www.wsj.com/articles/pharmaceutical-companies-buy-rivals-drugs-then-jack-up-the-prices-143009643.
87. Ibid.
88. Ibid.
89. A. Gordon Smith, "Price Gouging and the Dangerous New Breed of Pharma Companies," *Harvard Business Review*, July 6, 2016, online at https://hbr.org/2016/07/price-gouging-and-the-dangerous-new-breed-of-pharma-companies.
90. Derek Lowe, "Martin Shkreli Has One Idea, and It's a Bad One," *Science Translational Medicine*, September 21, 2015, http://blogs.sciencemag.org/pipeline/archives/2015/09/21/martin-shkreli-has-one-idea-and-its-a-bad-one.
91. Andrew Pollack and Matthew Goldstein, "Martin Shkreli All But Gloated Over Huge Drug Increases, Memos Show," *New York Times*, February 2, 2016.
92. Richard Anderson, "Pharmaceutical Industry Gets High on Fat Profits," *BBC News*, November 6, 2014, online at http://www.bbc.com/news/business-28212223.
93. Hagop Kantarjian, "The Price of Drugs for Chronic Myeloid Leukemia (CML): A Reflection of the Unsustainable Prices of Cancer Drugs: From the Perspective of a Large Group of CML Experts," *Blood*, First Edition Paper, Prepublished online April 25, 2013, online at https://doi.org/10.1182/blood-2013-03-490003.
94. Anderson, "Pharmaceutical Industry Gets High."
95. Angell, *Truth About Drug Companies*, 37–44; Mariana Mazzucato, *The Entrepreneurial State: Debunking Public vs. Private Myths in Risk and Innovation*, revised edition (New York: Public Affairs, 2015), 73, Fig. 7: Percentages of new drugs by type in the pharmaceutical industry.
96. Angell, *Truth About Drug Companies*, 75; National Institute for Healthcare Management Foundation, "Changing Patterns of Pharmaceutical Innovation," May 2002, at www.nihcm.org; and the FDA website, at www.fda.gov/cder/drmt/pstable.htm.
97. Angell, *Truth About Drug Companies*, 68–69; Eyal Press and Jennifer Washburn, "The Kept University," *Atlantic Monthly*, March 2000, 39, online at http://www.theatlantic.com/magazine/archive/2000/03/the-kept-university/306629/; and Peter S. and Michael H. Davis, "Why Don't We Enforce Existing Drug Price Controls?" *Tulane Law Review* 75, no. 3 (January 2001), online at https://papers.ssrn.com/sol13/papers.cfm?abstract_id=243040.

98. FDA Website, online at http://www.fda.gov/AboutFDA/WhatWeDo/History/Overviews/ucm304485.htm.
99. Angell, *Drug Companies*, 75–76.
100. Gøtzsche, *Deadly Medicines*, 172–73.
101. Ibid.; Gardiner Harris, "As a Patent Expires, Drug Firm Lines Up Pricey Alternative," *Wall Street Journal*, June 6, 2002; and "Two Fronts in Heartburn Battle," *New York Times*, August 20, 2003.
102. Gøtzsche, *Deadly Medicines*, 172–73.
103. Angell, *Drug Companies*, 78–79.
104. Goozner, *$800 Million Pill*, 46–48.
105. The $4000 figure for an Echocardiogram is based on personal experience. For cost comparisons see Medigo at https://www.medigo.com/en-us/procedure-pages/cardiology/echocardiogram.
106. Robert B. Reich, *Saving Capitalism: For the Many, Not the Few* (New York: Alfred A. Knopf, 2015). See the research at Robert W. Frenck, Jr., Alejandra Gurtman, et al., "Randomized, Controlled Trial of a 13-Valent Pneumococcal Conjugate Vaccine Administered Concomitantly with an Influenza Vaccine in Healthy Adults," *Clinical Vaccine Immunology* 19, no. 8 (August 2012): 1296–303, online at https://www.ncbi.nlm.nih.gov/pmc/articles/PMC3416075/.
107. See Robert Pear, "Bill to Let Medicare Negotiate Drug Prices Is Blocked," *New York Times*, April 18, 2007; and Elisabeth Rosenthal, "The Price of Prevention: Vaccine Costs are Soaring," *New York Times*, July 2, 2014.
108. Reich, *Saving Capitalism*, 23; and Angell, *Truth About Drug Companies*, 74–83; and Ray Moynihan and Alan Cassels, *Selling Sickness: How the World's Biggest Pharmaceutical Companies Are Turning Us All into Patients* (New York: Nation Books, 2005), 159–69.
109. Marc-André Gagnon and Sidney Wolfe, MD, Public Citizen Policy Brief, *Mirror, Mirror on the Wall: Medicare Part D Pays Needlessly High Brand-Name Drug Prices Compared with Other OECD Countries and with U.S. Government Programs* (Ottawa Canada: School of Public Policy and Administration, Carleton University, July 23, 2015), 11, online at http://www.citizen.org/documents/2269a.pdf. See also Congressional Budget Office, *March 2016 Medicare Baseline* (Washington, DC: Congressional Budget Office, 2016), online at https://www.cbo.gov/sites/default/files/recurringdata/51302-2016-03-medicareMedicare.pdf.
110. Pew Charitable Trusts and Fact Sheet, "Persuading the Prescribers: Pharmaceutical Industry Marketing and Its Influence on Physicians and Patients," November 11, 2013, online at http://www.pewtrusts.org/en/research-and-analysis/fact-sheets/2013/11/11/

persuading-the-prescribers-pharmaceutical-industry-marketing-and-its-influence-on-physicians-and-patients.

111. Dean Baker, "Firefighters and Prescription Drugs," *Truthout Blog*, Center for Economic Policy and Research, June 2, 2008, online at http://truthout.org/archive/component/k2/item/78463:firefighters-and-prescription-drugs; and Dean Baker, Truthout, "Liberals Working for the Right," *Truthout Blog*, Center for Economic Policy and Research, June 18, 2012, online at http://cepr.net/publications/op-eds-columns/liberals-working-for-the-right.
112. Congressional Budget Office, *Medicare Baseline by Fiscal Year* (Washington, DC: Congressional Budget Office, March 24, 2016), 1–2, online at https://www.cbo.gov/sites/default/files/51302-2016-03-MedicareMedicare.pdf.
113. Ibid.
114. UK Department of Health, "Pharmaceutical Price Regulation Scheme," December 21, 2015, online at https://www.parliament.uk/business/publications/written-questions-answers-statements/written-statement/Lords/2015-12-21/HLWS435/.
115. Ben Hirschler, "Exclusive—Transatlantic Divide: How US Pays Three Times More for Drugs," *Reuters*, October 12, 2015, online at http://www.reuters.com/article/us-pharmaceuticals-usa-comparison-idUSKCN0S61KU20151012.

Bibliography

Anderson, Richard. "Pharmaceutical Industry Gets High on Fat Profits." *BBC News*, November 6, 2014. http://www.bbc.com/news/business-28212223.

Angell, Marcia. *The Truth About the Drug Companies: How They Deceive Us and What to Do About It*. New York: Random House, 2005.

Arno, Peter S., and Michael H. Davis. "Why Don't We Enforce Existing Drug Price Controls?" *Tulane Law Review* 75, no. 3 (January 2001): 631–93. https://papers.ssrn.com/sol13/papers.cfm?abstract_id243040.

Baker, Allan, Justine Fitzpatrick, and Bobbie Jacobson. *Capital Concerns: Comparing London's Health Challenges with England's Largest Cities*. London: London Health Observatory, 2012. www.apho.org.uk/resource/view.aspx?RID=118051.

Baker, Dean. "Firefighters and Prescription Drugs." *Truthout Blog*, Center for Economic Policy and Research, June 2, 2008. http://truthout.org/archive/component/k2/item/78463:firefighters-and-prescription-drugs.

Baker, Dean. *The Savings from an Efficient Medicare Prescription Drug Plan*. Washington, DC: Center for Policy Research, 2006. http://cepr.net/documents/efficient_medicare_2006_01.pdf.

BBC News. "Life Expectancy Rises Again, ONS Says," October 10, 2011. http://www.bbc.com/news/business-15372869.

Blane, David, and Graham Watt. *GP Experience of the Impact of Austerity on Patients and General Practices in Very Deprived Areas*. Glasgow, Institute of Health and Wellbeing, University of Glasgow, 2012. http://www.gla.ac.uk/media/media_232766_en.pdf.

Brody, Howard. *Hooked: Ethics, the Medical Profession and the Pharmaceutical Industry*. Lanham, MD: Rowman and Littlefield, 2008.

Bussel, Reinhard, and Miriam Blumel. "Germany: Health System in Review." *Health Systems in Transition* 16, no. 2 (2014). http://www.euro.who.int/__data/assets/pdf_file/0008/255932/HiT-Germany.pdf?ua=1.

Chapin, Christy Ford. *Ensuring America's Health: The Public Creation of the Corporate Healthcare System*. Cambridge: Cambridge University Press, 2015.

Chapin, Christy Ford. "How Did Healthcare Get to Be Such a Mess?" *New York Times*, June 19, 2017.

Child Poverty Action Group. *Welfare Reform: What It Means for Families at Risk of Poverty*. London: CPAG, 2012. http://www.cpag.org.uk/sites/default/files/CPAG_factsheet_the%20cuts_May13.pdf.

Clover, Ben. "Three Trusts End Capita HR Contracts." *Health Service Journal*, September 30, 2014. https://www.hsj.co.uk/home/three-trusts-end-capita-hr-contracts/5075278.article.

Commonwealth Fund. "US Health System Ranks Last Among Eleven Countries in Measures of Access, Equity, Quality, Efficiency, and Healthy Lives." June 16, 2014. www.commonwealthfund.org/publications/press-releases/2014/jun/us-health-system-ranks-last.

Congressional Budget Office. *March 2016 Medicare Baseline*. Washington, DC: Congressional Budget Office, 2016. https://www.cbo.gov/sites/default/files/recurringdata/51302-2016-03-medicare.pdf.

Congressional Budget Office. *Medicare Baseline by Fiscal Year*. Washington, DC: Congressional Budget Office, March 24, 2016. https://www.cbo.gov/sites/default/files/51302-2016-03-Medicare.pdf.

Davis, Karen, Kristof Stremikis, David Squires, and Cathy Schoen. *Mirror, Mirror on the Wall: How the Performance of the U.S. Healthcare System Compares Internationally*. New York: The Commonwealth Fund, June 2014. http://www.commonwealthfund.org/~/media/files/publications/fund-report/2014/jun/1755_davis_mirror_mirror_2014.pdf.

Dorling, Danny. *In Place of Fear: Narrowing Health Inequalities*. London: Center for Labor and Social Studies (CLASS), May 21, 2013. http://classonline.org.uk/docs/2013_05_Think_piece_In_Place_of_Fear_(Danny_Dorling).pdf.

Dorling, Danny. *Inequality and the 1 Percent*. London: Verso, 2014.

Dorling, Danny. *Injustice: Why Social Inequality Still Persists.* Revised edition. Bristol, UK: Policy Press, 2015.

Dowler, Crispin. "Trusts Exit from Capita HR Contract." *Health Service Journal*, June 18, 2014. https://www.hsj.co.uk/finance-and-efficiency/trusts-exodus-from-capita-hr-contract/5072024.article.

Else, Liz. "Inequality: Of Wealth and Health: The Rising Affluence of the 1 Percent May Not only Mean There Is Less for Everyone Else. What Does Inequality Mean for Your Health? Special Report on Inequality." *New Scientist*, July 28, 2012. https://www.newscientist.com/article/mg21528752-400-inequality-of-wealth-and-health/.

Goozner, Merrill. *The $800 Million Pill: The Truth Behind the Cost of New Drugs.* Berkeley: University of California Press, 2005.

Gøtzsche, Peter C. *Deadly Medicines and Organized Crime: How Big Pharma Has Corrupted Healthcare.* Boca Raton, LA: CRC Press: Taylor and Francis Group, 2013.

Harris, Gardiner. "As a Patent Expires, Drug Firm Lines Up Pricey Alternative." *Wall Street Journal*, June 6, 2002.

Harris, Gardiner. "Two Fronts in Heartburn Battle." *New York Times*, August 20, 2003.

Henry K. Kaiser Foundation. "New Kaiser/New York Times Survey Finds One in Five Working-Age Americans with Health Insurance Report Problems Paying Medical Bills," January 5, 2016. http://www.kff.org/health-costs/press-release/new-kaisernew-york-times-survey-finds-one-in-five-working-age-americans-with-health-insurance-report-problems-paying-medical-bills.

Himmelstein, David, and Steffie Woolhandler. "The Bureaucratic Waste of ACA Quantified: The Post-launch Problem: The Affordable Care Act's Persistently High Administrative Costs." *Health Affairs Blog*, May 27, 2015. http://healthaffairs.org/blog/2015/05/27/the-post-launch-problem-the-affordable-care-acts-persistently-high-administrative-costs.

Hirschler, Ben. "Exclusive—Transatlantic Divide: How US Pays Three Times More for Drugs." *Reuters*, October 12, 2015. http://www.reuters.com/article/us-pharmaceuticals-usa-comparison-idUSKCN0S61KU20151012.

IMF. "World Economic Outlook Database," http://www.stiglitz-sen-fitoussi.fr/documents/overview-eng.pdf.

Institute for Health Metrics and Evaluation. "Healthcare Access and Quality Index Based On Mortality from Causes Amenable to Personal Healthcare in 195 Countries and Territories, 1990–2015: A Novel Analysis from the Global Burden of Disease Study 2015," *Lancet* 390, no. 10091 (July 17, 2015): 231–66. http://dx.doi.org/10.1016/S0140-6736(17)30818-8.

Jiwani, Aliya, David Himmelstein, Stefiie Woolhandler, and James G. Kahn. "Billing and Insurance-Related Administrative Costs in United States'

Healthcare: Synthesis of Micro-Costing Evidence." *BMC Health Services Research*, no. 14 (2014): 1–6. https://bmchealthservres.biomedcentral.com/track/pdf/10.1186/s12913-014-0556-7?site=bmchealthservres.biomedcentral.com.

Johnston, David Cay. *Free Lunch: How the Wealthiest Americans Enrich Themselves at Government Expense (and Stick You with the Bill)*. New York: Penguin Group—Portfolio, 2008.

Kantarjian, Hagop. "The Price of Drugs for Chronic Myeloid Leukemia (CML): A Reflection of the Unsustainable Prices of Cancer Drugs: From the Perspective of a Large Group of CML Experts," *Blood*, First Edition Paper, prepublished online April 25, 2013. https://doi.org/10.1182/blood-2013-03-490003.

Khazan, Olga. "Why Americans Are Drowning in Medical Debt." *Atlantic Magazine*, October 8, 2014. http://www.theatlantic.com/health/archive/2014/10/why-americans-are-drowning-in-medical-debt/381163/.

Light, Donald W., and Joel R. Lexchin. "Pharmaceutical Research and Development: What Do We Get for All That Money?" *BMJ* (*British Medical Journal*) 345 (August 11, 2012): 22–24. http://www.bmj.com/bmj/section-pdf/187604?path=/bmj/345/7869/Analysis.full.pdf.

Lowe, Derek. "Martin Shkreli Has One Idea, and It's a Bad One." *Science Translational Medicine*, September 21, 2015. http://blogs.sciencemag.org/pipeline/archives/2015/09/21/martin-shkreli-has-one-idea-and-its-a-bad-one.

Mazzucato, Mariana. *The Entrepreneurial State: Debunking Public vs. Private Myths in Risk and Innovation*. Revised Edition. New York: Public Affairs, 2015.

Mendick, Robert, Laura Donnelly, and Ashley Kirk. "The PFI Hospitals Are Costing NHS £2 Billion Every Year." *Daily Telegraph*, July 18, 2015.

Mintzberg, Henry. "Patent Nonsense: Evidence Tells of an Industry Out of Social Control." *CMAJ* 175, no. 4 (August 15, 2006). https://www.ncbi.nlm.nih.gov/pmc/articles/PMC1534100/.

Moynihan, Ray, and Alan Cassels. *Selling Sickness: How the World's Biggest Pharmaceutical Companies Are Turning Us All into Patients*. New York: Nation Books, 2005.

Mulholland, Hélène. "David Cameron Axes Equality Assessments in War on 'Red Tape'." *Guardian*, November 19, 2012.

Organization for Economic Cooperation and Development. *Country Statistical Profiles: Key Tables from OECD*. Paris: OECD, 2017. http://www.oecd-ilibrary.org/docserver/download/191100301e1t013.pdf?-expires=1500225822&id=id&accname=guest&checksum=BCB10C-83C4267695F3732C35249B3F25.

Organization for Economic Cooperation and Development. "Income Inequality." data.oecd.org/inequality/income-inequality.htm.

Organization for Economic Cooperation and Development. "Poverty Rates." https://data.oecd.org/inequality/poverty-rate.htm#indicator-chart.

Owen, J. "Crippling PFI Deals Leave Britain £222 Billion in Debt." *Independent on Sunday*, April 12, 2015.

Pear, Robert. "Bill to Let Medicare Negotiate Drug Prices is Blocked." *New York Times*, April 18, 2007.

Pew Charitable Trusts. "Persuading the Prescribers: Pharmaceutical Industry Marketing and Its Influence on Physicians and Patients," November 11, 2013. http://www.pewtrusts.org/en/research-and-analysis/fact-sheets/2013/11/11/persuading-the-prescribers-pharmaceutical-industry-marketing-and-its-influence-on-physicians-and-patients.

Pollack, Andrew, and Matthew Goldstein. "Martin Shkreli All But Gloated Over Huge Drug Increases, Memos Show." *New York Times*, February 2, 2016.

Porter, Wendell. "No, Obamacare Is Not Killing the Insurance Industry." *Wendell Porter Blog*. https://www.healthinsurance.org/blog/2016/03/01/no-obamacare-isnt-killing-the-insurance-industry/.

Press, Eyal, and Jennifer Washburn. "The Kept University," *Atlantic Monthly*, March, 2000, 39. http://www.theatlantic.com/magazine/archive/2000/03/the-kept-university/306629/.

Reich, Robert B. *Saving Capitalism: For the Many, Not the Few*. New York: Alfred A. Knopf, 2015.

Relman, Arnold S., and Marcia Angell. "America's Other Drug Problem: How the Drug Industry Distorts Medicine and Politics," *The New Republic* 227, no. 25 (December 2002): 27–41.

Rockoff, Jonathan D., and Ed Silverman. "Pharmaceutical Companies Buy Rivals' Drugs, Then Jack Up the Prices." *Wall Street Journal*, April 26, 2015. http://www.wsj.com/articles/pharmaceutical-companies-buy-rivals-drugs-then-jack-up-the-prices-143009643.

Rosenthal, Elizabeth. "How the High Cost of Medical Care Is Affecting Americans." *New York Times*, December 18, 2014.

Rosenthal, Elizabeth. "Paying Till It Hurts: A Case Study in High Costs, the $2.7 Trillion Medical Bill." *New York Times*, June 1, 2013.

Rosenthal, Elizabeth. "The Price of Prevention: Vaccine Costs Are Soaring." *New York Times*, July 2, 2014.

Sanger-Katz, Margot. "Signs of a Decline in Financial Distress Connected to Medical Bills." *New York Times*, January 15, 2015.

Saperstein, Tess. "Medicated Monopolies." *Harvard Political Review*, December 10, 2015. http://harvardpolitics.com/covers/medicated-monopolies/.

Silverstein, Stuart. "This Is Why Your Drug Prescriptions Cost So Damn Much." *Mother Jones*, October 21, 2016. http://www.motherjones.com/politics/2016/10/drug-industry-pharmaceutical-lobbyists-medicare-part-d-prices.

Smith, A. Gordon. “Price Gouging and the Dangerous New Breed of Pharma Companies,” *Harvard Business Review*, July 6, 2016. https://hbr.org/2016/07/price-gouging-and-the-dangerous-new-breed-of-pharma-companies.

Squires, David, and C. Anderson, *US Healthcare from a Global Perspective: Spending, Use of Services, Prices and Health in 13 Countries*. New York: The Commonwealth Fund, October, 2015. https://www.ncbi.nlm.nih.gov/pubmed/?term=Squires%20D%BAuthor%5D&cauthor=true&cauthor_uid=26591905.

Standing, Guy. *The Corruption of Capitalism: Why Rentiers Thrive and Work Does Not Pay*. London: Biteback Publishing, 2016.

Steinbrook, Robert. “The NIH Stimulus—The Recovery Act and Biomedical Research.” *New England Journal of Medicine* 360 (March 12, 2009). http://www.nejm.org/doi/10.1056/NEJMp0900665.

Stevens, Ashley J., Jonathan J. Jensen, and Katrin Wyller, et al. “The Role of Public-Sector Research in the Discovery of Drugs and Vaccines.” *New England Journal of Medicine*, February 10, 2011. http://www.nejm.org/doi/pdf/10.1056/NEJMsa1008268.

Stiglitz, Joseph E. *The Price of Inequality: How Today's Divided Society Endangers Our Future*. New York: W.W. Norton, 2013.

UK Department of Health. “Pharmaceutical Price Regulation Scheme.” December 21, 2015. https://www.parliament.uk/business/publications/written-questions-answers-statements/written-statement/Lords/2015-12-21/HLWS435/.

US Federal Trade Commission. *Generic Drug Entry Prior to Patent Expiration: An FTC Study*. Washington, DC: Federal Trade Commission, July 2002. www.ftc.gov.os/2002/07/genericdrugstudy.pdf.

US Senate, Office of the Chairman, Connie Mack. *The Benefits of Medical Research and the Role of the NIH*. Washington, DC: US Senate, May 2000. http://www.faseb.org/portals/2/pdfs/opa/2008/nih_research_benefits.pdf.

Weigel, David. “Max Baucus, Once a Foe of Single-Payer Healthcare, Belatedly Endorses It.” *Washington Post*, September 8, 2017.

Whelan, David. “Obamacare Could Cause Nonprofit Hospitals to Lose Their Tax-Exempt Status.” *Forbes Magazine*, September 17, 2012. http://www.forbes.com/sites/davidwhelan/2012/09/17/obamacare-could-cause-non-profit-hospitals-to-lose-their-tax-exempt-status-heres-how/#5b379e9217d3.

World Bank. “Health Expenditure Per Capita, 1995–2014.” http://data.worldbank.org/indicator/SH.XPD.PCAP.

CHAPTER 8

Big and Bigger Agribusiness: Farm to Table

Introduction

Back in 2011, Mark Bittman, writing in the *New York Times*, noted that the farm subsidy system was a joke: "Wealthy growers are paid even in good years, and may receive drought aid when there's no drought. It's become so bizarre that some homeowners lucky enough to have bought land that once grew rice now have subsidized lawns. Fortunes have been paid to Fortune 500 companies …"[1]

A year after Bittman's article appeared, Representative Stephen Fincher (R-TN) agitated, during a House Agricultural Committee debate, against food stamp assistance for the poor, although, in both the House and Senate version of the Farm Bill, nearly two million working families, children, and seniors had been denied food stamps. Fincher argued that this was proper: food stamps, he said, was an example of the government stealing "other people's money," or some people getting something for nothing. He cited the Bible to make his case: "The one who is unwilling to work shall not eat."[2] Despite Fincher's miserly stance toward the poor and the needy, he remained committed to subsidies for the rich. When it came to government handouts, he didn't object to something for nothing. Between 1999 and 2012, he was the second most subsidized farmer in Congress, collecting $3.48 million of other people's money.[3]

J. L. Luzkow, *Monopoly Restored*,
https://doi.org/10.1007/978-3-319-93994-0_8

Subsidizing Big Agribusiness: Monopoly on the Farm

Farm subsidies have been around for a while. They were originally intended as price supports for farmers during the Great Depression to help them avoid bankruptcy because of circumstances—such as the weather—beyond their control. The purpose, also, was to increase food supplies to help people avoid starvation. But long past the New Deal Era, farm subsidies and taxpayer support for agriculture continued, even when it had no ostensible purpose any more and was in fact helping to prop up windfall profits for corporate farms. The situation was mirrored and mimicked in a comic novel by Joseph Heller, *Catch 22*. In the novel, the father of Major made a good living not growing alfalfa: "The more alfalfa he did not grow, the more money the government gave him, and he spent every penny he didn't earn on new land to increase the amount of alfalfa he did not produce. [Each day, Mr. Major] sprang out of bed at the crack of noon … just to make certain that the chores would not be done."[4]

For years, one did not have to grow any crops to be treated as a farmer in the USA. In a short period of four years, between 2007 and 2011, according to figures released by the General Accountability Office (GAO), the US government paid about $3 million in subsidies to 2300 farms where no crops of any sort had been grown. Between 2008 and 2012, some $10.6 million was paid to farmers who had been dead for more than a year.[5]

Such aberrations were an anomaly of course, but subsidies for large corporations have been anything but anomalous. For years, US farm subsidies have been egregious and expensive, harvesting about $20 billion per year from taxpayers. Much of this money has gone to big farmers or corporate farms, which produce staple commodities such as corn and soybeans, concentrated in big agricultural states like Iowa.

Between 1995 and 2012, the US government spent over $277 billion of taxpayers' money on agricultural subsidies. The largest share of these subsidies by far, reflecting their political clout, went to a small number of large—corporate—operations: 75% of subsidies went to only 3.8% of US "farmers."[6] In an ironic note, the large producers who took a disproportionate share of subsidies, as Laura Etherton and the Environmental Working Group (EWG) have documented, used the federal dollars they received to buy out smaller farms around them, meaning that subsidies actually worked to displace small farmers to make large—often corporate farms—eligible for further subsidies, yet another example of how large corporate producers can minimize or eliminate competition and absorb more taxpayer dollars for themselves.[7]

Of the $277 billion plus farm subsidies gifted between 1995 and 2011, at least $81.7 billion went to subsidize corn; wheat and cotton growers received more than $32 billion each; and soybean growers received subsidies of more than $26 billion. Other subsidies went to rice, sorghum—grass used to feed livestock—peanuts, barley, tobacco, livestock, and dairy production.[8] In 2009, taxpayer costs for crop insurance programs alone rose substantially to $5.7 billion because higher premiums resulting from rising crop prices drove up premium subsidies to farmers, but this cost was driven even higher in 2011, almost doubling to $11 billion.[9] Moreover, unlike other agricultural subsidy programs, the federal crop insurance subsidy did not require caps, or payment limitations, which back in 2011 meant a boon for Big Agriculture. The GAO was able to show that just 4% of the most profitable farm operations accounted for 33% of all premium support provided by the federal government. For the same year, 2011, as noted by the United States Department of Agriculture (USDA), "farmers" made more than $98 billion in profit, a figure large enough to beg the question of why taxpayers should be subsidizing rich corporations.[10]

The EWG Farm Subsidy Database shows that farm subsidies for the period 1995–2014 were more than $322 billion, not counting the cost of research and statistical data provided by the government.[11] That is an average of more than $16 billion per annum, plus the annual $5 billion—minimally—in research support, plus the incalculable assistance helping seed companies like Monsanto, which have been able to get into Mexican markets and beyond thanks to the financial and commercial diplomacy of the USA.

But high as the costs of subsidizing Big Agriculture have been, the CATO Institute—a conservative think tank whose politics and instincts are more libertarian than Republican, and therefore even more anti-Big Government—has suggested they will be much higher than what we have already seen. This is despite the fact that the 2014 Farm Agricultural Act repealed direct payments—a substantial number of which had gone to farmers who did not suffer crop damage or even actively farm—and countercyclical payments, which were too easy for farmers to game and which over-compensated them regardless of whether prices rose or fell. But the new farm bill also created two new programs, Price Loss Coverage (PLC) and Agriculture Risk Coverage (ARC), that seemed to extend welfare for the rich, not reduce it. Producers of covered commodities—including corn, soybeans, wheat, and oats—could choose either program and be covered for either low prices, or low yields.[12]

The 2014 Farm Agriculture Act was largely friendly to Big Agriculture because it had many friends in Washington, among them Secretary of Agriculture Tom Vilsack, the former governor of the State of Iowa. The farm bill passed easily in the Senate, with sixty-eight votes, and comfortably in the House. Intended as a kind of reform bill, it did little to reform or reduce the big subsidies that propped up the outsized profits of Big Agriculture. It did abolish direct payments based on land ownership, banning subsidies to those "farmers" not actively engaged in farming or food production. But farmers were given more subsidized insurance, linking new subsidies to previous crop prices and productivity. Theoretically, the new farm legislation would save $23 billion over a decade, but since payments were linked to crop prices, and farm incomes were predicted to decline by 32% for the year following the passage of the new farm legislation, subsidies were almost a certainty to rise to replace falling incomes. In other words, rich corporate farms could look forward to (substantial) profits built into the system by guaranteed subsidies.[13]

If anything, the Farm Agriculture Act of 2014 granted more welfare to corporate farms, as well as to the insurance companies underwriting the agriculture sector. The government picked up 62% of a policy's premium on average; farmers paid 38%. Corporate farms benefited the most because premiums guaranteed up to 85% of benchmark revenues: even a bountiful harvest could bring handsome insurance redemptions—because a larger harvest would likely lead to lower prices that would kick in increased subsidies.[14]

This was precisely the point of the PLC program, a fundamental piece of the new legislation. Under PLC, farms would receive subsidies when corn, soybeans, and twelve other crops dropped below a target price. This all but guaranteed that farms would collect payouts, especially for corn and cotton, which previously were the same crops most often earning direct payments. The PLC program was especially advantageous to corporate farms, which now had the incentive to plant additional acreage—which presumed a lower yield—knowing the price support system would kick in additional subsidies to meet price benchmarks.[15]

The new law also included a program called ARC, which was added for "shallow losses" not covered by crop insurance deductibles, virtually removing any and all liability regardless of price or yield. If a farmer experienced a 15% "loss," i.e., missed an artificially high target price, and his crop insurance carried a 25% deductible, ARC would cover the difference or "loss". Farmers could not lose: whether choosing PLC or ARC, a farm had no liability. Farms did not pay for the cost of insurance, nor for the deductible, while target prices were virtually guaranteed at favorable rates.[16]

The new legislation was also a cash cow for the private insurance companies administering the crop insurance program, anything but a reform of previous practice. The crop insurance industry received $1.3 billion for administrative expenses—mostly paid by the government—just for 2011. In fact, this was its historical average, about a billion dollars annually for the first decade of the twenty-first century, with a 30% average return.[17]

The Farm Agricultural Act of 2014 was the reform act that wasn't. Taxpayers were liable for a significant share of payments that went to producers if they should suffer a "loss" of either income or yield. Under the new law, farmers could actually do better if there was widespread crop failure, or a loss of revenue from price decline (or collapse), since they were fully insured by government subsidy programs. The more that farmers "lost" from drops in yield or price, the greater the cost to the taxpayer. But the taxpayer also was liable when crop prices rose. That is because land values rise with the price of farm commodities, and that means that insurance premiums, largely paid by the federal government, go up.[18] It was *Catch-22* again.

Called a reform bill by Republicans, the farm bill of 2014 was denounced by many Democrats as bountiful for the rich—subsidies were simply reallocated—but punitive for the poor. This was because the farm bill stripped out food stamp spending altogether—putting this into a separate bill—despite the fact that wages for the middle class and working class had stagnated for decades, while prices for subsidized foods—and virtually all food commodities—had not. Realizing how much "fat" the rich retained even post-reform, Democrats were prompted to remark that Republicans were not so much against welfare as they were against the poor.[19]

Thinking back to FDR's four freedoms, especially the freedom from want, Paul Krugman put it even more starkly. For the Grand Old Party, "freedom's just another word for not enough to eat," or the freedom to be hungry.[20] As Krugman angrily put it, the Republicans were waging war against food stamps when House Republicans voted to slash them sharply back in 2013, while pushing to increase farm subsidies dominated by the corporate rich.[21] One might ask what Republicans could gain by depriving those already destitute enough to actually need food stamp assistance? Or why anybody could conclude that hungry people are hungry by choice, as the Republicans seemed to imply: after all, why would people not take a job if they were hungry?

So why did Conservatives target food stamps, or the Supplemental Nutritional Assistance Program (SNAP), the food stamp program's proper name? Although public spending as a share of gross domestic product (GDP) was falling, enrollment in SNAP grew from twenty-six million Americans in 2007 to forty-eight million in 2013—when Krugman was shaming House Republicans, falling off to about forty-five million in 2016. The cost of SNAP also rose from $17 billion in 2000 to $78 billion in 2012, declining to about $75 billion in 2015.[22]

For Conservatives, growth in SNAP should not have existed at all, after all the financial crisis and recession officially ended in 2009, and therefore, why would so many needy people require food stamps when clearly they were no longer needy? The rich are like that, of course, they see only shirkers in the poor, not in the 1% who caused the financial meltdown and Great Recession in the first place, driving millions of people toward dependency on food stamps. Nor do the rich see that post-2009 there was no recovery for the poor, not even for much of the middle class. Most of the gains between 2009 and 2016 went by far to the 1% and those who served them. Yet neither Congress nor the 1% acknowledged that millions of Americans were kept out of poverty only because of food stamps, or that because of the expansion of SNAP, hundreds of thousands of jobs were created, mostly in the private sector. The reason that SNAP rolls expanded, Krugman explained, was that,

> while the recession did indeed officially end in 2009, what we've had since then is a recovery of, by and for a small number of people at the top of the income distribution, with none of the gains trickling down to the less fortunate. Adjusted for inflation, the income of the top 1 percent rose 31 percent from 2009 to 2012, but the real income of the bottom 40 percent actually fell 6 percent.[23]

Never mind that SNAP kept people out of poverty, or that many people eligible for food stamps were actually working. The rich still insisted that welfare was bloated because it encouraged idleness. How else to put it when Paul Ryan, who apparently never went hungry or worked for minimum wage (which he has helped to preserve as a "minimum" wage), the chairman of the House Budget Committee at the time that SNAP was being curtailed, characterized the food stamp program as an example of turning a safety net into "a hammock that lulls able-bodied people to lives of dependency and complacency."[24] Was it possible that Ryan did not know that the previous year, on average, food stamp benefits were $4.45 per day? Or that almost two-thirds of SNAP beneficiaries were children, the elderly, or the disabled?[25]

The real welfare, as Paul Ryan knew, didn't go to the poor. The 2014 farm reform bill, according to the USDA Risk Management Agency, did not change much. If anything, farm subsidies were increased. They were simply channeled through different programs. The crop insurance program, which disburses more subsidies than other programs, now accounts for outlays of about $8 billion per year.[26] Subsidized crop insurance protects against low production, low revenues, and adverse weather conditions, covering more than a hundred crops, although corn, cotton, soybeans, and wheat are the most subsidized. Crop insurance also covers insurance premiums and the administrative costs of the nineteen private insurance companies offering policies to farmers.[27] Knowing that crop insurance is a welfare program for multi-millionaires, Congress has worked diligently to obscure the identities of the wealthy recipients, easily done by routing the largest portion of farm subsidies through the insurance program where the beneficiaries are not transparent.[28]

Subsidy amounts fluctuate but, according to the USDA, the ARC subsidy payout was about $7 billion for 2016.[29] PLC subsidies for 2016 were about $2 billion.[30] The USDA also manages farm conservation programs, providing subsidies that cost some $5 billion per year to the taxpayer. While some of these may be good ecologically, the largest conservation program, the Conservation Reserve Program, pays farmers $1.7 billion per year to keep millions of acres out of production.[31]

The total subsidies following the reform farm bill of 2014 add up to a minimum of $19 billion and as much as $25 billion annually, depending on price fluctuations, a sum that excludes about 67% of the cost of the conservation program. But if $19 billion seems like a relatively small amount of corporate-farm welfare, it should be remembered that crop insurance, price support, conservation subsidies, disaster relief, and commodity payments are only the beginning of welfare socialism for rich corporate farmers. Research and marketing support cost billions of dollars in addition. Note also that back in 2011 the farming sector netted $98 billion in profits, an indication that welfare, especially for the large corporate farms, was not needed.[32] Price support for corporate farms means keeping prices higher than they would be if government subsidies were not available to reassure agribusiness. And agribusiness has done well. Consider one of the largest corporations, Archer Daniels Midland, a recipient of government subsidy largesse. Its profit for 2015 was $1.8 billion, and this was a decline from 2014, when Archer Daniels reaped a hefty $$2.2 billion in profit.[33]

Over the two decades prior to 2014, farm subsidies totaled more than $320 billion. That represents a massive transfer of wealth from taxpayers to wealthy farmers, especially the top 4% of farms scoring a third of the total subsidies. The reform farm bill of 2014 did replace "direct payments" if commodity prices were to fall, regardless of how much farmers planted or how much prices fell, but some experts were predicting that the real costs to the taxpayer over the next decade would still be in the neighborhood of $195 billion. That is because savings from direct payment cuts have been shifted to an increase in crop insurance programs. Since the US government subsidizes about 62% of the premium costs of farmers—who buy insurance to shield themselves against price fluctuations—farmers can lock in high prices regardless of crop size or market conditions. The farm bill also extends the number of beneficiaries beyond corn, wheat, soybean, rice, cotton, peanut, and dairy farmers. It includes the fishing industry, alfalfa growers, and producers of biomass and sweet sorghum. And beyond that there is special peanut revenue insurance and funds to study the extension of insurance to cover losses because of food recalls or health advisories related to contamination. There is even insurance against business interruption for poultry producers. The result is that farmers will have little if any liability in case there should be "losses".[34]

All of these additions represent—mostly—transfers of wealth to corporate farms and those who manage them. But there are yet other kinds of subsidies as well. Sugar growers enjoy protectionist tariffs that spike domestic sugar prices by keeping out less expensive foreign sugar. Sugar growers also benefit from an allotment scheme that limits domestic sugar protection, helping boost sugar prices closer to targets set by the US government. If market prices fall below targets, the government is committed to buy sugar at the higher price, a subsidy to sugar producers and a significant cost to consumers. These kinds of tariff measures only "tax" American consumers indirectly, but they are not unusual and they are costly. Between 1998 and 2004, US butter was protected against foreign competition, resulting in US prices that were double international prices, and likewise US cheese, which for the same years was 58% higher than international prices.[35]

Subsidizing Sugar: How Sugar Went Sour

Sugar is the sweetest deal of all. Estimates are that protecting American sugar growers against foreign competition, plus the price support system mandated by government, has a cost to the consumer—who is also a taxpayer—of $3 billion per year, a significant amount of welfare and wealth transfer from consumers to the rich. There is also a collateral cost to consumers, their health. The high-fructose corn syrup industry did not exist before the early 1970s when the sugar price support regime was first implemented. The industry was born only because of the artificially high prices of sugar created by protectionism and sugar price support. Four decades later, high-fructose corn syrup, a cheap substitute for sugar, accounts for roughly half of all sugar consumed in the USA. Many clinicians and nutritionists believe it is no accident that the outsized consumption of high-fructose corn syrup has coincided with obesity, diabetes, and liver disease.[36] What is clear is that such pathologies as obesity and diabetes were not the health threats they have become since the widespread introduction of high-fructose corn syrup into soft drinks and foods typically called junk foods, many of which are in the American diet because they are cheap—and often addictive because of the sweetener.

Inflated sugar prices have cost American consumers up to $3 billion a year for well over three decades because of price support and tariffs, while the high-fructose substitute has cost many billions more because of health problems associated with its consumption. So how did the sugar industry, generally, whether cane sugar or corn growers, convince Americans that sugar was safe to consume and not a threat to their health? The strategy was simple: shift blame to fat.

The sugar industry paid scientists handsome sums in the 1960s to deemphasize links between sugar and heart disease, by promoting saturated fat as the chief cause of coronary heart disease. It was not until internal sugar industry documents were discovered by a researcher at the University of California in San Francisco, and published in September 2016 in *JAMA Internal Medicine*, that it was discovered that some five decades of research into the relationship between nutrition and heart disease were mostly shaped by the sugar industry. What the documents reveal is that the Sugar Research Foundation, also known as the Sugar Association, paid three Harvard researchers to publish a 1967 review of research on sugar, fat, and heart disease. Unsurprisingly, the articles that were given to the Harvard trio for review were handpicked by the Sugar Association. Right on cue, and with a fistful of dollars, the Harvard professors found minimal linkage between sugar and heart disease. The culprit according to them was saturated fats.[37]

One of the scientists paid by the sugar industry was Mark Hegsted, later the head of nutrition at the USDA, where in 1977 he helped draft a forerunner of the dietary guidelines of the federal government. A second scientist was Frederick J. Stare, who was the chairman of Harvard's nutrition department between 1942 and 1976. In 1964, John Hickson, a sugar industry executive, discussed a plan with other industry executives that would link high rates of heart disease with saturated fats and dietary cholesterol, while discrediting studies connecting high-sugar diets with coronary disease "through our research and information and legislative programs."[38] In 1965, Hickson formally began his campaign to debunk studies linking sugar consumption and heart disease by enlisting the Harvard researchers to write a review critical of anti-sugar studies. Paying the professors-nutritionists $6500, the equivalent of $50,000 in 2016 dollars, Hickson made it clear he expected the results to be favorable to sugar interests. Sharing early drafts with the researchers, Hickson was satisfied that his investment was well placed. The professors were coming to the desired conclusion, and why not; it had been paid for.[39] In this way, sugar entered the American diet, blinding Americans to the health hazards caused by the naked pursuit of self-interest and by the likely rise in human morbidity.

Fifty years later, reports showed that the food industry continued to influence "nutrition science." This time it was Coca-Cola's turn to bend the "research." Coke, the largest producer of sugary beverages, backed what it called a science-based solution to obesity, counseling more exercise and less concern with cutting calories. For those who remained unconvinced, Coca-Cola collaborated with scientists willing to promote its message in medical journals, academic conferences, and even social media like Twitter. To help its partner scientists, Coke provided considerable financial and logistical support to a nonprofit organization called Global Energy Balance Network (GEBN), which defied most medical practitioners by proclaiming that weight-conscious Americans should be less fixated about how much they eat and drink and concentrate more on exercise. The nonprofit's vice-president, Steven N. Blair, an exercise scientist, even stated that there was no compelling evidence that sugar-sweetened fast foods and sugary drinks led to obesity.

There was of course no compelling evidence that the consumption of sugar did not lead to obesity and type-2 diabetes. No doubt aware of this, Coke made a substantial investment in GEBN, though this was not readily disclosed by Coke. Not until requests based on state open-records laws that is: only then did two universities that employed leaders of Global Energy disclose that Coke had donated $1.5 million to start the organization.[40]

That was only part of Coke's campaign to support sugary beverages. From 2008, Coca-Cola provided about $4 million in funding for Dr. Steven Blair, a University of South Carolina professor, and Gregory Hand, dean of the West Virginia School of Public Health: both were founding members of GEBN. Its Web site, gebn.org, was also registered to Coca-Cola headquarters in Atlanta, Georgia, and Coke was listed as the site's administrator. Asked whether this fact meant that Coke had editorial control over the content of the network's site, the group's president, James O. Hill, professor at the Colorado School of Medicine, issued a reassuring rejoinder that Coke had registered the site because the network's members did not know how. This was a statement that might make most people wonder how GEBN's scientists could figure out that sugar consumption was healthy and that there was no compelling evidence otherwise. In a bit of pique, Professor Hill noted that, "They're (Coke) not running the show. We're running the show."[41] Dr. Blair added that Coke had no control over the work and the message of the network, and anyway he saw no problem with Coke's support since he and the group had been transparent about their relationship with Coke.

Well, almost transparent. Coke, it seems, had forgotten to disclose that it was supporting the work—and the "science"—of GEBN, an oversight that was "corrected" following an inquiry about sponsorship of GEBN's online site. The group's Facebook and Twitter sites, which had actively championed physical activity as the solution to chronic disease and obesity, remained silent about food and nutrition—read sugary drinks and junk foods—as causes of heart-related disease and obesity. The network, coincidentally, failed to reveal a relationship with Coke, although Rhona Applebaum, chief scientific officer of Coca-Cola public relations, had lauded the work of the group.[42]

Coke still did not retreat, relying on reputable scientists like Dr. Hill to make its case. After all, he seemed like a good investment. Dr. Hill was not only the GEBN's president, he was also a co-founder of the National Weight Control Registry, a long-term study of people who had lost weight. He served on committees of the World Health Organization and the National Institutes of Health. And the American Society for Nutrition even called him a leader in the fight against the global obesity epidemic.[43]

This was not necessarily reassuring for a number of other scientists. Barry Popkin, a professor of global nutrition at the University of North Carolina at Chapel Hill, explained that the tactics used by Coke were reminiscent of those once used by the tobacco industry, which also enlisted experts to become "merchants of doubt," as attorney and author Larry White once put it, about the health hazards of smoking.[44] Marion Nestle, professor of nutrition, food studies, and public health at New York University, was even more critical of Coke: "The Global Energy Balance Network is nothing but a front group for Coca-Cola. Coca-Cola's agenda here is very clear: get these researchers to confuse the science and deflect attention from dietary intake."[45]

An analysis published in the journal *PLOS Medicine* found that studies funded by Coca-Cola, PepsiCo, the American Beverage Association, and the sugar industry were five times more likely to find no link between sugared drinks and weight gain than studies whose authors had no reported financial links to the industry.[46] But GEBN continued to call itself the voice of science. It even provided links to two research papers providing strong evidence, it said, of the group's contention: if you want to lose weight, the key is to exercise, not reduce food intake. Unfortunately, each paper contained a footnote that the publication of the article was supported by the Coca-Cola Company.[47]

Coca-Cola, unashamed and undaunted, soldiered on. But then it encountered resistance it had not expected when voices were raised denying its claims to scientific legitimacy. In August 2015, the chairman of the nutrition department of Harvard's School of Public Health wrote a scathing letter, signed by thirty-six other scientists, criticizing Coca-Cola and the GEBN for spreading "scientific nonsense," a phrase that would seem to challenge the scientific credibility of Drs. Hill and Blair. Shortly thereafter, the American Academy of Pediatrics and the Academy of Nutrition and Dietetics, which had accepted millions of dollars from Coca-Cola, announced they were severing all links with the beverage company, begging the question of why they had accepted money from Coke in the first place. When GEBN emails were scrutinized, it turned out that Coke had named its leaders, created its mission statement, and even designed its Web site, signs that its relationship with the network was incestuous. The University of Colorado School of Medicine then announced it was returning a million dollar grant to Coke, while the GEBN announced it was closing its website.[48]

The vast majority of public health officials acknowledge that energy balance is an important concept: weight gain is about calories in versus calories out. But research by far concludes that the best way to maintain or lose weight is to consume fewer calories. Exercise increases appetite, making it likely that its advantages are linked to an increase in caloric increase. The best way to lose weight—and to maintain that loss—is to limit intake of high glycemic foods like sugary drinks—soda drinks especially—and other refined carbohydrates, which sharply raise blood sugar. Exercise is important, but it does not expend enough calories to maintain or reduce weight. A single can of Coke contains 140 calories, about ten teaspoons of sugar. To offset this, it takes three miles of walking.[49]

One rigorous analysis of the impact of physical activity on weight loss, published in the journal *Obesity*, recruited 200 overweight, sedentary adults and put them on an aggressive exercise program. The adults were instructed not to change their diets, so they could more accurately isolate the effects of exercise. Participants in the study were instructed to exercise five to six hours per week, doubling federal guidelines. The results were conclusive: men lost an average of 3.5 pounds after a year, and women lost an average of 2.5 pounds for the same period. Virtually, all who participated in the study remained overweight. The authors of the study concluded that diet mattered much more than exercise for weight loss.[50]

Corporations like Coca-Cola that sponsor "scientific" studies are not interested in science. They are interested in profit. They don't get involved because they are concerned with health and they want to maintain consumer consumption of their products. Coke is hardly the only corporate sponsor promoting health strategies that are profit-friendly, but it has certainly been successful in shaping—and subverting—the conversation about sugar when it comes to its soda beverages. It donated money to build more than a hundred fitness centers in more than a hundred schools across the USA. When the City Council of Chicago proposed a soda tax in 2012, to address the obesity problem in Chicago, Coca-Cola donated $3 million to establish fitness programs in more than sixty of the city's community centers. Coke was successful, the initiative to tax soda failed. Exercise, the company admonished, was the best antidote for obesity. Cheering on families in Chicago, Coke claimed the moral high ground. The battle against obesity and overweight begins, it said, "with the next push-up, a single situp or a jumping jack."[51] These were hardly bad things in themselves, but they were diverting public education and conversation away from legitimate science, while suppressing the truth about sugar through corporate-funded science or by shifting the conversation toward exercise as the best way to combat obesity and excessive weight.

For decades, the soda industry has argued that the obesity epidemic has multiple causes while evading its own responsibility toward a nation that is critically overweight. When Coke and Pepsi argue that Americans eat too much or that they exercise too little, such arguments are undeniably true. But it is also true that soda drinking is one of the biggest causes of the obesity increase. Science agrees that drinking soda is driving obesity and related diseases:

> Sugar-sweetened beverages (soda sweetened with sugar, corn syrup, or other caloric sweeteners and other carbonated and uncarbonated drinks, such as sports and energy drinks) may be the single largest driver of the obesity epidemic. A recent meta-analysis found that the intake of sugared beverages is associated with increased body weight, poor nutrition, and displacement of more healthful beverages; increasing consumption increases risk for obesity and diabetes.[52]

For a period of two decades, between the late 1970s and the late 1990s, the consumption of soda accounted for about half the total increase in calories in the USA. Consumption fell off after that, partially because of greater public awareness and rising costs, but a decade and a half later, in 2016, soda drinking had increased threefold for the typical American compared to the late 1970s.[53] That was because children and adolescents had been targeted extensively by soda industry advertising: so much so that in the mid-1990s children's intake of sugared beverages surpassed their consumption of milk. More than fifteen years later soda beverages accounted for 10–15% of all calories consumed by children and adults. Moreover, for children who regularly consumed one can or glass of a soda beverage per day, the likelihood of obesity increased by 60%.[54] Yet despite the science, the major producers continued to identify lack of exercise and poor eating habits as the major contributors to obesity, heart disease, and diabetes, while promoting studies that confirmed their denial of the dangers of overconsumption of sugared beverages.

The High Cost of Cheap Junk Foods: How Poor Health Enriches the 1 Percent

At a time when food production is as efficient as ever, and when high-quality food can be produced abundantly and cheaply, almost three-quarters of Americans are either obese or overweight. The reason? The American diet consists of too many junk foods—foods short on nutrients but high in calories. According to the data of the federal government in a report published in 2010 by the Dietary Guidelines Advisory Committee, breads, sugary drinks, pizza, pasta dishes, and "dairy desserts" are included among the top ten sources of calories among all Americans.[55]

Following the government report and a Harvard Health article publicizing it, the *New York Times* published an article in July 2016 by Anahad O'Connor, entitled "How the Government Supports Your Junk Food Habit," in which the author asked which ingredients were typically found in junk foods? The answer was corn, soybeans, wheat, and dairy. In their natural states, these products are hardly junk foods. But a high percentage of these foods are never eaten in their natural states, and this has especially been true of corn sweeteners, especially high-fructose corn syrup, which is derived from heavily subsidized corn. High-fructose corn syrup is in everything from breads, crackers, and cereal, to mayonnaise, ketchup and mustard, to ice cream, jams, cookies, soft drinks, and even yogurts and nutrition bars. Nothing, it seems, is excluded. O'Connor's conclusion? Government corn subsidies were helping to addict Americans to high-fructose corn syrup, and this was a significant contributing factor to obesity and diabetes, with predictable consequences for healthcare costs.[56]

Largely because of junk foods, and the government subsidies that help to underwrite them, the USA is today in the midst of a public health crisis. Obesity has become a national problem affecting adults and especially children. The obesity rates of children have tripled in the last three decades. Nearly 20% of children aged between six and eleven are obese, and the percentage continues to rise. The consequences of childhood obesity are immense. Obese children, for example, have arteries so thick they resemble the arteries of forty-five-year-old adults, making them susceptible to heart disease. Some 70% of obese five- to seven-year-olds have at least one of the risk factors for heart disease.[57]

The crisis cannot be fully measured in dollars, but Laura Etherton, Mike Russo, and Nasima Hossain published a report in 2012 on behalf of the US Public Interest Research Group (PIRG), "Apples to Twinkies 2012: Comparing Taxpayer Subsidies for Fresh Produce and Junk Food," which found that $150 billion per year was spent on problems related to obesity and comorbidities—heart-related problems for example—a sum that had doubled in the decade between 2002 and 2012.[58]

If predictions prove correct, and if there are no significant changes in policy, projections are that by 2030 half of all Americans will be obese and the USA will be spending an additional $66 billion a year on related medical costs.[59] There are a number of reasons for the production and consumption of junk food: consumer taste for one. But what the public clamors for can also be manipulated by industry, which spends millions promoting obesity-fueling empty calories—sugar coating for example—that are too often underwritten by federal subsidies. In 2011 alone, the US government spent more than $1.28 billion in subsidies that supported junk food ingredients, which brought the total spent subsidizing junk food between 1995 and 2011 to an outlandish $18.2 billion altogether. By contrast, between 1995 and 2011, the government spent only $637 million subsidizing apple production.[60]

By subsidizing junk foods—with minimal if any nutritional value—government spending has inadvertently supported obesity. This is especially true of corn syrup, high-fructose corn syrup, and cornstarch, all derived mostly from corn. Since 1995, the federal government has spent about $8.7 billion subsidizing corn that was turned directly into corn-based sweeteners and cornstarch.[61] When we add up the subsidies for commodities turned into junk foods, $18.2 billion between 1995 and 2011, $3 billion per year protecting sugar, and the increased costs of healthcare that are the result of eating junk foods—up to another $150 billion per annum as cited above, and then add the direct and indirect subsidies to Big Agribusiness, $19 billion and beyond annually, we begin to understand just how much we are subsidizing the super-rich, and how unaffordable they have become for all of us.

Subsidizing the Gentry Farmers of Britain

In the UK, the British have coddled and subsidized their own "farmers" much like the USA, but there is a substantial difference. The so-called agriculturalists and agronomists of Britain have a much longer lineage, and as a group, they are not only a landed elite, they also control most of Britain just as they did in the feudal era. In Britain, not much has changed, including inherited inequality—made worse by the coalition government of the Tories which has been intent, since it came to power in 2010, on maintaining the comforts and ease of the native aristocracy and the country gentlemen of Britain. There has developed something of a consensus that there are too few houses and that planning laws are overly restrictive. But there is also a counterview that too much of Britain has been bulldozed and set into concrete, and that the lands are less green and more odious every passing year. Land is scarce and becoming scarcer, the argument goes, until Britain simply runs out of the stuff.

This is, of course, a myth, easily dispelled by a look around. Many of the landowners of Britain are aristocrats who acquired their holdings through a quirk of ancestral good luck or who are at the long end of a succession that began with the Norman Conquest, or who benefited by the dissolution of the monasteries—a bit of good fortune during the sixteenth-century dispossession. There was also the wonderful benevolence of Parliament, which sanctioned the enclosures between 1688 and the Great Revolution and the final acts of the nineteenth century that removed much land from the commons through a centuries-long privatization. How the beneficiaries acquired their lands, whether by being well connected to Parliament, or by being on the right side of the religious struggles of the sixteenth century, or by the violence of the Norman Conquest, the result was the same: a landed elite that still controls much of the land of Britain.

All that was the bucolic past, but what about the bovine present? Like a number of American cousins, and through another quirk of good luck, and contemporary privilege, British aristocrats—be they major or minor gentry—are paid to keep their acreage off the market through a system of European Union (EU) agricultural subsidies. The result is a scarcity of land on which to build, and a consequence of that is not only a lack of decent housing, but a lack of plentiful food production. That is because in the EU—and that means in the UK pending departure from the EU—subsidies are given to landowners, to any who possess acreage, not necessarily to food growers. In Britain, it is a good thing to be a gentleman on the estates, one can command a handsome sum without having to bother about all those bad seeds, or problem fertilizers, or advocates of green farming and best ecological practices. At least one could do so until Brexit, after which farming—or not farming—might not be so lucrative.

The UK, it turns out, is not so developed after all. Only 10.6% of England and 6% of Britain are actually developed. Land is not so scarce, only permission to build is scarce. Which brings up a perplexing question for the British: why do so many people persist in believing that Britain is running out of land? And for that matter, who really owns Britain? How did its present owners come to control so much acreage, and what does that mean exactly for everybody else, especially for those who suffer from a housing shortage, or who lack even proper nutrition? The Labor Party—never mind the Tories, they are defenders of the status quo and the 1%—never speaks of the need for a land tax and never seriously mentions land reform. Jeremy Corbyn has hardly uttered a squeak about housing shortage, or even nutritional deprivation—through land reform, meaning redistribution, and land taxes—was once a great principle of the liberals.[62]

For Labor to omit reform of the land regime may be sacrilegious, but what should one conclude when Laborites avoid mention of a land value tax—when even an orthodox free trader, Martin Wolf, a *Financial Times'* financial correspondent, sees such a tax as the sine qua non of a rational land development policy. Not to levy a land tax against the landed elite is to squander an opportunity to tax the enormous wealth of this group of 1 percenters, whose wealth grows exponentially because of the scarcity of land. Landed aristocrats, subsidized by the EU agricultural system, protected by the British Parliament, have been escaping unscathed from land and inheritance taxes. Back in 2006, Martin Wolf argued that inadequate housing and absence of permission to develop land were intimately connected:

> In 2005, the average value of a hectare in mixed agricultural use in England was some £9,300. In residential use it was £2.46m. Such are the price distortions created by keeping the bulk of the population in urban reservations. Since society creates the increase in value, with the stroke of a pen, it should also obtain some portion of the benefits.[63]

Giving permission to develop agricultural land as residential property, and then taxing these lands based on higher valuation, would create tax revenues to build infrastructure, such as schools and highways. Developers of properties so designated would have an incentive to develop the property since they would pay the same taxes either way, even if they did nothing.

Four years later, after the financial crisis of 2007–2008, Martin Wolf's remarks resonated even more widely. To merely sit on land and watch its value go up incrementally, without adding any labor or capital improvement to it, was an intolerable form of rent-seeking. Wolf even despaired that he had become something of a minor aristocrat (and rent seeker) without raising an arm:

> In 1984, I bought my London house. I estimate that the land on which it sits was worth £100,000 in today's prices. Today, the value is perhaps ten times as great. All of that vast increment is the fruit of no effort of mine. It is the reward of owning a location that the efforts of others made valuable, reinforced by a restrictive planning regime and generous tax treatment – property taxes are low and gains tax-free.... So I am a land speculator – a mini-aristocrat in a land where private appropriation of the fruits of others' efforts has long been a prime route to wealth. This appropriation of the rise in the value of land is not just unfair: what have I done to deserve this increase in my wealth?[64]

The emphasis here should be on low property taxes and no taxes at all on the added value of land, which rises despite no efforts to improve it by its owner. The emphasis also is on the fact that keeping rural land undeveloped, by squeezing the British people onto urban reservations, pumps up land values in populated areas, amounting to an artificially created scarcity of land (for development) and inflating land values in (rural) undeveloped areas—which are untaxed—as the inevitable result. Land speculation is inevitable. The less land that is developed, the more that developed land is worth. And what makes it even more valuable is that the added value is not taxed, which fuels speculation further: "This is the most important way in which wealth is transferred from the unpropertied young to the propertied old," adds Martin Wolf.[65]

Britain's iniquitous system of land ownership is well known and it has been around for a while. In 1911, Herbert Asquith was moved to pass the Parliament Act, establishing the primacy of the House of Commons over the House of Lords, which was one of the staunchest defenders of landed privilege in Britain. A century hence and not much has changed, despite Asquith's noble attempt at reform. Of the sixty million acres in the UK, forty-two million acres are designated "agricultural" land and twelve million are called "natural wastage," such as forests, rivers, and mountains, which are owned by institutions like the Forestry Commission, the Ministry of Defense, and the National Trust. The remaining six million acres are known as the "urban plot," not a reference to a mystery novel but the densely congested lands on which the houses, factories, and offices of Britain are built. This "urban plot" represents some 10% of the landmass of Britain, compressed enough by any standards. But it is even worse than it sounds. Most of the sixty-two million people of the British Isles live on just three million acres. As Jason Cowley and George Eaton have been able to document, this means, in effect, that 69% of British acreage is owned by less than 1% of the population (0.28% to be exact), or some 158,000 families. Britain, in other words, belongs to the 1%; it is a virtual—as the authors put it—cousinhood, a concentration of ownership so extreme that it is unrivalled in Western Europe, with the possible exception of Spain. Never mind that the British lords of the cousinhood receive their own fair share of subsidies—something they fear they might lose because of Brexit—but their virtual monopoly of titles and land is also a primary cause of the housing shortage in Britain: which means high and ever escalating rents for those without the proper pedigree, while the lords serve tea on the manor.[66]

Britain therefore has an unenviable paradox. It has no shortage of land, but little of the precious stuff is available for development—for housing for the non-privileged—because the landed elite still has its eternal grip on land. The lament that the pastures of England have been covered in concrete remains untrue. In 2011, the UK's National Ecosystem Assessment conducted the most comprehensive survey of the country's natural environment and resources ever undertaken, concluding that only 6.8% of the land area of the UK could be classified as urban.[67] Low as this figure was, it actually overstated the case for development. In

England, as an illustration, 10.6% of the land was designated as urban, but 54% of that area was green space, consisting of parks, cemeteries, and sports pitches. Domestic gardens comprised yet another 18%, and water (rivers, ponds, and canals) consisted of another 6.6%. Altogether, when the accounting was done, 78.6% of English urban land was found to be "natural," not "built."[68]

Overall, in the UK, "enclosed farmland" accounts for the largest share of land by far, some 40%, followed by mountains, moorlands and heath at 18%, and woodland at 12%, a percentage that has doubled since 1945. These figures explain why the UK has the smallest and yet the most expensive homes in Europe. Some 90% of the population lives on 5% of the land, a number that is bound to have a profound negative impact on the pocketbooks of home renters and is equally profitable for those renting them out. As authors Cowley and Eaton concluded, "it is unsurprising that so many believe this is an overcrowded country in which rapacious developers have monopolized what little space remains."[69]

What has emerged is a system that is not only contrary to reason, but reflects the power and influence of its beneficiaries. It is no surprise then that the largest landowner in all of Europe is British. He is none other than Richard Scott, the 10th Duke of Buccleuch and the 12th Duke of Queensberry. He is the senior patrilineal descendant of James, Duke of Monmouth (April 9, 1649–July 15, 1685), the eldest illegitimate son of King Charles II and his mistress, Lucy Walter, who inherited his titles and landed estates upon the death of his father in 2007. Scott is the reputed grandee and custodian of at least 240,000 acres—estimates are as high as 280,000 acres—including the Queensberry Estate, with headquarters in Drumlanrig Castle, Dumfries, and the Langholm Estate on the Dumfriesshire–Cumbria border, worth an estimated £1 billion altogether.[70]

This might be enough to impress most of us, but the Duke of Westminster, who only has 133,100 acres on which he must make do, can console himself that his landed worth is somewhere close to £6 billion, while his Grosvenor Estate includes the most valuable real estate in London, in posh Belgravia and Mayfair. Even Prince Charles, who as the Duke of Cornwall owns 133,602 acres, can only claim a worth somewhat north of £1 billion, a frustration he will have to live with whenever the Duke of Westminster appears in his sights.[71]

Since these dukes and princes are at the summit of cousinhood and land ownership, we might conclude that these same individuals do not need nor would they accept subsidies from the taxpayer. Yet we would be mistaken. Under the auspices of the EU's Common Agricultural Policy (CAP), such a program of subsidies—dubbed "aid to aristocrats" by those with sympathies for the ultra rich—does exist, and it is not going away anytime soon. Up until Brexit, at least, the average British household has been contributing somewhere around £250 a year to the CAP program, most of which was going to wealthy landowners, including the titled dukedom.

The original intention of CAP was to support small farmers and to reduce Europe's reliance on food imports. To accomplish this, more than 40% (€55 billion) of the EU budget has gone to CAP. But what was a good intention has been transformed into a slush fund to maintain the lifestyle of assorted dukes, earls, and princes. That is because subsidy payments are based solely on acreage. There is no accounting of wealth, which makes the entire scheme the most regressive in all of Europe—the more acreage a lord owns, the greater the subsidy. Compounding this windfall, the EU's definition of "farmer" does not require landowner-farmers to actually get their aristocratic hands dirty by growing something like crops or any agricultural products.[72] Whether wheat is grown or pitches are organized for polo games or lavish croquet tournaments, it is all the same. The aristocrats are essentially paid whether they farm or not.

Naturally, how much they are paid might be a delicate matter, possibly inciting fanatics who think the grandees should at least grow a few potatoes in between the croquet wickets. In fact, when the *New Statesman* made a freedom of information request to the Department for Environment, Food and Rural Affairs (DEFRA) back in 2012, what they found out probably gave them a severe case of indigestion. The figures released by DEFRA for 2011 showed that the largest landowners received goodly amounts to purchase oats of the finest quality for their steeds. The Duke of Westminster, a multibillionaire, was paid £748,716 for his Grosvenor Farms, the Earl of Plymouth received £675,085, the Duke of Buccleuch some £260,273, the Duke of Devonshire £251,729, and the Duke of Atholl, who managed only an anemic £231,188 for his Blair Castle Estate. The Windsors also were in the queue. The Queen received a tidy sum of £415,817 for the Royal Farms and £314,811 for the Duchy of Lancaster, while Prince Charles reaped a harvest of £127,868 for the Duchy of Cornwall. Well compensated also was Saudi Arabia's Prince Bandar bin Sultan. He received £273,905 for his 2000 acre Glympton Estate in Oxfordshire, allegedly purchased with profits from the 1985 al-Yamamah arms deal between Saudi Arabia and Britain. All of the above subsidies paled, however, when compared to the proceeds taken by Sir Richard Sutton, who was paid £1.1 million for his Settled Estates, a 6500 acre property near Newbury inherited along with his baronetcy in 1981, despite having net assets of some £136.5 million.[73]

All these were predictable recipients, but there were strange outliers as well. One such benefactor of taxpayer largesse was an outsourcing company called Serco which had built a pipeline cashing in on the government's privatization of National Health Service services, courtesy of the British taxpayer and CAP. It received a land subsidy worth £2.7 million although EU member states were simultaneously cutting jobs, wages, and services according to the austerity policies of Brussels.[74]

But the EU and the British Tories are not oblivious to the concerns of the public waiting in the queue for housing assistance or job training. The EU had vowed to reform the program of "corporate" welfare by capping direct payments at €300,000 and also by ensuring that only "active" farmers would be eligible for subsidy. But even under these proposals, which went into effect in 2014, the EU continued to provide aid to landowners who derived only 5% of their annual revenue from agriculture. As for the CAP, the largest farms have been able to avoid it by simply restructuring, with barely a murmur from the Tories who derive much of their political sustenance from the gentry and baronet class. Life seemed to continue as it had for centuries, never mind the reforms. In 2014, the Queen still commanded £686,000 in subsidies from Brussels for Sandringham Farms on her Norfolk Estate. The Duke of Westminster, who died an untimely death a year later, and who had an estimated wealth of some £9 billion at the time, claimed £914,000 for his Grosvenor Farms, Tesco's biggest milk supplier. And then there is Sir Richard Sutton, a large claimant under CAP previously, who suffered no noticeable imposition in 2014, when he claimed another £1.8 million for growing wheat, barley, peas, and beans on his family farm. This hefty subsidy arrived just in time to help Sir Richard avoid any diminution of the family worth of £160 million. The Tory coalition government looked askance at all of this for good reason, they were not about to challenge the scions and lords with whom they were connected. The Work and Pensions Secretary, Iain Duncan Smith, who was simultaneously justifying and enforcing a £12 billion raid on welfare payments, managed, along with his family, to claim £159,000 for their Swanbourne Home

Farms, a subsidy which he apparently felt entitled to, while denying meager sums of welfare to the genuinely needy.[75]

If Secretary Smith was unaware of the needs people on public assistance have, he might have consulted his relatives. They were the recipients of EU largesse because they ran the family farm while the minister guarded the treasury against unwarranted welfare benefit intrusion. The farm business, which was run on the family estate, was partly owned by Duncan Smith's son, with Duncan Smith's wife as trustee. The family farm has received well over a million pounds sterling in taxpayer subsidies. To be precise, Swanbourne Home Farms, run as a partnership between the minister's in-laws, Baron and Baroness Cottesloe, brother-in-law Thomas, and cousin Richard Brooks, received €1,517,535 over a 10-year period in funding from the EU. Beyond that it also received grants worth tens of thousands of pounds sterling from Natural England, presumably for contributing to the greening of England.[76]

It could be that Brexit was supported because at least some British voters thought it mildly unfair to pay taxes to the coalition government, when Chancellor Osborne was proclaiming that nobody was going to get anything for nothing. In fact, the gentlemen farmers were getting quite a lot for nothing, sharing in the roughly €50 billion annually that the EU allocated to EU farmers. Considering that every British household was contributing some £250 per year to the EU, which then handed over subsidies to millionaires like the Duke of Westminster, the family of Minister Duncan Smith, and Sir Richard Hutton, Chancellor Osborne might have rephrased his views and asked why so many who had so little were subsidizing so few who had so much? The EU and its CAP, as Giles Fraser expressed it in the *Guardian*, was "socialism for the rich. It's a mechanism to buttress the aristocracy – who own a third of the land in this country – from the chill winds of economic liberalism." The European Union, said Fraser, "has become a huge and largely invisible way of redistributing wealth from the poor to the rich, subsidizing lord so-and-so's grouse moor, while redundancies are handed out to workers at Port Talbot (whose jobs the government can't help subsidize because of EU rules)."[77] With about £3.6 billion in EU subsidies going to UK farmers in 2015, and with a third of all farmland belonging to the baronets, it is easy to understand the ire of Mr. Fraser: the CAP is socialism for the landed aristocracy living high on the hog.[78] It is in fact a mammoth subsidy program enabling the rich to extract wealth from everybody else.

Patenting Life: Monsanto and Bigger Agribusiness

Monsanto, possibly the largest biotech company in the world, has become an example of a new monopoly company. Monsanto owns the key genetic traits of more than 90% of soybeans and 80% of corn planted by farmers in the USA. Its near monopoly grew from a clever strategy. Robert Reich noted the ruse: "[Monsanto] patented its own genetically modified seeds along with an herbicide that would kill weeds but not soy and corn grown from its seeds."[79] Initially, this saved farmers much money and time. But the purchase turned out to be costly. The soy and corn grown from Monsanto seeds did not produce seeds of their own. Farmers therefore had to buy seeds every season. Even if farmers did reserve their own seeds, they could not by law use them or plant them. As a result of what was effectively a monopoly, given patent protection, seed prices rose much faster than the cost of living. Monsanto's price for corn and soy seeds more than doubled in the first decade of the twenty-first century.[80] The cost of planting one acre of soybeans between 1994 and 2011 increased on average by 325%, while the price of corn seed rose by 259%.[81]

Monsanto's success inevitably helped lead to a decline in the genetic diversity of seeds. Yet another consequence was the rise of genetically modified traits in our food chain.[82] Further, as Monsanto acquired economic power, it also acquired political clout. It resisted a number of congressional attempts to require labeling of genetically engineered foods and to protect biodiversity as well. Instead, Monsanto globalized its reach, attempting to do in other countries what it had done in the USA, resisting moves to ban genetically engineered seeds. Monsanto sued other companies for patent infringement, and Monsanto lawyers sued farmers who theoretically saved seeds for planting or used them for replanting. To further establish and preserve its near monopoly, Monsanto successfully prevented independent scientists from studying their seeds, arguing that they would be infringing on Monsanto's proprietary rights.[83]

Officially, Monsanto argued it wanted to solve food shortages, especially as the world's population advanced ahead of its food supply, and the surest way to satisfy global food demands was through genetic manipulation to "improve" plant varieties. But Monsanto wanted to do much more than the genetic modification of plants. It wanted to own the results, or rather, it wanted the right to patent its genetically "improved" plants. There was a legal roadblock to doing this, however. Prior to a landmark decision by the Supreme Court in 1980, crops that had been genetically modified—transgenic crops—were not patentable because, as the courts had put it, life could not be patented. But in 1980 the court changed its mind. General Electric had filed a patent application for a bacterium that had been altered to consume hydrocarbons. The US Patent and Trademark Office had rejected the application because of a 1951 law stating that microorganisms and plant life were not patentable. The Supreme Court decision of 1980, however, was explicit: "Anything under the sun that is made by man can be patented."[84] This meant that life, microorganisms, plant life, and animal life, which naturally occurred in nature, could be patented, so long as Monsanto (or anybody) modified it in the laboratory.

Based on earlier US precedents, including the efforts of Monsanto, the European Patent Office (Munich) granted patents on microorganisms in 1982, on plants in 1985, on animals in 1988, and on embryos in 2000. In theory, these patents were granted only if the living organism had been modified by genetic engineering, but the reality was otherwise. The process had already gone well beyond genetically modified organisms (GMOs). Patents were now granted for non-transgenic plants, particularly if they had "medical" properties—hard to define in any case—which was in total violation of existing laws. According to Christoph Then, of Greenpeace, the common law system of patents was being revoked. In 2005, in an interview with Marie-Monique Robin, he explained:

> To get a patent, it is no longer necessary to present a real invention; often all you need is a simple discovery. Someone discovers a therapeutic use for a plant, the Indian neem tree for instance, describes it, isolates it from its natural context, and files a patent application for it. The deciding factor is that the description be done in a laboratory, and no attention is paid to the fact that the plant and its virtues have been known by others for thousands of years.[85]

Then's illustration meant that Monsanto was not only genetically engineering something new, as was required by law, but that it was patenting something quite old, which had been part of the commons and was entirely organic. In other words, Monsanto had devised a plan and had purchased the political influence to patent life, which under US and European patent law had historically not been permissible or legal. As an illustration of how the perception of legal definitions had changed, the US Patent and Trademark Office has been granting more than seventy thousand patents per year, about 20% of which have been for living organisms. Moreover, between 1983 and 2005, Monsanto secured 647 patents involving plants. As John Doll of the Patent Office told Marie-Monique Robin in 2004: "We now grant patents on genes and transgenic plants and animals, any product of genetic engineering."[86] When Robin responded that a gene is not a product, Doll replied that a company could patent anything, as long as it could isolate a gene in a laboratory: "once a company has been able to isolate the gene and describe its function, it can get a patent."[87]

That was only the beginning of Monsanto's campaign to restructure the agricultural national and global order—in its favor. In 1994, the company obtained a ten-year patent for its genetically modified (Roundup Ready) soybean seeds. The main benefit of these seeds was that they were resistant to Roundup Ready, a Monsanto pesticide: hence the name Roundup Ready soybeans. Two years later, in 1996, the European Patent Office followed the American precedent by granting a patent for Roundup Ready soybeans, ruling that the patent was applicable to a number of other crops including the following: maize, wheat, rice, soybean, cotton sugar beet rapeseed, canola, flax, sunflower, potato, tobacco, tomato, lucerne, poplar, pine, apple, and grape.[88]

The rulings of the US and European patent offices, however, signified a revolution that went beyond patenting seeds. Beyond patenting "life," they were also agreeing to patent Monsanto's intellectual property (IP) rights that the company had successfully argued were embedded in its seeds. The next step for Monsanto was to figure out how to enforce its IP rights. It first sold user licenses to seed dealers and then bought principal seed companies in order to secure its investment, and also to eliminate as much competition as possible. But Monsanto still had problems with farmers, who largely rejected the licensing agreements. Farmers were accustomed to reserving part of their crop to replant it the following year (except for hybrids), and this was often the prevailing practice in poor and developing countries. When the seed, however, contained a patented trait, such as Roundup Ready resistant seeds did, this created a dilemma for companies like Monsanto. In its own literature, the company complained that farmers who saved seed affected "competitive conditions." Monsanto implied that farmers saved seeds only in backward countries.[89]

But this was not true. In fact, it was so false that the head of Monsanto, Robert Shapiro, devised a "technology use agreement" that had to be signed by all farmers who bought Roundup Ready soybean seeds. The agreement, which dealers were compelled to present, provided for payment of a technology fee, set first at $5 and then at $6.50 per acre of soybeans. But there was another aspect of this agreement that farmers fiercely resisted. They had to agree not to replant any harvested seed the following year. Another clause required growers to use only Monsanto's Roundup Ready herbicide, not any of the many generics on the market, *after* the expiration of the patent on Roundup Ready in 2000. Farmers violating this agreement were subject to heavy fines, which were actively policed by Monsanto. The company reserved for itself the right to inspect and test all fields to be sure no farmer was in violation.[90] Monsanto imposed a heavy fine on violators or used litigation if there was resistance.

But the real coup de grâce was what was behind Monsanto's strategy all along, and this is when the company established not only a temporary monopoly, but one that was eternal and irreversible. Monsanto Corporation said that no farmer actually bought its transgenic (patented) seeds, farmers were merely leasing them, and therefore, they had to be returned to its owner. This was the basis of the company's insistence that it wasn't selling seeds, it was simply renting out the IP that was embedded in the seeds. In law, Monsanto was arguing that it was the permanent owner of the genetic information—IP—in the seeds it sold. The seed was divested of its "status as a living organism" and was designated a commodity with commercial value. Farmers, according to the corporation, were not buying Monsanto's seeds, they were purchasing access to Monsanto's IP. In effect, though seeds are used to feed the world's population, Monsanto was arguing that its clients were buying a license to use its patented genetic knowledge.[91] This required not only imagination and a redefinition of the meaning of deceit, but it provided a new definition for the properties of seeds. Seeds didn't only yield food to feed the planet, they also were a storehouse of knowledge that Monsanto was renting out.

Monsanto now had a strategy for taking over much of the food supply. Even worse, once it could patent life, it could claim that whatever was on the planet could be patented by Monsanto or some other corporation. It was the pharmaceutical industry all over again. Take the genetic material of one plant or seed, inject it into the genetic material of another, and there it is, a patent on life—and a form of life created in a laboratory, which under the new regime was legal, legitimate, patentable, fully acknowledged in law by Congress, and IP that belonged to Monsanto in perpetuity.

For Monsanto, however, this was only the beginning of its transgenic journey around the globe. There was profit to be made everywhere. Monsanto smelled this, and the US government was close at hand to help the company achieve its goal. The North American Free Trade Agreement (NAFTA), which was signed into law in December 1993 with the blessing of Bill Clinton, gave companies like Monsanto free access to the Mexican market. By itself, this was no more than a free trade agreement that should have helped Mexico and the USA, but companies like Monsanto were freely subsidized by the USA, giving US agriculture, and companies like Monsanto, a strategic advantage. It meant extending the monopolistic reach of Monsanto into Mexico by essentially making US patent law applicable there. This plus US subsidies to American companies meant that US agricultural commodities could undersell Mexican grown crops. Aided by the US government and supported by US law—and now international law—trade agreements like NAFTA trumped the sovereignty of all nations which were signatories.

In this case, it was Mexican farmers who were the victims of Monsanto's voracious appetite for market conquest. Biologists David Quist and Ignacio Chapela, in 2001, discovered that traditional Mexican corn, some 5000 years old, had been contaminated by Monsanto's Roundup Ready and Bt genes, genetically modified Monsanto seeds. The discovery was made in Oaxaca, where farmers adhered to traditional agriculture. Farmers had never bought seeds from outside Oaxaca, although they sometimes exchanged seeds among themselves. In Oaxaca, traditional corn was much healthier than the transgenic corn that had been planted in other parts of Mexico. Which was why in 1998 Mexico declared a moratorium on transgenic corn crops so the exceptional biodiversity of corn could be preserved. After all, the genetic cradle for corn was Mexico.[92]

But the sovereign power of Mexico in this case was not enough to protect its corn biodiversity. Industrial corn coming into Mexico from the USA already amounted to six million tons per annum, 40% of which was transgenic. This massive importation of corn, because of NAFTA, could not be stopped. The reason was simple, and not just because of NAFTA. American corn was heavily subsidized by the USA, providing more than $94 billion in corn subsidies between 1995 and 2014.[93] Local corn was threatened because US corn was being sold at half the price. Between 1994 and 2002, the price of Mexican corn fell by 44%. As a result, many small farmers had to abandon their farms and ended up in city slums, landless and jobless.[94]

There was a reason that the transgenic conquest was a danger for Mexico and its corn. If industrial corn, meaning an abundance of transgenic corn, became dominant, Mexicans would be forced to buy their fertilizers and insecticides from multinationals. Traditional Mexican corn would not grow otherwise, because it would not be resistant to imported insecticides. Mexican corn growers, in other words, would either have to buy corn seed patented by Monsanto, or they would have to abandon their farms because native corn seed and crops could not resist pests.[95] Mexican farmers had forfeited their freedom to farm using their own seeds, not by their own right to choose, but because of an agreement which they never signed—subjecting them to American subsidized corn—and Monsanto's practice of litigating against farmers accused of violating Monsanto's patented Roundup Ready products.

Green Revolution, Bad Seeds, and Patent Nonsense

Monsanto, like any producer of genetically engineered crops, has argued that the genetic modification of seeds has the potential to solve the world's food problems, for example, to overcome food insecurity globally by increasing yield per acre, largely by reducing food loss due to pests and blights, and also by resistance to drought. In sum, Monsanto has claimed that its products have helped to create the second Green Revolution.[96]

The initial Green Revolution was based on the work of Norman Borlaug. He was born on an Iowa farm and later hired by the Rockefeller Foundation as an agronomist. Borlaug had a single obsession: increase wheat production by creating varieties that could produce yields tenfold. He originally crossed Japanese dwarf variety Norin 10 with varieties grown in Mexico. This produced more kernels, but the weight of the more numerous kernels risked breaking the stems. The introduction of the dwarf variety reduced wheat stalks by three feet while—in 1910—wheat yields were increased from four hundredweight per acre to thirty-two hundredweight. But there were side effects because of the increased use of "phytosanitary products"—fungicides, pesticides, and insecticides—without which the miracle seeds were of little use. The problem was that to produce large amounts of kernels, the plant "had to be stuffed with fertilizers (nitrogen, phosphorous, potassium), which eventually brought about a decline in the natural fertility of the soil."[97] There were other problems: the plants had to be watered copiously, which depleted aquifers; the density of the kernels was manna for insect pests and fungi; and that meant the massive use of fungicides and insecticides. The obsession with yields finally led to a decline in nutritional values of the kernels and a reduction in the biodiversity of the wheat, some varieties even disappearing altogether.[98]

Despite this, the dwarf varieties that were produced spread around the world and India became the second largest wheat producer in the world, increasing production from twelve to twenty million tons between 1965 and 1970—and shortly after the turn of the century producing seventy-four million tons of wheat. According to Vandana Shiva, however, in *Seeds of Suicide*, this came at a great cost: exhausted soil, depleted water reserves, widespread pollution, and the spread of monocultures, all at the expense of food crops. The latter result meant the collapse of tens of thousands of small farmers, who ended up in slums because they could not afford the new model of farming. The first Green Revolution, whatever its merits, did not solve the world's food problems, and it was an unmitigated disaster for farmers in undeveloped countries like India.[99]

The second Green Revolution has been different, not led by the government agencies and the public sector but by Monsanto and other agribusinesses. The first Green Revolution did have the objective to sell more chemical products and farm machines, but its principal aim was to provide more food and food security. Although it came at the expense of legumes, India did produce more rice and wheat to feed people. But, as Vandana Shiva has explained, the second Green Revolution has little if anything to do with food security. Its only aim is to increase the profits of a company like Monsanto, as it attempts to impose its "law" around the world. And what is Monsanto's law? According to Vandana Shiva, it is,

Patent law. The company has always said that genetic engineering was a way of getting patents, and that's its real aim. … it is now pursuing in India. … it is testing twenty plants into which it has introduced Bt genes: mustard, okra, eggplant, rice, cauliflower … Once it has established ownership of genetically modified seeds as the norm, it will be able to collect royalties; we will depend on the company for every seed we plant and every field we cultivate. If it controls seeds, it controls food; it knows that, and that is its strategy. It's more powerful than bombs or weapons; it is the best way to control the people of the world.[100]

At the time of Shiva's interview in 2006, it was illegal to patent seeds—and life—in India. Patents meant monopoly, and if Monsanto or any company could patent life, or plants that had been grown for centuries, it could effectively deprive farmers of direct access to living organisms that they had planted for as many generations as anybody could remember. Patents also meant exclusion and ultimately dependency. Yet Monsanto found a way around the Indian obstacle: genetic modification or invention in the laboratory. Or, as Monsanto argued, IP belonged to the inventor, so long as the product was not found in nature.

An apt illustration of this was a patent held by Monsanto on a variety of wheat it had purchased from Unilever in 1998, that was used in India for the making of chapatis and cookies due to its low gluten content. The terms of the patent gave Monsanto the exclusive right to the growing, crossbreeding, and processing of this variety, which had originated in northern India. What had been part of nature in India, grown and processed freely, had now been pirated and then purchased by Monsanto, which now claimed ownership of the IP for this crop. In effect, Monsanto was making American patent law universal. It was also privatizing a part of nature, effectively removing a traditional crop from the commons. No wonder that Vandana Shiva summed it up in the following way:

The patent … encloses living things, such as plants that feed and heal people, and finally contributes to the exclusion of the poorest from the means of livelihood and even survival. As can be seen with food and medicine, as soon as a patent is filed, it means royalties and consequently an increase in price, which explains why food, crop maintenance products, and medicines were excluded from Indian patent law: this has enabled all to have access. The extension of the Western system of patents, advocated also by the World Trade Organization, directly undermines the economic rights of the poorest.[101]

Seedy Politics: Monsanto, Monopoly and the Revolving Door Syndrome

Like many corporations, Monsanto has left little to chance. The corporation has used political leverage to engage in trade wars as part of its effort to establish near monopoly conditions for its products universally. In 2007, WikiLeaks, as part of Cablegate, released documents showing that the US embassy in Paris, France, advised Washington to promote a military-style trade war against any country in the EU that opposed producing genetically modified crops. The request came from Ambassador Craig Stapleton, who was a co-owner of the Texas Rangers with George Bush between 1989 and 1998. Stapleton's wife, Dorothy Walker, was Bush's cousin. Stapleton's leaked cable came after France began moves to ban Monsanto's genetically modified corn.[102] Other leaked cables by WikiLeaks showed US diplomats working for genetically modified crops at the Vatican because of the resistance of US Catholic Bishops.[103]

To keep as much control as possible over seeds and food supply, Monsanto made good use of the revolving door syndrome, assuring that it would maintain a commanding presence in the corridors of Congress, and beyond. One illustration was Michael R. Taylor, who was appointed by President Obama to the position of Deputy Commissioner of Foods at the Food and Drug Administration (FDA), joining staff as attorney in 1980. Previously, he had been at the law firm of King and Spalding, which represented Monsanto. When he returned to the FDA in 1992 as Deputy Commissioner of Policy, he allegedly co-authored and signed a Federal Register notice that milk from cows treated with bovine growth hormone did not have to be labeled as such. He also ensured that the FDA would not interfere with the production of genetically modified foods. Jeremy Rifkin charged that this was a conflict of interest, but the FDA rejected the claim. Following his service at FDA, Taylor went to Monsanto as vice-president for public policy in 1998. Later, January 13, 2010, Obama appointed Taylor as Deputy Commissioner of Foods at the FDA.[104] Even the Supreme Court has felt the long hand of Monsanto. Supreme Court Justice Clarence Thomas was employed by Monsanto in the 1970s, and Associate Justice Elena Kagan previously had supported Monsanto's genetically modified alfalfa, helping to reverse a lower court ban on its planting.[105]

In 2011, Obama appointed Monsanto lobbyist Islam Siddiqui to the position of Chief Agricultural Negotiator in the Office of the US Trade

Representative. This was something of a shock because of the progressive image of the president. That is because in 1998, when Siddiqui was Under Secretary for Marketing and Regulatory programs at the USDA, he wrote the standards for organic food labeling that permitted genetically modified and irradiated food to be labeled organic. President Obama, however, had another surprise. He appointed Tom Vilsack as Secretary of Agriculture, although Vilsack was a major proponent of genetically modified crops and deeply linked to the biotech lobby. As Governor of the State of Iowa, Vilsack created a seed preemption bill in 2005 that blocked local communities from regulating genetically modified crops.[106]

Although many if not most US farmers think Monsanto is already too big, Monsanto does not think it is big enough. Its former German rival, Bayer, agrees. In late 2016, Bayer purchased Monsanto and entered into a $66 billion corporate merger, pending approval by some thirty nations. If anti-trust obstacles are overcome, the resulting company would own about 29% of the global seed market and 25% of the global pesticide market. Bayer-Monsanto would also control about 60% of the US cottonseed market. Add to these figures that 40% of the world's genetically modified crops are grown in the USA, where Monsanto already controls about 80% of the genetically engineered cornseed market and 93% of the genetically engineered soy market, and you have a recipe for control of the world's food supply.[107]

Should the merger be approved, it is hardly likely that the world's food markets will become more competitive, more innovative, or provide greater biodiversity and consumer choice. This is made more certain because much of the world's seed market not controlled by Bayer-Monsanto could soon be controlled by two other giant cartels: Dupont-Dow Chemical, which merged in 2015, and ChemChina, which acquired the Swiss company Syngenta in 2016. Although none of the mergers have received final approval, should they succeed these three agribusinesses alone will control about 60% of global seed sales and about 63% of global pesticide sales: hardly a recipe for so-called competitive capitalism.[108] Inevitably, seed and pesticide prices will rise, farmers will increasingly be squeezed into dependency and bankruptcy, and food baskets will inflate for typical families. Simultaneously, the new monopolies already present limitless opportunities for the extraction of wealth from global farmers and global consumers of food.

Yet, this is only part of the narrative. In 2015, the World Health Organization declared that glyphosate, the active ingredient in Roundup, Monsanto's herbicide, was probably carcinogenic in humans.[109] The state of California, where ten million pounds of glyphosate are applied annually, went much further. It decided to list glyphosate as a known carcinogen, a decision that Monsanto immediately appealed to the courts.[110]

Conclusion

Putting government to work to protect and extend patents, and then to extend them around the world through trade agreements, has made billions in profit for Monsanto and other corporations benefiting from the revolving door between government and industry. Subsidizing American agricultural production also is a giant assist undercutting Mexican and Indian and other farmers. Protecting target prices for (corporate) farms, which the government insures, is also a form of welfare capitalism: if the price is met, that is good for the corporation. And if it is not met, the federal government simply buys back the crop, which it helped to insure. All of this is costly. Between 1995 and 2014, the federal government spent more than $94.3 billion on corn subsidies. For the same period, it spent almost $40 billion subsidizing wheat and $35.7 billion in cotton subsidies. From these figures alone, we begin to get some idea how the super-rich, at least in agribusiness, manage to extract wealth and treasure from the rest of us.[111]

Subsidizing agribusiness, not applying anti-trust laws to deny monopolies to seed companies, allowing multinational companies like Monsanto to patent life—patents it then imposes universally through trade agreements—and manipulating the science of dietetics to conceal the health risks of sugar are forms of rent based on deceit. Permitting companies to label foods as organic when they are transgenic, not labeling transgenic crops as GMOs when they have been genetically modified, is deceitful and a betrayal of the public trust. Yet all these practices are widespread and becoming routinized, evolving into a rentier economy in which the privileged corporate super-rich, the new monopolists, have devised tools, from patents to IP, to impose rents on everybody else. Telling farmers that they are not purchasing seeds but renting the IP embedded in those seeds may be the world according to Monsanto, but it is not a world that we should embrace.

Notes

1. Mark Bittman, "Don't End Agricultural Subsidies, Fix Them," *New York Times*, March 1, 2011.
2. 2 Thessalonians, 3:10.
3. Aviva Shen, "Congressman Who Gets Millions in Farm Subsidies Denounces Food Stamps as Stealing 'Other People's Money'," *Think Progress*, May 21, 2013, at https://thinkprogress.org/congressman-who-gets-millions-in-farm-subsidies-denounces-food-stamps-as-stealing-other-peoples-bb26216147/.
4. Joseph Heller, *Catch-22* (New York: Simon & Schuster, 1999), 86; *Economist*, "Milking Taxpayers," February 14, 2015, at http://www.economist.com/news/united-states/21643191-crop-prices-fall-farmers-grow-subsidies-instead-milking-taxpayers.
5. Ibid.
6. Environmental Working Group, "United States Summary Information," *Farm Subsidy Database 2012*, online at http://farm.ewg.org/region.php?fips=00000. Also Laura Etherton, Mike Russo, and Nasima Hossain, *Apples to Twinkies 2012* (Washington DC: US Public Interest Research Group (PIRG), 2012), 2. "Ten Percent of Subsidy Recipients Collected 75% of the Subsidies, But Because USDA Reports That 62% of American Farmers Don't Pocket a Dollar in Federal Subsidies, Only 3.8% of Farmers [were] Being Paid Three Quarters of the Total Subsidies," http://www.uspirg.org/sites/pirg/files/reports/Apples%20to%20Twinkies%20vUS.pdf.
7. Brian Riedl, *How Farm Subsidies Harm Taxpayers, Consumers, and Farmers Too* (Washington, DC: Heritage Foundation, June 19, 2007), 6–7, at http://www.heritage.org/research/reports/2007/06/how-farm-subsidies-harm-taxpayers-consumers-and-farmers-too; Gilbert M. Saul, Sarah Cohen, and Dan Morgan, "Federal Subsidies Turn Farms into Big Business," *Washington Post*, December 21, 2006.
8. EWG, *Farm Subsidy Database*.
9. US Department of Agriculture Risk Management Agency, "Crop Year Government Cost of Federal Crop Insurance, 2002–2011," at http://www.rma.usda.gov/aboutrma/bud-get/cycost2002-11.pdf; Etherton, *Apples to Twinkies*, 5.
10. USDA, "Federal Crop Insurance, 2002–2011."
11. EWG, *Farm Subsidy Database*.
12. US Department of Agriculture, "Agricultural Act of 2014: Highlights and Implications, Crop Commodity Programs," at https://www.ers.usda.gov/agricultural-act-of-2014-highlights-and-implications/.
13. "Milking Taxpayers."

14. US Library of Congress, Congressional Research Service, *Renegotiation of the Standard Reinsurance Agreement (SRA) for Federal Crop Insurance* (Washington, DC) June 10, 2010, at http://farmpolicy.com/wp-content/uploads/2011/07/CRS_SRASummary_2011Aug12.pdf. See USDA, "Agricultural Act of 2014."
15. David Dayen, "The Farm Bill Still Gives Wads of Cash to Agribusiness: It's Just Sneakier About It," *New Republic*, February 4, 2014, online at https://newrepublic.com/article/116470/farm-bill-2014-its-even-worse-old-farm-bill.
16. Ibid.
17. Ibid.
18. Ibid.; EWG, *Farm Subsidy Database*.
19. Michael Tanner, "GOP Hypocrisy and the Farm Bill," *Huffington Post*, July 12, 2013, online at http://www.huffingtonpost.com/michael-tanner/gop-hypocrisy-farm-bill_b_3586544.html.
20. Paul Krugman, "Free to Be Hungry," *New York Times*, September 22, 2013.
21. Ibid.
22. Ibid.; Tanner, "GOP Hypocrisy and the Farm Bill."
23. Krugman, "Free to Be Hungry." See Annie Lowrey for the Math, "The Rich Get Richer Through the Recovery," *New York Times*, September 10, 2013.
24. Cited in Krugman, "Free to Be Hungry."
25. Ibid.
26. Budget of the United States Government, Fiscal Year 2017, *Analytical Perspectives: Budget of the US Government*, Table 29-1, Federal Budget by Agency and Account, at https://www.govinfo.gov/content/pkg/BUDGET-2017-PER/pdf/BUDGET-2017-PER.pdf.
27. US Government Accountability Office, *Crop Insurance: Reducing Subsidies for Highest Income Participants Could Save Federal Dollars with Minimal Effect on the Program*, GAO-15-356 (Washington, DC: GAO, March 2015), online at http://www.gao.gov/products/GAO-15-356. The full Report is available at http://www.gao.gov/assets/670/669062.pdf.
28. Bruce A. Babcock, "*Crop Insurance: A Lottery That's a Sure Bet*" (San Francisco, CA: Environmental Working Group, February 2016), 3–7, http://static.ewg.org/reports/2016/federal_crop_insurance_lottery/EWG_CropInsuranceLottery.pdf?_ga=2.72475792.246157226.1500401467-1093488400.1469977703; Chris Edwards, "Agricultural Subsidies," *Downsizing the Federal Government Blog*, October 2, 2016, online at https://www.downsizinggovernment.org/agriculture/subsidies.

29. US Department of Agriculture, Economic Research Service, "Data-Files: US and State-Level Farm Income and Wealth Statistics," online at https://www.ers.usda.gov/data-products/farm-income-and-wealth-statistics/data-files-us-and-state-level-farm-income-and-wealth-statistics/.
30. Ibid.
31. US Department of Agriculture, Economic Research Service, "Historic Data on Mean and Median Farm Operator Household Income and Ratio of Farm Household to US Household Income, 1960–2014," online at https://www.ers.usda.gov/data-products/farm-household-income-and-characteristics.aspx.
32. Editorial Board, "Senate Definition of Reform: Give Rich Farmers More Aid," *Bloomberg*, May 2, 2012, online at https://www.bloomberg.com/view/articles/2012-05-02/senate-definition-of-reform-give-rich-farmers-more-aid-view.
33. Archer Daniels Midland Company, "Letter to Stockholders Proxy Statement, 2015: Form 10-K," online at http://www.adm.com/en-US/investors/Documents/2015%20Annual%20Report.pdf.
34. Tanner, "GOP Hypocrisy and the Farm Bill."
35. Ibid.
36. Michael K. Wohlgenant, "Sugar Price Supports are Not So Sweet," *US News and World Report*, September 5, 2014, online at http://www.usnews.com/opinion/economic-intelligence/2014/09/05/sugar-price-supports-have-hidden-costs-for-economy-consumers.
37. Anahad O'Connor, "How the Sugar Industry Shifted Blame to Fat," *New York Times*, September 12, 2016; also Cristin E. Kearns, Laura A. Schmidt, and Stanton A. Glantz, "Sugar Industry and Coronary Heart Disease Research: A Historical Analysis of Internal Industry Documents," *JAMA Internal Medicine* 176, no. 11 (September 12, 2016), at https://www.researchgate.net/publication/308044447Sugar_Industry_and_Coronary_Heart_Disease_Research_A_Historical_Analysis_of_Internal_Industry_Documents; see also Robert McGandy, D. M Hegsted, and F. J. Stare, "Dietary Fats, Carbohydrates and Atherosclerotic Vascular Disease," *The New England Journal of Medicine* 277, no. 5 (August 3, 1967): 242–47, at https://nature.berkeley.edu/garbelottoat/wp-content/uploads/Mcgandy-1967-part-1-1.pdf.
38. Cited by Anahad O'Connor, "Sugar Industry Shifted Blame to Fat," *New York Times*, September 12, 2016.
39. Ibid.
40. Anahad O'Connor, "Coca Cola Funds Scientists Who Shift Blame for Obesity Away from Bad Diets," *New York Times*, August 9, 2015.
41. Cited by Anahad O'Connor, "Coca Cola Funds Scientists Who Shift Blame for Obesity Away from Bad Diets."

42. Ibid.
43. Ibid.
44. Ibid. Barry Popkin, *The World is Fat: The Fads, Trends, Policies and Products That Are Fattening the Human Race* (New York: Avery and Penguin, 2009); Larry White, *Merchants of Death* (New York: Beech Tree Books, 1988).
45. Cited in O'Connor, "Coca Cola Funds Scientists." For background, Marion Nestle and Mark Bittman, *Soda Politics: Taking on Big Soda (and Winning)* (Oxford: Oxford University Press, 2015).
46. Maira Bes-Rastrollo, Matthias B. Schulze, Miguel Ruiz-Canela, Miguel A. Martinez-Gonzalez, "Financial Conflicts of Interest and Reporting Bias Regarding the Association Between Sugar-Sweetened Beverages and Weight Gain: A Systematic Review of Systematic Reviews," *PLOS Medicine* 10, no. 12 (December 31, 2013), http://journals.plos.org/plosmedicine/article?id=10.1371/journal.pmed.1001578.
47. O'Connor, "Coca-Cola Funds Scientists."
48. Anahad O'Connor, "Research Group Funded by Coca-Cola to Disband," *New York Times*, December 1, 2015.
49. O'Connor, "Coca Cola Funds Scientists."
50. Anne McTiernan and Bess Sorenson et al., "Exercise Effect on Weight and Body Fat in Men and Women," *Obesity: A Research Journal* 15, no. 6 (June 2007), at http://www.onlinelibrary.wiley.com/doi/10.1038/oby.2007.178/full.
51. Cited in O'Connor, "Coca Cola Funds Scientists."
52. Kelly D. Brownell and Thomas R. Frieden, "Ounces of Prevention: The Public Policy Case for Taxes on Sugared Beverages," *The New England Journal of Medicine* 360, no. 18 (April 30, 2009), at http://www.nejm.org/doi/full/10.1056/NEJMp0902392#t=article.
53. David Leonhardt, "The Battle over Taxing Soda," *New York Times*, May 18, 2010.
54. Brownell, "Ounces of Prevention."
55. "Top 10 Sources of Calories in the US Diet," *Harvard Health Publications*, November 2014, based on the government's report of 2010, at http://www.health.harvard.edu/healthy-eating/top-10-sources-of-calories-in-the-us-diet; see also the full report, *Report of the Dietary Guidelines Advisory Committee on the Dietary Guidelines for Americans, 2010*, June 14, 2010, online at http://www.nutriwatch.org/05Guidelines/dga_advisory_2010.pdf.
56. Anahad O'Connor, "How the Government Supports Your Junk Food Habit," *New York Times*, July 19, 2016.
57. See World Health Organization, Information Sheet, *Obesity and Overweight* (Geneva: WHO, 2003), at http://www.who.int/

dietphysicalactivity/media/en/gsfs_obesity.pdf; Pam Belluck, "Child Obesity Seen as Warning of Heart Disease," *New York Times*, November 11, 2008.

58. Etherton, *Apples to Twinkies*, 1; see also Eric A. Finkelstein, Justin G. Trogdon, Joel W. Cohen, and William Dietz, "Annual Medical Spending Attributable to Obesity: Payer-And Service-Specific Estimates," *Health Affairs*, July 27, 2009, online at http://content.healthaffairs.org/content/28/5/w822.
59. "Series on Obesity," *Lancet*, August 26, 2011, at http://www.thelancet.com/series/obesity obesity; "Obesity 2015," *Lancet*, February 18, 2015, at http://www.thelancet.com/series/obesity-2015.
60. Etherton, "Apples to Twinkies 2012."
61. Ibid.
62. Jason Cowley and George Eaton, "How We Pay for Our Richest Landowners," *New Statesman*, September 19, 2012, online at http://www.newstatesman.com/politics/politics/2012/09/how-we-pay-our-richest-landowners.
63. Martin Wolf, "A Strong Case for a Tax on Land Values," *Financial Times*, January 5, 2006.
64. Martin Wolf, "Why We Must Halt the Land Cycle," *Financial Times*, July 8, 2010.
65. Ibid.
66. Cowley, "How We Pay for Our Richest Landowners."
67. Linda Davies, "Urbanization," *UK National Ecosystem Assessment, 2011*, Chapter 10, 362–63, at http://uknea.unep-wcmc.org/Resources/tabid/82/Default.aspx.
68. Ibid.
69. Cowley, "How We Pay for Our Richest Landowners."
70. Ibid.
71. Ibid.
72. Ibid.
73. Ibid.
74. Ibid.
75. Brendan Montague, "The Landed Gentry 'Jackals' Claiming Billions in Farm Subsidies," *DESMOGUKBLOG*, July 27, 2015, https://www.desmog.co.uk/2015/07/27/landed-gentry-jackals-claiming-billions-farm-subsidies; Hugh Muir, "Diary: Will IDS Speak Out Against 'Income Support' for Farmers?," *Guardian*, May 30, 2013.
76. Giles Fraser, "Why Our Landed Gentry Are so Eager to Stay in the EU," *Guardian*, April 21, 2016.
77. Ibid.

78. Muir, "Diary."
79. Robert B. Reich, *Saving Capitalism: For the Many, Not the Few* (New York: Vintage, 2015), 34.
80. William Neuman, "Rapid Rise in Seed Prices Draws US Scrutiny," *New York Times*, March 11, 2010.
81. Debbie Barker, Bill Freese, and George Kimbrell, *Seed Giants v US Farmers* (Washington, DC: Center for Food Safety and Save Our Seeds, 2013), 16, online at http://www.centerforfoodsafety.org/files/seed-giants_final_04424.pdf.
82. Rachel Tepper, "Seed Giants Sue US Farmers over Genetically Modified Seed Patents in Shocking Numbers: Report," *Huffington Post*, February 13, 2013; Reich, *Saving Capitalism*, 35.
83. Ibid., 35–36.
84. Cited in Marie-Monique Robin, *The World According to Monsanto: Pollution, Corruption, and the Control of the World's Food Supply*, trans. from the French by George Holoch (New York: The Free Press, 2012), 203.
85. Interview with Christophe Then, Robin, *The World According to Monsanto*, 203.
86. Cited by Robin*: The World According to Monsanto*, 203.
87. Ibid.
88. Ibid., 203–204.
89. Monsanto, *Pledge Report*, 2005, 42, online at http://www.monsanto.com/sitecollectiondocuments/csr_reports/monsantopledgereport-2005.pdf.
90. Robin, *The World According to Monsanto*, 204–205.
91. Daniel Charles, *Lords of the Harvest: Biotech, Big Money, and the Future of Food* (Cambridge, MA: Perseus, 2002), 185–87.
92. Robin, *The World According to Monsanto*, 244.
93. Environmental Working Group, *Farm Subsidy Database.*
94. Robin, *The World According to Monsanto*, 245.
95. Ibid.
96. Monsanto, *Pledge Report*, 2006, online at http://www.monsanto.com/sitecollectiondocuments/csr_reports/monsantopledgereport-2006.pdf.
97. Robin, *The World According to Monsanto*, 309.
98. Ibid.
99. Interview with Vandana Shiva (2006), in Robin, *The World According to Monsanto*, 310. See also Vandana Shiva, *Seeds of Suicide, The Ecological and Human Costs of Seed Monopolies and Globalization of Agriculture* (Navdanaya, 2006); Vandana Shiva, *Biodiversity: The Plunder of Nature and Knowledge* (Cambridge, MA: South End Press, 1997), 36–39

and 48–49, for an earlier iteration of similar themes. See also the most recent work of Vandana Shiva, *Who Really Feeds the World: The Failures of Agribusiness and the Promise of Agroecology* (Berkeley, CA: North Atlantic Books, 2016). This work challenges the customary arguments of Monsanto that genetically modified crops can solve global food shortages. On the contrary, they cause lethal damage to sustainable agriculture. See especially 33–37 and 85–110.

100. Interview with Vandana Shiva (2006), in Robin, *The World According to Monsanto*, 310–11.
101. Ibid., 312–13.
102. Jason Louv, *Monsanto vs. the World: Monsanto, GMOs and Our Genetically Modified Future* (NP: Ultraculture Press, 2013), 19.
103. John Vidal, "WikiLeaks: US Targets EU Over GM Crops," *Guardian*, January 3, 2011.
104. Louv, *Monsanto*, 22.
105. Ibid., 23; Joshua Frank, "Elena Kagan and Monsanto," *Counterpunch*, May 19, 2010, online at http://www.counterpunch.org/2010/05/19/elena-kagan-and-monsanto/.
106. Louv, *Monsanto*, 24.
107. Carin Smaller, "Bayer Tightens Control Over the World's Food Supply," *International Institute for Sustainable Agriculture Blog*, September 23, 2016, at https://www.iisd.org/blog/bayer-tightens-control-over-world-s-food-supply; also Organic Consumers Association, "US and Monsanto Dominate Global Market for GM Seeds," August 7, 2013, https://www.organicconsumers.org/essays/us-and-monsanto-dominate-global-market-gm-seeds.
108. ETC Group, *Seedy Characters* (Ottawa, ON: ETC Group, May 14, 2015), at http://www.etcgroup.org/sites/www.etcgroup.org/files/files/etc.-communique-seedycharacters-may2015.pdf; Tom Philpott, "Monsanto Now Belongs to Bayer," *Mother Jones*, September 13, 2016, online at http://www.motherjones.com/environment/2016/09/whoa-monsanto-about-get-swallowed-german-giant-bayer.
109. "Roundup Weedkiller 'Probably' Causes Cancer, Says WHO Study," *Guardian*, March 21, 2015.
110. State of California, Office of Environmental Health Hazard Assessment (OEHHA), *Glyphosate to Be Listed Under Proposition 65 as Known to the State to Cause Cancer*, CAS No. 1071-83-6 (Sacramento, CA: OEHHA, March 28, 2017), online at https://oehha.ca.gov/proposition-65/crnr/glyphosate-be-listed-under-proposition-65-known-state-cause-cancer.
111. Environmental Working Group, *Farm Subsidy Database*.

Bibliography

Babcock, Bruce A. "*Crop Insurance: A Lottery That's a Sure Bet.*" San Francisco, CA: Environmental Working Group, February 2016. http://static.ewg.org/reports/2016/federal_crop_insurance_lottery/EWG_CropInsuranceLottery.pdf?_ga=2.72475792.246157226.1500401467-1093488400.1469977703.

Barker, Debbie, Bill Freese, and George Kimbrell. *Seed Giants v US Farmers.* Washington, DC: Center for Food Safety and Save Our Seeds, 2013. http://www.centerforfoodsafety.org/files/seed-giants_final_04424.pdf.

Belluck, Pam. "Child Obesity Seen as Warning of Heart Disease." *New York Times*, November 11, 2008.

Bes-Rastrollo, Maira, Matthias B. Schulze, Miguel Ruiz-Canela, Miguel A. Martinez-Gonzalez. "Financial Conflicts of Interest and Reporting Bias Regarding the Association Between Sugar-Sweetened Beverages and Weight Gain: A Systematic Review of Systematic Reviews." *PLOS Medicine* 10, no. 12 (December 31, 2013). http://journals.plos.org/plosmedicine/article?id=10.1371/journal.pmed.1001578.

Bittman, Mark. "Don't End Agricultural Subsidies, Fix Them." *New York Times*, March 1, 2011.

Brownell, Kelly D., and Thomas R. Frieden. "Ounces of Prevention: The Public Policy Case for Taxes on Sugared Beverages." *The New England Journal of Medicine* 360, no. 18 (April 30, 2009). http://www.nejm.org/doi/full/10.1056/NEJMp0902392#t=article.

Charles, Daniel. *Lords of the Harvest: Biotech, Big Money, and the Future of Food.* Cambridge, MA: Perseus, 2002.

Cowley, Jason, and George Eaton. "How We Pay for Our Richest Landowners." *New Statesman*, September 19, 2012. http://www.newstatesman.com/politics/politics/2012/09/how-we-pay-our-richest-landowners.

Davies, Linda et al. "Urbanization," Chapter 10 in *UK National Ecosystem Assessment, 2011.* http://uknea.unep-wcmc.org/Resources/tabid/82/Default.aspx.

Dayen, David. "The Farm Bill Still Gives Wads of Cash to Agribusiness: It's Just Sneakier About It." *New Republic*, February 4, 2014. https://newrepublic.com/article/116470/farm-bill-2014-its-even-worse-old-farm-bill.

Dietary Guidelines Advisory Committee on the Dietary Guidelines for Americans. *Report of the Dietary Guidelines Advisory Committee on the Dietary Guidelines for Americans, 2010*, June 14, 2010. http://www.nutriwatch.org/05Guidelines/dga_advisory_2010.pdf.

Economist. "Milking Taxpayers." February 14, 2015. http://www.economist.com/news/united-states/21643191-crop-prices-fall-farmers-grow-subsidies-instead-milking-taxpayers.

Editorial Board. "Senate Definition of Reform: Give Rich Farmers More Aid." *Bloomberg*, May 2, 2012. https://www.bloomberg.com/view/articles/2012-05-02/senate-definition-of-reform-give-rich-farmers-more-aid-view.

Edwards, Chris. "Agricultural Subsidies." *Downsizing the Federal Government Blog*. October 2, 2016. https://www.downsizinggovernment.org/agriculture/subsidies.

Environmental Working Group. "United States Summary Information." *Farm Subsidy Database 2012*. http://farm.ewg.org/region.php?fips=00000.

ETC Group. *Seedy Characters*. Ottawa, ON: ETC Group, May 14, 2015. http://www.etcgroup.org/sites/www.etcgroup.org/files/files/etc-communique-seedycharacters-may2015.pdf.

Etherton, Laura, Mike Russo, and Nasima Hossain. *Apples to Twinkies 2012*. Washington, DC: US Public Interest Research Group (PIRG), 2012. http://www.uspirg.org/sites/pirg/files/reports/Apples%20to%20Twinkies%20vUS.pdf.

Finkelstein, Eric A., Justin G. Trogdon, Joel W. Cohen, and William Dietz. "Annual Medical Spending Attributable To Obesity: Payer-And Service-Specific Estimates." *Health Affairs*, July 27, 2009. http://content.healthaffairs.org/content/28/5/w822.

Frank, Joshua. "Elena Kagan and Monsanto." *Counterpunch*, May 19, 2010. http://www.counterpunch.org/2010/05/19/elena-kagan-and-monsanto/.

Fraser, Giles. "Why Our Landed Gentry Are So Eager to Stay in the EU." *Guardian*, April 21, 2016.

Guardian. "Roundup Weedkiller 'Probably' Causes Cancer, Says WHO Study." March 21, 2015.

Heller, Joseph. *Catch-22*. New York: Simon & Schuster, 1999.

Kearns, Cristin E., Laura A. Schmidt, and Stanton A. Glantz. "Sugar Industry and Coronary Heart Disease Research: A Historical Analysis of Internal Industry Documents." *JAMA Internal Medicine* 176, no. 11 (September 12, 2016). Online at https://www.researchgate.net/publication/308044447Sugar_Industry_and_Coronary_Heart_Disease_Research_A_Historical_Analysis_of_Internal_Industry_Documents.

Krugman, Paul. "Free to Be Hungry." *New York Times*, September 22, 2013.

Lancet. "Obesity 2015," February 18, 2015. http://www.thelancet.com/series/obesity-2015.

Lancet. "Series on Obesity." August 26, 2011. http://www.thelancet.com/series/ obesity.

Leonhardt, David. "The Battle over Taxing Soda." *New York Times*, May 18. 2010.

Louv, Jason. *Monsanto vs. the World: Monsanto, GMOs and Our Genetically Modified Future*. NP: Ultraculture Press, 2013.

McGandy, Robert, D. M. Hegsted, and F. J. Stare. "Dietary Fats, Carbohydrates and Atherosclerotic Vascular Disease." *The New England Journal of Medicine*

277, no. 5 (August 3, 1967): 242–47. https://nature.berkeley.edu/garbelottoat/wp-content/uploads/Mcgandy-1967-part-1-1.pdf.

McTiernan, Anne, and Bess Sorenson."Exercise Effect on Weight and Body Fat in Men and Women." *Obesity: A Research Journal* 15, no. 6 (June 2007). http://www.onlinelibrary.wiley.com/doi/10.1038/oby.2007.178/full.

Monsanto. *Pledge Report, 2005*. http://www.monsanto.com/sitecollectiondocuments/csr_reports/monsantopledgereport-2005.pdf.

Montague, Brendan. "The Landed Gentry 'Jackals' Claiming Billions in Farm Subsidies." *DESMOGUKBLOG*, July 27, 2015. https://www.desmog.co.uk/2015/07/27/landed-gentry-jackals-claiming-billions-farm-subsidies.

Muir, Hugh. "Diary: Will IDS Speak Out Against 'Income Support' for Farmers?" *Guardian*, May 30, 2013.

Nestle, Marion, and Mark Bittman. *Soda Politics: Taking on Big Soda (and Winning)*. Oxford: Oxford University Press, 2015.

Neuman, William. "Rapid Rise in Seed Prices Draws US Scrutiny." *New York Times*, March 11, 2010.

O'Connor, Anahad. "Coca Cola Funds Scientists Who Shift Blame for Obesity Away from Bad Diets." *New York Times*, August 9, 2015.

O'Connor, Anahad. "How the Government Supports Your Junk Food Habit." *New York Times*, July 19, 2016.

O'Connor, Anahad. "How the Sugar Industry Shifted Blame to Fat." *New York Times*, September 12, 2016.

O'Connor, Anahad. "Research Group Funded by Coca-Cola to Disband." *New York Times*, December 1, 2015.

Organic Consumers Association. "US and Monsanto Dominate Global Market for GM Seeds," August 7, 2013. https://www.organicconsumers.org/essays/us-and-monsanto-dominate-global-market-gm-seeds.

Philpott, Tom. "Monsanto Now Belongs to Bayer." *Mother Jones*, September 13, 2016. http://www.motherjones.com/environment/2016/09/whoa-monsanto-about-get-swallowed-german-giant-bayer.

Popkin, Barry. *The World is Fat: The Fads, Trends, Policies and Products That Are Fattening the Human Race*. New York: Avery and Penguin, 2009.

Reich, Robert B. *Saving Capitalism: For the Many, Not the Few*. New York: Vintage, 2015.

Riedl, Brian. *How Farm Subsidies Harm Taxpayers, Consumers, and Farmers Too*. Washington, DC: Heritage Foundation, June 19, 2007. http://www.heritage.org/research/reports/2007/06/how-farm-subsidies-harm-taxpayers-consumers-and-farmers-too.

Robin, Marie-Monique. *The World According to Monsanto: Pollution, Corruption, and the Control of the World's Food Supply*. Translated from the French by George Holoch. New York: The Free Press, 2012.

Saul, Gilbert M., Sarah Cohen, and Dan Morgan. "Federal Subsidies Turn Farms into Big Business." *Washington Post*, December 21, 2006.

Shen, Aviva. "Congressman Who Gets Millions in Farm Subsidies Denounces Food Stamps as Stealing 'Other People's Money'." *Think Progress*, May 21, 2013. https://thinkprogress.org/congressman-who-gets-millions-in-farm-subsidies-denounces-food-stamps-as-stealing-other-peoples-bb26216147/.

Shiva, Vandana. *Biodiversity: The Plunder of Nature and Knowledge*. Cambridge, MA: South End Press, 1997.

Shiva, Vandana. *Seeds of Suicide: The Ecological and Human Costs of Seed Monopolies and Globalization of Agriculture*. NP: Navdanaya, 2006.

Shiva, Vandana. *Who Really Feeds the World: The Failures of Agribusiness and the Promise of Agroecology*. Berkeley, CA: North Atlantic Books, 2016.

Smaller, Carin. "Bayer Tightens Control Over the World's Food Supply." *International Institute for Sustainable Agriculture Blog*, September 23, 2016. https://www.iisd.org/blog/bayer-tightens-control-over-world-s-food-supply.

State of California, Office of Environmental Health Hazard Assessment (OEHHA). *Glyphosate to Be Listed Under Proposition 65 as Known to the State to Cause Cancer*, CAS No. 1071-83-6. Sacramento, CA: OEHHA, March 28, 2017. https://oehha.ca.gov/proposition-65/crnr/glyphosate-be-listed-under-proposition-65-known-state-cause-cancer.

Tanner, Michael. "GOP Hypocrisy and the Farm Bill." *Huffington Post*, July 12, 2013. http://www.huffingtonpost.com/michael-tanner/gop-hypocrisy-farm-bill_b_3586544.html.

Tepper, Rachel. "Seed Giants Sue US Farmers Over Genetically Modified Seed Patents in Shocking Numbers: Report." *Huffington Post*, February 13, 2013. https://www.huffingtonpost.com/2013/02/13/genetically-modified-seed-patent-report_n_2678837.html.

US, Budget of the United States Government, Fiscal Year 2017. *Analytical Perspectives: Budget of the US Government*. https://www.govinfo.gov/content/pkg/BUDGET-2017-PER/pdf/BUDGET-2017-PER.pdf.

US Department of Agriculture. "Agricultural Act of 2014: Highlights and Implications, Crop Commodity Programs." https://www.ers.usda.gov/agricultural-act-of-2014-highlights-and-implications/.

US Department of Agriculture, Economic Research Service. "Data-Files: US and State-Level Farm Income and Wealth Statistics." https://www.ers.usda.gov/data-products/farm-income-and-wealth-statistics/data-files-us-and-state-level-farm-income-and-wealth-statistics/.

US Department of Agriculture, Economic Research Service. "Historic Data on Mean and Median Farm Operator Household Income and Ratio of Farm Household to US Household Income, 1960–2014." https://www.ers.usda.gov/data-products/farm-household-income-and-characteristics.aspx.

US Department of Agriculture, Risk Management Agency. "Crop Year Government Cost of Federal Crop Insurance, 2002–2011." http://www.rma.usda.gov/aboutrma/bud-get/cycost2002-11.pdf.

US Government Accountability Office. *Crop Insurance: Reducing Subsidies for Highest Income Participants Could Save Federal Dollars with Minimal Effect on the Program*, GAO-15-356. Washington, DC: GAO, March 2015. http://www.gao.gov/assets/670/669062.pdf.

US Library of Congress, Congressional Research Service. *Renegotiation of the Standard Reinsurance Agreement (SRA) for Federal Crop Insurance.* Washington, DC: June 10, 2010. http://farmpolicy.com/wp-content/uploads/2011/07CRS_SRASummary_2011Aug12.pdf.

Vidal, John. "WikiLeaks: US Targets EU Over GM Crops." *Guardian*, January 3, 2011.

White, Larry. *Merchants of Death.* New York: Beech Tree Books, 1988.

Wohlgenant, Michael K. "Sugar Price Supports are Not So Sweet." *US News and World Report*, September 5, 2014. http://www.usnews.com/opinion/economic-intelligence/2014/09/05/sugar-price-supports-have-hidden-costs-for-economy-consumers.

Wolf, Martin. "A Strong Case for a Tax on Land Values." *Financial Times*, January 5, 2006.

Wolf, Martin. "Why We Must Halt the Land Cycle." *Financial Times*, July 8, 2010.

World Health Organization, Information Sheet. *Obesity and Overweight.* Geneva: WHO, 2003. At http://www.who.int/dietphysicalactivity/media/en/gsfs_obesity.pdf.2.

CHAPTER 9

What Can Be Done?

Revolt of the Masses?

For several decades, accelerating after the financial crisis of 2007–2008, we have lived in an age of mass revolt. Leaderless for the most part, the revolt has targeted modern global rentier capitalism, which has evolved into a giant sucking machine, extracting wealth and concentrating it in the hands of a narrow elite, the super-rich. Based on the correct belief that the rules of modern capitalism enrich the already rich through excessive rent-seeking—and taking—and the slim (if any) opposition from politicians, economists, and most of the media, the masses are on the march. The question remains, however: will they march in the same direction?

It all began with the Occupy Wall Street movement, aimed squarely at the financiers who brought us a national, almost global calamity. Occupy Wall Street had great energy, fueled by anger and the feeling of alienation, as well as the fear of a jobless and insecure future. Leaderless, without an ideology, it fizzled and was thought dead. But it turned out that the sentiment felt by Occupy Wall Street was echoed throughout much of the West.

What followed were the *indignados* (the angry and defiant ones) in Spain and then mass movements in Greece and Portugal. These may have been led by primitive rebels, but millions were politicized overnight. The reason? Taking over a park or a street was not only a way to make a statement, a strategy to challenge power without relying on

J. L. Luzkow, *Monopoly Restored*,
https://doi.org/10.1007/978-3-319-93994-0_9

political parties that didn't represent a majority of people anyway. It also helped forge an identity that could be shared by millions of others, based on common grievances and a common assault on institutions that served only the elites. In a word, it was possible to articulate alternatives, to participate in mass politics that were deeply personal, and to forge collective identities even while rejecting the very notion of politics and the holding of power.

What emerged were people sharing similar narratives, similar voices of hardship and deprivation, similar stories about losing control over personal destinies, a collective sharing of needs and grievances. It was at least a beginning, a chord of dissent. It was a refusal to pretend that the system was all-inclusive, or that there was no alternative, or that the present relationships were in any way fair. It was an acknowledgment that too many were left out in the cold by institutions and ideas, neoliberalism and rentier capitalism, for example. It was an assertion that getting education and training, often very expensive, for nonexistent jobs, was inherently unfair. The dice were loaded, and the vast masses were not the beneficiaries. It was the beginning of a movement; based on exclusion and the increasing evisceration of democracy, it was an explosion of anger at media that ignored those left behind by de-industrialization, globalization, the victims of Big Money, especially Wall Street and the City of London.

There were, of course, failures. Some of them were acknowledged early on. The refusal to participate in established parties and conventional party politics left the super-rich in charge, with nobody mounting a challenge. Mass refusal left the field open to those the rebels wanted to get rid of. It meant the inability to articulate alternatives, the lack of a coherent ideology. The defense of radical individualism conflicted with the need to act collectively and to achieve collective goals. It was difficult, as it had always been, to square liberty and equality.

Primitive rebels have come from everywhere. They are young and old, urban and rural, educated and uneducated. They are the temps, the contract workers, working in call centers, rotated out so they will never collect benefits. The retail workers, the sales forces, whose lives will always be tenuous and who will never retire. Seasonal workers. Part-timers.

They are especially the young. Youth, with college degrees that have given them debt, but not jobs or income. Youth confronted by elites they will never join. Youth who wonder why they should attend colleges that lead to a lifetime of debt. Youth increasingly doing apprenticeships as baristas, stuck in low-paying jobs with no benefits. Often moving back to their parents' home.

Altogether these are the precariat, as Guy Standing refers to them. They have precarious lives, precarious living conditions, precarious education and training, precarious health, and precarious futures. They are the first generation to be worse off than their parents, and their children will do even worse. And they know this. They are the ones who bear the brunt of inequality, and they are sinking even further. They are the ones who were told to compete with Chinese workers. They rebelled, and for this, they were accused of being indolent, or even too stupid to get a proper training. Or they were accused of being drug addicts or alcoholics when they reacted to precarious living by resorting to drugs. Ignored by the media, they occasionally made it into popular culture. Danny Boyle's film, *Trainspotting*, for example.

The precarious classes come from US families that used to be the factory workers who made cars, or steelworkers working forges in Pittsburgh, or textile workers in the mills of the East and then the South: until the factories disappeared. When factories went and mines played out or were abandoned, so did the historical proletariat vanish, leaving their children behind to join the legions of the precarious.

The precarious classes used to be the small proprietors in small towns and average size cities. They used to be independent and be able to send their children to college. Then, the national chains came in. They put the mom and pop stores out of business. The national chains provided cheap services and products, but only because they were exploiting foreign labor, or American labor forced to compete with low-wage workers in low-wage countries.

Social Democrats and Marxists and fellow travelers on the Left have dismissed the precariat or precarious classes as reactionary because they are difficult to organize, lack a coherent ideology, and have abandoned the Left to vote for Donald Trump in the USA and for Brexit in the UK. Progressive Democrats and New Labor invite the precarious classes to recover their lost and abandoned solidarity and identities. But it is too late. The nineteenth-century and twentieth-century solutions they offer can never work, not in the twenty-first century when the industrial working class has mostly vanished, and the industrial unions no longer have the political clout, money, or will to defend the rights of workers.

Forging a new collective identity will be difficult, but when extreme inequality reached a boiling point after the Great Recession of 2008–2009, the legions losing their jobs and income, their homes, and their futures, soon discovered each other, aided by the social media. They were angry enough, energetic enough, mostly young. They lacked a unifying vision, but they refused to legitimize the given: the establishment, the plutocracy, the financiers of Wall Street and the City of London. They rejected the lies that told them to get an education and the necessary skills to match the jobs that were out there. But the indignant knew the jobs were not there, they were abroad, or nowhere. That was why they were resisting the institutions that surrounded them. Vaguely, they understood they were against rentier capitalism and that somehow the super-rich were conspiring against them. Vaguely, they understood that their fall was a result of the excessive rents that the corporate rich imposed on them in the form of their mortgages, their patents, the intellectual property (IP) rights granted them by government. Increasingly, the precarious classes resented the monopolies the 0.1% established in healthcare and communications, the fake degrees the super-rich offered in business colleges, the way the corporate rich privatized the commons in which publicly owned assets were transferred to wealthy elites by politicians the rich helped elect.

If resistance were to come it would be from this group, those who live precarious lives, who no longer believe in upward mobility, who are staring at *permanent* unemployment or underemployment, who come out of college, if they attend one, with a degree and a lifetime of debt. Resistance will not come from the *salariat*, those with a comfortable income and decent pensions, whose income is directly related to corporate profits and who can count on receiving company shares. They are too intimate with the elites, their fortunes too entwined with the super-rich. They will not rebel. Their lives are not precarious.

The proletariat—blue-collar working class—are part of the past, in which they continue to live. They remember a better past, especially when compared to a desperate present. They no longer resist, they are beaten and resentful. Too often they blame the wrong people for their predicament: blacks, immigrants, Muslims, and Jews. They are often prey to right-wing populism and neo-fascist politicians, potential tyrants who know how to manipulate the legitimate grievances of the fallen blue collars.

There are still the independent contractors, the technically skilled, the freelancers who contract out their services, but they also benefit from rent-seeking. They do share insecurity with the precarious classes and that makes them potential allies. They may join, but they will not lead the new rebels.

There is, also, an underclass that is genuinely downtrodden. They have not fallen, they were already at the bottom. They are the genuinely angry, those who cannot articulate their grievances because they have come to prefer their lives to reentry into a society they despise. Some might join a movement. They are not natural rebels. They have ceased to hope for a better future. For any future.

The Party Is Over: Time for a New Party

If primitive rebels are to become successful, they must share beliefs in common, have a critique of why present arrangements are unfair and unsustainable, and have a vision of change that is possible, desirable, and just, for a majority of people, and not only a self-chosen few. They must also have a unified strategy. That will mean a new political party, at the least a movement that captures an existing party (as a few operatives did in the Republican Party, and likewise the Conservatives in Britain). And a motivating principle that can reverse what is now the deepening resentment that has become America and Britain and is spreading to continental Europe.

The current system of rentier capitalism is irredeemable, beyond salvation. It has failed utterly to create a society that is fair for the majority. It has failed to provide equal opportunities for all. It has failed to distribute income and wealth in a way that is even close to just. It has failed to provide equal access to education. It has rewarded the rich with even more wealth, and it has taken away from those who have the least wealth to pay for the concessions of the elite. It has plundered the Earth and sold the falsehood that unlimited economic growth is a religion. And the reason all this has happened is what we have observed: a rentier economy in which the rich extract rents from everybody else. In a word, the prime motivation for change must be to transform utterly a system that relentlessly distributes wealth vertically, upward bound to the 0.1%, while arguing there is no alternative.

Meanwhile, mass forms of organization and protest have been whittled down. Professional craft guilds and craft unions have weakened or disappeared altogether. The industrial union is in serious decline as its membership and manufacturing have diminished. The right of assembly has been challenged by nervous states and the elites that guide them.

Somewhat ironically, churches remain as places where congregants can pool grievances, find fellowship and common ground, and pose moral alternatives to institutional degradation and political tyranny.

Political parties no longer have a unified platform, or even a stable constituency. Everywhere they are flattened, the more they change, the more they resemble each other. They squabble but in power they serve the same masters, invariably the 0.1%. They recruit from the same elites, the same upper classes that serve people mostly like themselves. Everywhere they have moved to the right, often in search of the very same citizens they have helped to marginalize, mostly by ignoring their grievances, often by catering to rentier capitalists such as the Street and the City. Even center Left parties have participated in this fraud. The Third Way Social Democrats in Germany, Blair's New Labour, and Bill Clinton's Democrats in the USA have mostly abandoned the working class in pursuit of a middle- and upper-class constituency. In doing so, they have ignored the wage stagnation of workers, the excessive inequality that has driven their despair, the increasing inability of even the educated to secure employment in the areas in which they have trained and studied. Proponents of the Third Way have even celebrated the affluent as the great creators of jobs and wealth. It doesn't matter how they acquired their wealth, or that they largely use it to extract even more wealth for themselves, rather than investing it in their employees and research and development (R&D).

It remains to be seen where Labor will go as Jeremy Corbyn takes the reins. He has appealed to the precarious classes for support, a kind of left-populism. But Labor is bitterly divided between moderates and progressives, an indication of the split in its electoral base. The same for the Democrats, split between Bernie Sanders' progressive supporters and backers of the Clintons and moderates. In the meantime, virtually all major parties in the USA and the UK are dominated by dynastic politics. They have become less and less democratic themselves. Donald Trump is an exception, but he became president by running against the Republican Party, by catering to the resentment toward the elitism of both parties, which brought him the support of working-class voters angry at conventional politicians and parties.

Once political parties stagnate and represent the interests of elites, they may well be beyond repair. Once they stifle critical debate, they cannot be part of the exit from the past. Once they become incapable of imagining an alternative future, or of offering a route to that future, they cannot represent the majority of us because they are beholden to the special interests that keep them in power. And when that happens they inhibit genuine public discussion, reinforcing the inequalities that already exist in education and in control of the media. The result is confusion, higher education that increasingly is vocational training, media that obscures or fails to clarify the difference between truth and propaganda.

When established parties do not represent significant segments of a population, when they are beholden too big money to help them to attain and remain in power, then they become increasingly irrelevant. In their place, new political parties begin to emerge to give a voice to the voiceless, to the multitudes of the precarious. To the left and the right, these parties will grow while conventional parties diminish. We have significant illustrations.

Beppe Grillo's Five Star Party, or Movement as he has called it, has had notorious success appealing to precarious populations in Italy. But Grillo and his movement have also been incoherent, blending populist messages, anti-globalism, and tirades against the corruption of political elites, with more conventional narratives that accept neoliberalism, or at least fail to oppose it. There is also Podemos in Spain, the "we can" party, that followed the mass protests of the *indignado*, the angry or indignant ones, against inequality and corruption of the political establishment. Podemos emphasized the full implementation of the 135th article of the Spanish Constitution, which stresses that all wealth, regardless of its ownership, must be subordinate to the people's interest. Anti-NATO, opposed to austerity budgets and neoliberal policies that benefit the elite rich, Podemos has polled more than 20% in national elections.

Syriza has had a similar profile to Podemos and even inspired the latter by opposing austerity measures, neoliberalism, and global finance, producing an electoral triumph that put Syriza at the helm of Greece. The Scottish National Party has also revived by invoking a similar agenda, taking seats away from New Labor after the latter had solicited support from the establishment.

Progressive parties have emerged for a reason. Old left parties have moved to the right, resulting in the mass desertion of its supporters. This has been virtually self-evident in the USA and the UK, where Bill Clinton and the Democrats, and Tony Blair and Gordon Brown and New Labor abandoned traditional working-class constituencies while appealing to a broad middle. But too many compromises with the financial elites and Big Business, too much adulation of wealth, too little concern for the groups they had abandoned, their insecurities and aspirations, created openings for populist parties, of left and right, signifying the end of the old left.

So far so good. Yet the broad detachment from party politics, the frustration that has exploded onto the streets from New York to Madrid, to Athens and elsewhere, have only fitfully had political success where it really matters, at the polls. Guy Standing may be correct that this is to be expected in the initial phase of mass discontent as popular resentment has erupted into symbolic days of protest.[1]

But there may be more to be worried about than merely symbolic protests. That is because the new wave of politics and protest since 2010 is a "rebellion" without a cause, or an ideology or project. As Ivan Krastev put it, "Protesting itself seems to be the strategic goal of many of the protests."[2] It is mostly about moral indignation, not a set of issues but a public performance. Many protestors are both anti-institutional and mistrustful toward the market and the state. They participate in demonstrations but disavow a politics of representation. They avoid established political parties and distrust the mainstream media. They reject all formal organizations. They prefer the Internet and local assemblies for decision-making. They not only mistrust leadership, they mistrust authority of any kind, including their own. Rhetoric and ideology are considered passé and distasteful. And here the revolts run into an obstacle. By mistrusting institutions and authority, protestors are reluctant to take power themselves. The longing for community conflicts with the desire to preserve individualism and personal autonomy.[3]

It will be difficult to transform primitive rebels into genuinely progressive political parties, especially when rebellion takes the form of right-wing populism, as it has in Denmark, in France, Germany, the Netherlands, Poland, the UK, the USA, and elsewhere. In all these nations, deep resentments are often fueled by nativist sentiment, distrust of elites, including left-leaning parties, and antagonism toward immigrants and migrants, who are typically seen as intruders, criminals, and freeloaders living off established welfare systems paid for by native-born citizens.

There are, however, energizing factors that have made possible the resurgence of progressive left movements. Globalization and the dominance of global finance and financial interests, neoliberalism run rampant, have helped to spark more than 800 mass demonstrations just between 2011 and 2015. The coincidence between the financial meltdown of 2008 and 2009, disrupting global financial markets and causing a massive shift of wealth toward the global financial elite (rent seekers), has inspired a number of these demonstrations. Many have turned into outright rebellion and rejection of the new global order, which seems everywhere to be run by the same financial elite we have observed throughout this book. Syriza in Greece swept to power because it alone was willing to confront and reject the power stranglehold of global finance, including the European Central Bank (ECB). A similar narrative happened in Scotland, where resentment still festers against the City of London and the political domination of financial interests, producing an overvalued exchange rate that has decimated industrial production and employment in manufacturing. Similarly, the independence movement in Catalonia has been sparked by hostility to global finance, this time in Madrid. The community behind this challenge is about more than nationalism. It wants security and the chance to be free of rent-seeking finance.[4]

There are several factors driving these fledgling parties and movements. Rights long fought for by unions, workers, and engaged intellectuals and the parties representing them have been diminished by states and elites almost throughout the West. These include fundamental rights such as the right to vote, under systematic attack by elites and Republicans in the USA and by Tories in the UK. They include the right to organize unions, under assault in the UK since Margaret Thatcher, and in the USA by a movement to expand right-to-work states. The right to assemble is increasingly shrinking and is under assault.

Today, the levers of power have shifted toward a rentier minority, and that shift has been accompanied by unprecedented inequality and the concentration of income and wealth in a distinct minority. None of this is sustainable, yet the modern state, a captive of the 0.1%, increasingly reduces the means of redress, which, in effect, vitalizes the movements that are challenging the financial and corporate elites.

What do the precarious classes need and want, whether overqualified college students preparing for jobs that don't exist or former members of the working class who have lost their employment permanently? Or minorities, or immigrant families deprived of access to income or status or rights? Or the underclass that has long abandoned hope?

They want income security, currently denied them by the rent-seeking paradigm dominated by finance. They want access to education that is not merely vocational training. They want education that is uniform and equal. Education that is public and not for profit, not controlled by the rentier class. They want public access to financial information and knowledge, and regulation of credit providers. They want work commensurate with their education and skills. They want dignity that includes universal healthcare. They want decent pensions for their retirement. They want a government that protects them, not a government in tow to the elites. Moreover, they know all this is possible! Social democratic countries in Europe have accomplished all this and more.

Abolish Undeserved Rents Collected by the Super-Rich

Rentier income is an undeserved income. It is a rent on all those not part of the 0.1% and those who serve them in managing the transaction economy. Taken together, the rentier class and those who serve them represent 10% of the population, but they control roughly 80% of national wealth in the USA and roughly half the national wealth in the UK. As the wealth of the 1% is increasingly concentrated, the lives of the middle class, including many former blue-collar workers, become more precarious: more job risk; more health risk; more pension risk. Increasingly insecure, the precarious classes—the precariat—will avenge themselves by voting for the likes of a Donald Trump. Or they will simply be in permanent revolt. And as they rebel, the USA and the UK will become countries in which economies become even less efficient. The East will rise, and its rise will accelerate. The West will continue its decline.

So what can be done?

Healthcare

It is getting late, but it is time to take rents out of healthcare: healthcare is inefficient and unfair when run as a business. Healthcare must be a universal right. Begin by limiting IP protection. Restrict the patent system dramatically. Twenty-year regimes for drugs are too long. Too many patents are granted for products that are not innovative: quite the contrary as we have seen with the development of drug therapies. Drugs and other products based on government research, or government-sponsored research, should benefit the public, and not just the holder of a government-approved patent.

Impose a higher tax levy on drug profits. Do not allow drug companies the right to count their marketing costs as expenses. Marketing is not research. Do not allow drug companies to advertise as they routinely do on television, and then pass the cost of advertising onto the consumer.

Regulate drug prices: Congress can do this. Let Medicare negotiate the cost of drugs. This would save at least $50 billion per year in rents currently and needlessly going to drug companies. Extend Medicare for all by creating a single-payer healthcare system.

Dramatically revise healthcare in the USA and in Britain so that it is not privatized. None of it. Healthcare should not be an opportunity for the super-rich to collect rents on medical consumers. This makes us all sicker as well as poorer. It means ultimately less access to healthcare and more bankruptcies.

Don't believe the rhetoric that single payer does not work because it is too expensive. The USA has the most expensive healthcare system in the developed world. And it is because of excessive rent collection by the super-rich. We don't need them.

Here is how to get rid of their rents. In a single-payer system, the government collects tax revenues from everybody, based on all income, corporate and individual, and administers the entire healthcare system. This is effective and inexpensive. Getting rid of for-profit health insurance companies would save roughly $400 billion per year in the USA. And removing corporate responsibility for healthcare will make corporations more competitive as well.

Not-for-profit hospitals? They are really for-profits. They just are not allowed to sell shares. Start levying taxes on them. Or force them to reduce their costs. Hospitals argue that they have to charge excessive prices to patients who have insurance so they can serve those who don't have insurance. But here is the point. In single payer, we are all insured, we have universal coverage, there is no need to worry about who will do the paying. The government will. Cost control? Again, single payer means hospitals have to negotiate prices with the government: that is how single payer works.

Intellectual Property Rights

Speaking of patents, government should not be licensing companies by allowing them to patent life, and then supporting trade agreements that extend these patents to other countries. Granting patents for transgenic seeds should also be carefully restricted, and this is a license for companies to control too much of the world's food supply. At the least, products derived from transgenic seeds should be labeled as such. At the least, life in any form should not be patented. Such patents do not represent advances in science, just examples of predation. And many patents are the result of knowledge generated by government research. They should not be windfalls for private gain, but benefits for the commons, from whence they came.

Agribusinesses should not possess monopolies on anything occurring naturally. Whatever occurs in nature should remain part of the commons, not an opportunity for profit. Patenting the IP embedded in seeds is another example of pure predation: it is a technique for extending monopoly. It does not contribute to food supply as much as to profit.

Subsidies for corporate farms should be eliminated, they are billion dollar companies. Not necessary to coddle them. Coddling the British gentry landed class is a subsidy clear and simple for millionaires and billionaires, some of whom have inherited their estates from a remote past.

Corporations, contrary to public knowledge, have not developed many of their so-called innovations. They have often relied on publicly funded research, yet they retain IP rights for themselves. Here is an illustration of rent-seeking (and taking). Between August 2012 and March 2015, Apple Incorporated "returned" more than $112 billion to investors, mostly hedge funds and private equity firms, neither of which had put a penny into Apple's original technology or productive assets. They had nothing to do with the underlying innovations that enriched Apple. That was because most of the innovations were developed by the federal government which created the bulk of the technologies that made the smartphone smart, including touch screens, GPS, voice activation, and even the Internet. Investors also had nothing to do with engineering and assembling the final devices. This was done by engineers in Silicon Valley and factory workers in China.[5]

I am not suggesting that Apple be nationalized. Only that since much of its wealth is based on the commons, it should be paying much more in corporate taxes: it should share the harvest. Instead, it incorporates subsidiaries in tax shelters, where it collects profits based on IP. The result is a minimal tax bill in the home country. In fact, Apple claims there is no home tax country, enabling it to ramp up its rent collecting.

And while we are on the topic of Apple, let us remember that Apple could generate tens of thousands, really hundreds of thousands of jobs, by assembling its iPhones in the USA instead of China. According to Apple, what would the additional cost be for the US consumer? Readers might recall the sum of $65. But Apple refuses, never mind that it, like many high-tech corporations, already has cashed in on the commons, enabling it to use technologies developed by the US government to make many billions for company executives and its investors, prime examples of rent-seeking and taking. Can the precariat change any of this? Yes, elect a government committed to taxing Apple on the immense profits it makes right here in the USA. Don't give free access to Apple products in the USA if it avoids taxes here. Sound like protectionism? Maybe, but it is one way to create many jobs in the USA and to make Apple into a responsible corporate citizen.

Finance

Rentier capitalism thrives in the finance and banking sector. Here are a few measures to reverse that. Criminalize insider trading and enforce the law. Write tighter laws specifying what insider trading means. Do not allow corporations to spend unlimited amounts of capital to buyback shares. This enriches the holders of shares, and it consumes trillions of dollars in buybacks better spent on human capital in the form of wages and R&D. Ultimately, insider trading costs jobs. It costs tax revenues too because under current rules the value of the shares granted to executives can be deducted against corporate taxes. These are all rents paid by everybody else.

When executive recipients of corporate shares sell these shares, the income they collect is called capital gains. These are taxed at about half the rate of earned income. This is a clear rent for no particular advantage except to the recipient of a corporate gift. Tax capital gains the same rate as earned income, which is how most of us are taxed.

Stop federal government support of derivatives. Knowing that large investment banks are too big to fail only encourages risk taking, while collecting bailout money such as in 2008–2009 was the biggest rent taking in history. And don't allow the big banks to have access to pension funds. This fuels the greed of the funds and also means that banks have to be bailed out when they fail.

Restore usury laws. Otherwise interest rates rise even when money should be cheap—and remains cheap to banks. Payday loan companies should not be allowed to levy interest rates that are often 100% and above. Renewing usury laws would stop this.

To avoid the problem of corporations hoarding cash abroad, levy taxes on companies at the point where profits are actually earned, at the point of consumption. This may amount to accounting adjustments, but it will prevent corporations shifting losses to high-tax countries and earnings to low-tax countries.

Start a Development Bank. Such a bank was used by the Roosevelt administration for big projects, such as bridges. Such a bank can be capitalized by floating bonds or a wealth tax. The projects that are subsidized by the bank can pay for themselves through tolls, such as on bridges (Golden Gate).

Tax Reform

Taxes are a huge super-rent levied by the super-rich on virtually everybody else, contrary to the rhetoric of the super-rich themselves. We have already mentioned capital gains taxes. They are a virtual gift to the ultra-wealthy, who receive a disproportionate share of their income as lower-taxed capital gains. At the least, these should be taxed as earned income. Remember that as much as 80% of capital gains go to the top 10% of the population in the USA, and more than 40% goes to the 1%.

Income tax rates should be capped at 60–70% as recommended by some economists not beholden to the 1%. There is no reason why a family earning a half million dollars per annum, or a half billion pounds sterling, should pay the same earned income tax rate as a family earning "merely" millions.

An increasing percentage of federal revenues come from payroll taxes, which fall predominantly on the middle and even poorer classes. Payroll taxes are not levied on most of the income of the 1%. Even in the case of earned income, there is a cap set at $127,000: any earned income above that is not subject to the payroll tax. Any unearned income also escapes payroll taxes. Yet payroll taxes undergird Social Security and Medicare. The solution seems obvious: raise the cap dramatically. Even better, tax all income, earned and unearned. This would make Social Security solvent. And it would be fair. A means to redistribute income and wealth, reducing inequality and risk.

Inheritance taxes? This amounts to one of the top rent-seeking areas. That is because a person can inherit the right to collect rents whether in the form of IP, land or physical property, or financial property, and this can be heritable eternally. This is one of the chief areas of inequality and a big corruption of democracy. For example, financial wealth and/or wealth in IP enables the super-rich to distort political campaigns and to buy influence. One thing to change in this area? Roll back and revoke *Citizens United*, a primary source of the distortion of American democracy. Also, as in the UK and in Europe, limit campaign spending, and limit the length of the political campaign season. And only allow individuals to donate campaign funds.

Wealth tax? This is a tax that has been levied to advantage in Europe. It is a redistribution device, necessary in a time of unparalleled inequality. It is also a device that can put capital to productive use that might otherwise be used only to collect more rents.

Protect Workers from Rentier Predators

The trend toward "workfare" has been pronounced in both the UK and the USA. Not only is it coercive and humiliating, it neither helps develop the economy nor does it help poor families. Forcing anybody to take a make-work job that pays little—or nothing as in the case of the UK's zero hours contracts, for few and dwindling benefits, does not contribute to anybody's well-being. Telling people they are unemployed because of their own fault—wrong training, indolence, no talent, or poor behavior—hardly contributes to developing real jobs. Subjecting individuals to means tests is quite simply mean; punishing the victim for technological change or for government ineptness or corporate indifference or malfeasance is also unfair and vindictive.

Raising the minimum wage or insisting on a "living wage"—as the British do—can help, but setting wages higher by fiat generally induces more automation, or outsourcing, or avoidance or even wage theft by deliberate job misclassification. In Britain, where the minimum wage has stagnated, as it has in the USA, it has been used as an excuse to limit employment, or to restrict or eliminate benefits.

In the UK where employers are obligated to pay a living wage since April 2016, which is really a higher minimum, employers have resorted to more flexible work paradigms—reduced overtime, bonuses, and benefits. The result is that employees are hardly better off.[6] Since almost half of "living wage" workers work in the hospitality or retail sector, it seems almost self-evident that these are and will be lower skill level jobs, difficult to organize, and easily replaceable. The "living wage" is not likely to be a long-term solution for hospitality workers and the vast majority of service workers.

So what can be done? Let's begin with education. The more equal the access to education becomes, the greater the equality in jobs and income. This seems self-evident, but in the USA especially, and in the UK, there is no such thing as equality in education. A good start would be to fund all schools equally and to put funding on a national basis. One way to do that? Integration of schools. A national public school system that is attended by all students. Sound impossible? Maybe! But the only way to get affluent whites to support quality education for everybody is to insist their children go to school with poor white and black children. And then maybe there will be equal opportunity after all. And not just in theory, not the equal opportunity to become unequal.

Equality in education will be a difficult mountain to climb. The reason? Once again, the rentier class has known for decades that education can be a tempting for-profit opportunity. But the rentier sees education as much more important than a place to make money. It is the place where the young are schooled in how to see the political cosmos. It is the locus where students can be taught that for-profit healthcare is a good thing, that government intrusion into the so-called free market is a bad thing, that government regulation portends the authoritarian, repressive state, that the distribution of income and wealth is a true measure of individual ability. Or to put it bluntly, education is the ideal place to legitimize the rentier and a rent-seeking economy—and to marginalize consideration of alternatives. The corruption of democracy *begins in the schools.*

Guy Standing once again provides an apt illustration of how education, in this instance in Britain, has been used to promote ideology, not critical thinking. In 2007, the *Financial Times* sent a correspondent to a state secondary school, Tower Hamlets in London's East End, one of hundreds of schools encouraged by New Labor to form school–business partnerships. Tower Hamlets had indeed formed a partnership with an American investment bank. A bank executive was the chair of the school's governing body and bank staff helped in classes and in mentoring of students. As the headmistress put it, for the school–business partnership to work there had to be a shared culture. A few months later, the bank went bankrupt after speculating with the money of millions of people and losing, precipitating the world's financial crisis that ruined tens of thousands of lives. The name of the bank? Lehman Brothers.[7]

Lehman Brothers is only a single example of what is becoming increasingly global: the commodification of education, transforming learning as critical thinking into vocational training. In a country such as the USA, where tuition inflation has been accompanied by a shift from government grants to private loans—another opportunity for Wall Street rent-seeking firms—students have to be concerned with income potential. Fixated on future income, dependent on student loans, increasingly drawn to high-income professions like banking and finance, students forfeit knowledge of public policy, history, politics, culture, and ultimately critical thinking, easy prey for the predators and their distorted view of the universe.

This is precisely the kind of issue that should consume the media. Government should be actively involved in providing free higher education for all qualified students. Industry should be much more committed to apprenticeships and to their future labor forces instead of looking abroad for cheaper labor, or importing skilled workers on special visas, punishing Americans with the same skills. And public schools should not be an opportunity for predation, as they are (increasingly) in the USA and UK.

A well-educated workforce presumes there will be jobs at the end of the academic ladder. However, we know this is not the case in the USA and UK, and even in some continental countries, as illustrated by France. So what can be done? It is tempting to agree with Guy Standing and others that in this post-industrial age, we are mostly post-union as well. And that other forms of worker protection and wage protection will have to be discovered in which workers can act in solidarity with each other. This will be difficult, even in an age of mass protests. We know some of the reasons: distrust of authority, of institutions, of leaders of all stripes, of the media, of any form of representation. But in an age of labor fragmentation, when large numbers of workers no longer work in massive factories, when unions are repressed or bypassed, as in right-to-work states in the USA, and when outsourcing is more common—and often used as a lever of negotiation, employee organization and solidarity is more difficult to accomplish than ever. Unless of course the government assists workers enough to help them negotiate with employers as equals. And that presumes that there is a political party—or parties—that actually believes in relative equality, and that has a chance to come to power.

Today, there is no such party in the USA. The possible exception is the progressive wing of the Democrats, led by Bernie Sanders, and he is vigorously opposed by the wing of the party that defends the rentier, not the population sinking into the precarious classes, which explains why so many voters abandoned the Democrats and committed political suicide by voting for Donald Trump. Moreover, Sanders is not even a Democrat, he remains an independent. And how could this be otherwise? His very sensible proposal to make universal healthcare accessible by expanding Medicare has been opposed by most of the Democratic establishment.

Over in the UK, it is much the same. Conservatives and so-called New Labor support the rentier class: New Labor cast its political future with the City of London. It never considered reversing Mrs. Thatcher's anti-union stance; instead, it supported workfare. And the Conservatives are largely funded by the rentier class in the City and beyond. Yes, Jeremy Corbyn can make a difference, he has sympathies for the precarious classes and understands the need for a new politics to represent them, but he is roughly in the same predicament as Sanders: despised by many Labor moderates.

Pessimism and even surrender need not be inevitable. The massive protests of the last decade or two, the vote for Brexit, the victory of Donald Trump, what are these but protest votes, protests that will become ever more violent as the precarious classes become the new dangerous classes if they remain as marginalized and forgotten as they are today. The political successes of Sanders and Corbyn represent the visible part of the future, and the power the precariat can obtain once they find their own political voice.

Here are some of the things that they and we should consider when at last the establishment is challenged for political power. We know that the income and wealth divide has become precipitous in just a few decades. The replay of the Gilded Age is blamed by some publicists and many professional economists on globalization and technological change. But there are exceptions such as Harvard professor Alexander Keyssar, and later Robert Reich and Nobel Prize winner Joseph Stiglitz, and they point to a larger truth. Here is how Keyssar has summarized the Great Divide:

> It's difficult not to see a determined campaign to dismantle a broad societal bargain that served much of the nation well for decades. To a historian, the agenda of today's conservatives looks like a bizarre effort to return to the Gilded Age, an era of little regulation of business, no social insurance and no legal protections for workers.[8]

Professor Keyssar has a point. All that is necessary is to take a quick look at a number of other developed democracies and we can see that they have not experienced nearly the income and wealth divides of the USA and the UK, though they are equally or more exposed to globalization than America. Denmark, France, Germany, and Sweden, for example, are far more exposed to global integration and also at risk of competition with China and other developing countries, yet none of these countries experienced the erosion or stagnation of wages that the USA is still facing almost a decade after the Great Recession. According to OECD figures for the years 1985–2008, measuring the growth in total compensation for manufacturing workers, the USA failed to register any gains at all over a period of more than two decades (and very little since 2008). For the same years, however, France registered a gain of more than 150%, Germany and the Netherlands just under 200%, and Denmark achieved gains of greater than 200%.[9]

The difference between the USA and European countries like Germany, the Netherlands, and Sweden is that the latter embrace government regulation as a good thing. They understand that corporations will do everything they can to establish monopoly and to limit competition, even while they employ the rhetoric that the government should honor competitive capitalism by leaving the market alone. Germany and other developed countries in Europe put a premium on long-term productivity growth, which means that profits should be reinvested in the real economy—remember the $3 trillion US corporations spent buying their own stock to pump up income of executives? Many Europeans advocate limiting corporate influence on government. They put a priority on long-term growth in wages—to accompany growth in productivity. This is the key to family prosperity, and family prosperity is the key to national prosperity. And they believe in protecting unions as the surest route to protecting jobs. They even promote worker membership on corporate boards of directors. This not only means the democratization of corporations, but it is the surest way to retain the social contract between workers and their employers. Give everybody a voice at the table, and capitalism can work because it is based on a social contract that benefits everybody.

But the USA and the UK have chosen to abandon the social contract, while developing a rhetoric that promises good things if only we stop an overly intrusive government. The 0.1% soldiers on, accusing would-be reformers of practicing class warfare, even as the super-rich scuttle the social contract that worked so well for decades. Armed with outlandish resources, from money to media, the super-rich spread myths to offset the growing consensus among the 90% that maybe it is better to have universal and affordable healthcare, or that the super-rich have too much, or that it is not globalization that is robbing the 90%, but rather US and British corporations that have been shifting risk to everybody else by suppressing wages, limiting the minimum wage, reducing food stamp eligibility in the USA, reducing or eliminating pension benefits, downsizing, outsourcing, hiring temps, opposing personal bankruptcy, lending fraudulent loans, and wage theft, all the while rejecting equality in education and converting learning itself into a for-profit opportunity for Wall Street banks.

Co-determinism: Protect Jobs by Democratizing Corporations

British and American corporations are unfair, divisive, selfish, and as a result unproductive. They have played a leading role in dividing their societies in ways that recall the rhetoric of Marx, even though they abhor that kind of language when they hear it in the words of their former employees. Corporations in both countries take a short-term view geared to raise share value and executive salary, but too often at the expense of their employees. What was once a more collaborative management style in both countries has been replaced by a more hierarchical command structure that discourages loyalty and concentrates only on the bottom line. By emphasizing top-down management styles, and deemphasizing long-term employment, by assuming that company knowledge is concentrated only at the top, and by believing that shareholders matter much more than workers and the communities in which they live, USA and UK corporations have ignored human capital investment, resulting in American and British loss of the productivity edge that both countries once enjoyed. The consequence of short-sightedness and short-term strategies has been disastrous for the USA and UK corporation, and especially so for their employees, as MIT economist Paul Osterman has argued: "The path of least resistance is not to invest in your workforce, not to invest in a career ladder, to squeeze on wages and benefits, to make your workforce more contingent and flexible."[10]

It is widely believed that the American model has lagged behind because it fails to harness the skills, knowledge, and capacity for innovation of its employees into a process of coordination and collaboration, integrating the collective abilities of all employees. Productive growth as it turns out requires sustained investment in research and innovation and long-term commitment to workers. It requires solidarity, mutual commitment, and a sense of common purpose.

Some American and British high-tech firms have acknowledged the value of their employees. But generally corporate executives in the USA and UK have treated their employees as expendable, ignoring the truism that an insecure workforce is unlikely to lead to sustainable well-being for most people, including the executives who run the corporations. Job satisfaction, long-term commitment to workers, supervisors who respect those they supervise are indispensable elements of company success. Working in harmony and with mutual respect assures psychological benefits such as job satisfaction, meaningful work, and collectively pursued goals, as has been widely recognized in Scandinavia, Germany, and elsewhere in Europe, though this has not been the practice in the USA or the UK.

A widely practiced system in Europe, co-determination, has embraced a much more congenial version of capitalism than American and British managerial bottom-line, short-term capitalism. In Scandinavia and Germany, where co-determination is widely practiced, non-management members routinely sit on hundreds of boards of directors of all the largest corporations. In Germany, half of the directors of German boards are rank and file employees. That means that Germany has the most democratized corporations in Europe. The result has been transformative: Germany does not pursue short-term gains at the expense of innovation. Because it values its employees, utilizes their knowledge, includes them in long-range planning, invests in them as apprentices—at company expense, and is committed to lifelong employment—and lifetime retraining where necessary, German innovativeness and competitiveness are second to none. The reason for all these transformations is because employees sit on boards, not as tokens but as equals. The boards become more responsive to their employees, who are not seen as temporary or seasonal or commodities, or as expendable: after all they represent a huge investment for companies. Boards do tend to be more contentious, but that is what makes companies more innovative. They work better than top-down management because knowledge is in the heads of employees at all levels, with the result that a company is more competitive. Co-determination implies a long-term perspective, and that means putting shareholders, employees, and the communities in which corporations are embedded ahead of executive compensation. It has also meant maintaining high wage levels and long-term employment, ensuring also compatibility within firms because of shared management and mutual commitment long term, including the reduction in costly labor strikes.

Ironically, co-determination was imposed by the Western Allies on Germany following the defeat of the latter in the wake of World War II. In retrospect, the reason seems obvious: prewar industrial and financial elites had supported Hitler and the Nazis. The antidote was to include employees on previously compromised boards of directors. And that was precisely what happened, first in the British zone and then in the US zone in West Germany. The strategy was endorsed by the Christian Democrats and later by the Social Democrats: the result was that a third of the boards of public companies with a workforce between 500 and 2000 contained non-supervisory personnel, and half of the directors of all larger enterprises, like Siemens and Daimler, included employees who were not in management roles.

Co-determinism worked so well in the coal and steel firms where it was initially implemented, that it became the permanent German corporate model. It had many advantages for German industry, but it was especially helpful for German workers—and fair. With employee directors sitting at the helm, industrial and financial firms became more responsive to all stakeholders, including shareholders, consumers, and workers who now had equal representation in boardroom decisions. With corporate objectives now representing broader populations, and with the increasing efficiency that co-determinism brought because of the increased usage of collective knowledge in a company, the new model spread throughout the German economy. Put bluntly, concluded historian and analyst Thomas Geoghegan, speaking of the revolutionary populist and democratized approach to collective management, the addition of employee directors worked because,

> They are responsible for other people. They are responsible for running the firm. They make up a powerful leadership class that represents the kind of people–low income, low education—who don't have much of a voice in the affairs of other industrialized countries.[11]

But do not take Geoghegan's word for it. The vast majority of German firms have embraced co-determinism because it works. It enhances profits, spurs growth, and increases innovation and productivity.

Co-determination improves employee loyalty and company intercommunication. It encourages company investment in employees because of long-term commitment to workers. Plants with works councils, which consist of employees elected by their co-workers to negotiate labor issues with management, have tended to be 25–30% more productive than those without works councils.[12]

Geoghegan's conclusions help explain the decline of productivity in the USA, which definitively abandoned a model of collaboration for one that diminished labor by treating it as a commodity. During the postwar era, 1949–1980, productivity growth, how labor, capital, and innovation come together, averaged 1.6% per year. During the following period, 1982–2009, the Reagan–Thatcher era of short-termism driven by share price and golden parachute cashouts, productivity grew about 1.1% per year.[13]

Nor has co-determinism hurt Germany's trade balance. By stressing R&D and innovation, by emphasizing long-term growth, and by sinking significant corporate sums into apprenticeship programs that add value and increase competitiveness, Germany has not been hurt by the China trade. It has been a net exporter to China, reversing an earlier profile that put Germany in the red in its trade with China. In the year 2007, Germany ran a $3.3 billion deficit, but that was transformed into a $12.7 billion surplus by 2011, largely through the sales of capital equipment—a strength of Germany—that also helped China raise its productivity.[14] By 2016, Germany became the largest exporter in the world, surpassing China, though its positive trade balance with China was later reversed because of a prolonged slump in the Chinese economy.

Co-determination is not only significant because it is efficient and profitable, but because it is about what economies should always be about: supplying work for everybody, enhancing satisfaction of all employees, and promoting the well-being of all members of society. This is the greatest virtue of co-determination: when companies understand that the value of any corporation is in the knowledge of its employees, then they are willing to support and consult those employees. After all, the value of any company is in the heads of those they employ. In the words of Robert Bosch, founder of the giant eponymous German engineering and electrical firm Bosch, "I am not paying high wages because I have a lot of money, but I have a lot of money because I pay high wages."[15]

Which is precisely the point. Germany has avoided becoming a low-wage country—as the USA has not—by adopting an industrial policy which is inclusive, and that acknowledges the advantages of industrial peace and prosperity by investing in its own employees, rather than discarding them to maximize short-term earnings. This means an active apprenticeship program and huge investments in future employees, producing a high employment ratio for youth compared to the UK and the USA, and even some European countries. In America, for example, where there is no strong commitment to the training of youth, who are mostly on their own, and convinced they have to go to college—at their own expense—fewer than 5% of young people train as apprentices, and almost all of these are in the construction trades. In Germany, the number of young people being apprenticed is closer to 60%—in areas as diverse as advanced manufacturing, IT, banking, and hospitality. Moreover, in Europe, what's often called "dual training," learning practical skills in a work environment, in addition to academic training, is a highly respected career path. Just as significant, the bulk of the funding for German apprenticeships comes from corporations.

The alternative in the USA is quite the contrary: abandoning communities and long-term employees for right-to-work states, reducing the workforce to minimize the wage bill, and transforming full-time jobs into part-time work, or contract work—the better to avoid benefits, such as health insurance. In the USA and the UK, without a clear industrial policy to promote the well-being of workers and their communities, without serious apprentice programs, without corporate willingness to participate in worker training—instead of complaining about the lack of skilled workers—neither country is a net exporter, both have high youth unemployment rates, and neither has a strategy to employ workers long term.

Establish Sovereign Wealth Funds: An Alternative and Better Future

In Chapter 1, we saw how Norway put oil revenues into a fund that serves the common good. Britain did the opposite, privatizing the revenues from oil, because the British state was a captive of the rentier class, intent only on extracting income for private accumulation and use.

In effect, Norway became a rentier state, but that meant it was not a captive of the rentier class. Notably, Norway was at least as efficient extracting oil and gas as Britain. *The Economist* described the Norwegian fund as possibly the most impressive instance of long-term thinking of any Western government. In 2017, the fund surpassed $1 trillion, making it the largest sovereign wealth fund in the world.[16] So far, Norway's fund has invested its oil and gas earnings mostly in foreign stocks, but it could easily ramp up investment in Norway—putting a share of earnings into reducing inequality and insecurity. But Norway does not need to do this for the obvious reason that it does not have the kind of inequality and insecurity that are all too pervasive in the USA and the UK! Why? It puts a brake on its rent seekers, the same predators coddled by the USA and UK. In Norway, for example, healthcare is universal, affordable, and efficient, perennially ranked well ahead of the USA. Norway does have a deductible of about $300 annually, after which physical and mental healthcare is free. Norway does not rely on private for-profit health insurance, sparing it one of the highest costs for healthcare in the USA. In a word, Norway's healthcare system works well because it excludes rent-seeking by the rentier class. Healthcare is not-for-profit but a citizen's right.

Norway's example demonstrates that where there is the political will, and responsible government—not captured by the rentier class—the public good can be served. Inequality need not be tolerated. Predation need not be a norm. The Norwegian sovereign fund means that the entire population can be and is economically secure, and not just the 1%. Britain could do the same, it could protect the British and not just the British super-rich. Had it done so it would now have a sovereign fund worth £450 billion in assets, more than Kuwait, Qatar, and Russia combined.[17]

If Russia can have a sovereign fund (as it does), then every country with any kind of resources could also establish a sovereign wealth fund. It is a matter of simply sharing rental income, whether by taxing it or granting concessions with the stipulation that profits must be shared with the public for the common good. After all, granting a concession for the extraction of mineral wealth to a corporation is already removing wealth that belonged to an entire nation. That wealth should be shared with all citizens, as was formerly done with drugs developed in the USA using government and government-funded research. Likewise, rental income of all kinds, IP for example, could be subject to fees and royalties. Or a stake could be taken in a failing bank, or for that matter in almost any company, especially those profiting from rent-seeking, by investing sovereign funds directly in such companies. Finally, it hardly needs repeating, governments could actively enforce existing anti-trust laws to ensure competition, preventing the kinds of monopolies that have occurred from drugs to telecommunication.

Establish Basic Income

Sovereign wealth funds can have another fundamental use. They can support a basic income mostly or entirely based on the wealth fund. This would have several desired effects. It would be emancipatory because an income would be provided to every citizen from birth, at least partially reversing economic insecurity that plagues a majority of British and American populations and many others in Europe. A basic income would also make it more likely that recipients would accept paid work that would supplement the basic income. For many, this would enable them to escape the poverty trap. It would also contribute to a kind of moral economy. Since all would have a basic income, there would be no stigma such as now exists in welfare states, where there is always a sense of shame attached to receiving welfare benefits. And since basic income would not be means tested, that signifies it would be a fundamental right, an entitlement to income that should be in the public domain to begin with. In a word, revival of the commons, or putting a priority on public wealth as opposed to its extraction by the rentier class.

The idea of a basic income has been around for a while, at least since Thomas Paine proposed it in 1797 in *Agrarian Justice*. His idea was "to create a national fund, out of which there shall be paid to every person, when arrived at the age of twenty-one years, the sum of fifteen pounds sterling, as a compensation in part, for the loss of his or her natural inheritance, by the introduction of the system of landed property."[18] The justification for this fund, said Paine, was that "every proprietor … owes to the community a ground-rent" on land and that payments should be made to "every person rich or poor" because land is "*the common property of the human race*."[19] All personal property accumulated by anybody, beyond what he produce with his own hands, "is derived to him by living in society" and he "owes on every principle of justice, of gratitude, and of civilization, a part of that accumulation back again to society from whence the whole came."[20]

Paine was an early defender of the commons. The payment to each and every person was no more and no less than a restoration of that part of the commons originally deducted by a previous generation. Paine thought of the payment as a kind of dividend on the collective work and wealth of all previous generations. In a word, the payment was a return to the "common wealth" that had been unfairly captured by rentiers.

A modern counterpart to Paine's proposal was introduced in the USA by Bruce Ackerman and Anne Alstott in 1999. They argued that all Americans should have the right to share in wealth accumulated by preceding generations and that "a single innovation once proposed by Thomas Paine can achieve what a thousand lesser policies have failed to accomplish."[21]

In the 1960s in the UK, Cedric Sandford proposed a negative capital tax payable on adulthood.[22] In 1989, Julian Le Grand and David Nissan took up Sandford's idea by proposing a start-up grant for young people.[23] In 1986, the Basic Income European Network (BIEN) was established to promote research and advocacy; it later evolved into the Basic Income Earth Network as its ideas became popular and its membership grew.[24]

Since the 2008 crash, the basic income has increasingly been touted as the antidote to rising inequality and insecurity, and to meet the challenges posed by rentier capitalism, which promises even more inequality and insecurity. In 2017, Guy Standing published *Basic Income: A Guide for the Open-Minded*, advocating for a basic income to remedy unsustainable and unfair growth in inequality.[25]

The idea of a basic income has always drawn critics. A basic income, they argue, diminishes the desire to work. It rewards the indolent. It unfairly taxes wealth producers whose capital is required to make a basic income possible. It slows economic growth by reducing productive capital that can be better invested in the economy. It is unsustainable because it would attract populations living in countries that do not have a basic income. It would be impossible to fairly determine eligibility: who would be included and who would not. In a word, a basic income gives the least deserving something they don't deserve, it gives them something for nothing.

Fair enough. So what can and should be done. Let's start with what we have: a system that already rewards the rentier, to such an extent that more and more wealth is concentrated in ever fewer hands. Inequality that is so extreme that it is growing the precarious classes to the extent they vote for demagogues, authoritarian leaders willing to exploit insecurities by pursuing extreme measures to fuel their own and others' xenophobia, a dangerous mixture as we know from the past. What we have is inequality that is extreme, precisely because super-rich rentiers have taken so much for themselves. In a word, they have been given a great deal for nothing, as we have seen throughout this entire book, whether in the form of undeserved patent rights, unearned IP rights derived from the commons, monopolies unchallenged by anti-trust laws, and tax regimes that favor the 0.1%.

Any criticism of basic income ideas should consult what we have in Western societies today: social assistance schemes that are fundamentally flawed because they are costly, inefficient, and inequitable. In fact, much of the money that goes into assistance programs actually is spent on the administration of those programs, not the recipients of the aid. Moreover, many if not all forms of social assistance are inadequately funded, and many are even punitive, stigmatizing those who must rely on these benefits for their survival. Then, there are the ubiquitous means tests to determine eligibility, and the humiliation of applying and then being rejected for assistance.

Too often, the most vulnerable of us don't even apply for assistance because of the too stringent rules for eligibility, and the meager sums of assistance on offer when eligibility is established. And as is widely known in the community needing assistance, receiving it too often does not mean that recipients will escape poverty. Workfare does not establish a career path. In the USA and the UK, especially, where workfare is common and is also harsh and punitive, the most vulnerable of us are forced into training for jobs that don't exist, and that offer no entrée into a future work path. What social assistance schemes ignore is that societies are unequal from birth: unequal education, unequal access to housing, anything but the equal opportunity theoretically offered in liberal societies. Low inheritance taxes seal the bargain. Much wealth is still inherited. And so is much poverty. With a basic income much of the poverty trap could be reversed. The least of us would have a platform on which to stand and an incentive to accept work to supplement the basic income.

Who would be eligible? Guy Standing proposes that "basic income or social dividend would be paid, individually, as a modest monthly sum. … The income would go to every legal resident, with a minimum residency requirement for non-citizens of … two years."[26] The income would be unconditional regardless of family status, work status, or age. Children would receive a smaller payment. Standing does not advocate a lump-sum capital grant because that would invite ill-advised splurge spending.[27]

Basic income should be universal because that is much more efficient and solidaristic. It would include the rich, they would simply give more back as taxes. A basic income scheme need not replace a current assistance regime, both could be run in tandem as means testing and behavior testing were phased out and basic income phased in.

Basic income is realistic. It can be thought of as a modest social dividend on the collective efforts of pervious generations who built the wealth we have inherited. Basic income would be paid for by capturing rental income, which is largely undeserved. Since rental income contributes little if anything to investment, innovation, or sustainable growth, basic income would be an alternative way to increase all three. That is because it would produce much more demand, leading invariably to rising investment, employment, and sustainable growth. And there is an added advantage: financial policies would be taken from the hands of the bankers and given back to elected governments willing to employ a basic income regimen.

Resorting to basic income would reduce social inequality and redistribute income and wealth in a more fair and sustainable way. Basic income would redistribute political power and increase personal freedom. It would decrease social insecurity. It would mean healthier people. And it would likely make them more tolerant of each other.

Basic Income: The Only Way Forward

Three major problems face Europe and the US today: slow growth or stagnation, unprecedented inequality, and dangerous populist reactions to migration, especially to non-European migrants and immigrants. Both the European Union (EU) and the USA (and beyond) have reacted to slow growth and stagnation in the wake of the housing and financial crises of 2007–2008 by employing quantitative easing (QE) policies. The ECB and the Federal Reserve Bank (FED) in the USA pumped billions of euros and dollars respectively into financial markets by purchasing mortgage-backed securities and government Treasuries. The plan of the ECB was to increase liquidity and to invest €315 billion in infrastructure. In the USA, the idea was to increase the liquidity of commercial banks so they would be encouraged to lend more.

In both Europe and the USA, liquidity increased, yet in the short run, and in the long run, QE was a failure, except for the rentier class. QE buoyed stock markets, and it pumped up the housing market, but the greatest beneficiaries of these policies were the super-rich, who held much of their wealth in market shares and physical property. In both Europe and the USA, growth remained slow, inequality widened to unsustainable levels, and migration continued to fuel populist reactions in populations whose social protections were under assault and whose economic futures were tenuous and unpredictable.

All these problems have seemed intractable in Europe and America. Inequality endures as a hindrance to growth because it constrains demand. It also contributes to government deficits because the super-rich can easily avoid taxes—remember their use of tax havens—while the poor don't earn enough to pay them. Inequality also contributes to migration from the South and East to the North and West in Europe. Although many EU countries need migrants because of low birth rates and aging populations, migration to the wealthier parts of Europe is inducing populism and xenophobia. Simultaneously, poorer countries are losing many of the youngest and most skilled of their populations.[28]

What is happening in the US parallels its EU counterpart, with some obvious exceptions since the USA is not part of the EU. Growth has been slow, even in the supposed uptick in the decade following the Great Recession. Wages for most of the population have stagnated. The unemployment rate is at 4.1% in late 2017, but that hardly reflects the reality of the job market where much of the population labors involuntarily in part-time jobs, many are over-educated for the work they are in, and the minimum wage has remained well below a living wage. In the USA, also, QE has helped inflate the stock market—and the rich who control much of the share wealth, while bankers new-found liquidity may be financing yet another bubble in the real estate market. All this has fueled xenophobia and overt racism in the USA, based on the precarious classes' perceptions that foreigners and minorities have been coddled by a protective welfare state.

According to Mark Blyth and Eric Lonergan, and a long list of economists stretching from John Maynard Keynes to Milton Friedman and beyond, the FED in the USA and the ECB in the EU should transfer money directly to people, not unelected bankers. Pumping money directly into lower-income families would address inequality, fuel demand, boost economic growth, and reduce migration in Europe where funds could be earmarked for low-income regions with high out-migration and low aggregate demand.[29]

Unfortunately, this alternative to QE has not been considered in the USA and the UK. Instead, the FED put $4.5 trillion into QE that increased asset bubbles and boosted the stock market, but also did nothing to mitigate inequality or to boost growth. It might have done better to give $56,000 outright to every household in the USA.[30] Much the same could be said of the UK, which diverted £375 billion to QE, but witnessed increased debt, asset bubbles, rising homelessness, and the spread of food banks. For the same capital, the UK could have provided some £50 to every legal resident in Britain every week for two years. Had the UK done so, claims Guy Standing, "Inequality would have been reduced, economic security improved, growth boosted."[31] He might have added that when it came time to get the UK's newly acquired assets (debt) off its balance sheets, inevitably spending cuts followed, and these in turn have driven public anger toward traditional political parties and the financial elite.

Most reasonable people, including many economists, have concluded what is obvious: traditional monetary policy and QE have not worked and an alternative is needed. In fact, a number of pilot programs implementing basic income paradigms have been implemented. One such scheme took place in Cherokee, North Carolina, a small town on a Native American reservation, when the tribal council decided in 1996 to distribute half its casino profits each year to all tribal members. After a modest start the fund grew until by 2015 each person was receiving $10,000 per year. Research found that this sum did not induce indolence. On the contrary, children of recipient families performed better in school than non-recipients and were less likely to commit crimes.[32]

Several pilot projects in India have produced similar results. Even a small basic income can improve nutrition, health, and healthcare. Children perform better at school. Adults become more productive. And basic income has produced a feeling of greater liberty, even liberation. Reduced risk and greater security do not produce rising indolence. On the contrary, they produce greater security and happiness, a sense of well-being and solidarity, hardly characteristics resulting from QE, or low interest rates, or the neoliberal, rentier model that we are all enduring today.[33]

Conclusion

What is needed today is a profound moral transformation. We need to repudiate the kind of selfishness that is justified by orthodox neoliberalism. We need to bypass political parties that bow to the 1%, especially the 0.1%. We need to recover our hijacked democracy. We need to rebuild the commons and to remember that the sky, the rivers and the oceans, the minerals in the ground, the land and Earth itself, once belonged to all of us: they can and should belong to us collectively again. We should reject monopolies. We should advance the public good over private greed. We should remember that public institutions like libraries, schools, museums, and parks serve all of us as equals, that they are part of the commons, that the knowledge in books, the art in museums, the grass and trees in our parks, the learning imparted in our schools, is part of our common heritage, an integral part of the commons, an indelible part of our identity, and that they should not become commodities for private gain any more than our children should be commodified (as consumers) for profit. For there can be no freedom, no liberty, no genuine emancipation, no democracy, if the common good is splintered into private gains for the advantage of a few. The latter is what we have, and it has failed.

Notes

1. Guy Standing, *The Corruption of Capitalism: Why Rentiers Thrive and Work Does Not Pay* (London: Biteback Publishing, 2016), 289.
2. Ivan Krastev, *Democracy Disrupted: The Politics of Global Protest* (Philadelphia: University of Pennsylvania Press, 2014), 3.
3. Ibid., 3–4.
4. Standing, *Corruption of Capitalism*, 290–91.
5. Rana Foroohar, *Maker and Takers: How Wall Street Destroyed Main Street* (New York: Crown Business, 2017), 123–24.
6. Sarah O'Connor, "UK Companies Look for Loopholes Around Living Wage," *Financial Times*, March 30, 2016.
7. Standing, *Corruption of Capitalism*, 264–65; especially Michael Skapinker, "How to Run a School-Business Partnership," *Financial Times*, December 3, 2007.
8. Alexander Keyssar, "The Real Grand Bargain, Coming Undone," *Washington Post*, August 21, 2011.
9. Bureau of Labor Statistics, *Inflation-Adjusted Total Labor Costs Per Hour in Dollars*, Chart 1.2: International Hourly Compensation Costs for

Production Workers in Manufacturing (wages, all benefits, social insurance expenditures and labor-related taxes) (Washington, DC: Bureau of Labor Statistics, 2011), online at http://www.bls.gov/fls/pw/ichcc_pwmfg1_2.txt; see also Organization for Economic Cooperation and Development, "Private Consumption Deflators," *Economic Outlook* 2011, no. 1 (Paris: OECD, December 2011), online at https://doi.org/10.1787/eco_outlook-v2011-1-en.
10. Cited by Steven Greenhouse, "The Challenge of Creating Good Jobs," *New York Times*, September 7, 2011.
11. Thomas Geoghegan, "Consider the Germans' Codetermination and Works Councils," *Harper's Magazine*, March 2012, online at https://coto2.wordpress.com/2010/03/23/consider-the-germans-co-determination-and-works-councils/; Thomas Geoghegan, *Only One Thing Can Save Us: Why America Needs a New Kind of Labor Movement* (New York: The New Press, 2014), 104.
12. George R. Tyler, *What Went Wrong: How the 1% Hijacked the American Middle Class ... and What Other Countries Got Right* (Dallas, TX: Benbella Books, Inc., 2013), 169–71.
13. Organization for Economic Cooperation and Development, *Economic Surveys: United States 2012* (Paris: OECD, 2012), Figure 15, online at http://www.oecd-ilibrary.org/economics/oecd-economic-surveys-united-states-2012_eco_surveys-usa-2012-en; Tyler, *What Went Wrong*, 162, chart 7.3, Annual average growth rate.
14. Floyd Norris, "China Trade Numbers Bear Watching, Up or Down," *New York Times*, September 16, 2011.
15. Cited by Daniel Schafer, "Keeping the Lights On," *Financial Times*, November 10, 2009.
16. *The Economist*, "Norwegian Blues," October 10, 2015, https://www.economist.com/news/business/21672206-now-easy-times-are-over-norway-must-rediscover-its-viking-spirit-norwegian-blues. See "Norway's Sovereign-Wealth Fund Passes the $1 Trillion Mark," *The Economist*, September 23, 2017, online at https://www.economist.com/news/finance-and-economics/21729458-5m-odd-norwegians-own-more-1-all-shares-world-norways.
17. Caroline Wedmore, *Funding the Future, How Sovereign Wealth Funds Benefit Future Generations* (London: Intergenerational Foundation, 2013), online at http://www.if.org.uk/wp-content/uploads/2013/11/A-British-Sovereign-Wealth-Fund.pdf.
18. Thomas Paine, *Agrarian Justice*, 2nd ed. (London: J. Adlard, 1797), 15.
19. Ibid., 12, 15.
20. Ibid., 24.
21. Bruce Ackerman and Anne Alstott, *The Stake-Holder Society* (New Haven: Yale University Press, 1999).

22. Cedric Sandford, *Economics of Public Finance* (Oxford: Oxford University Press, 1969).
23. Julian Le Grand and David Nissan, *A Capital Idea: Start-Up Grants for Young People* (London: Fabian Society, 2000); see also Anthony B. Atkinson, *Inequality: What Can Be Done?* (Cambridge, MA: Harvard University Press, 2015).
24. For a number of experiments in basic income provision, see basicincome.org.
25. Guy Standing, *Basic Income: A Guide for the Open-Minded* (New Haven, CT: Yale University Press, 2017).
26. Standing, *Corruption of Capitalism*, 309.
27. Ibid.
28. Ibid., 312. I am grateful to Guy Standing for much of this discussion. He has been a modern pioneer and advocate for social justice and the basic income.
29. Mark Blyth and Eric Lonergan, "Print Less but Transfer More," *Foreign Affairs*, September–October 2014, online at https://www.foreignaffairs.com/articles/united-states/2014-08-11/print-less-transfer-more.
30. Ibid.; Jeff Cox, "Fed economist: 'No Evidence That QE Works' as Central Bank Starts Unwinding Program," *CNBC*, September 19, 2017, online at https://www.cnbc.com/2017/09/19/fed-economist-no-evidence-qe-works-as-balance-sheet-unwind-starts.html. Saint Louis FED economist Stephen Williamson declared that QE produced bubbles, inflated the stock market, but didn't contribute to growth or the reduced inequality.
31. Standing, *Corruption of Capitalism*, 314.
32. John Sutter, "The Argument for a Basic Income," *CNN*, March 9, 2015, online at http://www.cnn.com/2015/03/01/opinion/sutter-basic-income/index.html.
33. Charlotte England, "Indian Government Survey Says Universal Basic Income Could Combat Poverty," *The Independent*, January 31, 2017.

Bibliography

Ackerman, Bruce, and Anne Alstott. *The Stake-Holder Society*. New Haven: Yale University Press, 1999.

Atkinson, Anthony B. *Inequality: What Can Be Done?* Cambridge, MA: Harvard University Press, 2015.

Blyth, Mark, and Eric Lonergan. "Print Less but Transfer More." *Foreign Affairs*, September–October 2014. Online at https://www.foreignaffairs.com/articles/united-states/2014-08-11/print-less-transfer-more.

Bureau of Labor Statistics. *Inflation-Adjusted Total Labor Costs Per Hour in Dollars*. Chart 1.2: International Hourly Compensation Costs for Production

Workers in Manufacturing. Washington, DC: Bureau of Labor Statistics, 2011. Online at http://www.bls.gov/fls/pw/ichcc_pwmfg1_2.txt.

Cox, Jeff. "Fed Economist: 'No Evidence That QE Works' as Central Bank Starts Unwinding Program." *CNBC*, September 19, 2017. https://www.cnbc.com/2017/09/19/fed-economist-no-evidence-qe-works-as-balance-sheet-unwind-starts.html.

The Economist. "Norwegian Blues." October 10, 2015. Online at https://www.economist.com/news/business/21672206-now-easy-times-are-over-norway-must-rediscover-its-viking-spirit-norwegian-blues.

England, Charlotte. "Indian Government Survey Says Universal Basic Income Could Combat Poverty." *The Independent*, January 31, 2017.

Foroohar, Rana. *Maker and Takers: How Wall Street Destroyed Main Street*. New York: Crown Business, 2017.

Geoghegan, Thomas. "Consider the Germans' Codetermination and Works Councils." *Harper's Magazine*, March 2012. Online at https://coto2.wordpress.com/2010/03/23/consider-the-germans-co-determination-and-works-councils/.

Geoghegan, Thomas. *Only One Thing Can Save Us: Why America Needs a New Kind of Labor Movement*. New York: The New Press, 2014.

Greenhouse, Steven. "The Challenge of Creating Good Jobs." *New York Times*, September 7, 2011.

Keyssar, Alexander. "The Real Grand Bargain, Coming Undone." *Washington Post*, August 21, 2011.

Krastev, Ivan. *Democracy Disrupted: The Politics of Global Protest*. Philadelphia: University of Pennsylvania Press, 2014.

Le Grand, Julian, and David Nissan. *A Capital Idea: Start-Up Grants for Young People*. London: Fabian Society, 2000.

Norris, Floyd. "China Trade Numbers Bear Watching, Up or Down." *New York Times*, September 16, 2011.

O'Connor, Sarah. "UK Companies Look for Loopholes Around Living Wage." *Financial Times*, March 30, 2016.

Organization for Economic Cooperation and Development. *Economic Surveys: United States 2012*. Paris: OECD, 2012. Online at http://www.oecd-ilibrary.org/economics/oecd-economic-surveys-united-states-2012_eco_surveys-usa-2012-en.

Organization for Economic Cooperation and Development. "Private Consumption Deflators." *Economic Outlook 2011*, no. 1. Paris: OECD, December 2011. At https://doi.org/10.1787/eco_outlook-v2011-1-en.

Paine, Thomas. *Agrarian Justice*. 2nd ed. London: J. Adlard, 1797.

Sandford, Cedric. *Economics of Public Finance*. Oxford: Oxford University Press, 1969.

Schafer, Daniel. "Keeping the Lights On." *Financial Times*, November 10, 2009.

Skapinker, Michael. "How to Run a School-Business Partnership." *Financial Times*, December 3, 2007.

Standing, Guy. *Basic Income: A Guide for the Open-Minded*. New Haven, CT: Yale University Press, 2017.

Standing, Guy. *The Corruption of Capitalism: Why Rentiers Thrive and Work Does Not Pay*. London: Biteback Publishing, 2016.

Sutter, John. "The Argument for a Basic Income." *CNN*, March 9, 2015, at http://www.cnn.com/2015/03/01/opinion/sutter-basic-income/index.html.

Tyler, George R. *What Went Wrong: How the 1% Hijacked the American Middle Class … and What Other Countries Got Right*. Dallas, TX: Benbella Books, Inc., 2013.

Wedmore, Caroline. *Funding the Future, How Sovereign Wealth Funds Benefit Future Generations*. London: Intergenerational Foundation, 2013. Online at http://www.if.org.uk/wp-content/uploads/2013/11/A-British-Sovereign-Wealth-Fund.pdf.

Index

J. L. Luzkow, *Monopoly Restored*,
https://doi.org/10.1007/978-3-319-93994-0

The manufacturer's authorised representative in the EU is Springer Nature Customer Service Centre GmbH, Europaplatz 3, 69115 Heidelberg, Germany. If you have any concerns regarding our products, please contact ProductSafety@springernature.com

Printed and bound by CPI Group (UK) Ltd, Croydon, CR0 4YY

05/10/2026

02228128-0014